eurotopia

Intentional Communities and Ecovillages in Europe

Edition 2005

Imprint

Volker Peters, Martin Stengel (editors and copyright):
***eurotopia*-directory: Intentional Communities and Ecovillages in Europe**
- Edition 2005
Ökodorf Sieben Linden, Bandau-Poppau: Volker Peters Verlag / 2005
ISBN 3-00-015401-9

Editorial address: ***eurotopia*-directory**
Ökodorf Sieben Linden
38486 Poppau | Germany
Tel.: +49-(0)39000-90621 Fax.: -51232
website: www.eurotopia.de
e-mail: info@eurotopia.de

Data survey and collection: Sandra Campe, Ute Janda, Ute Langkabel, Christiane Oberdorf, Volker Peters, Martin Stengel, Michael Würfel, Jörg Zimmermann

Translations: Alan Nothnagle; Kosha Joubert, Christiane Oberdorf, Martin Stengel

Data survey and conversion: Volker Peters

Cover design: Martin Stengel

Cover photo: Wolfgang Blöchl: Community of Ökodorf Sieben Linden (Germany)

Layout: Kosha Joubert, Julia Kommerell (+ Illustrations), Martin Stengel, Mona Ziegler

Printed by: Offset Druckerei Pohland, 86165 Augsburg, Germany
printed on 100% recycled paper

The Eurotopians

I arise in the morning torn between
a desire to improve the world or to save it and
the wish to delight in and enjoy it.
(E. B. White)

Table of Contents

Foreword

"Look the other person in the eye and become aware of the powers that are there... the gifts and strengths... which that person might not even be aware of... Just think what these powers could do to heal our planet... And imagine how good it would be to work together... on a common project, for a common goal... Just imagine how it would be to take shared risks... to work something out with fun and humour and laughter... to celebrate success, to overcome failure together, to forgive one another when mistakes have been made... and just to be there for one another... enjoying each other's joy..."

(from a meditation by Joanna Macy, deep ecologist and peace activist)

"Here it is, the *eurotopia directory*!" The name eurotopia is derived from the words Europe and utopia, as you can see in our logo. Utopia is a Greek word meaning "nowhere". It has come to mean an idealised but unrealised state of society. And we selected the continent of Europe because... well, because we happen to live here and understand its culture better than anyone else's, and because Europe has seen a lot of community activity over the past few thousand years...

We eurotopians see utopias as healthy as long as people take them as an inspiration – and then translate that inspiration into motivation for practical action. A utopia can be a guiding force for change. It should not be abused as a yardstick for judging real accomplishments against unrealistic ideals, so as to divide everything up into "good" and "bad" results until everyone finally loses interest. Utopias can get people excited about a new life. And we think it is essential to create new environments in which forward-looking and peace-promoting lifestyles can be developed.

This book is about real examples of how such lifestyles with their different approaches actually look. They were and are being initiated by people who want to live differently and change something. Perhaps, gentle reader, a longing, a vision, an idea of a different life has driven you to pick up this book of almost 500 pages. We hope that some of the thoughts and impulses recorded here will come alive: spreading the community thought, strengthening existing communities and helping to found new ones.

Our research

Since autumn 2003 we have produced and sent a mountain of letters, postcards and emails to 1,723 communities and 547 institutions in twenty-nine countries. About a quarter of them have replied, some only after repeated reminders. Our respondents decided for themselves on the questionnaire whether they wanted to be called a community, an ecovillage, an ecosettlement or something different, since such terms have a great deal to do with how they view themselves. We only challenged these labels, or recast them ourselves, when we discovered egregious contradictions to our own knowledge or to other information on the questionnaires. We ourselves are assuming that the minimum criteria for a "community" include the fact that the participants live together, that they are more than a family or a couple, and that the community's purpose goes beyond mere cohabitation. In addition, we have included small and also planned projects which are just starting down the path to community.

As this is the English edition of eurotopia we decided to limit the amount of communities mentioned in the chapter about Germany: we did not include some very small, most of the planned and those communities, that do not welcome more members. In the German edition of eurotopia you can find around 50 more of them.

We have done little to check up on the information printed here, and the communities themselves bear full responsibility for the content of their self-descriptions. The degree to which their self-evaluations match what you will actually find there depends not only on the condition of the community and its members at the time of writing, but also on your expectations. That's why we want you to decide whether a group is "politically correct" or whether there are other (good or bad) reasons to mistrust it: you, the readers, have a wide range of views and are conducting your search with different interests in mind. That's why we do not want to discriminate in our selection and pass judgement on individual projects. The philosophical and organisational makeup of the communities depicted in this book derives exclusively from the participation of communities in our survey, and does not necessarily reflect the current state of the community movement.

Overall, 311 communities in twenty-four countries found their way into the data section this time. More than half of them did not appear in *Eurotopia* 2000/01, and we have also included some fifty projects which have been founded since 2000. What if you know of communities which have not been included? There are a number of reasons why communities do not respond: First, we simply do not know them all. Second, some are not interested in visitors and new members. Third, some do not want to attract any additional attention to themselves. Fourth, some do not get around to answering or else they "misplace" the questionnaire. Fifth…

From our vantage point, the responses make it impossible to offer any reliable assessment as to whether the community movement as a whole is growing, stagnating or even shrinking. It appears as if general interest in solidarity-based and alternative lifestyles and organisational structures is on the increase, or at least that's the impression one gets from on-going media interest and the number of community seekers. But we are convinced that the community lifestyle still needs a major boost through active participation and the establishment of new groups. Nothing is perfect, but there are plenty of projects out there that are worthy of support. Please take both your search and the communities themselves seriously, and take account of their members' efforts and dedication.

You might be wondering why, in this age of instantaneous electronic communications media, the *eurotopia* index is still only appearing in book form. One reason is that currently a third of the communities we wrote to did not want to be published on the Internet and thus would not show up in an on-line data base. On the other hand an on-line eurotopia could be continously updated and would be very useful for travelling people. The question is, if users would be willing to pay an appropriate fee for such a service. Feel free to tell us your opinion! In any case for us personally, a real honest-to-goodness book is a very satisfying result from our 1,500 hours of work, particularly each time we hand it over to an interested person.

Structure:

On the first fiftyfive pages we have put together some thoughts regarding the topics of "community" and "ecovillage". First, Martin and Karen present some definitions in their articles "What is a community?" and "What is an ecovillage?" and go on to outline the characteristics of these two ways of life. In his essay on "The Rainbow Power of Community", Dieter takes a philosophical-sociological perspective on the dynamic interaction of human beings, the group and society, with a special angle on the development of an integrative understanding of community. The three following articles are dedicated to focal points of community life: Bill examines the connections between "Money, property and responsibility"; Lora breaks a lance for an active discussion over the existential issue of "Decision-making in consensus"; and Peter reports on a study devoted to the subject of "Communities as the lifestyle of the future" according to the criteria of an ecological evaluation.

While preparing this edition of *eurotopia* we were particularly concerned with emphasising community development. This topic is discussed at various points throughout the first section. The article "Forming a community" by Martin with his consultation tips, and "How to begin?" by Dieter invite each reader who is on the path toward community to dedicate him- or herself to the exciting processes of human togetherness and to transform old sorrows into new virtues. The only repeat from the last edition is Sven's satirical suggestions for community visitors, which rounds off the first section.

And as if this weren't enough already: As in the last *eurotopia* from 2000, we have included a special section on **community networks**. There you can find further information showing how the individual communities fit together, or how networking within the community scene looks. The **useful addresses** should also be helpful in locating further practical information around the topic of "living in community".

We hope that this book is exactly what you have been looking for. In any case, we here at the Club99 Community at Ökodorf Sieben Linden have stood behind it all the way, with hand, heart and soul. Good luck!

The Community-Seeker

A story for this book and its readers

told by Dieter Halbach

Stopping by a small co-operative bookshop recently I came upon a book with the modest title: "Eurotopia: An Index of European Communities". My heart skipped a beat: perhaps there was still a chance for me to find a new life before death? The salesman behind the counter looked at me through his nickel-rimmed glasses, his eyes half sympathetic, half amused, and said: "A good book for people looking for community! Yes, I was searching once myself... and what I found, I lost again. But I recently rediscovered part of what I thought I'd lost."

After this somewhat nebulous introduction, he began to relate his odyssey across the globe from one community to the next. He was nothing if not critical: no one could satisfy him on his quest for the perfect community. The politically correct communities lived in a wrong way and lugged around heavy ideological baggage; the economically successful ones were sandbagged with work and management and had turned conventional; the freaks were too stoned and chaotic for his taste; the spiritual communities were so obsessed with love that they had thrown sexuality out the window, and the sexually liberated communities had done the same with love.

My bookseller was just getting into high gear when suddenly a wistful, almost mystical smile appeared on his lips: "But after so many years of searching I've finally found it: my community! They're just a handful of people, but somehow they have managed to integrate all aspects of life." "Right, so why didn't you stay there?" I asked him. "They didn't want me," he replied. "I wanted the perfect community, but they wanted the perfect human being!"

A short time later, after many more questions, I stepped onto the street, the book under my arm. I felt funny inside. A blend of pain and joy, spiced with a pinch of fear, had settled onto my heart – which in turn was beating like a drum. Is this what the poets call "longing"?

"Only sunny eyes can see the sun," my bookseller called after me, laughing.

"And what about the butterflies in my stomach?" I wondered.

So on shaky legs I stepped out into the adventure they call life... my life, which has something to do with me and something to do with community.

What is "Community"?

A tentative definition and overview

by Martin Stengel

"The whole world is a commune. We all live in one world. Addressing this task, pulling this simple statement out of utopia and into the simple consciousness of yourself and everyone else will be our task and the task of future generations." *(Gogo Böhm / La Lix)*

What is "community"? "Well, that's obvious enough, isn't it?" I thought – and then I decided to head out in search of a more precise definition. The linguists tell us that "community" comes from the Latin word *communis*, which means "shared", "common", "general", "universal" and "public". Thus it's an antonym to the word *proprius*, i.e. private. It is related to the words *commune*, meaning "common property" and *communiter*, i.e. "in common with others", "jointly" and "generally". In modern-day Europe, a "community" is generally described as a group that shares something or whose members agree on specific characteristics, behaviours or interests.

In using this definition, we note that there are countless forms of communities on virtually every relationship level, existing for the most varied of reasons. There is scarcely a single human or other being who does not somehow belong to at least one community, if not to many. We grow up within families, with whose members we have a great deal in common; we earn our money in businesses together with others whose attitude is also aimed at earning money; we live in municipalities within state communities (whether we like it or not); or else we're members of the regional forest community.

The Institute for Sociology at the University of Münster describes groups of individuals who join together on the basis of similar interests so as better to achieve their individual goals as *social* communities. Such communities arise from private (football, scat clubs...), religious (churches, faith communities...) or political motives (parties, trade unions...) and as economic organisations (co-operatives, corporations...). They usually limit themselves to one aspect of the members' lives or one common task and do not touch on private matters – which doesn't necessarily mean that the local suburban garden club or co-operative won't give us an opportunity to meet our new best friend or even our mate.

Originally, and even today in some non-industrial cultures, all people are born into life communities encompassing more than one family. Life itself is firmly linked to membership in a tribe, a clan, a village, and a purely individualistic lifestyle is accorded little value. Such communities are classified as *primary*, i.e. as communities on the same social level as the family. Such a community's existential basis is often tribal property. Tasks are defined by the village community and fulfilled by the individual on behalf of this village community. People quite naturally live in and for the community and the community in turn feels responsible for the well-being of each of its natural members. Among other things, this concern expresses itself in traditional rituals through which new-borns or young men and women are formally admitted to the tribe.

What we are reporting on in *eurotopia* are groups of people who consciously and voluntarily decide to share their private time, ideas and values together and, to this end, to live together. Here we are referring to *intentional* or *voluntary* communities. Ideally, people who decide to live in such communities intentionally enter in on more intensive relationships with others, bond more closely with others, and voluntarily place part of their lives and actions in the service of the group's common good and thus in the service of other people. Ideally, they also pull back the curtain which normally surrounds private life and make themselves more visible to others.

"A community is a circle of people who know and accept each other and who support each other in their mutual growth – people who trust each other and dedicate a part of their energy to a greater whole."

(Corinna Felkl/Sieben Linden)

Community intensity

What about the level of intensity possible in living together in a community? There is a broad spectrum: from the *neighbourhood* and the (pragmatic) *flat-sharing community* all the way to the classic *commune* (whereby these terms may have different meanings from one place to the next). While settlements organised on a neighbourhood basis (such as the co-housing projects in Denmark) still put the family first, namely in a clearly defined territory – the family flat – in communes these private structures have largely been dissolved in both spatial and even social terms: members share common kitchens, they often take care of the children together and they earn the money in common.

While in eco-settlements most decisions are private (individual, family, household), the shared decisions in communes usually reach considerably further into such areas as procuring commodities, eating habits, professional activities or even child-rearing. The looser communities are thus sometimes described as secondary groupings, while communitarian living arrangements are included among the primary groupings, right along with the family and couple relationships. While secondary communities certainly can encompass hundreds or even thousands of members, the primary groups normally stay well below this on account of the greater intensity of their relationships.

The book you are holding in your hands was written by people who belong to two communities: the commune Club99, whose contractual terms reach far into its members' private lives, and also the surrounding village community – the Ecovillage Sieben Linden – whose goal is to become a 300-member organism made up of smaller communities. Thus hybrid forms are certainly possible and help to integrate different aspects.

Community consciousness and individuality

Communities are usually characterised by a group consciousness, by a not always easy-to-grasp concept of who "we" are as a group. A person as an *individual* (= "the indivisible one") maintains a living relationship with the surrounding community. If all goes well, as an individual person living in community I feel both that I am a self-responsible person with my own uniqueness and also that I am a part of a larger organism which possesses an exterior form and identity with which I can identify.

The experience of my own uniqueness within this field of give-and-take and the direct feedback of people I am well acquainted with gives me, as an individual, a clear awareness of who I am in the company of others and how others perceive me. Equipped with this knowledge, which continues to develop, I can then decide whether or not to become a "community-compatible individualist" who is aware of his strengths and weaknesses, his abilities and needs. I can embark on a voyage of mutual inspiration and enrichment together with my community.

According to the sociologist Hans-Peter Dürr, the secret of Nature's success is the "plus-sum game": within the overall context, the advantage of one is the advantage of the other. If I, with my dedication and my love, promote another member of the group, then that has a positive effect on the community environment and, ultimately, on me too. We are becoming increasingly aware of the negative experiences that go with the standard model of mutual competition and living at other people's expense. Humankind is becoming more aware of itself through the globalisation of its unavoidable mutual impacts. The result is that we stop viewing ourselves as being independent and start viewing ourselves as part of the *world community*.

Of course, there's no guarantee that things will work out this way. History is filled with examples of negative group consciousness. When "we" becomes a substitute for a missing positive self-awareness the result can easily be a dependence on the group's identity and strength with some nasty results. In other cases, communities/societies develop absolutist structures which suppress deviant attitudes and actions through punishment. We need only recall the wars of religion and the Inquisition, or the madness of fascist and racist systems in cultures all over the world.

These tendencies appear to be weaker or are at least harder to detect in our "civilised" societies. But even here membership in a group can lead to a situation where members develop a disparaging and even hostile stance toward people who think differently. Not even politically and spiritually enlightened groups/communities are immune to this. The nature of the boundary drawn between You and Me, between Us and Them determines whether a group becomes an enrichment for the whole (promoting peace) or else a threat (provoking war).

The vision of community

Many "intentional" communities have formulated a common vision, an utopia as an ideal vision of another world or another type of society. Thus community is not just intended to fulfil a need for more relationships but offers an experimental space for alternative models for living. The communes of 1968 were a response to the repressive normality of Germany's "Economic Miracle". They were experienced as islands of artfully expressed autonomy, non-conformity and freedom from domination. Rural communes were and still are responses and alternatives to the dependent life of urban culture with its jobs, its food and energy deliveries. The monasteries of the middle ages not only sheltered people hoping to exchange worldliness for chastity, but also socially critical people who were given the opportunity to develop their theories and conduct their research under the protection of the Church. Monastic orders developed whose members lived and practised their faith in common while rejecting the prevailing ecclesiastical norms and hierarchies.

Even today, most communities can be identified as model projects for future-compatible and society-changing ways of living. Many consciously present their experiences to the public. Not least, the shared and energy-amplifying aspect of a commonly formulated and sustained vision is significant for new community formation.

The communities you will find in *eurotopia* partly have many similar characteristics; but from another point of view, they also differ greatly from one another. On the backside of our questionnaires we sent the communities a list of keywords, the most relevant of which they were to mark with an "X". With this rough characterisation, we want to go beyond the mere self-descriptions and additionally provide our readers with a simpler overview. Of course, from this one could go into a whole range of statistical analyses of the way in which communities view themselves.

The 311 communities described in this index have marked their most relevant characteristics in the following way:

70 % describe themselves as "ecological"

41 % are "non-violent"

36 % view themselves as "spiritual"

31 % practise "organic agriculture" and

32 % "self-sufficiency"

35 % follow a "vegetarian" diet and 12% even follow a "vegan" diet

26 % do "peace work"

20 % have a "left-wing political understanding"

10 % are "anarchistic" as opposed to 4% which are "hierarchical"

7 % live in "free love"-relationships

One community (0.003%) is both "anarchistic" and "hierarchical" at the same time

Do we need communities?

We eurotopians maintain that the world needs communities, more communities than ever before! The greater the separation between people and cultures, the more destructive their individual and collective influence on one another and on nature seems to become. Over the course of the Industrial Revolution our attentiveness toward the common good has disappeared more and more. Humankind has become an economic factor and a calculable system component. From the perspective of the so-called powers that be and the media, but also in our own eyes, we are basically consumers (of superfluous assets), workers or employers, investors, home builders, money savers. Or else we are gifted, disabled, soldiers, security risks... In the process, we ourselves have elevated our individuality to a desirable trait in itself.

On the other hand, despite all our creativity, our desire for self-realisation, our search for more meaning in our lives, we are becoming more and more superfluous – we are even becoming a "problem" in our own right. We identify with symbols and objects, with having and doing, and yet we place great value on being as different as possible from other people. Individuality becomes competition: we don't want other people to be better off than we are, and war between individuals – as between states – is a "regrettably but unavoidable means" of securing one's existence.

But we can already see signs of a turnabout. As our consciousness becomes more global, and as humankind continues to recognise that our destinies depend on one another and that we are all heading down the wrong path together, a shared desire to think in new ways is starting to spread. Whoever holistically examines the causes of human misery will ultimately realise the necessity of a transformation of values: humans and humanity itself need more contacts and a deeper connection to other sentient beings. They need to be able to express their inner longings, to express the meaning of their lives through meaningful activities, through a link to nature and the natural foundations of life. They need peace with one another, co-operation, mutual support and a sense of community.

I don't want to suggest that voluntary communities, as described in this book, constitute a solution to all problems. And the fact that many people leave communities and that community initiatives fail certainly also means that the community principle is less than a perfect fit in many cases. But I am convinced that they offer a whole world of possibilities for the transformation we need and that they can be the nuclei of a new consciousness. They can be learning places for co-operative behaviours and laboratories for future-compatible lifestyles – both for groups as a whole and for the individuals within them.

"When all members sense a living balance among one another, then the community will become a place of great passion and profound satisfaction."
(Lillian Downey)

What is an Ecovillage?

by Karen Svensson

Ecovillages embody a way of living. They are grounded in the deep understanding that all things and all creatures are interconnected, and that our thoughts and actions have an impact on our environment.

Ecovillages are communities of people who strive to lead a sustainable lifestyle in harmony with each other, other living beings and the Earth. Their purpose is to combine a supportive social-cultural environment with a low-impact lifestyle. As a new societal structure, the ecovillage goes beyond today's dichotomy of urban versus rural settlements: it represents a widely applicable model for the planning and reorganization of human settlements in the 21st Century.

The deep motivation for ecovillages or intentional communities is the need to reverse the gradual disintegration of supportive social-cultural structures and the upsurge of destructive environmental practices on our planet. Underlying the concept of the ecovillage is the desire to take responsibility for one's own life; to create a future which, contrary to the depleting energies of the „mechanical" world dominated by organizational giants, is regenerative for the individual and for nature, and thereby sustainable into the indefinite future. A future which we would like to bequeath our children, so they, and in turn their children, may grow up as balanced and healthy human beings.

Ecovillages embody a way of living. They are grounded in the deep understanding that all things and all creatures are interconnected, and that our thoughts and actions have an impact on our environment. Based on this philosophy, ecovillages build on varying combinations of three dimensions:

- ***Ecology***
- ***Community (the social dimension)***
- ***Culture/Spirituality***

Today there are as many different versions of the ecovillage as there are ecovillages. Each has reached its individual level of development, and reflects the particular creativity and inspiration of its builders. While some ecovillages have been in existence for over 20 years, and are starting to present the picture of quite complete experiments in sustainable living, others are just starting to emerge.

Though in the past ecovillages may sometimes have been seen as rather marginal and idealistic settlements, we are gradually witnessing the advent of the „mainstream ecovillage", which integrates ecovillage principles while also fitting in with mainstream lifestyles and expectations (e.g.streamlined architecture; a mix of rental and privately owned housing; both shared and private facilities, including common and private gardens; mixed backgrounds, occupations and ages). These ecovillages allow for a diversity, both in societal composition and in people's individual focus and degree of participation in the community, which reflects mainstream circumstances.

The following section presents an overview of the three main dimensions of ecovillages, which are integrated with varying emphasis in different settlements. These dimensions also represent the three areas we can choose to focus on when establishing more sustainable lifestyles for ourselves in other settings (e.g. our family, neighborhood or organization).

The Ecological Dimension of an Ecovillage

The ecological dimension of ecovillages denotes people's connection to the living Earth: the soil, water, wind, plants and animals. It ranges from an expressed intention to save energy and recycle waste to a more all-round commitment to low-impact living, integrating village-based energy systems, water treatment plants, Earth restoration, permaculture (e.g. for food production) and ecological building.

Ecology means, among other things:

- Growing organic food as much as possible within the community bioregion
- Creating „living" homes out of natural, locally available materials, and using local (architectural) traditions
- Using village-based integrated renewable energy systems
- Ecological business principles (local green business)
- Assessing the life cycle of products used in the ecovillage from a social/spiritual and ecological point of view
- Preserving clean soil, water and air through proper energy and waste management
- Protecting and encouraging biodiversity and safeguarding wilderness areas.

Strawbale construction in Club99 (Ökodorf Sieben Linden)

The Social Dimension of an Ecovillage

The social dimension of ecovillages refers to people's desire to spend more time together, and to create a supportive environment where one can thrive both as a free individual and as part of a group. Ecovillages are small enough that everyone feels empowered. In the Western world, among the deafening noise of industrial concerns, over-communication and political megastructures, the voice of the individual person is often not heard. In an ecovillage, this voice is loud and clear. People are able to participate in making decisions that affect their own lives and that of the community on a transparent basis (i.e. with total openness).

For children, ecovillages provide a loving environment where they are involved in daily tasks such as gardening and building. This enables them to learn a variety of skills through practical experience. Learning to function as responsible members of a community also helps them think for themselves while at the same time remembering their place in the whole. Generally, ecovillages are able to foster a balance between personal freedom and one's responsibility to others, creating free and purposeful human beings who learn to identify and meet their own needs as well as those of the society they live in.

Social community means:

- Recognizing and relating to others
- Sharing common resources and providing mutual aid
- Learning to make good decisions and solve conflicts
- Emphasizing holistic and preventive health practices
- Providing meaningful work and sustenance to all members
- Allowing for a whole life for children, the elderly, and marginal groups
- Promoting lifelong education
- Encouraging unity through respect for differences
- Fostering cultural expression
- Green Economics

Economic Ramifications

The economic setup of ecovillages is often designed to fit a supportive social and family life by reducing financial requirements to allow a shift in lifestyle. One can cut down on commuting time by seeking work closer to home, even if it means a lower income, and reducing external work hours altogether. This in turn allows more social and family time, and can leave room for building up a local business. In practice, this setup often means adopting principles of voluntary simplicity, increasingly integrating work- and private lives, and creating income-earning occupations within the community. Partial self-sufficiency in the form of local food and energy production - combined with a strong communal network - provides an added sense of security for individuals or groups to dare tackle a change in economic setup. Sometimes a community will help launch new ventures by supporting its initiators during rocky beginnings. In many cases the creation of an alternative economic system can add to an ecovillage's independence from the global systems, and strengthen the community. Alternative economics are often based on the principle of gift giving and exchange, and therefore also directly related to social parameters and values.

Economic principles to support ecovillages encompass:

- Complementary currencies (LETS systems, Friendly Favors, ecovillage currency)
- Alternative banks
- Voluntary simplicity
- Local income-generating activities (green businesses, consulting)
- Expanded informal economy (communal meals, services) up to shared economy

The Cultural/Spiritual Dimension of an Ecovillage

Through the integration of Cultural and Spiritual principles into their fabric, many intentional ecovillages echo the re-birth of cultural traditions throughout the world, and return to a way of living where harmony with all living beings, including our Earth, is the backbone of daily life. Ecovillages embody a sense of unity with the natural world. They foster recognition of human life and the Earth itself as part of the larger cosmos. Though some ecovillages choose a well-defined spiritual path, many do not place the emphasis on spiritual practices as such. However, observing natural cycles, and respecting the Earth and all living beings on it, they tend to maintain, recreate or find new cultural expressions of humans' connectedness with nature and the universe.

Building a sweat lodge (Amerindian purification ritual)

Culture and Spirituality are expressed through:

- Fostering a sense of joy and belonging through rituals and celebrations following natural cycles (e.g. maypole, harvesting feast, Midsummer)
- Emphasizing creativity and the arts as an expression of unity and interrelationship to our universe
- Expressing a spiritual world view of global interconnectedness
- Respecting that spirituality manifests in many ways
- Respecting the expression of different cultures
- Facilitating personal growth and integral spiritual practices.

Traditional Villages

In the northern hemisphere, ecovillages are mostly of an intentional nature, as they try to re-build communities from scratch based on their chosen focus (ecological, social and/or cultural-spiritual). In the global South, 50-75% of the population is still living in villages whose social, cultural and spiritual fabric remains intact, and whose inhabitants largely survive on subsistence economies (supported by self-sufficient agricultural production). Farmers are increasingly forced to shift from polycultures to monocultures on the land.

The ecovillage concept provides viable alternatives to popular exodus and growing monocultures in the southern' hemisphere: networks of villages (e.g. Sri Lanka, Senegal, Burkina Faso, India) and progressive governments are today seeking to integrate ecovillage principles into the traditional village structures, to achieve a form of village-based sustainable development which meets people's basic needs with local resources, while also adapting to more modern requirements and market demands.

Sesame-processing plant at at the Senegalese NGO AAJAC-COLUFIFA, member of the Senegalese ecovillage network.

The rainbow power of community

On the significance of communal living today

by Dieter Halbach

The rainbow symbolises the new spirit of self-organised and integrative forms of community – "unity in diversity". While freedom and interconnectedness, the individual and the collective may have seemed like contradictions in the past, they increasingly harmonise in today's communities. Just like a rainbow with its shining colors, modern communities wish for individuals to develop their complete individuality. The goal of these new forms is not the blending of individual colours into a single, uniform shade. Nor are the individual colours separated and indiscriminately patterned, as in the case of extreme individualism. Instead, they complement and support one another in their radiance. Only in harmony with one another can they produce that harmonic and comprehensive work of art we know as a rainbow – a visionary tension between heaven and earth.

This rainbow power is the driving force of modern communal experiments – regardless of where they came from. It is a profoundly human and historical healing process rooted in openness and trust. Probably all the communities presented in this book have experienced these changes to the extent that they have addressed genuine human issues and have not closed their doors to the outside world for ideological reasons.

Some of the central themes discussed in the following chapters:

1. How can we understand and shape this dynamic composition of the individual and the group with their common goals embedded in society?
2. What is the deep and historical longing that the desire for community is rooted in?
3. What does the notion of integral community mean today?
4. What social issues do these experiments address? What special contribution do these new communities make to an integral and forward-looking culture?

Action by students of the Holma College for Holistic Studies in Sweden

1. A necessary balance: The magic triangle within the circle

Individuals, communal life within the group and the group's goals all combine to form a magic triangle within the circle of the world. If the flow between these poles and the surrounding territory is disrupted, then the balance in all areas will be disrupted.

Narim Hikmet has expressed this polarity in a poem which illustrates our image:

"To live individually and free like a tree
and brotherly and sisterly like a forest

... that is what we long for!"

individually and free like a tree

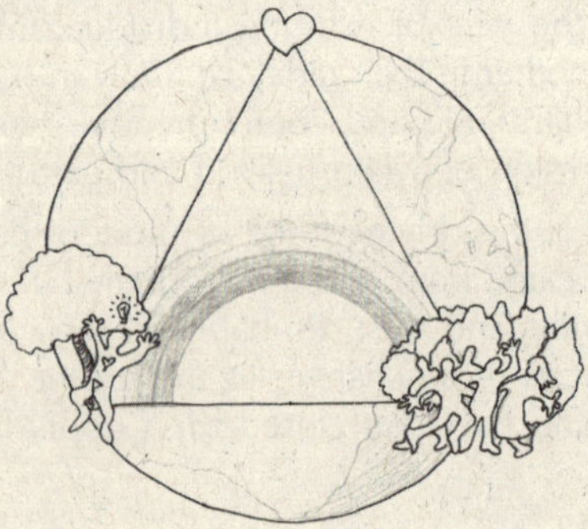

brotherly and sisterly like a forest

The magic triangle in the circle of the earth (inspired by the "thematic interaction" of Ruth Cohn and the "Quadrants of the great transformation" by Ken Wilber)

What are the starting positions of these poles in today's world and how does their interaction impact the formation of communities?

The individual:

One step at a time, the individual is emerging from the shadows of history. Until recently, this history has been one of suppression, disrespect and degradation for all earth's children. It has uprooted our self-esteem. But the age of Enlightenment raised a new demand:

"On this earth there is one single path which no one can take but you. Don't ask where it leads! Follow it!" (Friedrich Nietzsche)

Today, the individual is no longer thought of as a faceless fragment of a collective, but as a unique and multidimensional being. While once just a cog in the machine, he or she is slowly receiving a special voice, a heart, a soul, an erotic sexuality, a life story, a thinking mind and a spiritual dimension: that of his or her interconnectedness with all living things.

The group:

Today, there is a new longing for community, since – as we have all witnessed – modern individualism ultimately destroys the individual. Stripped from their living roots, individuals have merely been set free to pursue their own dependencies. *"The full development of the individual is a communal undertaking"*, chaos theory proclaims. In communities, the individual can find partners who help him or her to grow, fostering genuine empathy. Such an interaction calls for complete and complex personalities. The awareness of one's own inner voices, of one's own strengths and weaknesses harmonises with the diversity and co-operative skills of a group. Here, the individual can combine his or her strengths with the strengths of others in harmony, rather than succumb to conflict and rivalry.

The goals:

A community needs common visions in order to reach out beyond its own day-to-day existence, in order to work together in good and bad times, to admit weaknesses to one another and to grow through them. But unlike in traditional family and clan relationships, and unlike in purely functional work teams, these goals cannot be prescribed. The new intentional communities – this network of "selfelected affinities", as Goethe once called this quasi-chemical interaction of previously isolated individuals – are instead created out of a shared conception of humanity and the world. Closeness must be consciously created. That is why honest and continuous discussions on common values and tasks are the living foundation of the modern community idea.

The environment:

The social environment, which can be understood as everything from one's immediate neighbours all the way to the planet as a whole, is the breeding ground of every community. "No community can survive (except as an ideological fossil!) if it separates itself from the social framework to which it belongs. It draws its real justification from the service which it provides to society as a whole." (Donald Waters, founder of Ananda Villages.) Community does not end at one's own property boundaries (or at the boundaries of concepts, legal structures, relationships). A communal person always lives in community, wherever he or she happens to be. And the themes of one's own community are always historical and social themes, too.

2. The individual and the longing for community

Every human being carries a longing for interconnectedness within his or her heart. "Co-naissance – being born with others" describes our inborn brother- and sisterhood within the great net of life. All new-borns experience themselves as an integral part of this cosmos and are utterly dependent on the love and care of their surroundings. Every child seeks wholeness in a family and protection within a larger network of nurturing relationships and places. *"It takes a whole village to raise a child"*, says Sobonfu Somé of the Dagara people in West Africa. But at the same time: *"It takes a whole village to ensure the parents' spiritual health"*. Life in the lap of the tribal community was once the cradle of humanity and is deeply rooted in us as social beings.

"The community is the soul, the guiding star of my people... The goal of community is to ensure that each of its members is heard and the gifts which he or she has brought into this world are put to use in the right way. Without the sharing of these gifts the community dies. And without the community individual people no longer have a place where they can contribute what they have to give... But if we cannot pass on our gifts then we are blocked internally, which influences us in many spiritual, mental and physical ways. We are homeless, we have no place where we can go when we have the need to be seen." (Sobonfu Somé, "The Gift of Happiness")

Human existence is characterised by the pain of separation. Knowledge of oneself throws us back on ourselves. We emerge from Creation only to enter a state of fear – we are castaways in a strange world. We must all pass through this painful process of birth, both as individuals and as part of the human race. The infant must emerge from its unconscious existence as the giant and dwarf of its own world and realise that the world outside exists and does not obey its wishes. Humanity as a whole was forced to awaken from its dream of original unity with nature. For more than five thousand years now, countless traditional tribal cultures based on the principle of kinship and mutuality have been systematically wiped off the face of the earth.

Today's society with its global market and turbo-individualism threatens to uproot what little remains of this legacy. According to a world-wide study on happiness, people in the affluent societies lag far behind those in the poorer countries, where strong social bonds still exist (study by the London School of Economics).

A life totally bereft of community is not possible for us: without contact and co-operation we would "starve" in a spiritual and physical sense. In this respect, community is the elixir and glue of all social life, the warm current within our history, which allows us to move on no matter how bleak the outlook may sometimes be.

Alongside the prevailing trend toward individualisation, evolution of human society has also demonstrated a tendency towards more community. As a matter of fact, in today's globalised world, human beings are linked more closely together than ever before – in both good and bad ways. *"We have only the one world which we are creating together, whether we like each other or not." (Humberto Maturana)*

3. An integral approach to community in practise

The vision of non-violent communal life means expanding the community idea into a global community and co-operation with the earth as a living being. The progressive dissolution of all traditional bonds, all the way to social atomisation, provides both the opportunity and necessity of developing a new concept of community. But just as official social structures and world organisations have failed to constitute themselves on a solidarity-based foundation, communities have so far been unable to develop their social potential within the larger society.

Up to today, communities have often not been more than a brief visionary flash in the pan. Taken as a whole, they have had only little significance in regard to the share of the population they represent and the sociopolitical influence they bring to bear. In the past, many have been plagued by internal conflicts, personal overtaxing, scarce funds, and a lack of regional and social networking. Demands and stress come to dominate everyday life, which loses its visionary drive and degenerates to empty routine. As in any family drama, communal experiments can become their own worst enemies.

"Perhaps one of the greatest errors on the part of community planners was the fact that they expected too much from their concepts. No system can create virtue... Our intense interest should go to people as individual beings, not as part of a system. A system is only necessary to co-ordinate life... People must develop the communal spirit organically. The surest way for every new community is to give everyone the freedom to come together with others, each in his or her own way... But when people are supposed to do everything together and have the same opinion about everything, conflicts are sure to follow... Above all, we must not expect miracles. It suffices for the new way of life to be better than the old one." (Donald Waters/ Ananda Village)

4. The inner turning point in process of community

So how can we conceive of an integral communal model which is able to combine the variety and stability of a village, the interconnectedness of a tribe and the planetary culture of networks with the quest for personal growth within one group? A forwardlooking understanding of community must be structured openly with an eye to transforming the quest for community from an idealised group dictate to an experimental social concept with sufficient room for personal growth and social development.

The starting point is radical honesty and simplicity in personal interaction, the abandonment of every preconceived form. Otherwise the desire for community will end up like the bush in Bertolt Brecht's Keuner story: in his attempt to give the bush a round shape, the gardener keeps cutting it until it's round all right, but no longer a bush! The form threatens to stifle the content: you might cut too much!

The Arche community in southern France is an example of a community which has existed since shortly after World War II and which continues to uphold ambitious goals in regard to self-sufficiency and non-violence.

The following experience of two long-term residents represents a turning point in the communal idea:

"It becomes really difficult when you have to accept what's inside of you. To accept yourself means to accept others the way they are – and that's how communal life starts in the first place. Once you've reached this point, the form suddenly drops away. And the critical questions, the ones about the tractor and the electricity, aren't so important anymore. Because even if I really am on the "right" path, even if I genuinely want to live in harmony with nature, that doesn't help me one bit unless the motivation comes from a deeper place. When you live in a community, you have to abandon all preconceived notions. Only one thing is important: to work on what's inside of you. You have to let go of things in every respect. Only after you've abandoned the form do you start encountering each other in truth, in your real nature. That is brother- and sisterhood, because a community can only exist if all the members know each other as brothers and sisters." (Etienne and Brigitte, Arche Community in France)

*Now it's true that the down-to-*earth Arche communities are not classical therapeutic or New Age groups. Working on "what's inside" also means working on "content", on a binding praxis. "Abandoning form" doesn't mean abandoning communal and individual principles and goals. On the contrary, it means taking the

decisive practical step of freeing the content from its egotistical chains and contradictions and arriving at a human understanding of it. To be "radical" means to "reach for the roots", and the roots of today's crisises lie within us as human beings. In keeping with the inner attitude of "non-violent communication" (Marshall Rosenberg), we can connect to one another while addressing our needs as the original common source of our lives that lie behind our different positions. Community can be a special place where world-views do not collide but where instead a "world forum" takes place. Here we don't have antagonistic positions facing off against one another, but people who want to live together and who have an opportunity to look behind these positions and understand them.

"We are divided in our convictions but united in our doubts," Peter Ustinov once observed. Why do I sow peace but harvest conflict? Why is the other guy the way he is? And why am I the way I am? Why haven't the right arguments brought about the world revolution? Why can an objectively good concept lead to a subjectively wrong life? And why can a subjectively happy life have objectively negative consequences?

Historically, "communities" have been built up upon traditions, collective adaptation, ideologies and identification. The individuals with their individual truth were not included in this collective public sphere. The individual and the community were separated. These preindividual forms of community were and still are a hotbed of division, exclusion and thus war in all its many forms. "To be clear in our goals and soft on our people" – this integral communal idea is the common thread uniting a wide variety of communities today: it can be perceived over the whole spectrum of leftist communes to spiritually-oriented groups.

Many of the communities listed in this eurotopia catalogue are moving in this direction. In recent years, the idea has become a reality in the loose network of German communal projects ("Come Together"), in the world-wide Global Ecovillage Network (GEN), and in many other co-operative projects.

The new spirit of co-operation is no longer provincial and collectivist, but planetary and increasingly non-ideological: it includes all living beings. It is founded on the free and alterable will of its members. It provides enough space for self-discovery and personal development. Its structures are comparable to the concept of ecology: each individual is both a whole unto him or herself, and also part of a greater whole.

New communities are neither unstructured bunches nor hierarchical collectives. They are both "holistic" and "individualistic". Their structures experiment with grass-roots democracy and combine chaos, egalitarian communication and different layers of complex order including areas of competence. The basis for all this is human encounter and a profound perception of one another. Their networks do not grind to a halt at their own group boundaries but consciously include more and more groups and movements. Thus they ultimately link their fate with the evolutionary stream of humankind's possible (but not inevitable) growth in awareness of a "more comprehensive unity" (Teilhard de Chardin).

How do such communities function, and what inner attitudes are they based on? The following thesises are intended both to describe and inspire today's spirit of co-operation.

10 thesises on community formation

1. **Interconnectedness:** Community is not primarily defined by group affiliation but is an attitude of interconnectedness with other people and with life itself. It is constantly recreated by one's own inner work and openness toward others.
2. **Commitment:** The clear formulation of fundamental community goals and values helps bring like-minded people together, enabling them to use their power to realize dreams and their creativity together in synergy. Clear agreements ward off failure as a result of fundamentally different life concepts. Commitment to common goals and the interconnectedness of individual paths motivate and promote one another.
3. **Personal participation:** Community can only develop when I participate, when I dare to proclaim the big YES and the precise NO with my whole person. As long as we don't take this step, community will be nothing but an empty sideshow staged by "the others". This is an invitation to the critics in the back rows to step in and start playing leading roles themselves.
4. **Individuality:** Community does not develop from the desire to restrict personalities and to adapt them to a transcendent group identity, but rather from recognising our differences, our strengths and weaknesses as our common treasure.
5. **Unity in diversity:** The more diverse and powerful individuals are, the more stable and lively the community will become through a network of complex relationships. As in a biotope, the meaning of community lies in mutual amplification and co-ordination. Unity and diversity need each other.
6. **Inner community:** The ability to achieve "unity in diversity" corresponds to the inner awareness of one's own self as a diverse being: "I am many!" Understanding and integrating the various, often conflicting and fragmented inner voices into becoming a co-operating orchestra within oneself is the precondition for dealing openly with external adversaries. Rigid self-conceptions prevent community. Open self-conceptions make it possible to assume various roles within the total organism and to amplify one another: "We are one."
7. **Experimental formation of society:** Community includes both self-transformation and social transformation. No area of life and experience should be excluded so that the common dialogue can lead to human and factually appropriate solutions. Intimate human questions particularly require the healing light of mutual perception in order to free their potential from private bonds and injuries.
8. **Building of trust:** The ability to see the world through another person's eyes and with an open heart, to be able to open oneself up without giving oneself up, is the foundation of empathy and trust. Those who assume the risk of

supporting others in their goals and potentials can help banish petty nit-picking over inadequacies and problems. We can learn to enjoy and appreciate the distance between one another and to perceive one another within the scope of a larger horizon.

9. **Projection and disappointment:** The longing for community often stands in an inverse relationship to our ability to make it happen. Instead of fulfilling our own expectations and filling the gaps in our lives, community can end up as a mirror of our own fears and a challenge to our own growth. Those who look for US will find ME – and vice versa.

10. **Home:** Only once I can be entirely natural within community – abandoning all pretence and truly being myself – can I really say that I've arrived in community.

Community happening in this way only emerges when a process of conscious socialisation takes place from within the individual, when the individual opens him or herself to find resonance in the world. Mutual interconnectedness is a tendency which we encounter not only in communities and social movements, but also within human evolution itself.

5. The social meaning of communal projects

"We have learned to fly like birds and to swim like fish; but we have forgotten the simple art of living like brothers." (Martin Luther King)

Within this process, the relatively few communal projects in existence today (from comprehensive living communities and neighbourhoods, all the way down to project groups) are merely the conscious and organised expression of a broader evolution towards more co-operation and openness. Community always occurs when people place awareness of their interconnectedness at the centre of their lives, whether in love, in the family, in their careers or in politics. *"You, covered in the clothes and armour in which society, the state, the church, school, economics, public opinion and your own pride have placed you, indirect amongst others who are indirect, shatter the armour, become direct, may one person touch another." (Martin Buber)* Communal projects can promote this process by creating places of trust and understanding and by developing model integrative solutions out of a new spirit.

"I suggest that we develop world-wide research projects where a few hundred young, intelligent people are given the freedom to develop new comprehensive concepts and solution models for the existing problems." Thus spoke Aurelio Peccei, co-founder of the Club of Rome, in a speech before of the United Nations. By living and working together, communities are developing precisely such holistic blueprints for life, models containing an abundance of experiences on the inner connections of ecology, social issues, economics, politics and spirituality. Like a permanent "future workshop", new models are developed, tested and made accessible in daily praxis.

6. Building blocks for a future-compatible lifestyle

In the following sectors of society communities can serve a pilot function as developmental projects for a future-compatible lifestyle:

Ecological living and working

Many communal projects dedicate their entire way of life to bringing about a comprehensive ecological balance which cannot be achieved by standard individual efforts.

- o They assume that manageable and self-determined living contexts are needed in order to experience and show responsibility for the ecological consequences of one's own actions.
- o They attempt to reduce the consumption of space, energy, machines, packaging materials etc. through shared use.
- o They attempt to replace the addictive consumption of things through human encounters and more fundamental satisfaction.
- o They integrate their work and the needs of their own household into a common economy by, for example, dividing and upgrading housework, by a common household till, common decisions on large purchases and (partial) self-sufficiency.
- o They create self-determined jobs which can be integrated as far as possible into the social and natural habitat. By primarily producing for their own needs and those of their local area, they can, for example, help reduce traffic.

Social proximity and co-operation

Communal projects attempt to offset the prevailing competitive, individualised and anonymous workaday world with the values of co-operation, communication and personal encounter, thus helping to counteract social dissolution.

- They form "self-elected affinities" which can abolish dependence and rigidity in isolated nuclear families and provide children with an expanded protective and relational framework.
- They develop new conceptions of love, friendship and sexuality which bring fluidity to the boundaries of typical couple relationships and create an expanded area of trust.

Summercamp in the Waldhaus

- They create settlement and living forms in which spaces can be filled in many different ways and new contacts can occur. They also fill communal facilities with life.
- They develop networks of mutual support which can include old and young people, people in crisis, the ill and disabled, and also transform care fon one another from a purely private or state task to a shared, inter-personal undertaking.
- They develop methods of non-violent conflict resolution and mutual perception so that the social energy that is wasted in conflict can be replaced by the power of co-operation for the sake of a common future.
- They create spaces of synergetic thinking in which all human issues are concretely and comprehensively discussed and where social intelligence and a co-operative pool of ideas can be developed.

Democracy and self-determination in everyday life

Communal projects without executive personnel come alive through the conscious input of all participants and incorporate all areas of life into this process.

- o They detach leadership tasks from authority by distributing leadership tasks directly to the entire community, which in turn becomes the client and the "authority" that the individual leaders answer to.
- o They provide the necessary emotional work which is required to separate the practical decision-making process from the emotional background of a conflict, thus fostering confidence.
- o They work on a consensus basis, i.e. decisions are not made in crucial votes but through agreement (which does not necessarily mean that everyone has to have the same opinion) so that all the significant aspects of communal life are borne by everyone.
- o They are in a constant process of renewal which can and must adapt itself flexibly to all information and situations.

Economy and social justice

Communal projects develop models of sharing and common property in order to provide for social balance and mutual support.

- o In various ways they correct power imbalances in income and property relations through standardised wages, equalisation funds, a community of property, collective property or other mixed forms of shared and individual economy.
- o They seek to procure the communal ownership and management of existing and limited resources such as soil and water.
- o They emphasise the utility value of commodities and promote local added value and direct contact between producers and consumers.
- o They pursue self-help and co-operation, thus freeing themselves from dependence on employers and foreign interests.
- o They promote communal work, sweat equity and co-operative legal structures and thus fulfil essential functions which are increasingly being neglected as a result of the growing gap between declining state care mechanisms (public poverty) and increasing privatisation (private wealth).

Inner growth and holistic values

Communities provide an opportunity to transform the destructive energy of quantitative external growth into the idea of inner personal growth through daily praxis.

- o They attempt to substitute the emptiness of the individualised ego in its desperate quest for satisfaction with a renewed contact to one's own higher and greater self. Everyone joins hands in this quest.
- o They promote the non-submissive anchoring of the individual within a larger whole and thus provide the experience of mutual commitment.

- They experiment with various forms of lived spirituality beyond blind faith, repression and subordination.
- They develop a harmony of public and private values by creating an atmosphere of honesty and transparency surrounding inner human processes, including their shadow sides.
- They enrich their everyday life with culture, cultivating their own festivals, rituals, stories, songs and creativity, thus giving expression and meaning to their lives.

Communities can be viewed as microcosms in which a whole constellation of issues are bundled and placed within a human focus. They are social experiments which have managed to create a special free experimental space for themselves – a space which is impossible in the purely private sphere and unimaginable on a market economy or national basis. Communities also play an important role within social movements and non-government organisations. While civil society has roots to some extent in horizontal networks on a global basis, its orientation on certain broad issues means that it has few vertical roots in the substrate of life itself. The fact that widely diverse people voluntarily live together and share their life experiences is the really sensational aspect of communal projects.

Without falling into the trap of attempting to graft these experiences onto society as a whole, one-to-one, we can nevertheless conceive of communities as the nuclei of a new culture. They provide countless concrete examples and impulses over a broad spectrum of social issues. Above all, they can contribute the spirit of commitment and their unique social competencies to a broader process of renewal. Here new forms of thought and action are not being developed in isolation and abstraction, but together with the human being seen as a whole. We don't need new think tanks and ideological schools, we need "learning biotopes" in which a socio-ecological mixed culture of mutual enrichment and co-operation can develop.

In the spirit of a developed "unity in diversity", communities are also models of peace in a world that's out of joint. We don't need to invent new people – we "only" have to learn to perceive and recognise one another in our common humanity. First comes the experience, then the transformation; healing first, then morality.

A different world is possible – if we live differently!

Dieter Halbach: born in Berlin in 1953. First contacts with rural communes on hippie hitchhiking trips in the 1960s. He has lived and studied in various communities ever since. Co-founder of the →Sieben Linden ecovillage, →"Aufbruch – anders besser leben", →Come Together Network, seminars and consultation on community development: →"Hand in Hand, eurotopia-Gemeinschaftsberatung", editor of the journal "Kurskontakte-Eurotopia", musician, father of two daughters.

Money, Property and Accountability in Intentional Communities

by Dr. Bill Metcalf

While most people thinking of joining or forming an intentional community would admit that money, property and accountability are important issues, they are not generally seen to be as 'sexy' as issues such as power, gender relations, spirituality or decision-making. Many people wanting to live in intentional community are, in fact, trying to avoid such 'boring, bourgeois' issues as money and property — yet will find that they are crucial to community life. Only after people have been involved for some years in intentional community living do they fully appreciate the importance of these issues.

I have written about these issues at length in my latest book, *The Findhorn Book of Community Living* (Findhorn, UK: Findhorn Press, 2004), and I shall discuss money, property and accountability by using edited abstracts therefrom.

Money

Money is an issue within every intentional community — although perhaps not as big an issue as within the wider society. Most conflicts over money within intentional communities arise because of poor communication, unclear rules and weak norms. Some members can thereby feel that they are contributing too much or receiving too little, either in total or compared to others. The sources of this conflict include simply not having enough money, and disagreements over the allocation of money and financial responsibility between members, and between the individual and the collective. In some cases members agree to contribute different amounts, because they have different savings and/or income, but this requires additional trust.

There are two 'idealised' models of intentional community finance. In one individual members are responsible for the collective, while in the other the collective is responsible for the individual.

In the first 'idealised' financial model, each member is responsible for her/his own income, property and money, but contributes a stipulated amount to the collective purse, like a sort of tax. In intentional communities such as Redfield (UK), Wilhemina Ecovillage (Netherlands) and Associazione Culturale Torri Superiore (Italy), most of the collective income comes from member contributions. Each individual is responsible for her/his own expenses and communal charges, even if unable to work. Generally, property is private unless specifically collective. This is the most common financial model within newly developing ecovillage and cohousing communities around the globe.

In the second 'idealised' financial model, most or all income is earned by the collective, through communal businesses, and these funds are used to support members. Kommune Niederkaufungen (Germany), Darvell Bruderhof (UK), Communauté de l'Arche La Borie Noble (France) and residential staff members of Findhorn Foundation (UK) exemplify this system. Almost all members work for the collective which then feeds and houses them. Individuals either receive a personal allowance or simply request/take cash for private needs. If a member cannot work because of ill-health or old age, she/he is still cared for by the collective. Property generally belongs to the collective unless specifically allocated to individuals.

As with most such heuristic models, many intentional communities develop hybrid forms. At Damanhur (Italy), and ZEGG (Germany), for instance, some members work for and earn money from the collective while others work elsewhere but all income belongs to the individual who then contributes to the collective for her/his food and accommodation, regardless of from where that income came. At Ökodorf Sieben Linden (Germany), most members work for the collective, receiving wages from it and contributing equally to it, although a sub-group (Club99) pool all income and expenses. On the other hand, at most Kibbutzim (Israel) and at Kommune Niederkaufungen (Germany), all income goes into the collective regardless of whether the money was earned by collective or private enterprise.

Some intentional communities reduce their need for money by creating their own currency for internal transactions, while many others use local complementary currency systems such as LETS. Damanhurians have their own currency, the 'Credito', which increases their prosperity and, they believe, ethically anchors their exchange system to 'values linked to the sustainability of the planet, to the respect for Humankind and all living beings, to respect for work and the added value of well thought out products created with care and love'.

Property

Few countries have legal systems designed to facilitate property ownership by communal groups. In Israel, kibbutzim predated the establishment of the nation, so communal property-holding is well provided for within their legal system. In most other countries, however, intentional communities must rely on laws which were designed for co-operatives, churches, non-profit organisations and small companies. Some countries have recently enacted legislation to facilitate cohousing and ecovillages, usually based on laws applying to high-rise home units. Within these models, individual property rights are generally greater than the rights of the collective, and this can lead to problems.

In intentional communities such as ZEGG (Germany), Darvell Bruderhof (UK) and Findhorn Foundation (UK) almost all property belongs to the collective so some potential problems do not exist — but others may arise. Not everyone is happy not to own any 'real' property. At some Israeli Kibbutzim, for example, housing is being reassigned from the collective to individuals. While this solves one problem it creates others such as what control the collective will have on future transfers by sale or inheritance of this now private property.

Findhorn Foundation has been privatising its collective resources for many years although it still owns much property. Intentional communities, like other social groupings, must control who can be a member, and ensure that membership is used for the common good. This is relatively easy while most property is collectivised but becomes more difficult when property is privatised. Some intentional communities have failed simply because individuals have transferred their private property (housing) to others who are not interested in communal living, and who thereby drain the collective energy.

Another potential problem with collective money and property is that individuals may not feel responsible for it and may waste resources and not care for assets. The danger is that what is 'ours' is not the responsibility of any 'me'. This problem was well known within many communist societies and within many kibbutzim. In general, this is rarely a problem for small groups but can become serious as the group expands.

Damanhur has a hybrid system wherein most real estate is owned by a co-operative in which members hold shares, allotted according to their investments, and these can be reimbursed if a person leaves. Members believe that this ensures that 'ownership of communal property is not divided and that wealth remains in common, protected for those who have contributed to its acquisition'. On the other hand, Ökodorf Sieben Linden's property is all held by one of their four co-operatives or associations from which individual members rent living space. Private ownership is precluded under their statutes.

There is no 'best' model for how to deal with property within an intentional community but generally, the more property that is owned collectively, the closer the group will usually be in social, spiritual and cultural ways — although this may not be a causal relationship. This very closeness and interdependence, of course, is what many would-be and current intentional community members fear, which is why we have the dramatic increase in creative hybrid forms such as cohousing. I am not putting a value judgement on how any intentional community holds their money or property but it is an important issue with far-reaching implications. To naively start off with the unquestioned assumption that private or collective ownership is best, or worst, seriously limits an intentional community's social, environmental and political potential.

Accountability

All intentional communities require a degree of mutual trust and, ideally, each member should expect to be held personally accountable. In financial matters, within some less communal groups, this may be as simple as having the audited account books available to members. In more communal groups much more may be expected. Full income-sharing groups such as Kommune Niederkaufungen, Israeli Kibbutzim and Darvell Bruderhof require far more accountability because far more is at stake. Such groups might display all income and expense figures, and some groups hold meetings at which each member's productivity and consumption are discussed. I once attended a meeting in such a group when a member requested money to fly overseas to visit his sick mother. What would be a very personal decision for most of us was made by the group after discussing that person's contribution to the collective. He was given the money.

Accountability is crucial to good decision-making and governance within an intentional community. In brief, members who take part in decision-making should be held accountable — and those who are held accountable should be the decision-makers. In reality, however, some members may fear accountability so that they become passive observers in community governance, while others may take their accountability so seriously that they become a serious blockage to involving others in consensus decision-making. There are numerous excellent books on this thorny issue and many experienced consultants who can help an intentional community to achieve the optimum outcome.

I´m all for a shared economy. I´ve let go of everything anyway!

Of course, intentional community accountability also applies beyond finances and governance. Members of most intentional communities are expected to be accountable for what they say, for their relationships, for how they treat collective assets and even for how they interact intimately. Many people find this to be one of the less attractive aspects of intentional community life, feeling that their personal autonomy is constrained by the group, and that they are no longer free 'to be themselves'. There is some basis for this concern because accountability does entail the individual showing due respect to the collective — not a popular notion in our pathologically individualistic society. The catch is that it is individuals respecting the collective needs (and vice versa) that is essential to healthy intentional community life.

Conclusion:

Every intentional community requires money to get started and to maintain daily life, and property on which to live. Members need to be individually and collectively accountable, at least to other members and hopefully to humanity. As a general rule, the more collectivised are money and property, the more close-knit will be the group. On the other hand, unless such highly collectivised groups have very broad and transparent accountability, the more likely they are to encounter difficulties. There is a dynamic tension between individualism and collectivism, for which each intentional community and each member must find their own compromise.

Dr. Bill Metcalf is a sociologist and social historian at Griffiths University in Australia. He has devoted nearly all his adult life to the study of communities all over the world. He has conducted ethnographic studies and surveys in over one hundred community projects and has published extensively on the subject. He is the honorary president of the *Intrnational Communities Studies Association* and the international correspondent of Communities Magazine. His most recent work is *The Findhorn Book of Community Living* (Findhorn Press)

Consensus Decision Making

Leadership for Social Change

by Liora Adler

Have you ever felt trapped in a meeting, wishing you were anywhere else? Have you ever walked out convinced that you will never, ever attend one more meeting in your life? Have you ever noticed the power dynamics in groups, the egos, the personal investment, and wondered if there isn't a better way?

Most people have experienced these frustrations, often to the point of giving up on working in groups. In fact when asked to list their "favorite" complaints about meetings, people all over the world cite basically the same frustrations: a few people do all the talking (and deciding!), a lack of organization, nothing gets accomplished, what does get decided doesn't get implemented, late start, late finish, people go off on tangents, egos get out of hand, a waste of time, boring, too much in-fighting, shy people never get heard, people don't speak up in the meeting, but gossip about it afterward. These experiences are all too common.

Now imagine another scenario: People arrive to the meeting at the appointed time. There is a proposed agenda already posted for all to read. The room has been arranged with attention to comfort and beauty and seating is in a circle. After an opening in which everyone has a chance to speak, the proposed agenda is modified and confirmed by the group. People volunteer to keep track of the time, take notes, and write down items for the next meeting's agenda. Each proposal or item on the agenda is allotted an agreed upon time. The facilitator assures that everyone in the room has the opportunity to speak and creates a safe environment in which there are no personal attacks.

By prior agreement the group focuses on the benefit of the group as a whole, and the facilitator handles any attempted imposition of personal ego deftly. Conflicts are expressed in ways that add richness to the discussion. Emotional issues are exposed in a manner that allows members to feel supported. The facilitator makes sure the group sticks to the agenda and uses appropriate techniques to bring out the best intentions, wisdom and experience of all participants. There are periodic breaks, allowing members to socialize, stretch, do a dance or play a game. Decisions are made that everyone can support and the meeting ends with clarity about who will do what to enact the decisions taken, when the next meeting will be, and who will facilitate and plan the proposed agenda.

An impossible ideal? Not so. Groups all over the world have adopted the consensus method, a process by which an entire group of people can come to an agreement. Every person affected by the decision that is to be taken, engages in finding a solution she can say "yes" to. This "yes" means supporting the decision and taking full personal responsibility for its consequences. The input and ideas of all participants are gathered and synthesized to arrive at a final decision acceptable to all. Through consensus, we are not only working to attain better solutions, but to promote the growth of community and trust as well. Although there is some training and a continual learning process involved, these groups have found that the time and energy invested is well worth the effort. Their meetings can become fun and productive as well as important tools for transforming the passion of change-oriented groups into effective action teams.

Most ecovillages, utopian communities and groups focused on environmental and social change seek a horizontal leadership structure. This is an admirable goal. Nevertheless, without an adequate decision making process, which highlights transparency, integrity, participant and facilitator training, as well as active engagement of members, most of these efforts will fail. If the core values of the community are not reflected in its method for taking decisions, people become cynical and withdraw their energy and support.

In fact my travels all over the world since the late sixties, to scores of communities in every stage of development, have reinforced my conviction that the single

"I know where to go!"

most important aspect of successful community and social change is the human architecture. You can build the most earthy buildings, dream the most inspiring visions, mount up the compost and hang out the solar panels, but if the group dynamics, the decision making process, the balance of leadership, the respect for diversity is not flowing, there will be inevitable break down.

Building long lasting community using the skills of conscious human architecture involves choosing with awareness the raw materials, molding them with care, making use of them in appropriate ways, finding a harmonious blending, and adding the special quality that makes for "spirit" in a building or a group. What is exciting and challenging about this process is that it is always fluid, never stagnant; it ebbs and flows as life itself. It is nurtured by the deepening of safety and trust and by the personal awareness and self development of each member in service of the needs of the whole.

This is not to say that the ecological and other aspects of utopian projects are not important. We are not creating demonstration models of sustainable living if we do not deal with the core issues of how we obtain our food and water and its quality, how we deal with our wastes, produce our energy, build our homes, create economic sustainability, outreach to the larger community, restore the Earth. Without these aspects we can have fantastic meetings and still will not contribute significantly to the fulfillment of our ideals.

It is also not to say that consensus decision making meetings are the proper place to engage in deep therapy or personal conflict resolution. People who live together will especially need other forums for the resolution of personal differences, the clearing of individual and group issues that have become emotional, confused, ego focused or otherwise not appropriate for meetings primarily focused on the "business" of the group. There are many formats for these meetings, sometimes called "third meetings", "forums", "A-B conversations", "heart circles", "mediations" etc. It is in coming to terms with our "dark" sides that we are better able to share our light. These forums are essential complements to the type of consensus meetings we envision in this article.

Is consensus then the only good way to make decisions? Although I consider it (properly practiced) to be the ideal method, it is certainly not the only decision making technique available.

In fact, there are circumstances under which an "autocratic" or "oligarchic" (government by a few) decision might be called for. In general, any large group decision making process will require more time than that required for one or a small group of members to decide. It is important to develop criteria about which decisions concern the entire group and require its consent and which decisions can better be made by an individual or a committee.

Some communities prefer what they call "consensus minus one" or as in Lebensgarten Ecovillage "a thoughtful majority", where a decision can be reached if only 2 or 3 participants from a group of 25 or so, have concerns that do not impede them from supporting the decision of the larger majority. In some communities there are gradients of decisions. Some decisions require the support of all members, others require the support of at least 75% and other decisions a simple "majority." Most variations on what is sometimes called "formal consensus" seem to work, as they are in fact consensus processes with the allowance for a few "stand asides": differing opinions or concerns which do not challenge the basic integrity, values, or security of the group (and would require a "block" if they did). It is when we get to the "simple majority" alternative that we really have another process that may present obstacles in the long run for the group.

Why select the consensus process over the procedure we have come to venerate in our common conception of democracy: "majority rule?" In this process, it is possible that 51% of the vote goes to the "winner" while 49% become the "losers." While it is obvious that the 49% disaffected minority may have difficulty in fully supporting the decision taken by the 51% majority and may even attempt to obstruct its enactment, there is a further and even more significant difficulty that goes to the root of the dilemma. The very process of making decisions by majority rule embroils us in a competition for "votes." Each side makes efforts to gain the support of the "undecided," attempting to convince them of the unworthiness of the "opposition's" position (and often of their character as well!). Not a method that would normally support the ideals of cooperation, harmony, respect and integrity, which form the vision of egalitarian groups.

It is true that the consensus process may appear to "take longer." I believe it is time well spent to make the FIRST decision as effective as possible. How many of you have been in groups where a decision is "rushed through" without taking the

time to consider all of the possible options and consequences? How many remodelings of buildings, office systems, transportation networks, educational curriculums and a myriad of other structures that affect our daily lives, are a result of too little input by the users of these "systems", too little attention to the possible outcomes of the decisions, too little time spent taking into account the input of each of the participants in the decision making process. It may take longer in the initial stage, but making quality decisions that give honor to the "piece of the truth" that each person brings to the process will almost inevitably result in a more positive outcome, avoiding costly mistakes in time and materials.

Will the consensus decision process work in every situation? A resounding NO!

Just as a seed will not grow in certain types of soil, without certain nutrients, care and attention, the consensus process requires some minimum conditions for it to take root, and some loving care for it to flourish and blossom. Is there a willingness of all the participants to share power? If the entire group does not have the authority or the commitment to take decisions and enact them, the seeds will fall on barren soil. Are the "leaders" in the group willing to cede their "power" for the benefit of the group? Is there an issue of "founder's syndrome" which might impede other voices being heard? Is the group willing to look at the issues of "rank and privilege" in a way that honors all members? Is there a reason for the group to meet and a common vision? It is important to be able to remember this vision when the "honey moon period" has ended and it is time to work down more deeply into the soil. Is there a willingness to attend workshops to become effective facilitators and participants? Is there a commitment to do the personal work needed to differentiate personal from communal benefit and know how to support the group's search for solutions. Without these agreements the necessary nurturing, mulching, watering and even weeding when things go awry will be unlikely and the process will break down.

If your group cannot answer a resounding (or even a tentative) "yes" to the above questions, find another method for making your group decisions, or at least get some training and spend some time looking at the issues raised before moving forward with consensus.

Let's imagine that your group has been using consensus process, but the initial enthusiasm is gone and the mulching isn't piled on high enough and the weeds are starting to pop through, people are getting frustrated, tensions are beginning to build (or have reached a crisis stage) and the merry gardeners are desperate for some relief. Now what? Time to make, or remake the process agreements each group needs for effective functioning. Differing from the "essential elements" we have implied above, the process agreements require a commitment by members to operate under certain basic "rules" set by the group. These agreements often address the "favorite complaints" of group members mentioned at the beginning of this article.

Common ones might be:

- o All members have an equal opportunity to participate
- o Use a facilitator
- o Start and end on time
- o Stick to the agenda
- o No interrupting
- o Speak only for yourself
- o Seek a solution
- o Evaluate the process
- o Support training for facilitators and participants

There is much more to learn if your group wishes to embark on this path. This is true both for new groups and those who are ready to face the "shadow side" of consensus - what to do when your ideals do not match up to the realities, how to deal with "difficult members", how to deal with "founder's syndrome" or "rank and privilege" issues, how to do conflict resolution.

Be sure your group has clear agreements as to how members will participate in meetings. Develop effective meeting evaluation techniques that will enable the group to learn from its efforts. A brainstorm on "What we did well" and "How we can improve" is a positive method. Form a self-help group for facilitators in order to give each other constructive feedback. Foster an atmosphere of self-awareness and transparency. The time dedicated to these tasks will be repaid in a bountiful harvest of a garden abundant in the colors and fragrances of creativity, passion, and excitement.

AND, when the ever-shifting human architecture is fine-tuned and a telepathic connection begins to grow amongst group members and re-unions become vehicles for personal growth as well as effective means to grow community, the spirit of trust, harmony, respect, unity, peace, friendship, and positive action takes root, blossoms and scatters the seeds of change throughout the land...

Liora Adler: Dancer and lover of life, untiring world traveler, seeder of dreams and visions, spider woman, uniting movements and people.
For the last 35 years Liora has worked to create and promote tools for personal and social change and has shared her experience and knowledge worldwide, as a member of the Board of Directors of →GEN (Global Ecovillage Network), its representative to the UN, and as a founder of two ecovillage projects in Latin America. Her current workshops are "Consensus Decision Making as a Tool for Social Change", "the Art of Facilitation", "Building Authentic Community", "The Shadow Side of Consensus", and "Global Strategies for Earth Restoration". Liora Adler offers workshops in Europe on a regular basis. Write to <liora@lacaravana.org> for current course schedule.

Are communities a lifestyle of the future?

For the project team: Peter Dangelmeyer

A whole range of studies has emerged demanding a reduction of environmental consumption in the industrialised nations by 80 to 90% in order to help bring about globally sustainable and future-compatible lifestyles and economies. Only part of this reduction can be achieved through a technologically more efficient use of resources. Beyond that, we are all called upon to question our habits and demands in order to continue reducing environmental burdens and to create a peaceful, solidarity-based life on the local, regional and global level. As far as we know, community projects are using various means and focuses in order to deal with this problematic and to manage their economies in such a way as to keep the resulting damage to human beings and their environment as minimal as possible. They are on a good path – but they still have an immense amount of work ahead of them.

What do I really need to satisfy my needs? Can I answer for the consequences of what I consume? A thorough analysis of these questions provides us with an opportunity to begin reducing our material demands and instead to shift our focus to fundamental human needs. Here it becomes clear how closely ecology, economy, social issues and also culture are intertwined and how important it is to address all the demands of human life on a socio-ecological basis.

The research project "Communal Life and Economic Styles and their Environmental Relevance", which the Kommune Niederkaufungen (Germany) undertook in co-operation with the Scientific Centre for Environmental System Research at the University of Kassel, examined three large intentional communities: the →Kommune Niederkaufungen (KNK), the →Ökodorf Sieben Linden (ÖSL) and →Lebensgut Pommritz (LGP). German statistical data as well as three ecologically oriented families in Kaufungen served as points of comparison.

Main focus – environmental consumption

According to the concept of environmental space, our planet possesses a certain regenerative capacity. That means that there is a global damage limit – here, now and in the long term – which must not be surpassed if future generations are to encounter the same living opportunities we enjoy today. Since the concept of environmental space grants all people on this earth an equal right to the environment and its resources, this damage limit needs to be divided by the sum of all living human beings. This results in a defined maximum emission output which each individual human must stay within so as not to endanger the foundations of sustainable life.

In order to make the results quantifiable and comparable, the project only monitored the emissions of greenhouse gases (the so-called CO_2 equivalent). Since approximately 70% of environmental damage normally derives from residential living, nutrition and mobility, these categories were examined closely. In concrete terms, the greenhouse gas emissions were calculated with the help of process chains examining all emissions along a product's path, i.e. from the extraction of the raw materials required to manufacture the product all the way to its final disposal.

The illustration shows that the emissions from an average German household in these three areas lie six times above the sustainability level (as calculated from the environmental consumption concept). The eco-families produce significantly lower emissions – and the emissions of two of the three communities lie clearly below those of the families. The main savings potential lies in the category of living. But even the communities still need to make some major changes if they wish to claim that they are approaching the sustainability level.

The **"living"** field shows differences between KNK and ÖSL on the one hand and the German average on the other. The most important factors for this are building condition, the type of heating system and electricity consumption. The two communities live in well-insulated low-energy houses which were almost exclusively built or renovated using ecological building materials. They largely provide their heating and water-heating with regenerative energies and show a significantly reduced consumption of electrical current, which is in turn purchased from ecological energy providers. The LGP, whose large building has essentially been left in its original condition and is partially heated with an old coal furnace, stands out.

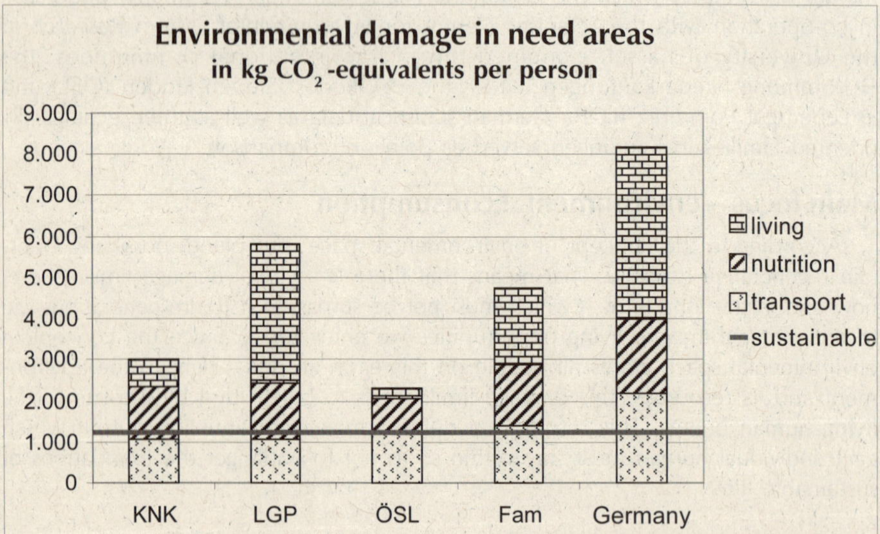

The **"nutrition"** field, which entails the global trade in foodstuffs and the elevated use of fertilisers in monocultures, has high environmental relevance. Organic cultivation methods show an approximately 25% lower emissions level compared to conventional cultivation. Depending on the type of product, food transports can represent anywhere from 5 to 40% of environmental damage. Particularly in regard to fresh foods, purchasing local products or – even better – planting a garden can help prevent a considerable share of these emissions. However, the lion's share of climate-relevant emissions derives from the consumption of milk and meat products. The following illustration shows the effects of various kinds of nutrition. On the national average, few people are vegetarians and even fewer are vegans (avoiding all animal products). This means that the consumption of meat and dairy products is extremely high. In communities considerably less meat is consumed. A considerable portion of the members follows a vegetarian or vegan lifestyle. At the ÖSL the proportion of vegans is particularly high. Meat plays a virtually negligible role and the consumption of dairy products is also very low.

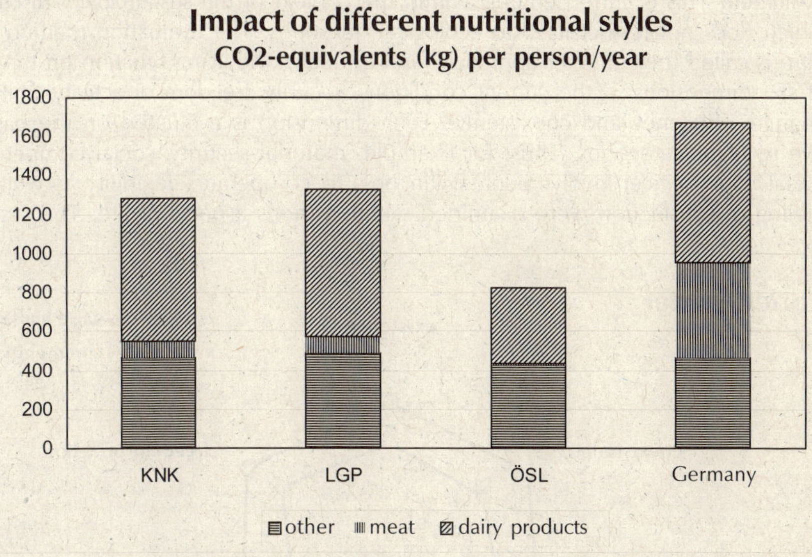

In the **"mobility"** field the ratio of kilometres to individual person is even higher in the communtities than the national average. This partially reflects the age structure. The more mobile age groups between twenty and fifty are more heavily represented than elsewhere, whereas elderly, less mobile people are rarely encountered in communities. In addition, the communities maintain various relationships throughout the Republic and elsewhere as well. Personal trips as well as networking activities between communities take their toll. However, through the choice of transportation (restricted air travel, frequent use of public transportation), "clean" auto fuels (natural gas, rape oil), car-sharing and a higher vehicle-occupancy rate, the resulting emissions are only half as high as the national average. Of course, the highest savings result from avoiding mobility altogether.

Focus – regional economic aspects

In the nutrition field, all three communities reveal a relatively high share of self-sufficiency from a biological perspective. Through the direct consumption, processing and conservation of their own fresh foods, the resulting process changes are considerably more environmentally friendly. The purchase of foodstuffs was examined closely in order to analyse the KNK's regional relationships. Through the development of its own supply network, almost the entire household is provided with organically grown products. A survey among suppliers showed that, as a commercial customer, the "Kommune" has been a consistent, reliable and friendly partner.

Focus – evaluation of social and economic sustainability

Alongside environmental damage, the economic and social situation was also evaluated. This occurred entirely within the context of the sustainability discussion which does not restrict itself to ecological questions. The evaluation method used here is called the "orienter approach" and evaluates the living situation on the basis of six "dimensions" – the current conditions, security, freedom of activity, ability to change, efficiency and coexistence. Each dimension is evaluated on the basis of five to eight categories. Thus, for example, material security, social competence, social and political involvement, willingness to co-operate, flexibility as well as a feeling of satisfaction were examined within various aspects of life. The result is

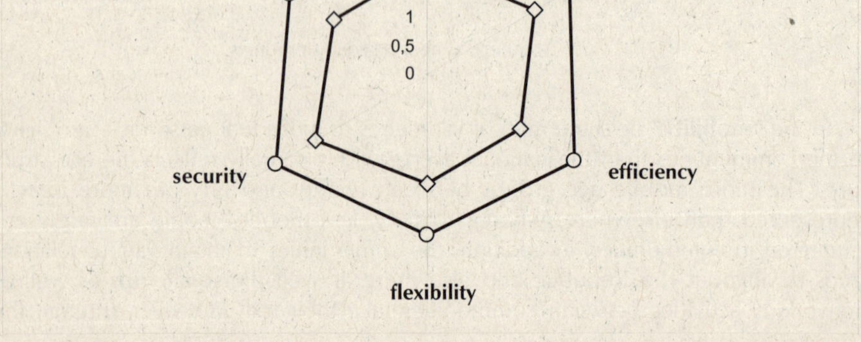

illustrated in the orienter star. The "0" on the scale is the minimum evaluation and "4" the maximum evaluation in regard to sustainability. These results show that according to these criteria the communities are much closer to addressing the demands of sustainability than the small households.

Focus – further development

In order to initiate a discussion within the community scene on the subject of "sustainable living", the research team invited large communities with various orientations (Christian, Anthroposophian, communes, ecovillages...) to a conference. Interest in the topic and in a mutual exchange was so great that the group of twenty people from ten projects decided to plan further quarterly conferences which would take turns meeting in each of the participating communities. The topic of "sustainable living" now plays an increasingly important role in all the participating communities. Developing a lifestyle which challenges conventional social values and replaces them with own value concepts is a challenge for the communities – and will become and remain one for society as a whole in the future.

Summary

Thus it is evident that communities, at least those which were examined during this project, can be viewed as models of sustainable development in two regards: as models in the sense of a concrete example for how living conditions can be designed – and as models in regard to what kinds of social transformations can be set into motion. The pioneer potential of communities, i.e. their focus on the future and their readiness to act, is one of the most important starting conditions for social change. Thus communities can take the stage as "eye-openers", as innovators and initiators. But they will only develop a political impact if they join hands and get involved in society.

I welcome your opinions, discussion contributions and criticisms. Further information on the research project can be found under: www.usf.uni-kassel.de/glww. A 17-minute film in German language was made on the project. You can get a copy from heidi-sieker@web.de.

Peter Dangelmeyer (49) lived in the Kommune Niederkaufungen for fourteen years and is currently involved in developing a large new commune in Waltershausen (→KoWa e.V.). He has been interested in the social significance of communities for many years. This research project provided him with the opportunity to study various aspects on a scientific basis and to shape some of his ideas. E-mail: dangelmeyer@web.de

How to begin – and what then?

The most important steps in building a community

by Dieter Halbach

"The matter is understood and has been judged to be good, the idea takes shape and is about to be put into practice – and suddenly people are standing in each other's way. The humane fails because of human nature." (Erich Mühsam)

Unfortunately, this diagnosis from 1919 on contemporary attempts to achieve a better life is still frequently accurate. Many well-intended community initiatives fail soon after they have started. Actually, everybody wants the same thing – they just want to do it in different ways!

You sit together, sometimes with complete strangers, conduct endless discussions – and your dream is lying there snoozing in the corner. You try to formulate a consensus on your common goals – and end up with non-committal generalities. You develop some concepts on how to implement your ideas and end up with formal plans devoid of any common spirit. These people are just too diverse...!? Time is pressing and the first enthusiasts are already heading for the exits. "When will we meet again?" (Maybe never?)

Even if it doesn't start this bad, many beginning errors come back to haunt you in the later stages of your communal life. Once you have set off with the "wrong" people or structures, you can't change course without causing a lot of hurt feelings (and often material losses).

Luckily there is considerable knowledge available on community development and the inner mechanisms of the human soul. This article has collected some experiences and suggestions on the first founding steps, but also on the dynamics of the further steps towards community development. Here are a few suggestions on what a useful approach to the matter might look like:

Seven first steps towards building a community

1) Clarify your own inner vision and personal motivation

The basis of your communication must always be clarity on your own goals and competencies. You particularly need an honest analysis of your deficiencies, your hidden motives and the compensatory expectations you place on others. Sadly enough, your beautiful official goals often do not match your personal expectations and self-doubts. Both sides need to be revealed from the beginning.

2) Look for a small group of like-minded persons whose motivation and group chemistry are in harmony (no more than 5-12 persons)

If the group is too large it's very difficult to arrive at a clear consensus. On the other hand, a small family or other symbiotic structures are too small to serve as a sole nucleus. What is important is the inner agreement and mutual recognition within this "core group". The determination to act together in full awareness of thematic and personal differences is the inner task of this group.

3) Determine the essential principles in common, i.e. formulate the vision clearly but leave the individual paths and free spaces open

Using a powerful vision as a foundation, this group should proceed to develop a basic concept which formulates all essential common goals but which also allows for sufficient individual freedom. If the project's fundamental goals and focal points are defined clearly enough, it becomes that much easier for interested persons to decide whether or not to join. This also means that there will be fewer rules, and less debate over how to implement them, as the community progresses. Rules on communication, decision-making structures and the necessary steps toward realising the project should be laid out at the beginning.

4) Look for capable core members with good people skills who want to share and realise the goals

This core or start-up group has the right to select further participants and determine the criteria for joining. It is important to develop a sense of one's own roots – a "healthy" sense of self – in order to take on a certain executive function which doesn't exclude others or appear arrogant (no more debates on principles).

5) Create a culture of trust through internal group work, appropriate communication methods and rituals

No concept, no structure and no vision can replace our ability to achieve authentic perception and communication. Internal peace work and personal growth are the essence of community formation. If conflict arises, it is worth seeking help from experienced people, e.g. from other communities or group therapies.

6) Get to know each other through shared work in practical projects

Life itself is our greatest teacher. No group should move in together without having experienced one another over an extended period of shared working and living (e.g. in other communities).

7) Define the starting group and create the path as you go

The expanded core group becomes the project's sponsor when it assumes the risks of direct action and establishes legal and financial commitments (particularly in regard to joining and leaving and between the first residents and sponsors/financiers). Competencies and leadership qualities must be recognised and areas of responsibility defined. A complex organism – a social sculpture – emerges in which all the components demand to be seen (e.g. through rituals of admission, recognition and appreciation).

But for all our enthusiasm and earnestness we should never forget our sense of humour and the fact that we are all seekers on an unknown path. All the errors we make are gifts to the group as long as we are prepared to look at them without bias and with courage.

"Standing up for that which you love deep in your heart, for the vision of your own life, for the vision of your own self and the world as you dream it to be – with all your strength, all your intelligence, all your eroticism, all your joy, and together with others: that's what I call a vision!" *(Susha Wolters, ZEGG)*

About putting your foot in it and illusory love affairs

or: How do I go about visiting a communal project ?

Good advice from Sven Borstelmann

"Yeah, hi – are you that project I've been hearing about? Listen, I'm calling from the motorway service area nearby. You see, I'm hitchhiking my way down south. And since I've always wanted to come over and check you fellows out sometime, I thought I'd kill two birds with one stone and drop by - OK? And uh... can someone buzz over and pick me up?"

"Well, you know, we've got something called a 'visitors' weekend' and the next one is in three weeks. You can sign up for that."

"Sorry, no chance, 'cause I want to be in Sicily by then – but come on, I'm sure one of you has got some time to spare – there are so many of you after all; I'll probably just be staying for a couple of days and I already visited one other commune once...."

OK: It really isn't all that hard – you've heard or read about a communal project somewhere. You call or write, arrange a date for the next possible visit, go there and spend a couple of days that will change the rest of your life.

There are a few things you can do to make sure that your visit is a good experience for you – and hopefully for the project you're visiting as well.

For example, you can think it through first.

Have you ever actually asked yourself why communities and other projects invest energy in visitors? Perhaps they want to get new people interested in them in hopes of expanding; perhaps they just want to be inspired by new faces, ideas and opinions; perhaps they want to make money of visitors, perhaps they even want to convert you, perhaps they just need some help with their work, perhaps perhaps perhaps.... Whatever the reason, neither they - nor you either – are going to set up this encounter out of mere charity.

In order to avoid disappointments, you can usually inform yourself beforehand about the project that interests you – for example, many projects have produced information material or self-descriptions which they are happy to post you on demand, and many of these pamphlets include helpful hints on visiting procedures. When setting up a visit be sure to be as clear as possible on the date and length of your stay as well on any financial aspects – this helps prevent plenty of exasperation later on.

During your visit you are bound to experience one or more disappointments, large or small – you might think that an alternative project really "should" have achieved this goal, or it "should" have solved that problem better than the rest of society (or at least better than you), you might find the group's "sense of community" underwhelming, you might be turned off by their computerisation or their diet, you might discover contradictions between their self-description and practical everyday life, or you might not experience the wildly romantic love affair you were secretly dreaming about. In other words, you may become a victim of your unexpressed expectations, which it can't hurt to think about in advance.

So what else can you do to make sure your visit is an all around success?

Here's an incomplete list of suggestions:

- o Avoid the "zoo effect": don't be too curious and pushy. Remember that you are in a place which is someone else's home. Or do you always show your visitors every corner of your apartment and spontaneously tell them about all the most intimate aspects of your daily life?
- o Observe written or oral instructions, even when their meaning is not immediately apparent (but when in doubt feel free to ask why things are done the way they are).

- Put your best foot forward, but don't put on an act and don't expect too much from yourself. Don't hide your own particularities, for example dietary habits, religious beliefs, or physical limitations.
- Realise that communal projects make "compromises" on a number of points in order to get along with one another, so forgive them a few shortcomings – just as you forgive your own.
- Try to develop a nose for potential "land mines" you are liable to put your foot into in the course of a project's daily life and try to avoid them. But if you do tread on one, don't take it too personally – it happens to everyone.
- Even if it sounds hackneyed: nothing opens doors better, nothing generates more trust and mutual understanding, than simply working together.
- Definitely contribute your expertise and ability, but don't force it on the community; whether you're at a plenary meeting or other group meetings, restrain yourself.
- Don't let this or any other tip stifle your exuberance!

Finally, remember that your visit has only shown you fragments of the project's life – in a different season, in other weather or in another frame of mind on your part the visit might have gone very differently. Perhaps certain group members were not at home, perhaps the project's atmosphere was influenced by a temporarily overriding topic – who knows how the next visit might have gone – or might yet go....

"Aim for the moon.
Even if you miss it, you will land between the stars."

Communities - self-descriptions

"And now, ladies and gentlemen, it is with great pleasure and great honour that we present to you our main attraction..."

Legend

	community in planning
	ecovillage
	ecosettlement
AZ	indicates the location of the community on the map
|	start a new line when writing the mailing address
	telephone number
	fax number
	Email
	homepage
	founding year
	located in the city
	located in a town/suburb
	located in the countryside
	behind it: size of the property (1 ha =10,000 m², 1ac =4,050 m²)
( )	*behind it in brackets:* the nearest large town
♀	number of women
♂	number of men
	number of children
	total number of members
	languages spoken in the community (besides the national language): g=German, e=English, f=French, i=Italian, s/sp=Spanish
	How many work inside the community?
	Who makes important decisions?
( )	*in brackets:* How are these decisions made?
	type of financing
	owner (of building/land)
	ideological/spiritual principles
	main areas of activity
	catchwords
☺	new members are basically welcome
	behind it: admission requirements for new members
	welcome work ing guests in exchange for board and lodging
( )	*in brackets:* do not explicitly offer board and lodging
	is part of the networks listed here
X	this community no longer exists or is no community any more
A-Z	country abbreviations, which are explained on page 415.
→	see entry in the index

Instructions for the Info Section

All of the information presented here comes **directly from the communities themselves and reflects their own self-assessment**. These are snapshots which reflect their situation at some point between November 2003 and April 2004. We have neither checked nor changed the communities' information, unless the communities wrote more than we have space to print. If individual bits of data are missing, this means that the communities did not send us this data. Since this book has developed out of translations from four languages into English, individual words – especially in the self-presentations – should not be taken too literally. We also ask for your forgiveness if we have made any mistakes in transferring the data from the questionnaires. Please let us know if you find any errors so that we can correct them in our next edition. *(For more information on data collection, see the foreword.)*

The communities are **arranged alphabetically** according to countries and according to the first letter of their names. A few Eastern European and neighbouring countries with only a few communities have been gathered together at the end. The map at the beginning of each country section offers a rough geographical overview of the communities presented here. If you are looking for a specific community and do not find it right way under the name which is known to you, then you should use the comprehensive index at the end of the book (see below).

In the grey-shaded bars you will find the names and addresses of the individual communities as well as all additional contact information. If the name is marked with an ✎ it means that the community is still in the planning stage.

The **telephone and fax numbers** ☎/📠 are listed in such a way that they can be used from all European countries equally, e.g. **+49-(0)4567-12345**:

+49 The plus sign stands for the numerals which are necessary in order to call abroad (in Germany it is "00"); next you will find the country code

-(0)4567 After the first hyphen ("-") there follows the regional code. A zero in parentheses is used for calls within the country, but is then dropped in calls from abroad. If it is not in parentheses, that means that it is also used in calls from abroad.

- 12345 After the second parenthesis you will find the extension number. If several numbers are identical except for the last digits, we have only printed the part after the last hyphen.

If you encounter any problems, please call the respective country's directory assistance for help.

Are you looking for a specific community? In the **Index** at the end of the book you will find communities not only under their complete names, but also under other standard terms – e.g. Kommune Niederkaufungen can be found both under Kommune Niederkaufungen and under Niederkaufungen. Boldfaced page numbers refer to the page on which the community is described.

Austria

FW Friedrichshof Wohnungsgenossenschaft
KB KEIMBLATT ÖKODORF
LG Garten Eden - Leben in Gemeinschaft
WW Wohnclub Wien

Friedrichshof Wohnungsgenossenschaft

FW

Römerstraße 1 | 2424 Zurndorf/Burgenland
☎ +43-(0)2174-7000-171 office@friedrichshof.at
-116 www.friedrichshof.at

1990 ca. 20 ha (near Neusiedel am See) ♀60 ♂50 40
150

g, e, sp., f
co-operative board, general assembly
limited common financing and individual co-operative
AAO
Administration, hotel, restaurant, museum, archive, psycho-social residential community, pottery studio, art studio, horse stable, renting, beekeeping
non-violent, meditation, yoga, adult education, pedagogical, seminar-house, mentally/psychologically handicapped persons, physically handicapped persons, social work: association „Burgenland Netzwerk Sozial mit WG", organic gardening, pottery, painting and boat repair, apiary, fitness room, jogging path, sport grounds, museum with space for rotating exhibits, tolerant, multicultural, open, communicative, variety

☺

The Friedrichshof offers visitors and residents a successful synthesis of town and country: with its dramatic history, evolving all the way from a Habsburg model estate to a communal living experiment, today its diversity and openness combine to make it a place of broad intellectual and social vistas.
Since 1990 the Friedrichshof residential co-operative (most members are former communards) has owned and operated the approx. 20 ha property, rents apartments, sells lots and administers the facilities. Decisions are made by the general assembly and the board. However, one does not have to be a member of the co-operative to live at the Friedrichshof.
Since the commune's dissolution families, couples, singles, single parents and flat-sharing communities have been living here. We have freelancers and artists, there's a seminar hotel, a country inn, a mail order business for natural products, a boat repair workshop, an apiary, an integrative social project with a flat-sharing community and day workshops, as well as a horse stable. The co-operative also owns an art collection and operates a small museum with permanent and temporary exhibits. The children have a large space for playing and exploring, the young people have a youth club, there's a bathing pond, a playing field, a place for bonfires, a sauna and the PAN cultural association. Those who wish to do so attend yoga and meditation meetings. There are many opportunities to join in or else to organise activities on one's own.
We are a place with great potential – everyone can work to realise his/her ideas and dreams on a peaceful, humanitarian and ecological basis, and always full of love. Come and see!

☺ Renting a flat, purchasing a lot, house construction, independent of membership in co-operative

Keimblatt Ökodorf Info-Office Wien KB

Johann-Strauß-G. 33/3 | 1040 Wien
(project centre: Altenmarkt 95, 8333 Riegersburg)
☎ +43-(0)676-6015647 dialog@oekodorf.or.at
www.oekodorf.or.at/

2002 30-50 ha planned (near Jennersdorf) ♀2 ♂3 1 6

g, e, sp., it.
everyone in common (consensus) shared income
sustainability, peacefulness, self-development
ecological, self-managed, non-violent, spiritual, inner growth, free love, organic diet, vegetarian diet, vegan diet, pedagogical, crano-sacral therapy, organic gardening, alternative energy, ecological construction, joinery and other handicrafts, singing, dancing, making beautiful things out of wood (instruments), humour

☺

We are a consensus-based group which has decided that the time is ripe for an ecovillage in Austria. We're looking for like-minded people!
Our competencies include: farming and gardening, permaculture design, project and community experience, association management, public relations, healing,

pedagogy, art, crafts, joy in learning and long-term contact to other ecovillage projects. The ecovillage should provide living space for 150 to 300 people in the spirit of sustainability, peacefulness and self-development. Because of the climatic and socio-geographic conditions, we have chosen the southern Burgenland/south-east Steiermark region as the optimal site for the ecovillage.
Our plan to realise this ecovillage can be broken down into three phases:
Phase 1: The core team of 6 to 12 determined persons gets together and selects an appropriate property for a project centre (farm) which will serve to anchor the project in the region.
Phase 2: We move into the project centre (status: 19/2/05), after which the project presents itself to the "general" public and garners the necessary support (e.g. the local authorities). The core team locates the ecovillage's permanent site and develops a detailed project plan and a permaculture design.
Phase 3: Construction and growth phase of ecovillage.
The ecovillage is open to everyone who is willing to support our basic consensus. Request information about our regular introductory meetings!

→ See also description of network "**GEN**"
☺ orientation on sustainability and peacefulness

Verein Leben in Gemeinschaft

LG

Barbara Strauch | Ziegeleistr. 35 | 4020 Linz
☎ +43-(0)650-4133283, -(0)732-611297 ✉ barbara.strauch@aon.at
www.leben-in-gemeinschaft.net, www.garteneden.net

2000 (near Linz)

g
mixed model
work on the theme of „community"
ecological, self-managed, inner growth, self-sufficiency, permaculture and forest garden, alternative energy, ecological construction, trans-generational, integrative, conflict treatment

☺

"It takes a whole village to raise a child."We have found life in a the nuclear family and as a single too taking, and that's why we've decided to achieve social stability through community.
Since we didn't have enough money to buy a large property, in June 2002 we founded an association and looked for a residential co-operative to get involved in. Small flat-sharing communities are now developing. However, in order to realise all aspects of our vision (economic, ecological, social and cultural) we are planning larger projects at various locations (ecovillages). But even our community-building and planning process gives us a taste of true community.
We are involved in communication and conflict resolution, create "spaces" for individuality and community, and work to promote social and economic solidarity and self-determination. Consensus is the basis of all our decisions. Project manage-

ment, discussion structures and attention to gender-specific views all help us in this process.
Our most important concern is a trans-generational life with children of different ages, with younger and older adults and with old people. We want to be a part of nature and know that our human needs for belonging and well-being are being fulfilled. We cannot possess the earth – we can only use it while we are here. We think the best way to use it is to do so sustainably, lovingly and as a community.

☺ everyone who feels attracted to us is welcome

Wohnclub Wien

WW

Forum für intelligente Planung | Franz-Josefs-Kai 31/39 | 1010 Wien
+43-(0)1-5334524 office@wohnclub.at
-15334524-5 www.wohnclub.at

1998

g, e
individual financing
none
care-providing, health, leisure
ecological, spiritual, inner growth, meditation, yoga, adult education, seminar-house, social work: unemployed, health centre, permaculture, new technologies, ecological construction, wellness centre, young and old, assisted living, jobs

☺

The "Wohnclub Wien" is a practical residential model for young and old with an integrated economic life and active involvement of the surrounding community. The size of one's flat can be adapted over the course of one's life by attaching and detaching living and working modules. We have a large kitchen, a laundry and repair service as well as child, sickness and old age care to offer. The establishment of companies brings jobs.
This living form is designed to ensure flexibility, promote social life, offer enough room for one's private sphere and also guarantee individual needs. Each module is 26 m² big and has all the necessary hook-ups. The individual modules can be combined at will. Ranging from a garçonnerie to a loft, these combinations can create different and alterable residential and office floor plans. Neighbours or groups can set up their communal spaces as they wish and then change them again.
With this living project we also want to help launch a new community. We are open to all people as long as they accept a lively communal life made up of different ideas on how to live this life. Since we want to emphasise the themes of community and well-being, we intend for our project to become a place where tolerance and intellectual freedom can be practised.

☺ readiness for this kind of living and working

Belgium

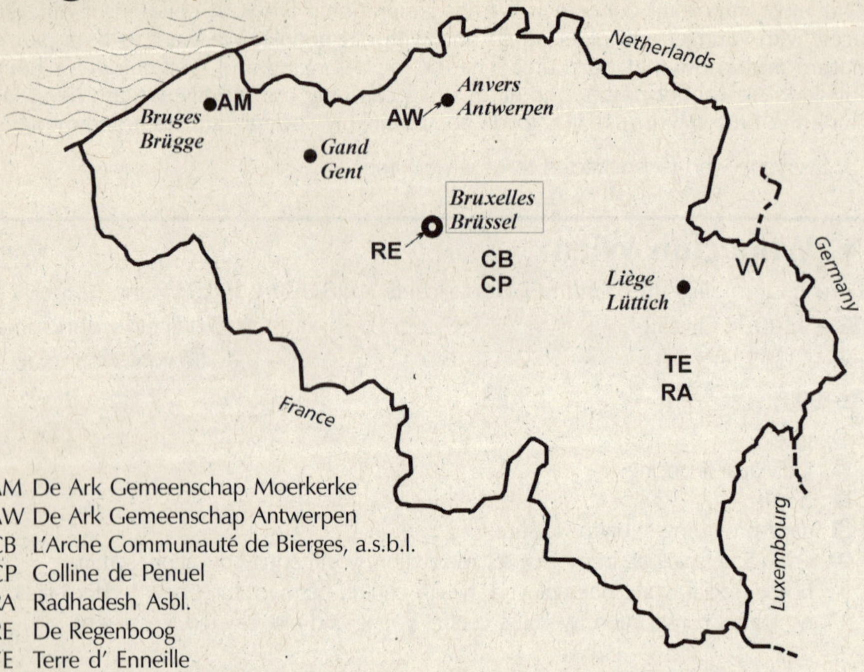

AM De Ark Gemeenschap Moerkerke
AW De Ark Gemeenschap Antwerpen
CB L'Arche Communauté de Bierges, a.s.b.l.
CP Colline de Penuel
RA Radhadesh Asbl.
RE De Regenboog
TE Terre d' Enneille
VV La Communauté de la Verte Voie

Colline de Penuel

CP

Rue de Nil, 55 | 1435 Mont-Saint-Guibert

☎ +32-(0)10-659424 — penuel@village.uunet.be

1982 — 7 ha (near Ottignies-Louvain-la-Neuve) — ♀2 ♂3 — 9 — 14

f, e, dutch, g — all voluntary

everyone in common (majority vote/consensus)

individual financing, accommodation fees, donation — rented/leased

Catholic Church of Belgium

silent retreats ("Poustinia"), prayer, receiving guest groups, ecological use of grounds (nature preserve)

spiritual, christian

☺ ( )

La Colline de Pénuel is made up of several families who prefer prayer in a secluded area and who welcome persons seeking to spend time in seclusion. They have a chapel, so-called "Poustinias" (rooms and hermitage) and 7 ha of grounds. It is a place of peace not far from a town (5 minutes to Louvain-la-Neuve and 30 minutes

to Brussels). All people are welcome: Christians, believers in other religions, non-believers... We give them the opportunity to go into silence from time to time in order to live more intensively and to receive inspiration and — for Christians — to develop an intensive loving relationship with Jesus and God.
The reception of individuals is complemented by additional activities, particularly the reception of groups and managing the grounds according to ecological criteria. Some members devote themselves to non-violence and peace work. La Colline de Pénuel is linked to the Church through the town's bishop. We basically have 4 residential houses on the site (we're still looking for an additional one). Additional people take part in our lively association life without living here.

☺ openness to Catholic community, part-time volunteer work, financial independence, liking prayer in secluded area

De Ark Gemeenschap Antwerpen

AW

Sportveldlaan 21 | 46BE-2530 Boechout
☎ +32-(0)3-454-3402 ark.antwerpen@moso.be
-3275

1974 (near Antwerpen) ♀15 ♂15 30

- f, e, g, dutch — all 30
- one part of the group (consensus)
- state subsidies, limited common financing — common property
- Arche according to Jean Vanier, openly ecumenical-Catholic, open to other religions
- community living with people with learning disabilities
- spiritual, christian, ecumenical, inner growth, pedagogical, mentally/psychologically handicapped persons

☺

This community is a member of the International Association of Arche Communities, founded by Jean Vanier. Our community consists of three community houses and a "conference centre". In each house we accommodate six mentally handicapped persons and between two and four "assistants" who have chosen to share their lives with them. The assistants come from various countries and decide for themselves how long they want to stay in our community. Life in our houses revolves around the handicapped and is grounded in a Christian spirituality (from a Catholic standpoint) which is very open, also to "non-believers". The community has many friends and contacts with other communities throughout the world. Life here is very simple: a life in which the human being stands in the centre, which offers opportunities for personal and spiritual development, in which people get to know each other, in which we learn to appreciate one another in both our differences and our similarities ...

→See also description of network "**Arche following Jean Vanier**"

☺ probationary period, spiritual openness, motivation to share one's life with people with a mental disability

De Ark Gemeenschap Moerkerke

AM

Vissersstraat, 71/1 | 1BE-8340 Demme (Moerkerke)

+32-(0)50-581884 | info@arkmoerkerke.be

-5814052 | www.arkmoerkerke.be

1993 | 4 ha (near Bruges) | ♀5 ♂5 | 10

dutch, f, e, g | 5

everyone in common (majority vote, consensus) | limited community financing

common property

ecumenical

farm with fields and animal husbandry

ecological, self-managed, spiritual, christian, ecumenical, inner growth, meditation, adult education, pedagogical, mentally/psychologically handicapped persons, environmental protection, self-sufficiency

The Ark community of Moerkerke includes the "De Barke" residential house for mentally handicapped persons and their attendants, and the "'t Hoevetje" workshops for the promotion of creative, practical and social skills.

→ See also description of network "**Arche following Jean Vanier**"

☺ adaptation to communal life

De Regenboog

RE

Norbert Gillelaan 20 | 1070 Bruxelles

+32-(0)2520-6586 | marc.vantente@skynet.be

1974 | 0,05 ha | ♀5 ♂3 | 8

dutch, f, (e, g) | none

one part of the group (consensus) | limited community financing

property of individual community members

broad ecumenical orientation (pluralism), but Christian-inspired

secondary and university instruction, communal life, hospitality

non-violent, ecumenical,inner growth, vegetarian diet, adult education, professions: teaching

☺

The Rainbow is a community with different living forms. It has 5 goals:

1. Community: a shared daily life, displaying loyalty and trust toward each individual and the community, continuously developing our lives.
2. Justice: how can we contribute to the creation of a society in which each individual can live a fulfilling life in respect and freedom and realise it within the community?
3. Non-violence: it is the only way to overcome hatred and violence, both in the community and in society.

4. Deepening: seeking a credible religion for the liberation of modern human beings - through practice, sharing with one another, individual prayer and liturgy - as an answer to the superficiality and manipulation in our society.
5. Utopia: the vision of a new world of peace, justice and love seems possible, even though this search may be long and open-ended.
We want to live in moderation and in solidarity with the poor and oppressed everywhere in the world and also show hospitality to the outcasts of our own country. The three people holding main responsibility are Christians, even though this is not a precondition. The community as a whole would like to be pluralistic, i.e. ecumenical in the broadest sense of the term (Christian churches, other religions, indepenent seekers).

☺ practising a simple lifestyle in solidarity, non-violence, pluralism, a sense of justice, respect for community structure

L'Arche Communauté de Bierges, a.s.b.l. CB

Rue Saint-Pierre, 14 | 14BE-1301 Bierges
☎+32-(0)10-401453 arche.bierges@belgacom.net
-401558

1974 | 0,5 ha (near Wavre) | ♀9 ♂14 23

f, (e) | 21

one part of the group (consensus) | common purse/individual financing

rented/leased

ecumenical-Catholic

housing and occupying mentally handicapped persons, living and working on a fraternal and familiar basis

christian, ecumenical, pedagogical, mentally/psychologically handicapped persons, physically handicapped persons, conventional gardening, sports, arts & crafts (candles), bakery, kitchen

☺

The "Arche" tries to give everyone a "home" in its small flats and family-size houses, which are integrated into the town or village. The Arche increasingly allows everyone to find his or her roots and a place of belonging, which is also important for people with disabilities. In this advantageous context disabled people gradually succeed in developing a positive self-image and discover that they have value and their lives have a meaning. Working in workshops promotes the unfolding and independency of handicapped people. It helps to bring structure to their live and gives them confidence. The usefulness of the work brings them respect and recognition from others. Our work is of a crafts nature and is adapted to the rhythm and abilities of the people living with us.

→ See also description of network "**Arche following Jean Vanier**"
☺ motivation and ability to live in community with people with learning disabilities

La Communauté de la Verte Voie

VV

Verte Voie, 13 | 4890 Thimister
+32-(0)8744-6505 bao@swing.be
-5378

1973 0,4 ha (near Verviers) ♀4 ♂3 6 13

none
everyone in common (consensus) individual financing
property of individual community members
cultural-creative, changing the world
managing a property, communal life, education
ecological, left-wing political understanding, non-violent, organic diet, adult education, pedagogical, seminar-house, peace-work, one-world development, mentally/ psychologically handicapped persons, physically handicapped persons, social work, environmental protection, organic gardening, new technologies

☺

The community of La Verte Voie (The Green Path) is a co-operative which owns a large house in a rural area. Since its founding in 1973 it has had the following goals: First, to provide a common home for approximately 20 persons: families, couples or singles, young people and the elderly ... Second, to create a place which would provide a local learning centre for adults, particularly in regard to continuing education in the areas of environmental protection, consumption, social support, recycling, active education etc. The members of our community all have careers of their own or work within the family and/or for themselves. Each member has a complete living area. All members take care of the rooms and the gardens, share tools and buy their groceries together. The various projects are discussed and coordinated in a weekly meeting. Our community is open for new members who dare to go for new experiences and who are genuinely prepared to give of themselves.

"De bouche à oreille" (part of "Culture et developpement")
☺ autonomy on an emotional, relationship, material and financial level; interest in social issues, politics and culture

Radhadesh Asbl.

RA

Chateau de Petite Somme | 6940 Septon Durbuy
+32-(0)87-322926 radhadesh@pamho.net
-322929 www.radhadesh.com

1980 50 ha (near Liége) ♀40 ♂40 9 89

f, e, dutch
one part of the group (selected governing committee reports to assembly)
common property

Hare Krishna
spiritual activities: making Krishna consciousness known outside, Indian boutique, cafeteria, restaurant, bakery, library, Collegium Bhaktevédanta
spiritual, meditation, yoga, vegetarian diet, pedagogical, seminar-house, construction

Krishna is a name for God, the highest being. The God Krishna appeared 5,000 years ago to found the religious service of Bhakti-Yoga. The tradition of honouring Krishna is based on the world's oldest writings: the Vedas. Krishna appeared at the court of Shri Caitanya Mahaprabhu. He spread Bhakti-Yoga through the mantra "Hare Krishna ..." Lord Caitanya said beforehand that this movement would spread to all towns and villages of the world. This prophecy was realised through Shrila Prabhupade. He spread the Bhakti-Yoga movement throughout the world under the name of the Hare Krishna Movement (or ISKCON), which enabled its members to develop a "simple life with true spirit" (Shrila Prabhupade). The Hare Krishna Movement follows the Hindu tradition of people who honour Krishna (they are called Vaishnavas).

→ See also description of network "**ISKCON**"
☺ the desire to discover the Krishna consciousness; respect the conditions of communal life

Terre d' Enneille

TE

Grande-Enneille 102 B | 6940 Durbuy
+32-(0)86-323457 benoit.laduron@skynet.be
-323456 users.skynet.be/ecovillage-eden

1992 4 ha (near Durbuy) ♀8 ♂4 4 16

f, e
everyone in common (consensus) individual financing
common property
ecological
managing a 41 ha nature preserve
ecological, meditation, peace-work, environmental protection, organic agriculture, organic gardening, alternative energy, ecological construction

☺

Terre d'Enneille is a shared community settlement welcoming friends of nature and organised as a co-operative. It is an eco-spiritual village without creed or collective doctrine. We do not represent a new sort of religion or cult. We see ourselves as a meeting and experiential place gathering people with different spiritual paths or practices. We believe that when we align ourselves to our charter's values, and share generously with one another, we can create a lifestyle that respects the individual, the collective and the environment. We each consider ourselves to be self-reliant and responsible for a part of the planet which we must manage as ecologically as possible, preserving nature and its biodiversity.

Eden

Living in community means starting fresh every day,
being aware of the atmosphere of pure voluntariness
and taking your own decision to be an active participant.
Who wants to join?

"Self-sufficiency – we all share in the potato harvest"
Bruderhof-community (UK)

Denmark

AM Andelsforeningen Møllegården
FV Fjordvang
HL Hertha Levefællesskab
LA Udgården - Lading Andelsboligfor.
SH Svanholm
SL Den Selvforsynende Landsby
VL Valsølillgård

Andelsforeningen Møllegården

AM

Resendalvej 16 | 8600 Silkeborg
☎ +45-86 85 30 91

2002 | 19 ha (near Silkeborg) | ♀4 ♂6 9 19

e, g
everyone in common (consensus)
common property
peacefulness
developing grounds, house construction, forestry

none
individual financing

ecological, self-managed, left-wing political understanding, non-violent, inner growth, environmental protection, organic agriculture, organic gardening, organic farming, animal friendly husbandry, forestry, alternative energy, ecological construction, humour, handicrafts (farming, blacksmithing), art, circus

7 km east of Silkeborg near Resenbro lies the old watermill. The mill doesn't work anymore. There are lakes filled by springs alone, which we are very proud of.
We are a community still in its birth state, 9 children and 11 grownups ranging from 1 to 67 in age. We live in temporary settlements (e.g. caravans) of ca. 50m² per family, but with a 600 m² farmbuilding desperately in need of restoration, giving the possibility of 6-7 apartments.
We would love to receive any help restoring and building or even babysitting ...
We are circus artists, artists, storytellers, farmers, light workers, social workers, workers, mothers and fathers and children and horses and sheep and goats and pigs too.
9 ha of the land is farmland, 8 ha is forest and 2 ha are two lakes. We even have a small waterfall - the best shower in the area!

→ See also description of network "**LØS**"

Den Selvforsynende Landsby

SL

Højgårdsvej 27, Hundstrup | 5762 Vester Skerninge
+45-62243620
kontakt@selvforsyning.dk
www.selvforsyning.dk

2002 | 15.6 ha (near Odense) | ♀5 ♂5 | 7 | 17

dan., e

everyone in common (consensus) | limited community financing

cooperative

house construction, farming, gardening

ecological, organic diet,self-sufficiency, permaculture, animal friendly husbandry, ecological construction

„Den selvforsynende landsby" means The Self-Sustaining Village. Since 2002 we have been preparing to establish an ecological and permacultural village on the island of Funen in Denmark. We have bought a farm with 15 ha of land which we will take over in May 2004, by which time we expect to have received all necessary permits from the authorities. On 3 ha of the land we expect to be permitted to build up to 26 houses. The area is situated next to the village of Hundstrup, about 15 km north-west of the town of Svendborg.
We are at the moment 11 adults and 7 children in the group. Most of us plan to build straw-bale houses. Each family will build their own house, some with the help of a professional. Everything will be designed and established along permacultural lines. From the farm land we plan to provide most of our food and firewood. All the residents are to participate in the farming work along with their

other employment. It will be possible to establish small firms on the grounds. We hope that the village will be full of life and activity and that a community spirit will arise between people of different ages and educations.

→ See also description of network "**LØS**"
☺ 3,400 Euros as investment and financing of own house

Fjordvang

FV

Skyumvej 101, Skyum | 7752 Snedsted
☎ +45-97936919 fjordvang1@post.tele.dk
www.members.tripod.com/Fjordvang

1999 16 ha (near Thisted) ♀3 ♂2 1 6

dan., e, f 4
everyone in common (consensus) limited community financing
common property
heaven on earth
course centre, eco-farming, construction
ecological, self-managed, inner growth, organic diet, seminar-house, peace-work, permaculture, organic farming, ecological construction, humour

☺ ( )

We want to develop and pass on our life experience within our own circle, among the local population and world-wide. We are working toward the development of the inner potential of the individual human being. We want to make creativity, joy, and love bloom in an active and spiritual community. We are striving to transmit our knowledge and understanding of health into the new millennium on a physical, psychical and spiritual level. We want to build houses and a community house according to permaculture principles. The community's members are to live in the houses. The community house should become the framework for the community's activities and for a support group. We want to organise courses, seminars and conferences which take the entire human being – from ecology to health all the way to spirituality – as their starting point. We want to establish a refuge, offer therapy and take part in local and global networks.
Fjordvang is located in the north-west of Denmark: one of the pearls of Denmark in regard to its powerful energy and the view it offers of seven megalithic graves, the blue Limfjord, and the protected Skyum Mountains. Up here the sky is high and the light is one of a kind. We live between the fjord and the raging North Sea.

→ See also description of networks "**LØS**" and "**GEN**"
☺ confidence in the present

Hertha Levefællesskab

HL

Landsbyvænget 14 A, Herskind | 8464 Galten
+45-86 95 45 20 Allanelm@hotmail.com, hertha@get2net.dk

1994 16 ha (near Århus) 80

dan., e

individual financing Village foundation

Acceptance of the presence of developmentally retarded people & acceptance of decision making on an anthrophosophic basis

Reverse integration with young developmentally retarded people

After many years of preparation, Hertha Community finally broke ground in 1995 and established itself with a solid core group and a strong village support group around it. Since then the community has grown up around a co-house with 13 young mentally retarded people. 45 persons live within the area and many more are connected to the place in different ways. Our relations to the nearby village of Herskind are functioning very well. The co-operation with the municipality and the other local authorities is friction-free. Hertha is characterised by its focus on social ecology rather than practical, physical ecology, even though this is also important in the village, particularly concerning buildings.
The community rests on two main principles: the first principle is that Rudolf Steiner's anthroposophy is the philosophical basis for this place; most decisions are made on this special foundation. The other principle is that both the community and its daily life are characterised by the practice of "reverse integration", an acceptance of the fact that developmentally retarded human beings are a central part of the village.

→See also description of networks "**LØS**" and "**GEN**"

Svanholm

SH

Økologisk Produktionskollektiv | Svanholm Gods, Svanholm Allé 2 | 4050 Skibby
+45-47566-670 guestgroup@svanholm.dk, kirstenh@svanholm.dk
-47566-607 www.svanholm.dk

1978 460 ha (near Frederikssund) ♀31 ♂31 45 107

dan., e, g, dutch 30

everyone in common (consensus) shared economy (shared income and capital)

the community

ecology

organic farming, forest work, work outside community

ecological, self-managed, left-wing political understanding, organic agriculture, animal friendly husbandry, forestry, alternative energy, ecological construction

In 1978 100 people came together to purchase the property in Svanholm with 253 ha of fields and 194 ha of forest and park land. We wanted to create an integrated

lifestyle and a genuine community in which we decide for ourselves how we want to live and work. It is a place where our children can romp around with animals in the fresh air. Our goal was to develop a rural production system based on common work and a shared economy as well as on common decision-making.
Ecological agriculture is our main interest. We cultivate maize and cereals, fruits and vegetables. Around 70 adults and 45 children between the ages of 0 and 70 live in Svanholm. Beyond that we have several long-term guests living here. We live in groups, residing in various houses on and around the property. A blend of families, couples and singles share their accommodation in group sizes ranging from five and twenty. Each has his/her own (bed)room and shares the kitchen, bath and living room with the rest of the group. All proceeds from our businesses as well as the wages and salaries of those who work outside the community go into one till. This money is then used to cover all expenditures. The plenum is the executive authority. We do not vote but rather discuss our way to a consensus.

→ See also description of network "**LØS**"
☺ please ask

Udgården - Lading Andelsboligforening

LA

Udgården 22 | 8471 Sabro
☎ +45-86949618

1992 | 17 ha (near Âarhus) | ♀18 ♂13 | 24 | 55

dan., e, g, f, sp. — none
everyone in common (majority vote/consensus)
common purse and individual financing — community
ecological, nothing more
ecological, self-managed, non-violent, organic diet, environmental protection, organic agriculture, organic gardening, organic farming, animal friendly husbandry, alternative energy, new technologies, ecological construction

The Udgården is a small ecological community consisting of a farm and 16 apartments just outside a small village in Central Jutland. We are approx. 30 adults and 30 children, 20 cows, 10 sheep, 20 chickens and some dogs.
Each family has its own apartment, but we dine together on weekday evenings. These meals are mainly ecological and consist of products from our own farm (beef, mutton, vegetables etc). The farm is run by all of us together and all work is done voluntarily in our leisure time. All adults have full-time jobs outside the Udgården.
The apartments are of a low-energy construction: double insulation, super-low-energy windows, and floor heating. Heating is based on a combination of solar panels and a wood-pellet stoker. Rainwater is collected from all roofs and used in our toilets and common laundry.
We have no common religious or ideological reference. What we have in common is the desire to lead a less polluting and polluted lifestyle.

→ See also description of network "**LØS**"
☺ only financial

Valsølillgård

VL

Knud Lavardsvej 94 | 4174 Jystrup
+45-53628777
-53628777

1983 1500 m² (near Jystrup) ♀9 ♂10 18 37

g, dan. none

everyone in common (majority vote (we rarely all disagree))

limited common financing common property

various professions

ecological, non-violent, organic diet, one-world development, Gestalt therapy, organic agriculture, organic gardening, alternative energy

Valsølillgård is located in a rural area in the centre of Zealand some 70 km from Copenhagen. The farm originally belonged to the estate of Skjoldenæsholm and the foundations are probably 300 years old. The buildings were no longer suitable for a modern farming operation. Thus in 1983 it was sold to a group of young people who wanted to develop a residential and working community here. In keeping with the spirit of the times, their ambitions tended toward establishing a production collective and for around 10 years they devoted a great deal of energy to this project and, of course, to remodelling the buildings into flats. The dream of jobs and their own production facilities on the farm cost them blood, sweat and a lot of money, but it never became viable. Today they all work off the farm.
But in contrast to hundreds of other, similar projects from this time, they succeeded n restructuring and reorganising the lives in such a way that although they were forced to abandon some of their original ideas, the living and house community still exists. The houses have been divided up into autonomous living units and their organisational form is a flat-sharing community with common property. Only 4 adults have remained from when the farm was purchased. But otherwise the community is very stable. The residents have remained unchanged for 6 years, most of them have lived here for more than 12 years and the majority of the residents are between 40 and 50 years old and remain active in peace and environmental campaigns. Despite private flats, we have many shared interests and communal activities. Our house community is above all a children's paradise.

☺ good chemistry, ecological attitude

Finland

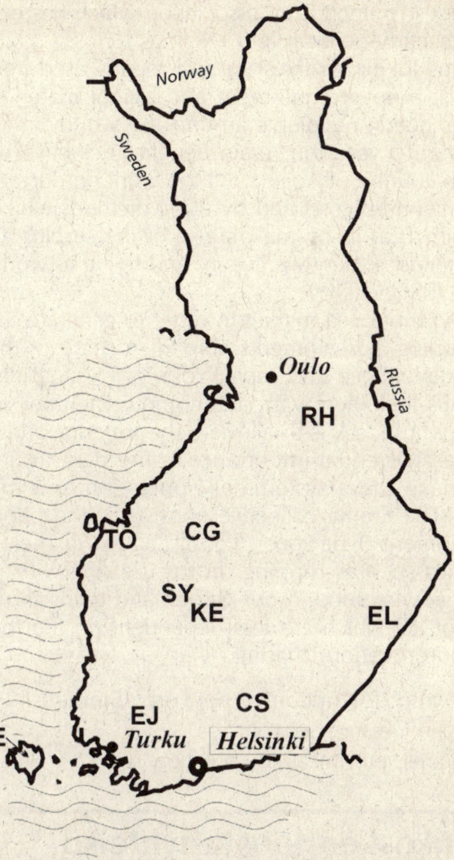

CG Palveluosuuskunta Casa Grande
CS Sylvia-koti
EJ Emmaus-Jokioinen
EL Enonkosken luostariyhteisö
KE Keuruu Ecovillage
ME Meridiana
RH Rauhala
SY Suomineito-yhteisö

Emmaus-Jokioinen

EJ

Humppilantie 339 | 31600 Jokioinen
☎ +358-(0)3-4386457 emmajokioinen@yahoo.co.uk

1978 0.5 - 1 ha (near Forssa) ♀3 ♂6 9

fin., e, swed., sp., slowen. — all

everyone in common (consensus) — limited community financing

rented/leased

DIY, anti-fascist, anti-authoritarian

recyling, second-hand shop, gardening, development co-operation

ecological, self-managed, anarchistic, feminist, vegetarian diet, vegan diet, peace-work, organic gardening, construction, social: internship; handicraft: bike repair, furniture repair, simple metal work

☺ ()

Emmaus Jokioinen is an association which has existed for over 25 years. It is neutral in both party-political and religious terms.
Emmaus Jokioinen fixes up and repairs used items such as clothing, tools, kitchen utensils, hospital equipment and school materials, which it then delivers as aid to various needy recipients around the world.
For over 10 years our main beneficiaries have been the war refugee camps in the African country of Angola. All the work on our premises is done on a voluntary basis with minimum costs and by using methods which harm the environment as little as possible. That is, by making use of the surplus and waste produced by the hyper-consumerist society we live in, and trying to work in harmony with the spirit of DO-IT-YOURSELF (DIY).
We also run a flea market in order to generate some income to help cover the costs for sending aid shipments abroad. A share of the revenues is also used to finance the maintenance and repair costs of existing infrastructure and tools.
Emmaus Jokioinen is an autonomous member of the international Emmaus movement, whose task is to alleviate the suffering and want afflicting various marginalized peoples. Of equal importance is the fight against the structures and mechanisms that make these systems of oppression and marginalization possible in the first place. The Emma collective consists of the people living in Emmaus Jokioinen (at the moment 5 persons). People active in the collective are engaged in different activities such as running distros (dealing with punk/hc-music and political literature), growing food in our garden and trying to develop autonomous, self-governing ways of life which are less dependent on the formal (monetary) economy. Mutualism, co-operation, sharing.

→See also description of network "**Emmaus**"
Vegan Organic Network
☺ non-religious, meat-free nutrition

Enonkosken luostariyhteisö

EL

Ihamaniementie 848 | 58180 Ihamaniemi
+358-(0)15-446558 — luostariyhteiso@kolumbus.fi
-446558 — www.kolumbus.fi/luostariyhteiso/

1994 — 2 ha (near Savonlinna)

- fin, g, e, swed.
- everyone in common (consensus) — shared income
- rented/leased
- meditative
- retreats, worship and prayer, gardening, handicrafts, visitors
- ecological, spiritual, christian, ecumenical, meditation, seminar-house, environmental protection, organic gardening, weaving, sewing, hiking, skiing

☺

The Monastic Protestant Community in Enonkoski began in February 1994 in a former Primary School building in the village of Ihamaniemi.
The purpose of the Community is to be a place for rest, relaxation and prayer. The Community accommodates guests and arranges silent retreats as well as other spiritual and religious occasions.
Women, men and married couples who are fit for work will be accepted as charity workers, test members or as full members to The Monastic Protestant Community.

☺ member of Ev. Luth. Church, ability to work

Keuruu Ecovillage

KE

Kivijärventie 300 | 42700 Keuruu
+358-(0)14-736571, -736573
keuruunekokyla@co.inet.fi
www.ekokyla.tk

1997 — 52 ha (near Keuruu) — ♀17 ♂11 — 11 — 39

fin., e, swed., g, f
everyone in common (majority vote) — individual financing
association
ecological with spiritual interests
community activities, maintenance, organic garden
ecological, non-violent, spiritual, inner growth, meditation, yoga, organic diet, vegetarian diet, vegan diet, peace-work, alternative medicine, art therapy, herbs, self-sufficiency, permaculture, organic agriculture, organic gardening, organic farming, animal friendly husbandry, forestry, alternative energy, pottery, goldsmith workshop, sports, art, media, courses, happenings, concerts etc.

☺ ()

Keuruu Ecovillage is located in a beautiful Finnish landscape beside a lake and is surrounded by wild forest. Keuruu Ecovillage Association bought the old Kivijärvi farm with its almost 30 different buildings in 1997. The oldest buildings date back to the beginning of the 19th century. There is a lot of room for visitors and good possibilities to organize courses and happenings.
The aim of the Keuruu Ecovillage is to promote a sustainable, communal way of life. The community has no political or religious ideology. We have members of all ages whose common interest is to live close to nature on an ecological basis. There is also much interest in personal and spiritual growth.

→ See also description of network "**GEN**"
SKEY
☺ acceptance of our ecological and ethical principles

Meridiana

ME

Thorsten Krüger | Sjökvarteret | AX-22100 Mariehamm, Åland
+358-457-3425916
projekt@meridiana.info
http://www.meridiana.info

2004 (near Mariehamm)

- swed., g, e, fin.
- all who are concerned (consensus)
- none
- ecological, self-managed, non-violent, self-sufficiency, permaculture, alternative energy, new technologies, ecological construction

☺

Our project „Meridiana“ came into existence in the autumn of 2004 with the objective of founding an ecological settlement on the Aland Islands. In the next few years we want to accomodate 10-20 inhabitants. The Aland Islands - situated in the beautiful nature of the „Schärengarten“ inbetween Sweden and Finnland - form a self-governed, swedish-speaking region within Finnland and are demilitarised and neutralized in accordance with international law.

Through our project we want to emphasize a way of life in which the precious knowledge of the „Schärengarten“, that has evolved over centuries, is joined to the possibilities of today in the spirit of the Agenda 21: a sustainable, ecological development, that has its roots in local activities.

Through a high degree of self-sufficiency and the use of local raw materials and products we aim at reducing the environmentally polluting and uneconomical need for transport and use of energy.

May a way of thinking in cycles and ecological principles become a key to our personal growth instead. In harmony with nature we want to find joy of life in creative simplicity.

We welcome all free-thinking and creative guests and friends, who in their own way and together with us want to contribute to the realisation of our project!

☺ openness and readiness for the experiment

Palveluosuuskunta Casa Grande

CG

Hoikanperäntie 290 or 495 | 43800 Kivijärvi
+358-(0)14-457136
-457140
anneli.nasi@casagrandepalvelu.fi
www.casagrandepalvelu.fi

1991 3.5 ha (near Jyväskylä) ♀5 ♂3 1 9

- fin., e
- 8
- everyone in common (consensus)
- shared economy, individual money
- common property
- belief in the power of the spirit of God, cultivating and protecting a piece of land
- electronics for industry, riding lessons and assemblies

ecological, non-violent, spiritual, messianic, adult education (languages), pedagogical (home instruction), peace work through prayer, social work (for children and young people needing help), animal protection, environmental protection, self-sufficiency, organic agriculture, organic gardening, organic/animal friendly husbandry, alternative energy (as goal), electronics, sewing, felt-making, knitting, skiing, ice skating, horseback riding, humour

We moved to live together as a community in autumn 1991 according to the verses of the Holy Bible, Acts 4, 32-35. We have managed together through the love of the Almighty God the Father, who has given us power and energy for every day. No one among us has needed medical care nor medicine, because our healing has come through trust in the name of Yeshua, the original Hebrew name of the Son of God. It is translated as "the Saviour" in English, "el Salvador" in Spanish, "der Retter" in German and "o Soter" in Greek. Because we love God, we want to obey His word which He spoke through His Son, Yeshua Messiah, and which is written in the Holy Bible. Our most important goal is eternal life, but we want to be a good example of knowing God better and better, of living in love of God, and of wanting to cultivate and protect land (Gen.2, 15, Rev.11,18). We still seem to live in a somewhat complicated way, but we are going on in faith and in hope. We have she-goats for our milk needs, sheep for wool and beehives for honey. We have riding horses as a wholesome hobby for the children and adults around us. We also prepare protective electronics devices under a subcontract for the needs of industry and for earning the money we need in order to acqire a larger farm and a simple life.

☺ trusting in God and his son Yeshua, sharing everything with us, probationary period

Rauhala

RH

Pentti Heikkinen | Pinlajavaarantie 11 | 88400 Ristijärvi
+358-(0)40-8487651

1990 | 90 ha (near Kajaani) | ♀4 ♂1 8 13

e, fin.
everyone in common (discussion) — individual financing
common property
Jesus and his Disciples. Seeking God's will.
forestry and ecology
christian, forestry

Religion is the most important thing in our community. Faith in God and Jesus, being his disciples. Understanding what that means today, seeing his times and their darkness. We see the moral and ecological collapse. God and Jesus want the people who believe in him to lead a life that does him justice.
Our next priority is practical work. It should be ecologically sustainable. We work in forestry. We also use the wood to generate energy. We own 90 ha of forest. We gather a great deal from nature and work with our hands. We plant vegetables and

we fish. Our family also includes two gardeners. We gather berries and mushrooms.
If you are seeking a logic for your life and new paths for yourself in the midst of this mess, then please call us. We'll talk to you.

☺ For us, the most important thing in life is to find God and Jesus

Suomineito-yhteisö

SY

Kaijantie 283 | 63700 Ähtäri
☎ +358-(0)6-5330601, -(0)50-5849286 (mobile) ✉ marketta.horn@6net.fi, hhattila@saunalahti.fi, juissi67@saunalahti.fi
Fax -5335323 www.athari.fi/suomineito

1997 — 10 ha (near Ähtäri) — ♀3 ♂4 — 7

- g, e, fin., swed. — all
- everyone in common (consensus/majority decisions)
- limited common financing — rented/leased
- none, the ecological lifestyle unites us
- animal husbandry (sheep, goats, chickens), farming, house and garden work
- ecological, self-managed, feminist, non-violent, spiritual, ecumenical, organic diet, permaculture, organic gardening, ecological animal husbandry, alternative energy, sheep shearing, wool processing, farm holidays, seminars

☺

We are an ecological flat-sharing community with 7 adults around 50 years old, but we hope things are changing and there will be younger people coming and assuming responsibility. We are on the lookout for some enthusiastic people who will regard this place as their home and seize the opportunity to build their own new community on the foundations of the old. We live in the countryside, on the grounds of a former pension house 7 km from Ähtäri (5,000 inhabitants) and 320 km from Helsinki or Turku. We want to contribute to the continued existence of life on this planet. We protect the glorious nature around us through as much self-suffiency as possible (permaculture) and by living in natural ways. Our large main building has many workshops and flats but there is still a lot of potential for setting up working rooms and workshops.

You can also spend your holidays with us. The rooms are furnished with recycled fittings and have a view to the lake. There is a cosy dining room, a small library, weaving and sewing rooms, a room for woodworking, large sun terraces, two saunas and a chapel.

The property includes 800 metres of lakeshore, a rowboat, fishing opportunities, bicycles, a barn with sheep, goats and chickens, as well as cats and dogs. We also have an exhibit on permaculture and ecological flat-sharing communities in Finland. Different natural therapies are available depending on the season and the people.

→ See also description of network "**GEN**"
Communes in Finland
☺ ecological outlook

Sylvia-Koti

CS

Kyläkatu 140 | 15700 Lahti
☎ +358-(0)3-883-130
info@sylvia-koti.fi
-1315
www.sylvia-koti.fi

1970 — 11 ha (near Lahti) — ♀30 ♂30 80 140

fin. — nearly all
colleague (consensus) — shared income
Foundation
anthroposophy
Anthroposophic health education
ecological, self-managed, spiritual, christian, anthroposophic, organic diet, adult education, pedagogical, mentally/psychologically handicapped persons, social therapy, therapy, organic gardening, handicraft, art

Sylvia-Koti is a living community for and with children who need special attention. At the moment we are caring for some 75 children and young people. Our co-workers live in family-like settings together with the children and young people. There is a school and there are activities in workshops, as well as a varied social and cultural life in Sylvia-Koti. We are part of the Camphill movement.

→ See also description of network "**Camphill**"
☺ good health, interest in people with developmental difficulties and in anthroposophy

"Happiness is doubled by sharing."

France

AA L'Arche de St. Antoine
AB Communauté de l'Arche La Borie
AC L'Arche à Cognac
AS Le Sénevé
BC Beau Champ
BL Bio-Lopin
BZ Bazian-Gemeinschaft
CA Carine Laloe, Alain Emery
CL Centre Lothlorien
CO La Ferme du Collet
CS Communauté le Sappel
DY Coopérative Cravirola
EC EcoLonie - Centre Ecologique Internat.
EP Emmaus-Peupins
FC Francischu
FL Communauté de l'Arche La Flayssière
GC Communauté de la Grande Chouannière"
LA Les Amis de la Douceur
LN La Lune Nette aux Lunettes
LS Proména les Sources
MA Le Moulin de l'Auro
MC Monastere de Cantauque
MG Eurocoop Longo Maï
ML Community in planning
PV Communauté de Pain de Vie
SN Communauté le Surgeon
SU Communauté de Sus
SV La Source de Vie
TF Les Trois Fontaines
VD La Val Dieu
VL Communauté Vitulettu

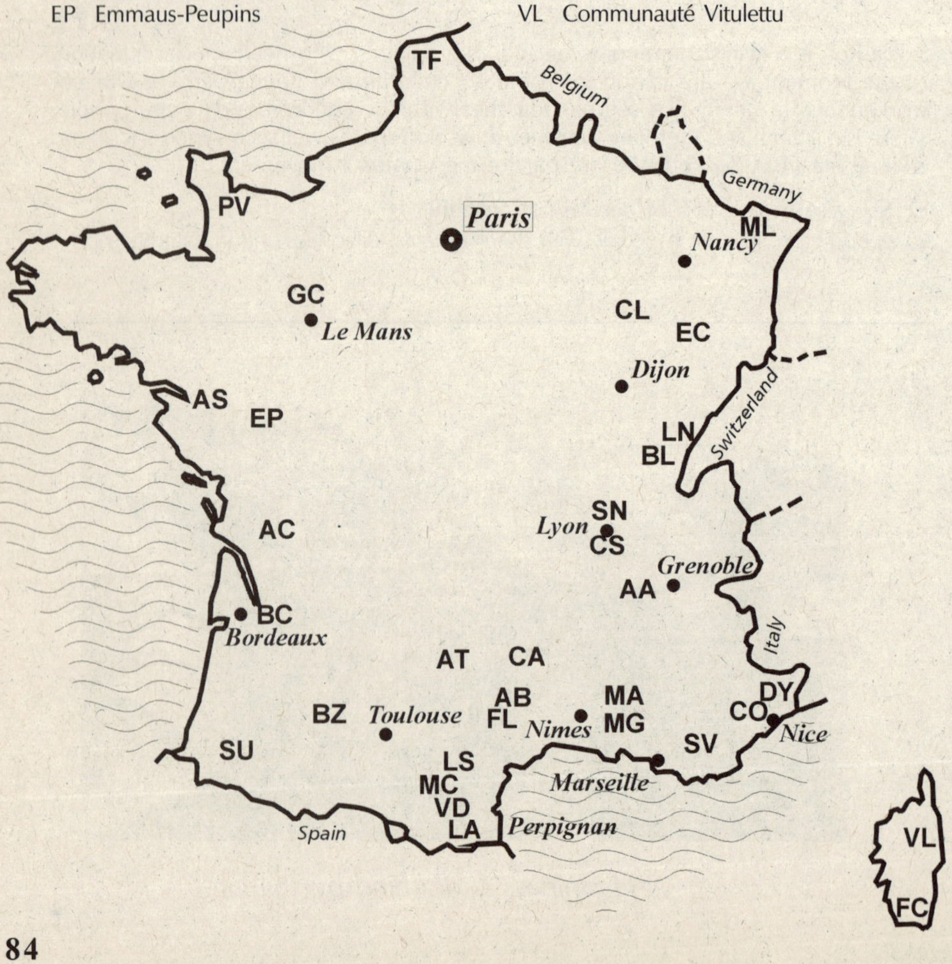

Bazian-Gemeinschaft

BZ

32230 Louslitges
☎ +33-(0)56270-9513
-9541

1994 | 48 ha (near Auch) | ♀3 ♂2 | 6 | 11-13

g, f, e

everyone in common (consensus)

individual and shared financing of certain areas — common property

construction, grounds, vegetable garden and orchard, kindergarten, school

ecological, self-managed, non-violent, organic diet, vegetarian diet, pedagogical, animal protection, environmental protection, organic gardening, alternative energy, ecological construction, apiary, music

☺ ( )

10-13 people live in Bazian on a permanent basis. We also have members who do not live here. Our community language is German. We aim for: to be able to live a high degree of authenticity, individuality and honesty in community. This entails finding room for emotional processes of both individuals and the group as a whole, whilst at the same time taking care of the children, and meeting the practical demands of a simple rural co-operative life. We place great importance on the benevolent and attentive care of our children in their growth and their individual development. The key concept here is: independent activity in a prepared environment instead of "school".
We supply ourselves with tasty fruits and vegetables from our own large organic garden over most of the year. We are also largely self-sufficient in the handicraft department. Our living space is limited but can be expanded. Guests are only welcome after making a prior appointment.

☺ consent of residents/members, financial independence, ecologically oriented, drug-free

Beauchamp

BC

Lieu de Beauchamp | 24610 Montpeyroux, Dordogne
☎ +44(0)5.53.82.69.98 — bonjour@beau-champ.com
www.beau-champ.com

1991 | 8 ha (near Bordeaux) | 2-6

e, f

everyone in common (consensus) — property of individual community members

permaculture

permaculture, gardening, ecological building, new technologies, green wood processing

We are looking for people actively interested in permaculture to help with building up a permaculture site on 8 ha of woods and meadows. There is a partially rebuilt house using many alternative and traditional techniques, partially established gardens employing a variety of organic methods, partially created orchards that are beginning to produce fruit, and a forest which supplies us with firewood, building material, compost, mulch and which is a joy to work in. If you would like to come and add your bit, please write, including an IRC/stamp and some information about yourself ... the whys, hows, whens, what ifs and how longs. We are also looking for investors / co-owners to create a sustainable future.

Bio-Lopin

BL

39570 St.-Maur-Jura
+33-(0)3-84442392 www.aricia.fr/bio-lopin
-84442392

1991 17.5 ha (near Lons Le Saunier) ♀4 ♂4 3

f, e, g, it. 6
everyone in common (consensus) individual financing
property of individual community members
none
farming, hotel, workshops etc. on organic building
ecological, self-managed, non-violent, spiritual, organic diet, pedagogical, environmental protection, organic agriculture, organic farming, alternative energy, ecological construction, construction, artistic activities

The community has not sent a current selfdescription.

RFEV (French ecovillage network)

Carine Laloe, Alain Emery

CA

Le Rabies | 48240 Saint Privat de Vallongue
+33-(0)4-66450127 causses-cevennes.com/rabies/default.htm

1992 70 ha (near Florac) ♀3 ♂2 5

f, e, g, sp., port. all
everyone in common (consensus) individual financing
common property
ecological, organic diet, vegan diet, adult education, seminar-house, therapies: spiritual psychology, transpersonal natural health care, animal protection, environmental protection, self-sufficiency, organic agriculture, alternative energy, ecological construction

( )

This old mountain village, idyllically located at an altitude of 900 m in the heart of the Cevennes National Park, lies at the confluence of two mountain streams, is isolated and quiet, was excellently restored and is open to receive people who eat no animal products or subsidiary products (vegan), who use no animal materials and who respect vegan ethics, as they are well known in the Anglo-Saxon countries (a lifestyle without animal exploitation).
We rent comfortable guest houses from Easter to the end of October, and according to availability thereafter. There are solar showers, a library and special rest places within the village.
Food is provided in a small vegan organic foods shop, as at the evening dinner table, at the plentiful breakfast and picnic.
There is an opportunity to become acquainted with the following areas: vegan cuisine, ecological gardening, collecting wild plants, gathering chestnuts and developing a universal consciousness in everyday life. One can take part in relaxation meetings, art therapy, wellness massage and foot reflex zone massage. In addition, there are courses on life hygiene, the hall is rented to groups (for yoga, education etc.), and evening events are organised on topics such as ecological building, fairy tales etc.

Association Graine de vie

Centre Lothlorien

CL

Domaine le Moiron | 52800 Foulain
+33-(0)3 25 03 40 86 centrelothlorien@wanadoo.fr
- 32 49 91 www.centrelothlorien.com

2002 14 ha (near Chaumont, Haute-Marne) 3 3

f, e, dutch 4

one part of the group (consensus) limited community financing

property of individual community members

none

organic gardening, renovation, education centre (courses and workshops), supporting people in search of their path through life

ecological, self-managed, spiritual, esoteric/New Age, anthroposophic, meditation, yoga, vegetarian diet, pedagogical, seminar-house, peace-work, one-world development, mentally/psychologically handicapped persons, therapies: alternative medicine, environmental protection, permaculture, organic agriculture, organic gardening, alternative energy, ecological construction, professions: gardener, teacher, entrepreneur; athletic activities: hiking, biking, tennis; artistic activities: sculpture, painting, arts & crafts

Translated, Lothlorien means "Flower of the Golden Woods" (Tolkien), a place where peace, quiet and harmony reign and where travellers may find strength and good counsel. Lothlorien is a community and educational centre. Our common basis is the desire to live in harmony with nature, to respect all living things and to create a society which shows friendship to all people. Lothlorien is an international, ecological and spiritual community which would like to reach out to everyone who is searching. Our centre offers courses, events and a resting place where all people can find their way back to themselves and then continue on their path through life. Lothlorien lies in the Haute Marne, a thinly settled natural paradise with many footpaths, including the pilgrimage paths of Santiago de Campostella and Joan of Arc. The 14 ha grounds contain a castle, a guest house, a chapel and various workshops.

NAR, NELK

☺ work 30 hrs per week, 500 Euros per month for all expenses, individual development

Communauté de l'Arche La Borie

AB

La Borie Noble | 34650 Roqueredonde
☎ +33-(0)4-67440989

1948 450 ha (near Lodève) ♀8 ♂8 10 26

f, e, g, sp. all

everyone in common (consensus) shared economy (shared income and capital)

common property

non-violence in the spirit of Gandhi

farming, animal husbandry,

ecological, non-violent, spiritual, ecumenical, inner growth, meditation, organic diet, vegetarian diet, adult education, peace-work, non-violent actions, environmental protection, self-sufficiency, organic agriculture, animal friendly husbandry, construction, singing, dance, handicrafts: tailoring, pottery, woodworking, spinning

☺

La Borie Noble is the oldest of the L'Arche Communities of Lanza del Vasto and was founded by him after his encounter with Gandhi. Lanza del Vasto and his wife Chanterelle lived here. La Borie Noble and La Fleyssière are located in southern France on a plateau bordering on the Larzac, which is known for its extreme climate. A major portion of the community's nutritional needs are produced on a 50 ha compound on stony and largely infertile soil: bread, vegetables, eggs, butter, cheese. The community owns a herd of cows and a team of work horses. The members cultivate various handicraft traditions, which contribute to self-responsibility by helping the members to provide themselves with a roof over their heads as well as clothing. One speciality of the community is that during the daily work a bell regularly strikes the hours, and for a brief moment there is silence so that the members can pause and become aware of the here and now. Interested persons can take part in the communal life during the special encounter weeks. In addition, events are organised on specific themes.

→ See also description of network "**Church & Peace**"
L'Arche according to Lanza del Vasto
☺ one-year stay, local training, mutual agreement

Communauté de l'Arche La Flayssière

FL

34650 Joncels
☎ +33-(0)467444090

1978 | 15 ha (near Montpellier, Béziers) | ♀4 ♂4 8 16

f, g, it., sp., e — all
everyone in common (consensus) — shared economy (shared income and capital)
common property
non-violence, inter-religious dialogue
farm work, garden, cheese making, pottery, seminars on non-violence
ecological, ecological, non-violent, spiritual, ecumenical, inner growth, meditation, yoga, organic diet, vegetarian diet, adult education, peace-work, organic gardening, organic farming, alternative energy, ecological construction, pottery

☺

The La Flayssière Community is part of the international L'Arche Movement, which was founded by Lanza del Vasto following his meeting with Gandhi. The community's members are attempting to implement non-violence in as many areas of their life as possible. This includes respect for nature, our fellow human beings, our children and ourselves; a simple life; inter-religious dialogue as well as dedication to justice, peace and the preservation of creation. The focal points of our work are organic farming and gardening, dairy cows and milk processing in our dairy, a small pottery workshop, various seminars and yoga courses.
Our daily routine is characterised by periods of meditation and ecumenical prayer, shared meals, various kinds of work and - depending on the season or the occasion at hand – various cultural offerings, children's activities or preparing for celebrations. The community members maintain a common purse and make decisions on the consensus principle. Solar cells and a wind power station to generate "clean" energy are under construction.

L'Arche according to Lanza del Vasto
☺ agreement with the principles of the Arche

Communauté de la Grande Chouannière

GC

72170 Ségrie
+33-(0)243333965

1999 | 35 ha (near Le Mans) | ♀4 ♂1 2 7

f, g, e, sp. | 4

in common (consensus) | individual financing

rented/leased

farming with draught horses, direct marketing

ecological, self-managed, non-violent, organic diet, vegetarian diet, adult education, environmental protection, organic agriculture, organic gardening, organic farming, animal friendly husbandry, alternative energy

The ecovillage consists of two economically independent groups which share an ecologically managed farm. Our common basis is an association aimed at becoming non-violent in our relations with nature, with other human beings and with ourselves. There are common activities such as festivals and political actions.
Our work on the farm currently includes: farming with draught horses, hand-milked dairy cows and goats, cheese making and bakery, vegetable growing, blacksmith shop, chickens, school farm, horse circus.

Communauté de Pain de Vie

PV

Sommervieu | 27, rue St. Pierre | 14400 Bayeux
+33-(0)31925419

1976 | 6 (near Bayeux) | ♀20 ♂30 15 65

f | 10

everyone in common (helpfulness and consideration)

shared economy based on Providence | rented/leased

Catholic faith

vegetable garden, people in difficult situations

christian, social work, construction, apiary

We live here together as a group – as men, women, singles, couples, children, consecrated brothers and sisters, priests. We want to be a people who worship the Lord Jesus, in the Eucharist, in the sacrament of love, together with the poor and weak. It is very simple: we choose to devote ourselves, like Christ, to a radical life, in keeping with the Gospels, which, when it is lived, gives God the honour and prepares the reign of Him who is coming. The "Bread of Life" community was founded in 1976 following the conversion experience of its founders, Pascal and Marie-Annick Pingault. They began leading their lives like the first apostles, true to the brotherly communion and prayer. In 1984 the community was officially recognised by the Catholic Church. In early 2000 it included 15 houses in France and some 50 on all the world's continents. There are a great many ways to get involved, including a variety of offerings for young people.

☺ Catholic

Communauté de Sus

SU

11, Route du Haut Béarn | 64190 Sus-Navarrenx
+33-(0)55966-1428 sus@douzetribus.com
-2034 www.TwelveTribes.com

1983 8 (near Oloron St. Marie) ♀30 ♂30 40 100

f, e, sp. all

everyone in common (consensus) shared economy (shared income and capital)

common property

we are part of the „Twelve Tribes Community"

gardening, shoemaking, construction, trade ...

Recreating all aspects of the communal life of Jesus' early followers

☺

The little village of Sus is located near the Spanish border with a view of the Pyrenees. Here one can often see herds of sheep with their shepherds. Since 1983 140 people of different nationalities and backgrounds have lived here together, gathered in the hope of bringing about that life of love and peace which the Son of God promised humankind on earth.
These people no longer live lonely and alienated from one another in a society for which independence and materialism are the highest gods. We, the members of this small tribe of human beings, practice various handicrafts and live together simply by sharing everything, just like the first disciples of Yashua (the Hebrew name for Jesus).
Our doors and hearts are open to all visitors, so you are welcome to come by sometime - whether for a day or forever....

→ See also description of network "**Communities of the Twelve Tribes**"
☺ people who live the Gospels as disciples of Yashua

Communauté le Sappel

CS

Le Grand Champ | 69510 Soucieu-en-Jarrest
+33-(0)478051608
sappel.j@tele2.fr
sappel.free.fr

1989 (near Lyon)

f 6

one part of the group (consensus) individual financing

common property

Catholic spirituality

offers for children in disadvantaged parts of town

spiritual, christian, adult education, social work: with poor people; artistic activity: painting, theatre

The Sappel Family is a movement within the Church whose calling lies in responding to the spiritual needs of Fourth World families. The Sappel Family consists of two communities: the "Sappel" Community, which is recognised as a "community of the faithful", is open to all lifestyles (families, singles); the "Good News" Community is called upon to found a religious congregation for women. It draws its energy from the memory of Père Joseph Wrésinski and endeavours to remain true to his stance toward the people of the Fourth World. The most disadvantaged have a right to find a place for themselves within our Christian community. Because Christ revealed himself to them, they have a place in the heart of the Church. Beyond that, they can help us enter the mysteries of the forgiveness and love of God. This vision commits us to rebuild our lives using those who suffer most as a starting point. The tools needed for this are:

- solidarity with the people of the Fourth World and assistance in the defence of their rights (work, housing, health, children etc.)
- creating a place where the most disadvantaged can pray and grow in their spirituality
- training Fourth World priests in France
- founding small prayer brotherhoods

☺ Catholic, desire to work with poor people

Communauté le Surgeon

SN

9-11, Allée des Cardons | 69120 Vaulx-en-Velin
+33-(0)78791670, -(0)78808823
-(0)78791670

1970 900 m² (near Lyon) ♀8 ♂7 15

f, it. 1

everyone in common (majority vote) limited community financing

property of individual community members

Christian communal life
everyone is employed outside the community, accepting minors into the community; meetings to discuss issues
ecological, left-wing political understanding, non-violent, spiritual, christian, ecumenical, pedagogical, mentally/psychologically handicapped persons, physically handicapped persons, social work

☺

The community of Le Surgeon took form in 1970 in the encounter of people of all backgrounds (disabled persons, former prisoners, religiously oriented students, ...). Individual and communal prayer is the basis for our actions. We are stimulated by our differences and each of us - in our personal and professional lives - tries to cultivate hospitality towards needy people. We try and we give these processes the time they need to resolve conflicts through the principle of non-violence. Our common values are expressed through our individual and communal commitments within society: the broader justice, the right to be different, respect and patience for the poorest in our society, attention to those who suffer, mutual responsibility... We have also created a solidarity fund. We have set aside time for specific rituals: five Saturdays chosen at the beginning of the year to reflect on a common theme, festive events (Christmas, Epiphany, Easter), birthdays, hikes and a three-day excursion in the spring, and the opportunity for weekly encounters (prayers, meals, etc.). We are linked to the network of Christian grassroots communities of France and the living and family communities network of France and Belgium.

Nationale Vereinigung der Basisgemeinden
☺ concept, have time available for the community, financial autonomy

Communauté Vitulettu

VL

20234 Pietricaggio, Corsica
+33-(0)495-359331
vitulettu@european-shamanism.org
www.vitulettu.org

1997 | 4.5 ha (near Cervione) | ♀7 ♂4 3 14

g, f, e | 11

everyone in common (consensus) | limited community financing

property of individual members, rented / leased
gardening, sheep rearing, forestry, apiary, seminars
ecological, self-managed, spiritual, inner growth, organic diet, vegetarian diet, organic gardening, animal friendly husbandry, forestry, alternative energy, construction, European shamanism

☺ ()

Ever since 1997 we have been living in an abandoned Corsican mountain village on the edge of isolation. It is located in the Castagniccia at an elevation of 800 m on the edge of the Caldane Massif (1,750 m). We own the village centre and lease the surrounding land with its orchard terraces, gardens, and the sweet chestnut forest. We own a herd of sheep, keep bees, engage in organic farming and forestry. We live a simple, self-determined life without a link to the public power supply network (we may soon have a solar energy system), with compost toilets and running spring-cold water. It is very close to nature and sometimes we're at its mercy; sometimes we live outside from morning to evening (sometimes overnight), and in winter the road is so icy that we can't get away. We strive for a lively co-existence through, among other things, our effort to start with ourselves when we have conflicts, i.e. to ask ourselves: "Why does what someone else says bother me so much?" We are an open spiritual community without denominational ties. For example, we use the village chapel for prayers and the threshing-floor and the surrounding nature for shamanistic rituals. We offer seminars almost year-round, which we announce over the Internet (www.Ines-Deutsch.de). For visitors we offer a campground with our "open-air bathroom" (washbowl, shower, compost toilet).

→See also description of network "**Come Together**"
☺ openness to self-realisation, acquaintance period

Community in planning

ML

Pia Rennollet and Werner Brengel | Moulin de Loutzviller | 57720 Loutzviller
☎+33-(0)387967524

2000 35 ha (near Saarguemines F; Zweibrücken D) ♀2 ♂1 3

g, f, e 3

everyone in common (consensus) limited community financing

property of individual community members

none

farming, horses, seminars, farm shop

ecological, self-managed, non-violent, spiritual, esoteric/New Age, inner growth, organic diet, vegetarian diet, adult education, therapeutic pedagogy with horses, animal protection, environmental protection, self-sufficiency, permaculture, organic agriculture, organic gardening, organic farming, animal friendly husbandry, forestry, alternative energy, construction, renovating building and mill, horseback riding, construction site art, communication in partnership with horse, crossing boundaries

☺

The Moulin de Loutzviller is a dilapidated mill with 26 ha of adjoining meadow land. We live here in the Franco-German border region. We cultivate a total of around 35 ha biodynamically, producing vegetables, potatoes and grain for people and animals. We still cultivate the land with tractors, but in the future – as far as possible – we want to work with our horses. We have a large experimental vegetable garden. We are looking for other meaningful life concepts so that we can live with a clear conscience.

Autonomy is important to the extent that it can be realised. One of our goals is to develop our own food and energy supply. We seek to build a community in the size of an extended family within which we can develop and complement one another. In order to achieve this we are looking for people with empathy, pioneer spirit, imagination, energy and a genuine love of people, animals and plants. 20 horses play an important role in our mill life. Our other animal co-residents include goats, chickens, a duck couple, dogs and cats. A gradually stabilising seminar operation is one of our financial supports. In terms of content, our course offerings range from living and working with horses and natural consciousness, all the way to therapies and alternative healing methods. We have made it our goal to make "borderline" experiences accessible, and to expand and cross these borders.

☺ empathy, pioneer spirit, imagination, energy, love towards people, animals and plants

Coopérative Cravirola

DY

06430 La Brigue
+33-(0)4-93047065
-93047065
cravirol@club-internet.fr
www.cravirola.com

1996 | 10 ha (near Tende, Nizza) | ♀4 ♂4 8

f, e, g | all

everyone in common (consensus) | shared income

property of part of the group

building a better world

farming, cultural events (music, theatre, visual arts)

ecological, left-wing political understanding, conventional agriculture, conventional farming, alternative energy, construction, artistic activities: music, theatre, visual art

☺

Cravirola, the site of an alternative project, is a farm in the middle of the mountains. It was built upon the foundations of an abandoned hamlet in the south-western French Alps. Here a small group of individuals of various origins are experimenting with alternatives to conventional social life. A blend of pragmatism and ideology, our project does not ascribe to any particular dogma: we are not religious, vegetarian, and belong to no particular political group, even if our sympathies strongly tend toward the left. Our will and our dedication reveal themselves in daily life in our decision for a location and a way of life in keeping with our convictions.

☺ humour

ECOlonie - Centre Ecologique International

EC

1 Thietry | 88260 Hennezel / Vogesen
+33-(0)3290700-27
-94
ecolonie@aol.com
www.ecolonie.org

1989 | 21 ha (near Darney) | ♀5 ♂7 6 18

f, e, g, dutch | approx. 15

one part of the group (consensus) | common property

vision containing ecological and spiritual elements (non-dogmatic)

organic garden, artistic workshops, creative courses and yoga ecological, spiritual, vegetarian diet, pedagogical, seminar-house, environmental protection, permaculture, organic agriculture, alternative energy, new technologies, ecological construction, construction, artistic activities: workshops

The community was founded in 1989. It is situated in the heart of Western Europe, in the middle of a beautiful hiking and nature area in the French Vosges Mountains near the town of Darney, 80 km south of Nancy.
Ecolonie views itself as a unique place for encounters of and with people from all countries who are interested in the issues of nature (thinking sustainably), art (creativity) and spirituality (mysticism). Interested persons can come to Ecolonie as guests or as either temporary or permanent participants. Everyone who works here receives free room and board. The permanent residents do not receive a salary.
Ecolonie is an organisation. The community places great value on the individual's own responsibility and, among other things, seeks to be a means to bring about the self-awareness and transformation of consciousness. It owns many buildings and properties in and around the valley of the Ourche River. A diversity of activities give form to efforts for a meaningful and constructive communal life.
Everyone who is interested in working together towards this goal is heartily welcome.

☺ one month of work with us, during which we can discuss all the little preconditions

Emmaus-Peupins

EP

9 Rue de la Tannerie | 79700 Mauléon
+33-(0)4981-9821 olivier.emmaus.peupins@wanadoo.fr
-9676

1977 (near Mauléon, Bressuire) 70

f, e all

one part of the group

individual financing community

principles of the Emmaus Movement: hospitality, solidarity, work ...

collecting/selling second-hand items in shop; recycling boxes, wood pallets, etc.

mentally/psychologically handicapped persons, physically handicapped persons, social work: living together with people from marginal groups

The community has not sent a current selfdescription.

→ See also description of network "**Emmaus**"

☺ the desire to share daily life with persons facing challenges; the ability to communicate. Creative, artistic activity makes it easier for new members to fit in.

Eurocoop Longo Maï

MG

Mas de Granier | Caphan | 13310 St. Martin de Crau
+33-(0)4904727-42
-23
lmcrau@wanadoo.fr
www.longomai.org

1973 | 23 ha (near Arles) | ♀4 ♂4 | 8 | 16

f, g, e, it., sp. | all

everyone in common (consensus) | shared income

common property

no spiritual/ideological principles

organic vegetables, alternative forms of trade, sheep rearing, making preserves, solidarity actions

ecological, self-managed, left-wing political understanding, non-violent, organic diet, peace-work, one-world development, organic agriculture, organic farming, alternative energy

Between the Alpilles and Camargue lies the Crau Plain. It was once the estuary of the Durance before it became a tributary of the Rhone near Avignon. Today, France's last "steppe" is threatened by the expansion of the surrounding towns and industrial areas. We have been living on the Mas de Granier farm since 1990 and cultivate 20 ha of land. From October to April a herd of sheep grazes on the meadows before it withdraws to the summer meadows in the mountains. During their absence we use this land to produce organic hay. The sheep dung is used as fertiliser on the fields and in our gardens. We grow organic vegetables year-round on 3 ha. We process fruits and vegetables from Mas and the other Longo Mai co-ops in our cannery. This facility is also regularly used by other organic producers. The unscrupulous price policies of the large distributors displace small farmers from the agricultural sector and have led to the creation of huge industrial monopolies.
In response to this, we are developing a direct marketing system in order to create solidarity-based relations between consumers and producers. Weekly vegetable baskets create a bridge between town and country. Our regular contacts with local grass roots initiatives and trade unions have brought about actions against war, for the rights and against the exploitation of the "Sans Papiers" and impulses for a sustainable regional development model. In the coming years we are planning the construction of a house and alternative energy projects.
We expect interested persons to bring plenty of time with them.

Longo Mai

☺ the desire to live with values other than "Metro, job, sleep ..."

Francischu

FC

20131 Pianottoli-Caldarello, Corse du sud

1993 | 8 ha (near Bonifacio) | 2-12

- g, f, e, dutch — best: all
- everyone in common (consensus) — limited community financing and individual
- rented/leased
- faith in love (Agape and Eros)
- garden, firewood, bread-baking, canning, cheese-making, hide-tanning, sausage-making, animal care, sailing
- inner growth, helping people to help themselves, sailing, self-sufficiency, organic agriculture, organic gardening, animal friendly husbandry, trust, freedom, humour etc.

☺ ( )

So many people come here to become commune members over the holidays. This is least stressful with people from other communities. We particularly enjoy tender loving couples and children. Our cats and dogs are usually the most important first "contacts" for children. Children have an easier time understanding that sheep, goats and chickens are slaughtered someday. Yes, we admit: we slaughter our beloved animals, eat them with gusto and are thankful for their hides.
For us, there's nothing romantic about not having a computer. It just doesn't fit in. We have no telephone, no car, no electricity, nor do we miss them. Many visitors (winged doves) enjoy the fact that they can come here and pull the plug on industrial civilisation. Some of us like to go about our work naked and without pretence (work is such an ugly word... we could just as easily say dancing, playing, meditation), hiking down to the water and swimming over to "St. Yves": our ketch (a two-master) is sailing again.
We have received an eviction notice for our hill with its huts and caves (0.5 ha). The owner has no basis for claiming that she needs it herself since new building is prohibited on account of the airport located 3 km away.

→See also description of network "**Come Together**"

☺ self-development (dealing with childhood problems), openness, enjoying activity and movement (as far as possible)

L'Arche à Cognac

AC

Rue de l'Anisserie | 16100 Chateau Bernard
+33-(0)545361500 aac.resp-assistants@wanadoo.fr

1998 ♀20 ♂15 15 50

f all

one part of the group (majority vote or consensus depending on importance)

a Christian/Catholic community which respects each individual's religious confession

living with mentally disabled persons

christian, pedagogical, mentally/psychologically handicapped persons

☺

We provide mentally disabled people with the opportunity to develop their own life goals both on the personal and professional level. For this we have a production workshop, a repair service, a school and 4 residential houses in the town of Cognac.

In our view, each person has unique value and possesses equal dignity and equal rights. In order to realise these values, the Arche is committed to a communal life which places great value on people's relations to one another (in terms of education but also friendship). Personal relationships, combined with individual goals, make it possible for humans to unfold their potential on three important levels: the civil, the medical and the spiritual.

We offer you the opportunity to give a little bit of your time (1 month, 6 months, 1 year ...) to others by serving them in the form of voluntary service or an internship.

To become a long-term "assistant" in the Arche requires not only professional skills but also the decision to live with disabled people on a more than just pedagogical basis, because the assistants share their daily lives with the care recipients. We can offer room, board, health insurance and a monthly allowance. "Assistants" can gain further expertise through practical experience but also through the network's internal training courses.

Those who would like to give part of their time and themselves profit from this experience when it comes to finding or focusing their personal and professional goals.

→ See also description of network **„Arche following Jean Vanier"**

☺ sharing community goal (community life)

L'Arche de St. Antoine

AA

Saint Antoine l'Abbaye | 38160 Saint Marcellin
+33-(0)47636-4552 arche.de.st.antoine@wanadoo.fr
-4290 www.arche-de-st-antoine.com

1987 1 ha (near St. Antoine) ♀15 ♂13 20 48

f, e, sp.
all affected persons (consensus) shared income
Vermieter
non-violence, Christian with an openness toward other religions
hostel, training in and practice of non-violent actions
ecological, left-wing political understanding, non-violent, spiritual, christian, ecumenical, inner growth, meditation, vegetarian diet, adult education, seminar-house, peace-work, organic agriculture, artistic activities: song and dance

☺

St. Antoine is a community in which life is oriented towards non-violence. Hospitality is our calling and main activity. The Arche community was founded by Lanza del Vasto in 1948 following his meeting with Gandhi. Singles and couples who have decided to join this communal living experiment do the necessary work, simplify their needs, pursue reconciliation, prayer and spiritual development along with singing, dancing and celebrations. They participate in political actions for justice and peace in co-operation with other non-violent groups. The community members of the Arche of St. Antoine are Christians of various denominations who feel that they have been called to religious reconciliation and respect for the individual life paths of individual people. Visitors are received in a large building in lovely medieval St. Antoine l'Abbaye.

→ See also description of network "**Arche following Lanza del Vasto**"
☺ mutual acquaintance during an internship

La Ferme du Collet

CO

06260/2 La Penne
+33-(0)49305-8893, -8450

limited common financing, individual/family
ecological, self-managed, non-violent, organic diet, self-sufficiency, permaculture, alternative energy, ecological construction, professions: farmer, baker, carpenter, architect; artistic activities: music (beginner), arts & crafts in future

We are two families, i.e. 4 adults and 4 children, and since September 2001 we have been living 70 km north-east of Nice at at altitude of 750 m. We live a simple life and are searching for simple ecological technologies. All other families with the same goals are sincerely welcome.

La Lune Nette aux Lunettes

LN

39170 St. Lupicine
☎ +33-(0)384421765 — erika.ofek.com/log20010608-20010714.php
Fax -(0)384421765

1996 — 2.75 ha (near St. Claude) — ♀2 ♂2 children 2 total 6

g, e, it., f, sp. — 1
everyone in common (consensus) — limited community financing and individual
property of individual members and of persons not living on-site
more Amerindian than anything else, e.g. the 4 elements as a guideline, vegetarian if possible
garden, renovation, tepee production
ecological, self-managed, non-violent, spiritual, yoga, organic diet, vegetarian diet, permaculture, organic gardening, alternative energy, ecological construction, handicraft: jewellry, weaving, tepee sewing, bead sewing, basket weaving, dream-catchers; sports: swimming, ping-pong; art: drawing, painting, carving

☺

A small community with large houses in the French Jura in the midst of wild and beautiful nature. Supplied with electricity from the stream, drinking water from the spring, with wild herbs and vegetables from the Fukuoka-inspired garden, we live following the rhythm of the four elements. Fires burn all year round in the tepees; the bright rooms of the houses serve as studios for art, handicraft and tepee building, as well as for shelter from the raw Jura winter.
We cook, eat, and attend to the most important household tasks in partnership with our holiday and working guests. Musicians, poets, roofers, bricklayers and travellers: all are welcome to spend some time here and decide for themselves whether they would like to pay money or work for their keep.
It is possible to join the co-operative with money and to help give form to this place; it is dedicated to the spirit of the earth.

☺ you can either buy a stake in the owners' association with 15,000 or become a simple community member for approx. 10 Euros per day for room and board

La Source de Vie

SV

Chemin des Riaux | 83570 Carcès (Var)
☎ +33-(0)494043432

6 ha (near Brignoles) — ♀1

f, european — 1
one person (majority vote) — shared income
common property
ecological and spiritual
experimental garden, compost, permaculture, renewable energy, house construction

ecological, self-managed, non-violent, spiritual, inner growth, organic diet, vegetarian diet, adult education, pedagogical, seminar-house, peace-work, one-world development, social work (RMI, young people) therapies (gentle alternative medicine), animal protection, environmental protection, self-sufficiency, permaculture, organic agriculture, organic gardening, alternative energy, new technologies, ecological construction, handicraft (manual work with the earth and construction), sports activities (hiking, biking), artistic activities (theatre, dance, pottery, painting), exchange with other countries

I am a person who for the past ten years has been dreaming of creating a place to live in community with others on my own little property. It is an area of 6 ha in natural surroundings with vineyards, a forest and olive trees. The heart of this community will be an old farm building made of stone (a "bastide") which provides room for around 12 people. It will be a guest house with a conference space and handicraft workshops. The land shall be used as an organic farm with vineyards and an olive grove. The planned centre will also be for children and old people. In 2004 I hope to set up a compost centre (Jean Pain method) and an experimental garden. I am looking for people with profound knowledge of permaculture, composting, organic farming etc.

RFEV (Resau francais d´eco-villages)
☺ strong ecological and communal motivation

La Val Dieu

VD

11190 Rennes le Château
+33-(0)468-742321 lavaldieu@aol.com
-742321 www.lavaldieu.com

1984 52 ha (near Limoux) ♀4 ♂3 2 9

e, f 3

everyone in common (majority vote) individual financing

common property

hostel, yoga classes, garden

ecological, self-managed, inner growth, yoga, organic diet, vegetarian diet, seminar-house, animal protection, environmental protection, organic agriculture, organic gardening, organic farming, animal friendly husbandry, forestry, alternative energy, ecological construction, humour

☺ ()

Lavaldieu is a beautiful place with a great deal of history, both ancient and contemporary. It has attracted various people who would not necessarily have chosen to live together otherwise. It is the coalescing force of the group, the love and commitment we feel which keep us together through the hard times, and in exchange we are graced with its beauty. Our goals are many and varied. We all want to maintain Lavaldieu as a beautiful place and keep it open for people to visit, re-energise, to take a holiday, to rest at the guesthouse and campsite. But we are equally concerned with managing the land in an ecological manner. The two farmers now keep chickens, pigs of an old breed and horses, they are breeding. We are still building personal housing, developing an ecological sewage unit, researching the history of Lavaldieu, keeping the forest from invading our fields while trying to earn enough money to do all of this.

☺ financial and ideological

Le Moulin de l'Auro

MA

930, Chemin de la Muscadelle | 84800 L'Isle s/Sorgues
☎ +33-(0)490206151 ✉ lemoulindelauro@wanadoo.fr
-(0)490207057

1976

f

one part of the group (majority vote) — common property

ecumenical, mentally/psychologically handicapped persons

Le Moulin de l'Auro accommodates 50 women and men with mental disabilities (moderate to serious) and the assistants who take care of them. The community aims to create an environment for living and working conducive to the personal growth and flourishing of disabled people in the spirit of the „Arche Community Charter". Le Moulin de l'Auro is linked to the state-run social services and is administered by an association whose members are mostly friends of the community. They support the community's operations with their respective professional expertise.

→See also description of network "**Arche following Jean Vanier**"

"Each blade of grass has its own angel, who leans over it and whispers 'grow, grow!'" Talmud

Tree-planting in Tamera, Portugal

Le Sénevé

AS

La Carizière | 44690 La Haye Fouassière
+33-(0)24036-9839 seneve@club-internet.fr
-7870 www.multimania.com/seneve

1984 3 ha (near Nantes) ♀34 ♂20 54

f, e 51

one part of the group (consensus) state financing

common property

Christian-ecumenical but open to other interreligious orientations

living with mentally/psychologically handicapped adults

spirit., christian, ecumenical, pedagogical, handicapped persons

We, the Le Sénevé community, which belongs to the Jean Vanier Arche movement, share our lives with handicapped persons. We form households including mentally and physically handicapped people who suffer from their "being different" and their limitations. This form of living together exists in the spirit of peace and brotherhood. The common goal of all Arche communities is to receive hurt and disturbed persons in order to offer them a dignified existence with a genuine home and an employment opportunity. In our communities of sharing with oneanother everyone has the opportunity to grow according to his or her own rhythm and to develop on all levels. The Arche's pedagogy is based on the concept of hope. There are Arche communities world-wide: in India, Japan, Africa, Australia, North and South America and in many European countries, twenty-three of them in France. We stay in regular contact with one another. Although our communities differ greatly from one another, they are united by the common respect and love for the weak. For us, living with handicapped persons means living in a Christian way.

→ See also description of network "**Arche following Jean Vanier**"

☺ readiness to live in community with adults with learning disabilities

Les Amis de la Douceur

LA

domaine de | 66230 Serralongue
+33-(0)468396256 enthousiasme@wanadoo.fr
-468396256

1964 21 ha (near Perpignan) ♀2 ♂2 4

f, e all

everyone in common (consensus) shared income

common property

vegan, gentle ("douce")

gardening, household, guest house, book publication

ecological, non-violent, spiritual, esoteric/New Age, inner growth, organic and vegan diet, animal protection, environmental protection, organic agriculture/gardening

Les Amis de la Doceur — „the friends of gentleness", that is quite a goal! Here every kind of violence and cruelty is avoided. The most beautiful virtues are united in the harmony being promoted here. We let ourselves be inspired by the stars in the sky, by the earth, the rivers, trees, flowers and birds. They teach us to help one another and grow.
Our projects include: growing lots of organic fruit, vegetables and flowers; taking care of our animals.
Le domaine de Maman Terre is an old farmstead situated at an altitude of 850m in the forested mountains of the Hant Vallespir in the eastern Pyrenees, it is isolated, and very peaceful. We can offer our vegan / vegetarian guests simple accomodation in our hut in summer, and invite volunteers to help us in our daily tasks. Our diet is exclusively vegan and drug free, including such harmful products as alcohol and tobacco. We prefer visitors to our community to contact us in advance preferably by post or e-mail telling us a little about yourself.

☺ group harmony, commitment to a vegan ecological and organic lifestyle

Les Trois Fontaines

TF

6 rue de l'Ecluse | 62164 Ambleteuse

+33-(0)321-999299 arche3fontaines@netinfo.fr

-333963 www.fraternet.org/arche3font/

1973 ♀40 ♂38 78

f, e all approx. 80

one part of the group (conference with the decision making group)

ecumenical with a Catholic tradition

mentally disabled, social involvement

spiritual, christian, ecumenical, mentally/psychologically handicapped persons

The "Three Springs" Arche is a community of the French Arche Association (founded by Jean Vanier). It is made up of 150 members: disabled people, assistants, volunteers, professional staff, friends. A shared life with mentally disabled people stands at the project's centre, a simple everyday life with meals, social evenings, leisure activities... The building is everybody's home. During the daytime everyone participates in various workshop activities: production (furniture shop, vegetable garden, mail-order) or art (wood, pottery, paper). The community encompasses 7 homes in which one can live either in the city or by the seaside. The community offers those who wish it the opportunity to deepen their spiritual life within the Catholic tradition. It offers a brotherly life on the basis of volunteerism, simplicity, mutual exchange and respect for differences. We are trying to create a unity with our shared life by embracing our individual cultural, intellectual and religious differences. People can turn to us in order to arrange a half or full-year stay as a volunteer or intern. These co-workers receive room and board, share in the social security system and receive monthly compensation.

→ See also description of network "**Arche following Jean Vanier**"
☺ working with people with disabilities in the spirit of the „Arche"

Monastère de Cantauque

MC

Domaine de Cantauque | 11250 Villebazy
+33-(0)468-316961
-316960

1975 | 150 ha (near Carcassonne) | ♀6 ♂6 12

f | 12

individual financing | rented/leased

Christian-Orthodox, ecumenical

devotion to God, religious studies, farming, working on the house

ecological, non-violent, spiritual, christian, ecumenical, organic diet, vegetarian diet, social work., environmental protection, self-sufficiency, organic agriculture, organic farming, forestry, alternative energy

Le Monastère de Cantauque is a community of Christian-Orthodox monks, founded in 1975. Its goal is to provide monks with a place to live under the aspect of spiritual self-realisation and to offer laypersons a place of spiritual and moral orientation. The monastery's religious focus and praxis are the two thousand year-old tradition of eastern Christianity. Gandhi's non-violence is viewed as a modern rendition of the central message of Christ's gospels. Ecology is lived as a necessary resistance to the threats against Man and his environment, caused by today's materialistic ideology. The monastery is located in the south of France on a gigantic rural estate. The community is active in farming and arts & crafts. It operates a hotel and accommodates people with psychological and social problems.

→ See also description of network "**Church & Peace**"
☺ Orthodox faith and monastic calling

Proména les Sources

LS

Les Illes | 11220 Montlaur
+33-(0)468240492 gewoba@wanadoo.fr

1993 | 35 ha (near Carcassonne) | ♀3 ♂4 2 9

f | none

everyone in common (3/4 majority in issues affecting shared property)

individual financing | association

everyone is free

construction, renovation, gardening, (alternative) energy, farming is possible

ecological, non-violent, inner growth, alternative energy

Our ecovillage developed from a community.
We have been living in a peaceful, romantic lateral valley of the Corbières since 1993. The land is stony, the soil is heavy: clay with limestone. We draw water from

our own spring. So far we have 4 solar installations in operation. We're planning a small water power station. The countryside grows and blossoms 12 months out of the year. A beautiful pond invites one to linger...
9 persons (5-63 years) live together as good neighbours in four autonomous households. All the residents own their houses and gardens. Each family is financially independent and is responsible for itself.
The rest of the land (some 32 ha) belongs to the sponsoring association. A few construction sites (southern slope) are still available for purchase. Starting in 2005 we will be able to integrate 1-2 new families. Only then will new buildings be possible. But not before that, since the settlement and our relationships must grow slowly.
Together we attend to the expansion and maintenance of our shared property, such as paths, the spring etc. Mutual help is a matter of course.
Everyone is absolutely free in spiritual matters. We have a yurt for meditation.
An extensive library (mainly in the national language) is on hand.
Please, we only want really interested people by appointment; no curiosity-seekers! We have no accommodations for visitors.

🌍 Reseau des Ecovillages
☺ We have building land for sale to 1-2 families (starting in 2005)

"Courage is the strength to let go of what you're accustomed to."

Germany

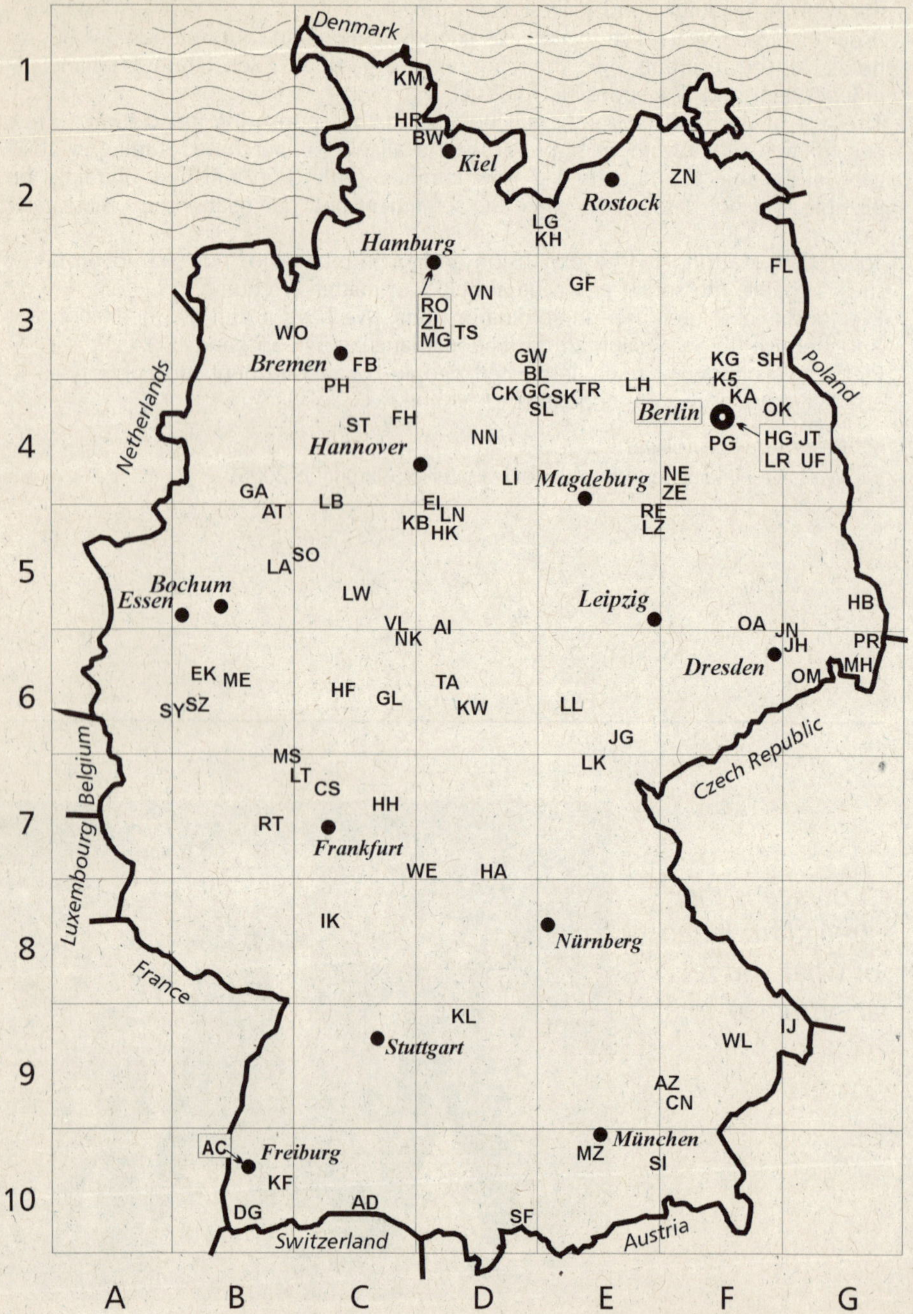

1
2
3
4
5
6
7
8
9
10
A
B
C
D
E
F
G
Denmark
Netherlands
Belgium
Luxembourg
France
Switzerland
Austria
Czech Republic
Poland
Kiel
Rostock
Hamburg
Bremen
Hannover
Berlin
Magdeburg
Bochum
Essen
Leipzig
Dresden
Frankfurt
Nürnberg
Stuttgart
Freiburg
München
KM
HR
BW
ZN
LG
KH
FL
RO
ZL
MG
VN
GF
TS
WO
FB
PH
GW
BL
CK
GC
SK
TR
LH
KG
SH
K5
KA
OK
HG
JT
LR
UF
PG
ST
FH
NN
LI
NE
ZE
RE
LZ
GA
AT
LB
EI
LN
KB
HK
SO
LA
LW
VL
NK
AI
HB
OA
JN
JH
PR
MH
OM
EK
ME
SY
SZ
HF
GL
TA
KW
LL
JG
LK
MS
LT
CS
HH
RT
WE
HA
IK
KL
IJ
WL
AZ
CN
AC
MZ
SI
KF
DG
AD
SF

AC Adidam Center&Bookstore *B10*
AD Agnus Dei *C10*
AI Lebens- und Agrarkulturelle Initiative e.V. *D5*
AT Arche Tecklenburg *B5*
AZ Aham-Zentrum *F9*
BL Gemeinschaftliches Leben e.V. Blütlingen *D3*
BW Basisgemeinde Wulfshagenerhütten *D2*
CK Kommune Karmitz *D4*
CN Connection-Medien-Zentrum *F9*
CS Casa Soluna *C7*
DG Delphin-Gemeinschaft - Wege zu Gott *B10*
EI Wassermühle Eime GbR *D4*
EK Emmaus Gem. in Köln *B6*
FB Finkenburg *C3*
FH Friedenshof-Kommunität *C4*
FL Feuerland *F3*
GA GRAL-Gemeinschaft *B4*
GC Hofgem. Gr. Chüden Nr. 4 *D4*
GF Haus der Gastfreundschaft *E3*
GL Galions e.V. *C6*
GW Gemeinschaft in Güstritz (Wendland) *D3*
HA Camphill Dorfgemeinschaft Hausenhof *D7*
HB Holderbusch *G5*
HF Hof Fleckenbühl *C6*
HG Anthropos. Hochschulgruppe Haus Bornstr. 11 e.V. *F4*
HH Sozietät Herrnhaag *C7*
HK Kürbisprojekt *D5*
HR Hof Rossee *C1*
IJ simhacalam academy *G9*
IK ISKCON Heidelberg *C8*
JG Jakobgut *E6*
JH Johannishöhe *G6*
JN Lebens(t)raum Gemeinschaft Jahnishausen *G5*
JT Lebens(t)raum Johannisthal *F4*
K5 Kommune 5 *F4*
KA Wagendorf Karow *F4*
KB Kommune Buchhagen *C5*
KF KommFrei e.V. *B10*
KG Kommunität Grimnitz *F3*
KH Dorfgem. Klein-Hundorf e.V. *E2*
KL Gem. in Klosterzimmern *D9*
KM Kommune am Meer *C1*
KW KoWa e.V. *D6*
LA Laakenhof *B5*
LB Gemeinschaft am Lambach *C4*
LG Lebensform Gemeinschaft *E2*
LH Land Rausch GbRmbH *E4*
LI Hofgemeinschaft Lindenhof *D4*
LK Verein z. Förderung ganzheitl. Lebensweise u. Kulturpflege *E7*
LL Beginenhof "Lieselotte" *E6*
LN Hof Luna *D5*
LR Therapeutische Lern- und Lebens-Gemeinschaft *F4*
LT Lahn-Taunus Gemeinschaft *C7*
LW Laurentiushof Wethen *C5*
LZ LebensGut Lübnitz e.V. *E5*
ME Mutter-Erde-Gemeinschaft *B6*
MG Villa Magdalena *D3*
MH Kulturfabrik Mittelherwigsdorf *G6*
MS Projektzentrum Maibacher Schweiz *B7*
MZ Miravillage-Zentrum *E10*
NE Noyana Gemeinschaft *F4*
NK Kommune Niederkaufungen *C6*
NN Sonnenhof *D4*
OA Umweltzentrum Ökohof Auterwitz e.V. *F5*
OK ÖkoLeA *F4*
OM Osho Manjusha *G6*
PG Pretschener Gemeinschaft *F4*
PH Zentrum PrinzHöfte *C4*
PR Lebensgut Pommritz *G6*
RE Projekt Reetz *E5*
RO Brot & Rosen. Diakonische Basisgemeinschaft. *D3*
RT Kultur- und Tagungshaus Rauenthal *B7*
RW Projekt Regenwurm *D10*
SF Stamm der Likatier *D10*
SH Gut Stolzenhagen e.G. *F3*

SI Lebenshof Siboling *E10*
SK Stallkultur e.V. *E4*
SL Ökodorf Sieben Linden *E4*
SL Club99 *E4*
SO Netzwerk Anders Leben Soest *C5*
ST Lebensgarten Steyerberg *C4*
SY SSK - Sozialistische Selbsthilfe Köln *A6*
SZ Sozialistische Selbshilfe Köln-Mülheim - SSM *B6*
TA Trauringja- Forsthaus Triesch *D6*
TR Traumschule *E4*
TS Demeter Hof Tangsehl *D3*
UF Ufa -Fabrik *F4*
VL Villa Locomuna *C5*
VN Vindorf *D3*
WE Generationsübergreifende Wohnanlage Eisingen *D7*
WL Hofgemeinsch. beim Waller *F9*
WO Lebensgemeinsch. Woldhof *B3*
ZE ZEGG - Zentrum für experiment. Gesellschaftsgestaltung *F4*
ZL Zeitlos e.V. *D3*
ZN Zar Nekla Die Zweite *F2*

Adidam Center& Bookstore

AC

Moltkestraße 28 | 79098 Freiburg
+49-(0)761-383-8886 info@dawn-horse.de
-8887 www.dawn-horse.de

1997 110 m² (near Freiburg) ♀7 ♂9 1 17

e, g 3

everyone in common (majority vote) individual financing

rented/leased

Path of Adidam

life of commitment within a community

non-violent, hierarchical, leader/guru, spiritual, esoteric/New Age, meditation, yoga, vegetarian diet, adult education

☺ ()

The German Adidam Centre is situated in the middle of Freiburg. It includes a public area with a beautifully designed bookshop and an area for community activities with a temple as its sacred core.
There are public introductory events every Tuesday at 8:15 p.m., plus lectures and music every Thursday at 8:15 p.m.

→ See also description of network "**Adidam**"
☺ study and participation in introductory course

Agnus Dei

AD

Hof Sankt Joseph | Spittelsberg 1 | 78351 Bodman-Ludwigshafen
☎ +49-(0)7773-920683
adams@haus-samaria.de
-5805
www.communitas-agnus-dei.de

1980 (near Konstanz) ♀15 ♂6 10 31

g, e, f
everyone together, part of the group (consensus)
shared economy (shared income and capital) rented/leased
Catholic Church
prayer, music, radio work, farming, receiving guests, midwifery, school
self-managed, non-violent, christian, inner growth, meditation, organic diet, peace-work, one-world development, organic gardening, music, liturgical singing, radio work, home for pregnant women in need, midwife practice, free consultation office, Jemael-Werk

☺ ()

The AGNUS DEI (Lamb of God) community has been in existence since 24th April 1980 and has 20 members. There are also 10 children from two families. Our path is guided by the Imitation of Christ. Every day we deepen our relationship to God in prayer, through the sacraments of the Church and through reading the Holy Scriptures. This profound bond to God nurtures our ability to practice brotherly love toward one another and toward all people. Those of our activities which are directed into the broader world also have a higher meaning. We currently reside in two houses on Lake Constance and maintain a settlement in Ecuador.

The Jemael-Werk represents an additional spiritual project. It is a network for a "culture of love" in co-operation with "people of good will".
The "Haus Samaria" in Irndorf takes its place within the framework of this organisation. It welcomes pregnant women in distress in order to provide them with an alternative to abortion. In Congo we are currently caring for 500 war orphans through our African staff. Further staff members in Kinshasa are occupied with social tasks... Among its many activities, the music group "Sarah music&art" works with Jewish and Palestinian musicians in the Holy Land and is particularly involved in peace service. The monastery bakery in Bodman offers full-grain goods and "fair trade" products. Radio work, a "Jemael branch office" in Brussels (with a focus on Africa) and other commitments, particularly in the field of spirituality, complement our other activities.

→ See also description of network "**Come Together**"

☺ membership is a question of calling which is examined by all sides over an extended period of time

Aham-Zentrum

AZ

Schloßanger 3 | 84168 Aham
☎ +49-(0)8744-8550
-8530

1999 | 2200 m² (near Landshut) | ♀4 ♂2 1 7

g, e — 80%

everyone in common (consensus) — individual financing

property of individual community members

we are Christians and pray

psychotherapy, administering the centre, communal life

ecological, self-managed, christian, ecumenical, meditation, vegetarian diet, peacework, one-world development, therapy

☺ ()

We are a community which has formed around Jesus Christ. Most of us are psychotherapists, both in regard to our training and our work. We mostly work with couples and also provide training in this area. We are attempting to develop a spiritually-anchored psychotherapy and are working with methods which can also be learned by laypersons.
The central principle of our communal life is the way we devote ourselves entirely to Jesus. We do not reject the established Christian institutions, nor are we dependent on them. The authority which we follow is our heart, which has been touched by Jesus.
The property where we live is located on the edge of a village; it was once an elegant court building, then served as an inn for many generations; we have now transformed it into an OPEN CLOISTER.

The living areas for our community members are located on the upper floor. People undergoing a profound personal crisis can join the community for longer or shorter periods of time, and can let themselves be borne up by the daily structure (four prayer and meditation times), by personal conversations, perhaps also by helping out with the house, yard and garden.
We welcome contacts with other communities.

☺ intensive acquaintance over a long period of time

Anthroposophische Hochschulgruppe Haus Bornstr. 11 e.V.

HG

Bornstr. 11 | 12163 Berlin
☎ +49-(0)30-85965045
www.bornstr11.de
-85078802

1983 | 1000 m² | ♀17 ♂14 7 38

g

everyone in common (consensus)

individual financing

foundation

youthful, Anthroposophian (not mandatory)

cultural group for (joint) projects, cleaning/renovation

self-managed, anthroposophic

☺ ()

We are a cultural initiative located in a formerly self-administered house (1984-2000). Thanks to an inheritance, it belongs to the Anthroposophical Society of Germany. The Society then left it to a group of students who, during the house occupation period in the late 1970s, founded a self-administered residential project for the promotion of Anthroposophical co-operation and cultural work. Today it is mostly lived in by young people undergoing career training. The administration is currently limited to a small circle, however there is still space for initiatives, for cultural work and a shared, considerate, people-friendly lifestyle. Rental profits go to the Youth/Anthroposophy Foundation.

☺ young people in the college/training phase

Arche Tecklenburg

AT

Apfelallee 23 | 49545 Tecklenburg
+49-(0)5482-7700 tecklenburg@arche-deutschland.de
-974024 www.arche-deutschland.de

1986 (near Osnabrück) ♀16 ♂7 23

g 13

everyone in common (special decision-making process)

public funds and donations

Christian-ecumenical

living together with mentally disabled people

christian, ecumenical, mentally disabled

The house at Apfelallee 23 originally belonged to the nearby moated castle of "Haus Mark", the birthplace of the 19th century social reformer Friedrich von Bodelschwingh. 8 persons with a mental disability, and 6 assistants in charge of supporting them, make up the house community. In 1993 we opened our second house.
In our house communities we live and work together, pray, celebrate birthdays and Christian holidays, enjoy each other's company, argue together, suffer together and learn to accept each other. Our daily routine is characterised by a regular rhythm: on working days our disabled community members travel to the nearby workshop for disabled persons. In the meantime, the assistants attend to the house and garden. Prayer, team meetings and supervision are all part of our working days. Sunday is dominated by attendance to local church services and the Sunday evening prayer in the Ledde village church.
The community is based on friendship with God and members' relations with one another and within a large circle of friends. Thus our numerous contacts and encounters form a major aspect of our communal life.
Our membership in the international Arche Federation is also very important. Regular visits from representatives of the international Arche, contact to other Arche communities and encounters on days of reflection and training courses within the federation help us on our way.

→ See also description of network "**Arche following Jean Vanier**"

☺ simple lifestyle, Christian-ecumenical orientation, psychological resilience

Basisgemeinde Wulfshagenerhütten

BW

Zum Wohld 4 | 24214 Wulfshagenerhütten
+49-(0)4346-368000 www.basisgemeinde.de
-368001

1973 2.5 ha (near Kiel) ♀17 ♂14 23 54

g, e, f, sp., russ., ukrain. all

all members decide together (consensus)
shared economy (shared income and capital) common property
we are Christians
wood workshop, vegetable growing, household, common child-rearing
ecological, self-managed, non-violent, christian, ecumenical, peace-work, organic agriculture, alternative energy, joinery, movement, sports, dance, political involvement, music

☺

The grassroots community in Gettorf is a Christian living community in the north of Germany. Adults and children, families and singles live together in the buildings of a former orphanage and attempt to share all the spheres of their lives and all their property according to the example of the first Christians. The community's members and guests all work inside the community in a workshop for wooden toys and vehicles, in the household, in our own kindergarten, in the organic garden and in janitorial work. The community is open for seeking people and draws them into its daily rhythm. All visitors are expected to take part in the common work and in the meals, and they are also invited to take part in the prayers.
The community is linked to a growing network of Christian communities, for example to a community in El Salvador and to Christians in the Ukraine. In Germany it is above all involved in peace work and in the anti-nuclear power movement. We experience the sharing of joy and sorrow, work and celebration, and listening to one another as the foundation of peace and justice. Instead of offering a programme, we invite all visitors to join us in our ways and to share our life. In 1990 a branch community was founded in East Berlin and in 1996 another was founded in the western Ukraine (grassroots communities of Prenzlauer Berg and Gäa).

→ See also description of network "**Church & Peace**"

Beginenhof „Lieselotte" LL

Schloßallee 1 | 07407 Tännich/ Thüringen
+49-(0)36744-22474 beginenhof.thueringen@t-online.de
-22475 www.beginenhof-thueringen.de

1999 6 ha (near Erfurt, Weimar) ♀15 2 17

g, e, russ. 8
one part of the group (consensus)
individual and limited common financing common property
feminist, anti-violence, ecological
garden, field, forest, goats, conferences, workshop, healing
ecological, feminist, non-violent, spiritual, organic diet, seminar-house, peace-work, organic agriculture, organic gardening, organic farming

☺

We draw upon the tradition of the medieval Begines, spiritually and economically independent women who lived in large and small communities. They were active in intellectual, craft and social professions.
In 1998, a modern Begine farm was founded in Thuringia, 30 km south of Erfurt and Weimar. The protected, 250 year old farm consists of 3,000 m² of residential and usable floor space including 70 guest rooms. It also includes several fields and meadows, a tract of forest, a park, a swimming pool, a vegetable garden, a herb spiral and labyrinth, plus some goats and chickens. A health section is in the process of being built.
We are a group of feminist-oriented women from different backgrounds and generations. We are striving for ecological and economic sustainability in our life and work. We want to make a contribution to the creation of a world that treats women better. At the moment we are 15 women and 2 children; the project is intended for 30 Begines. Women who have experienced violence can find special protection here.
Our goal is to create jobs for women. We are planning business start-ups in the craft, social, gastronomic, health and educational fields.
Alongside our daily work, our celebrations of the seasonal festivals play an important role. We have gained a certain reputation for our "Rauhnächte" ("wild nights") with the New Year's Eve party and our Women's Culture Days and summer night ball, exuberant parties which attract (female) visitors from near and far.

Verband i.Gr. "Beginenh öfe"

Brot & Rosen. Diakonische Basisgemeinschaft.

RO

Projekt „Haus der Gastfreundschaft" | Fabriciusstr. 56 | 22177 Hamburg
+49-(0)40-69702085 basisgemeinschaft@brot-und-rosen.de
-69702086 www.brot-und-rosen.de

1994 400m² ♀4 ♂1 5 10

e, f all
everyone in common (consensus) shared income
rented/leased
Christian/ecumenical
solidarity with homeless refugees, simple life, solidarity and peace work
anarchistic, left-wing political understanding, non-violent, christian, ecumenical, peace-work, social work: support of (illegalised) political refugees, deaconry work

The Diakonische Basisgemeinschaft Brot & Rosen (=Bread & Roses) in Hamburg is a small ecumenical-Christian community. Since 1996 we have been living in a rented house that used to belong to the church community. Our communal life is characterised by dedicated commitment to justice, peace, and ecology, communal meals and devotion. We want to live and work with people who are excluded from society and who have not been granted their fundamental rights. Up to eight homeless refugees can be accommodated by us regardless of their legal status. The community's members pay for their own expenses as an income co-operative through part-time work. The expenses and rent of our "guests" is financed by contributions from our friends' and supporter group. We want to live simply so that others may simply survive. Through our consciousness-raising work, for example during our open evenings, we strive to be our "guests'" mouthpiece and to champion pacifism, non-violence, and justice. At the same time we are trying to join forces with other initiatives to make a difference in public life and in the Christian parishes around us.

→ See also description of network "**Church & Peace**"

Camphill Dorfgemeinschaft Hausenhof

HA

Hausenhof 7 | 91463 Dietersheim
+49-(0)9164-99840, -998411 info@hausenhof.de
-998410 www.hausenhof.de

1987 50 ha (near Neustadt/Aisch) ♀40 ♂40 20 100

g, e 50

one part of the group (consensus) individual financing

association

Anthroposophic

living and working with disabled persons

ecological, self-managed, anthroposophic, mentally/psychologically handicapped persons, organic farming, animal friendly husbandry

We are developing forms of community, living and working designed to help disabled and non-disabled persons to lead a self-determined life together and in dignity.
We do not primarily see disability as a shortcoming but rather as a special expression of a person's individuality. Physical and mental limitations can lead to a situation in which a person's self becomes distorted so that he or she appears disabled on the outside.
The Camphill village community of Hausenhof admits adults who are viewed as permanently disabled or who may be multiply disabled and who indicate that they would like to join the community for an extended time.
Living together:
A house community of up to 10 disabled people forms around a family with its own children or around singles, together with interns and persons performing alternative (non-military) service. The house communities' family-like structure, which also includes the staff's children, gives the residents a sense of security and belonging.
Working together:
Work becomes meaningful when human activity addresses the needs of other people. Disabled people need assistance so that they can join in the work process. Work processes are designed in such a way that everyone can make an appropriate contribution and become as autonomous as possible. The farm and garden are

cultivated according to biodynamic principles.
Celebrating and learning together:
One central power source for the community's life and work is a cultural life based on a Christian foundation. Daily, weekly and annual rhythms are experienced and shaped in a conscious way. Culture plays a central role in all areas of daily life.

→ See also description of network "**Camphill**"
☺ suitable as staff or care recipient

Casa Soluna

CS

Dorn-Assenheimer-Str. 29 | 61169 Friedberg / Bauernheim
☎ +49-(0)6031-6867-93, -30(AB) www.soshona.de

2002 (near Friedberg) ♀1 ♂1 2 4

g, e
everyone in common (consensus)
individual financing, limited common financing rented/leased
MitMachZirkus SOLUNA, communal networking, massage, health advice, meditation
ecological, non-violent, spiritual, meditation, tantra, sexuality, free love, organic diet, vegetarian diet, peace-work, organic gardening, MitMachZirkus (participatory circus), juggling, health consultation

☺

Home, healing, happiness. A home for the people who live here and their guests. We want to build a home in beautiful surroundings, for relaxation and reenergising, to feel good in. It is to be the nucleus for our tribe/community: a community network location, meeting place, celebrations, communication with the world, library, media centre for and about community, friendship circle/tribal archive, open house for our children and those of our guests.
Garden: as much ecological self-sufficiency as possible, closed cycles which can be experienced by children and grownups.
Healing: ecological whole foods diet, beauty and sensuality in daily life, development of mutual communication structures in order to keep human, particularly love-related themes in motion; nutritional advice, meditation, foot reflex zone massage.
MitMachZirkus SOLUNA
We want to realise a large, future-oriented residential and living community in the Wetterau. We are interested in welcoming more people.

→ See also description of network "**Soshona Freundeskreis**"
regional community network

Club99

SL

Ökodorf Sieben Linden | 38486 Bandau
☎ +49-(0)39000-90621 club99@siebenlinden.de
-51232 www.siebenlinden.de

1999 4 ha (near Salzwedel) ♀3 ♂5 1 9

g, e, f, it., isl., dutch, africaans 5

everyone in common (consensus) shared economy

co-operative = common property

holistically ecological, self-responsibility, the private is political

self-responsibility in all areas

ecological, self-managed, anarchistic, left-wing political understanding, non-violent, spiritual, inner growth, yoga, free love, organic diet, vegan diet, adult education, forum, animal protection, self-sufficiency, permaculture, bio-vegan gardening, ecological construction, straw bale building, handicrafts for self-sufficiency, work horses, apiary, music, publishing eurotopia!

☺

Club99 is a neighbourhood within the Sieben Linden ecovillage which is based on common agreements. These agreements relate to the communal life on our grounds. They form the basis for an experiment with the goal of developing an environment which serves the healing of the earth in all its effects and which at the same time respects all humans, living beings, and elements. We are striving for the development of complete self-responsibility, which also means refusing to accept any and all victim status.
How do I contribute to violence, exploitation, suffering - through my lifestyle, my thoughts, my silence, my actions and my inaction? What can I learn from the mirror

Club99 in their selfbuilt strawbalehouse

which the world holds up to me? What do I really want, beyond outside influences and pre-programming? How can I make it happen - with respect towards all other beings? We would like to draw the conclusions and emphasise love instead of consumption, a dedicated and fulfilled life instead of self-pity, plus inner greatness, fulfilment and above all the zest of living.
In our material day-to-day lives this means: a satisfyingly simple lifestyle based on lower consumption rather than higher production; increasing self-sufficiency; the use of local, compostable and recyclable materials; a common economy; a responsible treatment of and co-operation with animals; genuine manual labour through a pleasurable synthesis of brain and brawn; high spirits without drugs and nicotine, and much more.
And because we aren't yet what we want to become, we are looking for others who want to commit themselves wholeheartedly to the contradictions of life and join with us in our joyful reaching out for the stars!

→ See also description of network "**Come Together**"
Ökodorf Sieben Linden
☺ We accept people who join our agreements and whose participation makes us genuinely happy (1-year probationary period)

Connection-Medien-Zentrum

CN

Hauptstraße 5 | 84494 Niedertaufkirchen
☎ +49-(0)8639-9834-0 — schneider@connection.de
8639-1219 — www.connection.de

1991 — 1300 m² (near Mühldorf am Inn) — ♀3 ♂4 1 8

g, e — 5
varies
individual financing — property of individual community members
publishing work, particularly PC and telephone
ecological, spiritual, inner growth, meditation, vegetarian diet

The Connection Community revolves around the operation of the publishing house of the same name. We publish the magazines "connection" and "connection special" alongside the book series "connection books", which deals with such issues as community, connection, spirituality, ecology and politics. Employment is only possible for persons with professional knowledge in these areas or else who have the long-term intention (as interns) to acquire them by working with us.
Alongside our publication work we also stage celebrations, seminars, an annual course in the writings arts and large events (e.g. The Oneness Gathering).
Our community is federally organised into two or three flat-sharing communities which are relatively autonomous in many social matters. We live in a village of some 200 people located 6 km from the nearest train station, 90 km from Munich, and operate a car sharing scheme with 2-3 community cars.

Holon
☺ professional specialisation in publishing work

Delphin-Gemeinschaft - Wege zu Gott

DG

ÖKODORF-Institut für Wohnprojekte |
Alpenblickstr. 12 | 79737 Herrischried - Niedergebisbach
+49-(0)7764-933999 meyer@gemeinschaften.de
-933388 www.gemeinschaften.de/delphingemeinschaft.htm

1995 7 ha (near Schopfheim) ♀6 ♂6 2 14

g, e, f 4

everyone in common, part of the group (consensus, inner voice, higher self)

shared economy rented/leased

all religions are of equal value

music teaching/production, publishing house, child care, garden/ permaculture, kitchen

ecological, self-managed, non-violent, spiritual, ecumenical, meditation, yoga, organic diet, vegetarian diet, adult education, self-sufficiency, permaculture, organic gardening, ecological construction, music, research on community development

☺

The Wiesental is a good starting point to shore up our community here. The population is tolerant, ecologically and spiritually open. We are surrounded by a very beautiful landscape and our children like attending the Waldorf School.
Our central goal: we support each other on the path to GOD, and help with others who desire the same. One contribution to this is the creation of a larger interspiritual community consisting of smaller communities of various spiritual orientations. Its range is not arbitrary. Instead, our framework is provided by the commandments which are the same in all world religions (see the world ethos of theology professor Küng).
Learning from history: the community can only develop if we do not keep reinventing the wheel. That is why we are learning from other communities (failed and successful ones) and pass this knowledge along through seminars, consultation etc. for those seeking and founding communities of their own.
Commitment to... a) the region: co-operation (e.g. hometown association, church, fire brigade). Discovering which of our region's needs are currently not being satisfied (e.g. ecological producer-consumer co-op). Then initiate this as a complement (not as competition) to existing enterprises... (please ask for further information). However, our landlords don't want to sell the 7 ha farm right now, that's why we're looking for a new moderately priced property. Or, since southern Baden is very expensive: some land on the edge of an organic farm where we can set up yurts/ simple buildings and, in return, help out on the organic farm.

→ See also description of networks "**Come Together**" and "**GEN**"

informal network of interspiritual ecovillages

☺ spiritual openness and tolerance,interest in the simple life, work with everyday addictions

Demeter Hof Tangsehl

TS

Biologisch-dynamische Landwirtschaft | Tangsehl 2 | 21369 Nahrendorf
+49-(0)5855-1278 HofTangsehl@t-online.de
-379 www.tangsehl.de

1987 130 ha (near Lüneburg) ♀8 ♂4 4 16

g, e all

one part of the group (consensus) individual financing

rented/leased, association and/or bank

Anthroposophy

farming/gardening/forestry, cheese dairy, housekeeping, sales, animal husbandry, school classes,

ecological, self-managed, non-violent, spiritual, christian, anthroposophic, organic diet, adult education, seminar-house, animal protection, environmental protection, organic agriculture, organic gardening, organic farming, animal friendly husbandry, forestry

☺

In the here and now we are a DEMETER enterprise with many ideals, and in the here and now we are very busy keeping our head above water economically. In the growing future, more and more people are settling on the farm; some will work with us, others are customers, still others are artistically active in the landscape (www.lebendigesland.de), they develop the "Oberuferer Christ's Birth Play" with the farm people and perform it in the cow barn, practice the art of celebrating festivals and much more.
We offer apprenticeships within the framework of free training (DEMETER) in farming, gardening, the cheese dairy and home economics. There is a guest house, which has been used by school classes up to now (farming internship); in the future it should also be available for seminars and conferences.
In the here and now we are very dependent on petroleum (tractors, commercial vehicles) and atomic energy (cheese dairy, refrigerators). In the future, we hope that Frithjof Bergmann's ideas will flourish among us and we will see the development of a "Centre for New Work" (www.newwork-newculture.net). People who are no longer "needed" in industry help us build our organic gas system, fashion new horse-drawn farm implements etc. They learn about farming, animal husbandry, gardening etc. People come who want to "ground" themselves and who want to contribute their knowledge from the "old working world" to the new village. From March to October we offer an introductory farm tour every last Saturday in the month at 2:30 p.m.

☺ open to Anthroposophy and spirituality

Dorfgemeinschaft Klein-Hundorf e.V.

KH

Klein-Hundorf 6 | 19205 Gadebusch
+49-(0)3886-2533

1989 | 10 ha (near Gadebusch) | ♀12 ♂8 | 18 | 38

g, e, rus., swed., poln. — 2-3

everyone in common (consensus) — limited community financing

partially leased, partially common property

none

garden, fieldwork, building, renovating, development work, planning, administration, improving communication

ecological, self-managed, chaotic, organic diet, self-sufficiency, organic agriculture, organic gardening, alternative energy, joinery, pottery, smithy, basket weaving, music

We own a large, little used and poorly maintained manor house, three self-built clay houses and two single-family houses. The rest of us live in trailers with extensions. We live on approx. 3 ha of garden and meadow near more or less congenial neighbours. We have a co-op and a farming operation.
In the summer it's a little paradise; in winter life withdraws almost completely into nuclear families and small groups. Although there is a certain wish for more communal life, more shared work, more common culture, the Klein Hundorfers have a hard time coming together.
We – i.e. a small group from the larger project – are writing this description for the whole group, even though some of us, e.g. Norbert, don't know what concrete information they should pass on to interested people about the Klein Hundorf village community and thus are against putting an entry into the eurotopia guide. But we're still here (the people and the place). We're working on a concept for this beautiful place and its people (including a construction and settlement concept in the long term). We're still looking for glowing examples and ideas.
Our plenum takes place every Tuesday at 4 p.m. For more information, contact Jörg, Wolf, Jemila, Karen B. or Carsten. May our seeds grow into strong trees and brilliant flowers!

Kommuja

☺ 1 year probationary period, then entry fee with co-op membership, it's important to grow into group, thus visit us frequently beforehand

Emmaus Gemeinschaft in Köln

EK

Geestemünder Straße 42 | 50735 Köln
+49-(0)221-9711731 info@emmaus-koeln.de
-9711733 www.emmaus-koeln.de

1959 5000 m² ♀5 ♂12 1 18

g all

one part of the group decides in consensus/maj.

shared income association

socialist

collection and sale of used items of all kinds

self-managed, left-wing political understanding

The community is open to people who – for whatever reason – have succumbed to the pressure of our performance-oriented society, e.g. people without shelter and/or work, drug addicts, alcoholics, the mentally ill, ex-prisoners etc. It provides therapy, living space, assistance in dealing with personal affairs in conjunction with meaningful and manageable employment. In our society, which is characterised by increasing pressure to succeed and the dissolution of social bonds and responsibilities, we view the possibility of living and working in a community as a necessary alternative.
Thanks to their long-term experience, those responsible for the planning and implementation of our activities possess the requisite qualifications; they have been living in the community – some of them together with their families – for many years. This willingness to live under one roof with disadvantaged persons greatly contributes to the success of the Emmaus Community in Cologne.
The requirements for admission to the community are the availability of living space and the willingness to integrate oneself into the community and accept its principles, particularly the principle of common work, through which members earn their keep. Alongside free room and board, community members receive a weekly allowance and a monthly supplement both for special expenses and as start-up money for when they leave the community.
Community members share all the community's values. An increasing sense of belonging can counteract personal and social destabilisation and marginalisation and individuals can be placed in a position where they can plan and take charge of their lives anew.

→ See also description of network "**Emmaus**"
☺ consideration and following of the community rules

Feuerland

FL

Ausbau 13 / Stoltshof | 17326 Brüssow
+49-(0)39742-81611 kommune.feuerland@t-online.de
-81613

1993 6.5 ha (near Prenzlau) ♀4 ♂3 1 8

g, e 5

everyone in common (consensus) shared economy (shared income and capital)

association

juice press, garden, house and farm

ecological, self-managed, left-wing political understanding, feminist, non-violent, inner growth, self-sufficiency, organic gardening, alternative energy, felt and textiles

We live on a beautiful farm in the Uckermark region, offering a lot of possibilities for our plans and ideas.
We are united by a common economy (we pay in and out of a common purse), the consensus principle, and the perspective of a self-sufficient life with as few dependencies as possible. We want to break down patriarchal structures and regularly divide into men's and women's groups in order to work on particular areas independently of one another. Even if we don't see ourselves as a therapy group, we try to integrate "radical therapy", a self-help concept for women (FORT) and men (MRT) into our communal life in order to promote dominance-free communication.
We cultivate a garden and some pasture for ourselves. At the moment we have two horses, three milk sheep, one pig and one dog living with us. We have an apple press, an engineering office, and construction sites on the farm. The maintenance and expansion of our buildings (the residential house, barn, the women's living house as well as the so-called conference house) are a constant field of work. Every day we learn something new: about ourselves, about living together, and while working... Sometimes we feel overtaxed, we often feel happy and we keep very very busy. We want to grow as a community.

Kommuja
☺ 6 months to get to know each other

Finkenburg

FB

Finkenburg | 27321 Thedinghausen-Eissel
+49-(0)4204-1497 finkenburg@verden-info.de
-(0)4231-6898001

1989 1 ha (near Bremen) ♀3 ♂6 1 10

e, norw., port. (bras.) 5

everyone in common (consensus) limited community financing

common property

ecological, self-managed, anarchistic, left-wing political understanding, feminist, non-violent, chaotic, organic diet, alternative energy, ecological construction, table tennis, cultural work, playing

☺ (✋✋)

The Finkenburg is an old free-standing farm house in the Wesermarsch region east of Bremen. It has existed as a communal project since 1989. At the moment it is occupied by ten permanent residents. We view ourselves as a political commune project and view our way of communal life as an alternative blueprint for a more social, ecological and solidarity-based society. For us, self-determination and free space for the individual as well as accepting different needs are the foundations of this goal. Our decisions are arrived at on an equitable basis and by consensus. The house and land are shared property and we run them ourselves. We have developed in such a way that a portion of our members work off the farm, e.g. in social welfare fields, as gardeners or as a school pupil. One of the women living here works as a writer. Other than that, we have a juice press, a pottery workshop and the editorial office for the regional magazine "Överblick" (s. www.oeverblick.de), which was founded by one of our members. "Överblick" also provides a position for the Voluntary Ecological Year (FÖJ), offering people up to age 27 the opportunity to live with us for a year and get to know our project.
We cultivate fruit and herbs on our land and brew our own beer. We live together with 4 cats, 2 fattened hogs and quite a few anarchistic chickens. On our meadow we also have two friendly ponies and sheep as part-time guests.

Kommuja

☺ introductory visit, probationary week, probationary period (1/2 year)

Friedenshof-Kommunität

FH

Hammerstein Str. 3 | 31535 Neustadt-Niederstöcken

+49-(0)5073-7022

-924131

1991 | 3 ha (near Hannover) | ♀5 ♂4 9

g, e | 3

everyone in common (consensus) | shared income

property of individual community members

- inter-religious, non-violent (L'Arche of Lanza del Vasto)
- household, organic farming, ecological building improvements, guests, educational work, home economics
- ecological, self-managed, non-violent, spiritual, inner growth, meditation, yoga, vegetarian diet, adult education, peace-work, self-sufficiency, organic gardening, organic farming, ecological construction, woodworking, spinning, weaving, media

In the mid-1980s we formulated the desire to realise our dedication to peace, justice and the preservation of Creation in our personal lives. We found an example for such a lifestyle in the French "Arche Communities" as conceived by Lanza del Vasto. The Friedenshof orients itself on the Arche idea, however it has made some compromises in the way it seeks to realise it. A further cornerstone is our own "Rule" which orients us toward the divine. The Rule helps us in our efforts to transform ourselves and to make an impact on the world.
12 years have passed. We are living in a 250 year-old half-timbered house on 5,000 m^2 of land with a garden, a pasture, a greenhouse and a workshop in the middle of a small village some 35 km north of Hanover.
We have found a new way of life which differs from the prevailing one in many respects.
Making money, consumption and bought entertainment have declined in importance – fulfilment through meaningful activities, through community and a spiritual quest now have a new value. We are also attempting alternatives in organic gardening, clay building and alternative healing techniques.
We hope that our experiments will provide a small contribution to the necessary reformation of the world society.

- Friendship Circle L'Arche according to Lanza del Vasto
- ☺ probationary period, individual spiritual search

Galions e.V.

GL

Brunnenstr. 3 | 36323 Grebenau-Bieben
☎ +49-(0)6646-919025
Fax -919027

1988 | 1.5 ha (near Bad Hersfeld) | ♀2 ♂3 5

- g, e — none
- everyone in common (majority vote, consensus in individual cases)
- limited common financing — Gemeinschaft
- none
- care of house, farm, garden
- ecological, self-managed, anarchistic, left-wing political understanding, non-violent, chaotic, inner growth, meditation, organic diet, peace-work, physically handicapped persons, animal protection, environmental protection, organic gardening, alternative energy, ecological construction, joinery, physiotherapie, back school, massages

☺ ( )

The GALIONS e.V. farm community is located on the edge of a small village with 300 inhabitants, but it is not beyond all civilisation. At the moment we have 5 adult human beings and 4 cats living here. We formerly had children here and also kept livestock. This is still possible.
We live organically, partly as vegetarians and only smoke outside the house. Our house remodelling follows ecological guidelines. We hold a weekly plenum. The organic garden, currently on the back burner, is looking for new people interested in gardening. We order our organic groceries through a food co-op.
The property is owned by the association. We pay 500.00 Euros per person and month into the association till out of which we then finance all expenses, aside from cars and tobacco.
People with children, animals, ideas and crafts skills are sincerely welcome. Our condition: take personal responsibility for everything you contribute. The sky's the limit to possibilities provided you bring initiative, drive and/or cash.

Kommuja
☺ ecological outlook, interested in natural nutrition, caring for plants and animals

Gemeinschaft am Lambach

LB

Am Lambach 14 | 32051 Herford-Eickum
☎+49-(0)5221-33438 www.lambachgemeinschaft.org.

1995 0.66 ha (near Herford) ♀3 ♂2 3 8

g, e, f none
everyone in common (consensus) shared income
Association
one's own profession, garden, child, building
ecological, self-managed, left-wing political understanding, non-violent, organic diet, vegetarian diet, peace-work, supporting refugees, environmental protection, ecological construction, music, non-violent actions, „Lebenslaute" („Sounds of Life") group

☺

We wanted to realise our utopias of a non-violent society not only through political commitment but also in our daily lives. For example, this means sharing our income in order to balance wage inequalities in different types of work and to provide individuals with some time off (e.g. for child rearing). It means loosening small family structures. It also means consuming fewer resources, for instance by sharing living space, consuming relatively little, using ecological building materials and mostly travelling by bicycle or train.
In living together we think it is important to respect the needs of individual persons within the framework of our basic understanding of a considerate treatment both of one another and of nature. In the evening we eat together (everybody cooks except the children). Once a week we meet for 2-3 hours in order to make decisions and to exchange important information.

In 1995 we purchased a small farming property on the edge of the town of Herford. It is surrounded by fields and we are located only fifteen minutes by bicycle from the train station.
Our professions are in the social service and handicraft fields. We all care for the large garden and the chickens.
Our shared activities include the non-violent actions of the "Lebenslaute" group (political actions with predominantly classical music), Castor (anti-nuclear transport) blockades and participating in and organising local politics ("energy without the atom", activities against public oath-taking by the German army, supporting refugees etc.). Socially disadvantaged persons have the – temporary - option of living together with us.

Gemeinschaft Heckenbeck

HK

Schulstr. 5 | 37581 Bad Gandersheim
☎ +49-(0)5563-6170, -999539

1984 — Dorf mit 450 Einw. (near Göttingen) — ♀25 ♂20 — 30 — 75

- g
- individual financing
- Inside the GeG there are house, farm and flat-sharing communities
- everything is possible
- ecological, self-managed, non-violent, spiritual, inner growth, meditation, free school, seminar-house, therapy: various physical and psychotherapy methods, ecological construction, humour, handicrafts: pottery, spinning, weaving, art: sculpture, painting, other: many communication groups

☺

Over the past 19 years the small village of Heckenbeck (450 residents) has witnessed the arrival of new people (families and individuals) who have set up numerous alternative groups, initiatives and creative projects. Alongside the traditional village structures one can currently observe the following initiatives: a Free School and kindergarten, the "Sounds of Silence" association with a meditation house, the "World Stage" cultural centre, a building community ("Lebens-räume Heckenbeck GmbH"), a joint doctor's surgery, building and craft firms, a drumming group, women's and men's groups, meditative dance, a forum, clan meeting, plenum, council etc...

There is a broad spectrum of living arrangements (residential courtyards,

flat-sharing communities, traditional living). The initiatives and projects are autonomous. Some are open to new people, others are not. They organise themselves and feel linked to the network in various ways.
The initiatives and projects can be classified under five focal points which have arisen on the basis of common visions: creativity, communication, living and working, teaching, spirituality. These 5 areas are linked together by the theme of healing with which everyone is preoccupied in one way or another.
The network is currently seeking a consensus in regard to common goals, structures and visions.

☺ we desire that the "new" respectfully adress the "old" and "new" in the village

Gemeinschaft in Güstritz (Wendland)

GW

Landstr. 6 | 29462 Güstritz
☎ +49-(0)5843-1574, -444
-444
wendland-wind@t-online.de

1993 | 7200 m² (near Lüchow-Dannenberg) | ♀3 ♂4 | 4 | 11

g, e
none
everyone in common (consensus)
limited community financing and individual
asssociation
linked to the world (ecumenical)
gardening, house, wood, foil tunnel, construction (hay barn)
ecological, non-violent, organic diet, vegetarian diet, vegan diet, environmental protection, organic gardening, alternative energy, ecological construction, painting
☺ ()

In 1993 the community purchased a residual farm including outbuildings on a large property in Güstritz near Wustrow. We wish for it to be possible to live in several separate units of different sizes. It is important for us to create a large common room and sufficient accommodations for guests. A reed bed system has been built, and a solar energy system, combined with a wood gasification plant, is in operation. We are involved in building a wind power station nearby. We want the community to be open, flexible and as non-ideological as possible. It is intended that both tighter and wider circles of people should form around the five to twelve older and younger people who feel part of the community. Belief in the divine life within humankind and and nature is important to us. Thus we want to share spiritual and religious variety in their concrete forms accompanied by a free and creative dialogue on our experiences. It goes without saying that political + ecological consciousness are important factors in the way we live our daily lives - doesn't it?

→ See also description of network "**Come Together**"
☺ ideologically open

Gemeinschaft in Klosterzimmern

KL

Gutshof | 86738 Deiningen
+49-(0)9081-290 1062 kontakt@zwoelf-staemme.de
-272849 www.zwoelf-staemme.de

2001 28 ha (near Nördlingen) ♀31 ♂25 54 110

g, e, f, sp., port. 30

all persons together, part of the group (consensus) shared economy

property of individual community members

We live according to the primitive Christian model as a community

organic farming (vegetables/grain, animal husbandry), renovation/remodelling, furniture assembly firm, own school

ecological, self-managed, non-violent, primitive Christianity, organic diet, self-sufficiency, organic agriculture, organic gardening, organic farming, animal friendly husbandry, alternative energy, furniture assembly, carpentry, folklore music, Israeli circle dances, dance workshops

☺

In the summer of 2000, after keeping a lookout for a large enough farm for several years, we purchased the large estate of Klosterzimmern in the Nördlinger Ries in Bavaria. This estate is like a small village with several residential houses, barns and halls, a grain silo, a mill and an electrical turbine. We would like to return this estate to its former glory and beauty and soon hope to set up own bakery, joiner's shop or farm store. We cultivate a variety of vegetable and grain varieties on our 28 ha of land. We also keep cows, goats and sheep.

The ongoing work on our buildings reminds us of the daily restoration which is taking place in our hearts. The Son of God gradually replaces our stony, selfish heart with a heart of flesh which can love others without end. We wish our common life to be a taste of the coming age in which there will be no more injustice and greed.

If you long for a new beginning in your life and sense that your soul needs healing, please come visit us! We would like to get to know you and share our wonderful life and our hope with you!

→ See also description of network **"Communities of the Twelve Tribes"**

☺ Everyone is welcome! We are united by our shared faith and our communal life.

Gemeinschaftliches Leben e.V. Blütlingen

BL

Dorfstr. 30 | 29462 Wustrow
☎ +49-(0)5843-7780

1995 | 0.8 ha (near Lüchow) | ♀3 ♂2 5 10

g, e, sp.
none
everyone in common (consensus)
limited community financing
association
home economics
ecological, self-managed, left-wing political understanding, non-violent, organic diet, organic gardening, alternative energy, ecological construction

☺

Our community is joined together by the co-existence of small and big people (we have three families at the moment) on an old farm in the Wendland which we have expanded and remodelled according to ecological principles. We are striving for an ecological household and both design and care for the land adjacent to the house with its variety of gardens and several small animals. We seek equitable living conditions and are working to develop a resource and environment-saving lifestyle which does not suppress the needs of the individual.

☺ sympathy

Generationsübergreifende Wohnanlage Eisingen

WE

Ilse Fischer | Spessartstr. 17-19 | 97249 Eisingen
☎ +49-(0)9306-981138

1998 | (near Würzburg) | ♀6 ♂4 4 14

g
none
everyone in common (consensus)
individual and limited community financing
none
all working members employed elsewhere
ecological, self-managed, non-violent, organic diet

☺

After a long preparatory phase (1 ½ years) and a lot of coming and going, a solid group has formed, consisting of 8 adults and 1 child. The group's members share the goal of improving and/or changing their previous life situation (single household, nuclear family, alone with child). To this end, we transformed a former old people's home into a trans-generational, independent residential facility with social and ecological goals. The house community belongs to the association "Der Hof", an association promoting, supporting and advising alternative lifestyles. Our common life has gone through ups and downs since late 1998. All tasks relating to the house, such as maintenance, administration, cleaning etc. are attended to by the residents. We hold action days at regular intervals to take care of major tasks, such as gardening, renovating the house etc. together. We have mandatory monthly meetings where we solve problems. Beyond that, such activities as barbecues, festivals and birthday parties take place spontaneously. Participation is voluntary. We continually discuss the form of our communal life. We discuss conflicts and seek new paths. On the whole, we are a cross between a normal condo block and a living community.

☺ interest in house community, 2 flats for sale

GRAL-Gemeinschaft

GA

Glandorfer Damm 5 | 49536 Lienen-Kattenvenne

☎ +49-(0)5484962466 gral-kattenvenne@gmx.de

2001 | 2.5 ha (near Münster-Osnabrück) | ♀5 ♂3 4 12

g, e, f, sp.

everyone in common (consensus) | limited community financing

rented/leased

ecological, spiritual, organic diet, permaculture, organic gardening, amicative, non-educational, authentic, undogmatic

☺

We are a community of small and large people living on a farm between Münster and Osnabrück with plenty of space for all our needs. We came together through Amication, an outlook on the world whereby everyone belongs to him or herself and all phenomena of life are of equal value (www.amication.de). Under this umbrella, both small and large individualists – spiritual and rational, eco and motorised, raw and cooked, loud and quiet, sad and happy – live here together. We come together every week in the orga house meeting or in the SVT (self-responsibility training) for psychodynamics and celebrate seasonal festivals, birthdays, life and ourselves. Beyond that, we have a large property which is partially cultivated on a permaculture basis and which is creatively designed.
We are part of the GRAL network which is made up of various people, individuals and groups, from all over Germany, all of whom feel they are part of Amication.

☺ Amication

Gut Stolzenhagen e.G.

SH

Lüdersdorfer Str. 5 | 16248 Stolzenhagen
+49-(0)30-44036767 contact@gut-stolzenhagen.de
www.gut-stolzenhagen.de

1999 | 3.8 ha (near Berlin) | ♀5 ♂12 9 26

g, e | none

everyone in common (majority vote) | limited community financing

common property

clay building, dance seminars, guests, self-administration

self-managed, organic gardening, ecological construction, expressive dance, pluralistic, non-ideological, humour

☺

We want to resettle the old estate in Stolzenhagen. The land (approx. 3.8 ha) and the buildings are the property of the Stolzenhagen Estate Co-operative (= us). The estate, with its 11 (to some extent) empty buildings and the gardens, provides considerable space for developing neighbourhoods which would in turn assume responsibility for the renovation, design, economy and administration of their houses. Are we even a community? We have neither common meals nor common work; we have few common ideals and no community vision. So far, only a few of us actually live full-time on the estate. Most commute between Berlin and Stolzenhagen and are rarely seen in wintertime. However: we have a common kitchen and bath, common rooms, a common open area, we discuss and decide matters in common at our member assemblies and generally get along very well together.
Stolzenhagen is idyllically located in a hilly, forested landscape, right next to the Lower Oder Valley National Park. From elevated points one has a view across the Oder Valley and over to the Polish woodlands. The Schorfheide-Chorin Biosphere Reserve begins 5 km further west.
You can find complete information on our website. We share the property with the "Wohnhof auf dem Gut Stolzenhagen" (see description).

☺ co-op stake of 2,500 Euros

Haus der Gastfreundschaft

GF

Alte Dorfstr. 6 | 19370 Dargelütz near Parchim
+49-(0)179-4072506 (7.00 - 7.30 pm) www.die-schenker.de

1994 | ½ ha (near Parchim) | ♀3 ♂6 9

g, e, f | 7

everyone in common (consensus when possible) | varies

"moral" rights of use

spiritual non-violence

alternative social work, collection and use of "remnants"

☺

The "Haus der Gastfreundschaft" ("Hospitality House") is part of the movement of people who only exchange gifts with one another (the so-called "Schenker" or "Giver Movement"). This means non-violent sharing in order to live in an overall responsible manner. We believe that it is only possible to be really happy by following our conscience in our path toward an overall responsible life (as "a healthy cell in the world organism"). The foundation for this is doing away with all conflict of will among human beings (violence, competition and account settling), which can never show who is right or wrong (morally) and which is not our business anyway. The "freedom and responsibility of the individual" means doing what needs to be done in a situation without having to hold back because of somebody else. In any case, structures based on the state (power) and money (the "achievement principle") don't fit in.
We live according to three lifeforms: 1.) "Pilgrims", without money and "papers", with posters on the street... 2.) "Hospitality Houses" for virtually unconditional sharing with the needy... We only "own" houses or land according to "moral rights of use", i.e. through their organic integration into the context of life (without purchase, binding contracts...); we only live on remnants, gifts and our own production, with neither electricity nor a water linkup... 3.) Self-sufficient "village families" as a "survival model" for humankind... a first seedling of this is the "Nature-Peace-Zone" in Pommritz.
Our movement is open for people from the most diverse religious or ideological backgrounds and it has "spiritually non-violent" links to Jesus, Tolstoy, Gandhi, "Peace Pilgrim", "L'Arche" (Lanza del Vasto), Catholic Worker, Emmaus...

→ See also description of network "**Emmaus**"
Friends of L'Arche (Lanza del Vasto)

Hof Fleckenbühl

HF

35091 Cölbe-Schönstadt
+49-(0)6427-92210 info@suchthilfe.org
-922150 www.suchthilfe.org

1984 | 145 ha (near Marburg) | ♀25 | ♂100 | 20 | ca. 150

all
everyone together/part of the group (consensus)
limited common financing | common property
farming, handicraft, administration
ecological, self-managed, non-violent, hierarchical, christian, buddhist, anthroposophic, meditation, organic diet, therapy: according to animal protection/ environmental protection, environmental protection, organic agriculture, organic gardening, organic farming, sports: football, art

Hof Fleckenbühl was purchased by Synanon from the city of Kassel in 1984. It has been managed according to the guidelines of bio-dynamic agriculture since 1985. All the farm's products are marketed at the farm store and at its branch stores in the surrounding towns.

The Hof Fleckenbühl addiction rehabilitation programme recently detached itself from the Synanon organisation and became independent, all the while maintaining its fundamental principles. The only precondition to joining the community is the desire to remain sober.
We accept new members at all times - day and night. We also accept addicted parents together with their children. In this case, however, we make an exception from the normal procedure and ask for advance contact and an interview. Members can stay as long as they feel is necessary.
In contrast to conventional therapeutic facilities, our addiction rehabilitation programme is a self-help community without a financial sponsor and without hired professional personnel. Our people give themselves their own structure and work towards common solutions for their addiction problems. Within the framework of a common household economy we strive to develop a variety of projects and small enterprises in order to secure our economic existence. Besides helping to contribute towards costs, these small enterprises are also intended to lead the farm residents employed in them towards meaningful and reality-oriented work. By working in the administration, the enterprises and other fields of activity, addicted persons acquire qualifications allowing them to find employment off the farm. At the moment, qualifications and training programmes are being offered in the following areas: organic farming and animal husbandry, gardening, cheese making, the bakery and natural foods, transport, and a ceramics workshop. Training also takes place within the framework of the administration.
"The Game" is a regularly occurring discussion group in which each resident participates. Here we discuss interpersonal and personal experiences and problems in complete openness. The Game is a hierarchy-free space, i.e. all members are equal and there is no discussion leader. The meetings have an equalising and stabilising effect on the individual and thus on the community as a whole.

☺ no drugs, no violence, no tobacco

Hof Luna

LN

Wilhelm R. Bertram | Im Siek 10 | 31085 Everode
☎ +49-(0)5184-958958,-950133 hof-luna@t-online.de
-950122 www.landleben-ev.de

1987 130 ha (near Alfeld, Hildesheim) ♀3 ♂6 9

g, e 9

one person

individual financing leased/property of individual members

none

farming, farm shop, weekly market, cheese dairy, bakery, sweat lodge ceremonies, public relations, construction, renovation

ecological, hierarchical, organic diet, environmental protection, organic agriculture, organic gardening,organic farming, remodelling and renovation

☺

Heinrich Bertram bought this farm for 1,250 Talers in 1795. In 1987, Wilhelm Bertram – his seventh-generation descendant – took over the farm from his parents and has been running it according to biodynamic principles ever since.
9 people live here today. The farm's main features are a herd of dairy cows, fields for growing grain and vegetables and also a farm shop. There is also a small cheese dairy and a bakery. As on any farm, our daily life is pretty labour-intensive. The farm is beautifully located in a low mountain landscape approx. 1 hour south of Hanover in a village with 500 inhabitants. We are supported and sponsored by the "Land-Leben e.V." association.
One of our concerns is nature conservation and/or healing the earth and its inhabitants. Using a moist biotope, fruit trees and hedges we are creating habitats for rare bird species and insects. Endangered wild herbs grow on specially selected land areas.
Regular sweat lodge ceremonies provide an opportunity to make an intensive bond with the 4 elements and to purify oneself physically, mentally and spiritually.
In this way – and also through a Vedic fire ritual – we seek to create an inner harmony with our work on the soil.
At the moment we are building and renovating the farm buildings in order to provide space for further seminars and events.

☺ probationary work week

Hof Rossee

HR

c/o Nicola Hieronimi | Rossee 1 | 24360 Barkelsby
☎ +49-(0)4351-880812 nicola@hof-rossee.de

2001 1.2 ha (near Eckernförde, Kiel) ♀5 ♂4 7 16

g, f, dan., e, norw. 3,5

everyone in common (consensus) shared economy (shared income and capital)

common property

very mixed

construction, gardening, children, outside work, kitchen

ecological, anarchistic, left-wing political understanding, feminist, non-violent, anthroposophic, yoga, organic diet, vegetarian diet, pedagogical, ecological construction, construction

☺

For the past two years we have been living on a farm near Eckernförde, located 4 km from the nearest beach and 25 km from Kiel. At the moment we are still largely experimenting with living our everyday lives, caring for and supervising the children. One of our main projects is to expand and modernise a stable building. It will be used for common rooms and several apartments of different sizes.
Aside from that, we are considering various other work areas, such as a food co-op, candle making and a sewing workshop, but have not yet implemented them. We produce what we need in common and have a shared capital economy.
We're basically a pretty mixed group with either a spiritual or political background. What brought us together was the desire to take a common path where we don't

all dicker around as individuals or in nuclear family structures but instead assume responsibility for ourselves and, not least, for the children.
We would like to grow. If we make full use of our expansion potential we will be able to accommodate around twenty persons. We organise regular "building weeks" (e.g. in loam and wood construction). We welcome every helping hand, although it would be a good idea to give us a call first.

Kommuja
☺ Willing to take part in shared economy, probationary period

Hofgemeinschaft beim Waller

WL

Stockham 2 | 84381 Johanniskirchen
☎+49-(0)8564-940711 hofgemeinschaft@wallerhof.de
-940711 www.wallerhof.de

1998 1 ha (near Pfarrkirchen) ♀3 ♂3 8 14

g none

everyone in common (majority vote, consensus)

limited common financing and individual common property

living as a family, architecture, geomanty, supervising construction, aiding disabled children, technical drawing studio, private physical therapy, alternative body therapy

ecological, non-violent, spiritual, christian, ecumenical, inner growth, meditation, yoga, organic diet, seminar-house in planning; mentally/psychologically handicapped persons, physically handicapped persons in short-term care; therapy, environmental protection, organic gardening, alternative energy, ecological construction, construction

☺ ()

We are a community consisting of 3 families and live on a four-sided farm in the lovely Rottal in Lower Bavaria. The former residential house and the stable building have been divided into 4 residential sections. Each family has ecologically remodelled a section as a living area, which it now owns. Thus one unfinished unit is still available.
We are looking for open, friendly and community-oriented people who would like to develop this unit and fill it with life. All further buildings are community-owned and are used in common. However, they can still be developed and are thus waiting for shared use, whether for vocational purposes, as a community kitchen etc., for self-development. The families are at the centre of our community, and together we celebrate seasonal festivals, harvest days, meditation and other undertakings. We gather regularly for organisational meetings and self-organised theme evenings.

Hofgemeinschaft Groß Chüden Nr. 4

GC

Dorfstr. 4 | 29416 Groß Chüden
+49-(0)3901-82942 www.alternativeninderaltmark.de

1993 4.5 ha (near Salzwedel) ♀3 ♂5 3 11

g, e 5

everyone in common (consensus) individual financing

rented/leased

seminar house, felt workshop, food co-op, mail order bookshop, joinery, garden, children

ecological, self-managed, organic diet, seminar-house, felt-making, greenwood furniture-making, books

☺

Despite financial and personal links to the Ökodorf Sieben Linden, the former Ecovillage Project Centre has turned into an independent project. Our communal life is based on sympathy and individuality, not on principles.

The farm has a living area of 450 m² and offers a variety of trailer lots. We operate a conference centre ("de´ bunte vier"), a mail order book shop, a felt workshop (Filzefanz), a greenwood joinery ("Wuchs & Werk"), and now a firewood business and food co-op ("EVG Immersatt e.V."). In addition, we like to spend our time with children, animals, our garden and many other lovely things in life.

We would be delighted if even more nice, "alternative" people would come to the Altmark and thus continue to expand the existing loose regional network. At the moment we are not looking for new co-residents, but we'd be happy to meet new people in our immediate surroundings... We help people as much as possible in their search for a flat, a farm or a community, supplying them with organic food, arranging contact with the Altmark Free School (primary school & kindergarten) etc. It's a patchwork of alternative diversity in and around us. Please – no unannounced visits!

networking with communities in region

☺ personal sympathy

Hofgemeinschaft Lindenhof

LI

Allmende e.V. | Presseweg 6 | 38170 Eilum
+49-(0)5332-3547 lindenhof@eilum.de
-6224 www.eilum.de

1979 120 ha (near Braunschweig) ♀5 ♂3 4 12

e, f, g 7

everyone in common (consensus) limited community financing

rented/leased

Bioland farming and vegetable gardening, bakery, direct marketing self-managed, left-wing political understanding, organic diet, environmental protection, organic agriculture, organic gardening, organic farming, alternative energy, ecological construction

Together we operate a large Bioland enterprise (120 ha) with farming, animal husbandry, a garden, bakery and direct marketing. We have two residential houses: several of us live together as a family with our own household and others live in a flat-sharing community. Important decisions are made by the entire group on a consensus basis. Our life is based on producing everything we need in our own entrprise. Because of economic constraints, we have less personal freedom than we'd like and little time for cultural or political activities. Still, together with the non-profit Allmende Assocation, which owns the farm, we keep managing to organise a varied programme which leaves its mark on the region.
Anyone who would like to combine a gardening internship or training with us, or who has already had training or professional experience and would like to help develop one of our work areas, is welcome to inquire about the possibilities.

Kommuja
☺ available living space

Holderbusch

HB

Dorfstr. 36 | 02906 Waldhufen OT Jänkendorf
+49-(0)3588-259402 fboltz@t-online.de oder Holderbusch-eV@gmx.de

1998 22 ha (near Niesky/Görlitz) ♀2 ♂3 1 6

1

everyone in common (self-responsible) limited community financing

property of individual community members

animal husbandry, farming, gardening, permaculture, joiner's workshop, locksmith's shop, youth work, education, healing

ecological, self-managed, non-violent, inner growth, adult education, environmental protection, self-sufficiency, permaculture, organic agriculture, organic gardening, organic farming

General conditions: A farm on the edge of town with ca. 22 ha of fields and pasture, barns and workshops scattered around the immediate neighbourhood. The aim of our project is for the people living here to assume full responsibility for their own lives. We provide space and the material conditions. According to our articles of association, our goals are "sustainable economy and the promotion of cultural variety". In concrete terms, we are in the process of developing a subsistence economy with permaculture gardening and farming (including a forest-edge garden); workshops (a metal working and cabinet making shop) for our own needs and for social work have largely been completed and are ready for use. One important theme here is healing through physical work. During the summer months we offer holiday camps, work camps and seminars.

Our farming operation encompasses animal husbandry with horses and ponies, sheep and small animals; c. 10 ha of fields are currently in cultivation using wage labour according to organic farming criteria and can be transferred to personal use on a short-term basis.
Living expenses are borne according to ability and are largely earned through agricultural work. Aside from the household till we have no shared economy.
Our nutrition is self-determined, there are no formal guidelines. However, we try to rely as much as possible on our own products (also on an exchange basis with other organic farms in the region).
The project offers a vast variety of opportunities, it is open and offers space to people with a variety of ideas and projects undertaken in the spirit of self-responsibility.
Guests are welcome at all times (after phoning). For talking, discussion, criticising as well as for working with us or experimenting, or to gain a first impression.

→ See also description of network "**Come Together**"
☺ self-responsibility

ISKCON Heidelberg

IK

Forum 5 | 69126 Heidelberg
☎ +49-(0)6221-384553
vipula@pamho.net
www.iskcon.de

♀4 ♂3 7

e, g
7

everyone in common (consensus)

all covered by donations and sale of books/food
rented/leased

Vaishnava (life philosophy of ancient India)

praying and singing to god, producing and distributing vegetarian/sanctified food, distributing religious books

self-managed, non-violent, leader/guru, spiritual, meditation, yoga, vegetarian diet, spiritual care with community members, wide range of life consultations, meditative music on the streets

☺

Most people know us as the "Hare Krishna Movement" since the "Hare Krishna Mantra" is important to us and we often sing it on the streets. But hardly anyone knows that our spiritual tradition (Vaisnava) can be traced back over 5,000 years; its origin lies in the period when the Vedic culture flourished in India.
Nearly every country has centres, temples and farm communities belonging to the International Society for Krishna Consciousness (ISKCON). After many of us moved away from Heidelberg, we had to give up our large temple some 5 years ago and move into a flat. At the moment there are 7 of us. We devote much of our time to the centre, our shop and our vegetarian party service. There is also a large congregation of around 100 people; some of them come regularly (e.g. to our Sunday festivals every week) and take part in our activities. Others only visit us now and then.

We expect the centre's residents to maintain Vedic principles, i.e. a vegetarian diet and no mind-altering substances, unregulated sexuality or games of chance.
We are currently planning to buy a house in order to offer more residential opportunities, expand our party service and disperse knowledge on Vedic culture better known (e.g. through cooking courses, music seminars, yoga, meditation, Ayurveda, Vastu etc.).

→ See also description of network "**ISKCON**"

☺ vegetarians, non-smokers, no drugs, participation in spiritual schedule and religious practices, acceptance only after long mutual acquaintance

Jakobgut

JG

07952 Ranspach
☎ +49-(0)37432-22676
-22676
jakobgut@oadien.de
www.oadien.de

1997 | 7 ha (near Plauen) | ♂4 | 4

e, g

everyone in common (consensus) | limited community financing

rented / leased, property of individual members

none

organising self-sufficiency

pluralistic, addiction-reducing, christian, chaotic, self-sufficiency, organic gardening, forestry, alternative energy, ecological construction, construction, art-individual: addiction work, therapy

☺

We have an estate with an adjoining field and an orchard plus an inn in Ranspach/ Vogtland. This is a softly intertwined landscape of hills and valleys. There are mineral springs nearby, thus the local town was once a pilgrimage site. We are looking for people who would like to enrich us. It would be great if we could find someone who would organise our self-sufficient food supply in the long term and enjoy doing it. This area is leading a rather pathetic existence. People can visit us for a while to recover from stressful modern culture. Our land is also a source of building clay.
Heinz wants to start an association to benefit the socially disadvantaged and disenfranchised. He is on the lookout for a social worker, educator or someone of this sort.
Those who would like to help us can look at our website and see what we need.

☺ women for demographic reasons

Johannishöhe

JH

Natürlich leben und lernen e.V. | 01737 Tharandt
☎+49-(0)35203-37181 ✉info@johannishoehe.de
Fax -37936 🖳www.johannishoehe.de

1992 4.5 ha (near Dresden) ♀2 ♂3 1 6

g, e, russ., f 3 x 0,5

everyone in common (consensus) limited community financing

usufruct by the ass. "Grüne Liga", Berlin

ecological, non-violent

environmental education, nature market, farming (goats), gardening, office work

ecological, self-managed, non-violent, chaotic, organic diet, adult education, seminar-house, peace-work, environmental protection, self-sufficiency, alternative energy, ecological construction, non-smoker house, music, circus

☺

We, the residents and also members of the association "Natürlich Leben und Lernen" ("Live and Learn Naturally") wish to combine a more ecologically conducive lifestyle in a community with self-determined education work here on the Johannishöhe. Bit by bit, this dream has become a reality through the efforts of many people.
We want to use the educational events for children and adults which we organise and conduct on the Johannishöhe to provide our participants with a conscious and respectful attitude toward themselves, other people and the earth we live on. Our educational work is rooted in the notion of living everyday life in an ecological fashion. For example, we produce a good portion of our own food. We keep chickens and goats for our own needs and also cultivate a garden.
Our house is equipped with a wood-fired central heating system, solar collectors, a photo-voltaic system and a compost system. In this area, too, we seek long-term independence.
Two young people and two adults live together on the Johannishöhe. We are committed to new social approaches, e.g. in energy and agricultural policy and also for the ecological development of our town and region. Thus we organise a market in Tharandt with products from direct marketing enterprises and craftspeople from the region.

☺ ecological outlook, 1 year trial period, co-operation in the conference house

KommFrei e.V.

KF

Jenneweg 10 | 66113 Saarbrücken
☎+49-681-9101451 ✉kommfrei@gmx.de
Fax +49-681-7096453 🖳www.kommfrei.de

1999

everyone in common (consensus) shared economy

ecological, non-violent, organic diet, seminar-house, peace-work, environmental protection, organic gardening, alternative energy, ecological construction, handicraft, art, handling conflicts (forum, GFK, mediation)

☺

The "KommFrei e.V." association is a growing group of currently some 15 persons of different ages who in the future would like to live and work together as a community. We are neither a cult nor a spiritual or church community, nor do we follow any other ideology. We were brought together by the desire to dissolve the conventional framework of the nuclear family and single life, of old age and nursing home, and create new social structures, while always remaining open to people who live in these structures (small families, singles).
We consciously wanted to live in an ecological community of 30 to 60 persons which would encompass all age groups. By implementing our idea of a communal, ecological large-scale household, we would like to develop into a model project for a sustainable lifestyle. We are thus following the tradition of the "Kommune Niederkaufungen" near Kassel.
The qualifications of our group's members are many and varied, which is why the most diverse professions come together in our community: e.g. architecture, energy planning, biology, farming, gardening, health, social welfare, electricity, carpentry, furniture making, construction and computer technology.
We would like to set up our places of employment on the same property as our flats and/or in the near vicinity in order to create a decentralised economic unit and develop a new living culture.
We would like to create encounter spaces for a vibrant exchange with the population and promote regional networking on a cultural, economic and social level. As adult, responsible citizens, we endeavour to become a natural part of the region.

☺ none

Kommune 5

K5

Falkenberger Weg 5 | 16230 Breydin OT Trampe
☎ +49-(0)334151-60956, -55024, -55077

2003 — 0.6 ha (near Eberswalde) — ♀2 ♂2 — 3 — 7

3

everyone in common (consensus) — individual financing

ecological/holistic

ecological building, self-sufficiency, alternative education and school models, permaculture, environmental education, spirituality, art

☺ ( )

Kommune 5 is a small, relatively young community of people who live on approx. 0.6 ha of land in Trampe, 7 km from Eberswalde. Our living community's goal is to develop a genuine alternative to the existing societal system. Inhuman, capitalistic structures long to be replaced by ecological-holistic alternatives. Our fields of work and interest include: ecological building, self-sufficiency, alternative child-rearing and school models, a shared economy, new relationship structures, permaculture, environmental education, spirituality and art. We make decisions by consensus. We work and live on a simple level, although fun and games will always get their fair share. We practice tolerance and are thus open to new, exciting encounters. What we're looking for are people who want to join us in realising their dreams.

Kommune am Meer

KM

Esgrusschauby 15 | 24402 Esgrus
+49-(0)4637-963734 vielmeerev@foni.net

2002 8.000 m² (near Flensburg) ♀3 ♂2 2 7

g, e 0-2
everyone in common (consensus) shared economy
common property
left, i.e. non-New Age, feministic is also good
used book mail order (outside), construction
ecological, self-managed, anarchistic, left-wing political understanding, feminist, vegetarian diet, organic gardening, ecological construction, construction

Since the spring of 2002 we have been living and working on a three-sided farm near Flensburg (and just 6 km from the beach!). There are now 7 of us, including 5 adults. We wouldn't mind being more. We view ourselves as a political commune. That means, for example, that we don't want to "go native" out here in the country but instead seek political and cultural contacts with groups from town AND country. We also want to experiment with forms of living together as an alternative to isolation, the nuclear family and profit-seeking.
So far we have largely been busy working on the house, earning money on the outside and organising our daily life. In the long term, we hope to develop ways of earning money on the farm, too. We are planning a used book mail order business and something to do with building.
Otherwise, we agree with Finkenburg: The fact that we're appearing in this book together with other projects does not mean that we agree with their principles or belong to them in any way. This particularly applies to ZEGG.

Kommuja
have to fit in, probationary period

Kommune Buchhagen

KB

Buchhagen Nr. 4 | 37619 Bodenwerder
+49-(0)5533-1400 buero@kommune-buchhagen.de
www.kommune-buchhagen.de

1997 3.5 ha (near Hameln/Holzminden) ♀4 ♂2 3 9

g, e, german language of gestures 2
everyone in common (consensus) shared economy (shared income and capital)
common property

- ecological living, leftist politics
- vegetable gardening and permaculture, bicycle hotel, building our own house
- ecological, self-managed, left-wing political understanding, inner growth, organic diet, environmental protection, self-sufficiency, permaculture, organic gardening, ecological construction

☺ (✋✋)

We have been living in a beautiful area at the centre of the Weserbergland since 1997. Here we occupy the former workers' houses on the grounds of an old estate. The property also includes an old water mill, a barn and stables, as well as 3 ha of land with a large vegetable garden and a young forest garden which we cultivate on a permaculture basis.
We also have a handful of sheep, some ducks and a couple of beehives.
The mill building is currently being restored and transformed into a cultural and event centre with a café. Aside from the communards, this cultural project involves a wide range of people from the region.
Our barn houses a carpentry/joiner's work shop which we share. In addition, we operate a small guest house with 12 beds for passing cyclists (Weser Bike Path) and groups.
Our permanent residents include 4 women, one of them in a wheelchair; 2 men, one of whom is gay; and 3 children aged 6, 6 and 15. We usually have another one or two long-term guests, and one of them is an FÖJ member.
What unites us is our shared economy, our willingness to discuss matters within and with the group, to grow from this experience and to make consensual decisions, as well as an ecologically responsible lifestyle.
Once we are finished refurbishing it, our residential building will provide enough room for about 20 persons and we hope to be able to share our life and our house with more people.

- Kommuja
- ☺ mutual sympathy, openness

Kommune Karmitz

CK

Karmitz Nr. 8 | 29482 Küsten
☎ +49-(0)5864-288

1990 | 4.5 ha (near Lüchow) | ♀6 ♂4 10

- e
- everyone in common (consensus) — shared financing of all areas of life
- partially rented / leased, partially common property
- self-sufficiency, juice press

☺ ✋✋

We are a commune which, with changing occupancy, has been living on an old farm in the Wendland for the past 13 years. We are 10 adults, one part-time teenager, two dogs, a cow, ducks, chickens, cats, trees, bushes, meadows, gardens etc. We are expending a great deal of energy on feeding ourselves organically and among other things work together in our juice press. That's harder than it sounds, so several of us also work in other professions. We have high political ideals: no hierarchy, mutual respect and acceptance, non-violence in word and deed, the consensus principle, active solidarity with non-dogmatic leftists, applied social criticism, anarchy!, and much much more... Sometimes we achieve our ideals, but usually we just nip at their heels. We have a ketchup faction, potato crisp eaters, lots of smokers, drivers, drinkers and always people who don't think that's good at all. We want to – and have to! – get along splendidly together since we share the responsibility for our living conditions, our money, our property and our well-being. Without the ability to stand back and see yourself, you might as well forget it. We're pretty happy to have found and developed this way of life.

Kommuja

active participation in the communal project

Kommune Niederkaufungen

NK

Kirchweg 1 | 34260 Kaufungen

+49-(0)5605-80070 info@kommune-niederkaufungen.de

-800740 www.kommune-niederkaufungen.de

1986 7 ha (near Kassel) ♀29 ♂26 18 73

e, f 49

everyone in common (consensus) shared economy (shared income and capital)

rented / leased, common property

ecological, socially compatible, emancipatory

construction, furniture workshop, metal working, kindergarten, carpenter's workshop, conference centre, vegetable, livestock, sewing workshop, consulting, kitchen, architectural office, administration

ecological, self-managed, left-wing political understanding, non-violent, organic diet, adult education, pedagogical, one-world development, environmental protection, organic agriculture, organic gardening, alternative energy, ecological construction, construction, handicraft

Niederkaufungen is a village near Kassel. 55 adults and 18 children live together in a commune located in a large building complex in the village centre. The project has been existence since 1986. We view ourselves as a non-dogmatic leftist group. The group as a whole orients itself neither toward a specific communal tradition nor to any particular spirituality. The foundations of our communal life are: A common purse, consensus decisions at all levels, a leftist political understanding, the dismantling of small family and gender specific power structures, non-violent communication and constructive conflict resolution.

We live in residential groups, we eat our meals together, and once a week we come together for our plenary meeting. Over the years we've built up a varied spectrum of working groups and collectives (conference house, child care centre, kitchen, building collective, carpenter's shop, repair shop, architectural office, administration, sewing and leather workshop, vegetable garden, cheese-making). We feel it is important to offer ecologically and socially compatible products and services. In the meantime we have also realised several meaningful ecological measures: renovating and insulating the buildings according to biological construction principles, the installation of a local heating system and an industrial wood furnace, the installation of rainwater collectors etc.

You can either order our self-presentation brochures "In Gefahr und größter Not" and "Der Traum ist aus" from us or download it from our website.

Kommuja
☺ leftist political understanding

Kommunität Grimnitz

KG

Grimnitzer Str. 15 | 16247 Joachimsthal
+49-(0)33361-70626 info@kommunitaet-grimnitz.de
-72094 www.kommunitaet-grimnitz.de

1997 2.5 ha (near Eberswalde/ Angermünde) ♀3 ♂3 6

g, e, russ., sp. 3-4

everyone in common (in consensus when possible)

limited common financing leased and/or association property

ecumenical/Christian

international encounters, regional community economy, youth and adult education, ecological economy

non-violent, christian, ecumenical, adult education, seminar-house, (youth) guest-house, peace-work, organic gardening, ecological construction, reed bed system

☺

We live near the beautiful Grimnitz Lake in the centre of a village on the edge of small town in Brandenburg. Our estate consists of numerous outbuildings, park land, gardens and fields. The coach-house, which has been remodelled into a 24-bed (youth) guest house and which is complemented by a small campground, a table tennis barn and volleyball field, houses our main areas of work: We organise international encounters in the areas of justice, peace, the preservation of creation and human rights (including overseas projects). Our regional educational work deals with alternatives to the impoverishment of structurally deprived regions as a result

of globalisation (community economy), with theological training including the dialogue between theology and economy, the natural sciences and ecological farming. We are also pleased to invite other groups who are dealing with similar issues and who are curious about communitarian life to hold conferences here.
Tolerant cohabitation in the spirit of Jesus and with a spirituality to match is our main project, teaching us to become reflective and dedicated Christians with all the social consequences this ideal entails. For this we are looking for further responsible members of various generations and family statuses. In our small town, we have been accepted as a "cultural factor" with political responsibility.

Kommunitäten (in development stage)
☺ recognising our articles of association and community rules, active participation

KoWa e.V.

KW

Kommune Waltershausen | August-Bebel-Str. 4 | 99880 Waltershausen
+49-(0)3622-200504 kowaev@freenet.de
-209492 www.kommune-kowa.de

2003 1,7 ha ♀5 ♂10 2 17

g, e, f, sp. 12
everyone in common (consensus) shared economy
common property
leftist, undogmatic
garden, household
ecological, self-managed, anarchistic, left-wing political understanding, feminist, non-violent, chaotic, meditation, organic diet, adult education, physically handicapped persons, environmental protection, self-sufficiency, organic gardening, forestry, alternative energy, ecological construction, construction, music, energy consultation office

☺

Kommune Waltershausen

Since April of 2003 some 15 people have been involved in rebuilding a former doll factory on the edge of the Thuringian Woods. The factory halls and a few trailers provide living space for 20 persons. All in all, some 50-60 people will one day live in the old brick factory, along with offices and workshop, with a good link to the local public transit network. That means that we want to grow – up to 100 people. In our view, life in a commune gives us an opportunity to exert political and social influence. We want to take active control of our lives, treating both human beings and nature with responsibility and consideration. This means challenging our consumption habits and creating space and time for human and social needs. Once a week, aside from the organisational plenum, we hold a meeting designed to cultivate our communication and relationships and also to tell each other how we feel. Alongside our construction work, we are gradually developing our own collective work areas. We are thinking in terms of a tailoring workshop, a culture café, the renaturation of our grounds, a construction company and a conference centre. Some of us are already collecting wood for our wood-fired heating system and are planting a garden to supply our vegetable needs. Our basic principles include a shared economy, the consensus principle and the rejection of all hierarchies.

Kommuja

☺ Willingness to share in common economy and to learn

Kultur- und Tagungshaus Rauenthal

RT

Hauptstraße 6 | 65345 Eltville-Rauenthal

+49-(0)6123-74412 Info@kuta-rauenthal.de

-75587 www.kuta-rauenthal.de

1988 (near Wiesbaden) ♀8 ♂5 4 17

g, e, f 4

everyone in common (consensus)

limited common financing, project financing

association property, leased by individuals

none, but ecological, leftist, autonomous, shamanistic and other roots

conference house, garden, sheep rearing, construction, courses

ecological, self-managed, left-wing political understanding, feminist, non-violent, spiritual, buddhist, esoteric/New Age, chaotic, inner growth, sexuality, organic diet, adult education, seminar-house, organic gardening, organic farming, animal friendly husbandry, alternative energy, ecological construction, martial arts, theatre courses and performances, cultural work, socio-cultural centre

☺

We have purchased, restored and remodelled a former village inn in the Rheingau near Wiesbaden as an association status. Here children and adults live together as a flat-sharing community. We operate a conference house which can accommodate up to 20 persons. As a socio-cultural centre we have our own programme of events and courses. Beyond this we raise milk sheep and have a cheese making shop, and we are endeavouring to supply ourselves with our own vegetables. Several of us are active in other fields, such as solar and control technology, social

education, health, astrology, ceramics, wood, theatre and horses. In our community we seek to realise both justified individual interests and ideas and try to develop and implement our shared dreams.
We range from A as in anti-auto and auto driver, bio-freaks, chlorine-free, diligent, energetic, flesh-eaters, generous, heartfelt, individuals, jolly, kabbalistic, leftist, macaroni, nature lovers, organisational talents, political, quarrelsome, relaxed, shamanistic, theatre loving, unusual, vegetarian, woolly, x-citing, yin and yang, to Z as in zigzag.

BDP - Bund deutscher Pfadfinder

(Feb. 2000 they where booked solid); no firm criteria, but rather qualities: tolerance, open, living with children, assuming responsibility, communicative)

Kulturfabrik Mittelherwigsdorf

MH

Hainewalderstr. 35 | 02763 Mittelherwigsdorf

+49-(0)3583-510735 www.fabrik.readme.de

-510736

1997 7500 m² (near Zittau) ♀4 ♂5 2 11

e, g 2

everyone in common (concensus minus one) shared and individual financing

property of individual community members

cultural work

self-managed, alternative energy, ecological construction, art actions, cultural events, cinema, festivals, dance and music events, men's and women's groups

This is what we're planning in the Kulturfabrik:
We want to counteract the growing isolation in our society (almost half of all households today are single-person households) and try out new forms of communal living. We want to treat our sewage ourselves, minimise and compost waste, use our own well, and in the future we want to generate part of our own electricity. We want to use ecologically recyclable building materials. As far as possible we wish to supply our food from organic production sources or else grow it ourselves. We view ourselves as a cultural project and organise film, music and art events..

Prospective members should take time to get to know us and accept guest status, a probationary period, and open communication

Laakenhof

LA

Enningerstr. 41 | 59269 Beckum-Neubeckum
+49-(0)2525-2560

1995 — 28 ha (near Hamm) — ♀4 ♂3 3 10

g, e — all
everyone in common (consensus) — shared economy
rented/leased
vegetable growing, fruit, milk cows, cheese making, chickens, marketing
ecological, self-managed, left-wing political understanding, feminist, non-violent, organic diet, organic agriculture, organic gardening, organic farming, animal friendly husbandry

We have been running the Laakenhof as a commune according to Bioland guidelines since 1995. The farm is located 3 km outside of town, surrounded by our vegetable fields and meadows which, sadly, are divided by a high-voltage transmission line. The meadows border on a forest and there is a quarry pond behind the vegetable field where one can bathe in summer.
We keep 10 cows and process the milk into cheese in our farm dairy. We also farm 12 ha of land. 2 ha of this is for vegetables, 750 m^2 is taken up by a foil house and ¾ ha is orchard. We keep 150 hens (breeding and raising them) and 4 pigs over the summer months. We sell the products through subscription boxes and market stands. We each work independently in our own work areas. We all share the housework, e.g. we each take turns preparing our daily common lunch. Our commune is an open group of people who want to live autonomously and free of hierachies. We are committed to a just, non-violent society and would like to participate in the development of alternative approaches. We consider it important to network with other groups. The consensus principle and a shared economy are important components of our communal life. This requires constant communication and addressing other people's needs. We would like to live in a permanent commune with 10 adults + children.

Lahn-Taunus Gemeinschaft

LT

Baumgarten 1 | 35796 Elkerhausen

1977 — 1 ha (near Limburg)

e, f, sp.
everyone in common (consensus) — shared economy (shared income and capital)
Mother Earth is the property of all
gardening, making firewood
organic gardening, free love, natural health care, fasting (-hiking)

The Lahn-Taunus-Gemeinschaft has been in existence for over 20 years. People come and go, but we remain just a handful of people. Our working areas include collecting and sawing (fire)wood through muscle power, organic gardening, living

within the cycle of nature with our tree bark-compost toilet etc. New members don't have to bother with wage labour: just live and work with us. Don't worry about too much drudgery: there's plenty of fun and relaxation.
Because of bad experiences with a few particularly sloppy residents/guests, we expect a certain minimum of daily tidiness in regard to food. Perhaps we could, by arrangement, bring back a lovely tradition from the log cabin days of the 1980s: in the book "The Sisters and Brothers of Ata Are Waiting for You" the people on the imaginary island don't take food from the table themselves, but are tenderly fed by the people next to them, one after another! This way there's enough food for everyone and no one need go hungry! We have an undogmatic diet which leans toward raw fruits and vegetables, plus wild herbs (in the spirit of Franz Konz), and in the winter we occasionally eat something warm, too.
Finally, we've got the vague idea of buying a (motor) sailing yacht (maybe we'll rent one first). Co-buyers or people with sailing experience: get moving! Closer is the dream to buy an island. Region still to be agreed over.

→ See also description of network "**Come Together**"
☺ tolerance and pleasure in cuddling

Land Rausch GbRmbH

LH

Dorfstr. 18/20 | 16845 Roddahn
☎ +49-(0)33973-80929 landrausch.hof@web.de
-80930

1992 | 0.7 ha (near Rathenow/Neuruppin) | ♀2 ♂4 | 4 | 10

g, e, f, sp. | 5
everyone in common (consensus) | shared income
common property
ecological building, psychotherapy, education, cinema, conference centre, organic gardening, ecological waste water technology
ecological, self-managed, organic diet, adult education, free school, seminar-house, Gestalt therapy, self-sufficiency, organic gardening, alternative energy, ecological construction, cinema, local politics

☺

We are a colourful assortment of currently six adults and four children aged from five to forty-eight years. Aside from the desire to live in the country, we are united by the wish to develop and experiment with communal living and working perspectives. Our skills and interests are varied: clay construction, solar energy, educational work, cultural activities, cinema, psychotherapy, gardening, juice-press, landscape planning, ecological building, and sheep rearing.
Now that we've finished our first building phase, we are currently developing our professional perspectives: Part of our group is working on developing a "centre for environmentally-friendly building" on the farm. One member of our group is operating a psychotherapy practice, another is participating in the development of a regional newspaper. In addition, we operate a simple self-supplier house for groups. We also have a film club on the farm, providing regular film showings, and a free school in the village.

☺ probationary period

Laurentiushof Wethen

Diemelstr. 3 | 34474 Wethen/Diemelstadt
☎ +49-(0)5694-1566 | wethen@t-online.de
Fax -995433 | www.wethen.de

1959 | 9.000 m² (near Warburg / Westf.) | ♀22 ♂15 | 17 | 54

g, e, f, russ. | 2

everyone in common (consensus) | shared income

association

Christian/ecumenical, church

peace work

ecological, self-managed, non-violent, christian, ecumenical, peace-work, one-world development, social work, environmental protection, self-sufficiency, organic gardening

☺ ()

The Laurentiuskonvent is made up of a number of communities with a total of some forty members. It is one of the active communitarian movements which emerged within European Christianity after the Second World War and take effect till today. A group of currently eight adults and eight children is living on a farm in the centre of the North Hessian village of Wethen among its ca. 500 inhabitants. The structure of our everyday life is that of an extended family in which, however, the characteristics of the nuclear family are preserved. The adults work partially in their own professions outside the group, partially on the farm. The attempt to bring about an intensive group dynamic process within the house community is linked with the effort to integrate ourselves into the village. In 1984 we purchased the neighbouring property, also an old farm; a further house community of the convention has been formed there. It also offers the opportunity to receive individual guests for longer or shorter periods of time, who would like to get to know the Laurentiuskonvent and the ecumenical grassroots community in Wethen.
A neighbourhood group made up of friends and interested persons who have settled in the Wethen area over the years, the "greater Wethen group", is closely linked to the house communities. Together they see themselves as an ecumenical grassroots community. Their members are united by their readiness to dedicate themselves to social, political, and church issues in the spirit of the biblical term Shalom. An informational brochure reports on new developments from time to time.

→ See also description of network "**Church & Peace**"

Communities in the EKD

☺ Christian/ecumenical orientation

Lebens(t)raum Gemeinschaft Jahnishausen

JN

Jahnatalstraße 4a | 01594 Riesa - Jahnishausen
+49-(0)3525-529525 ltgj@gmx.de
-529525 www.ltgj.de

2001 3 ha (near Riesa) ♀13 ♂4 5 22

g, e, f 2

everyone in common (consensus) individual, limited community financing

common property

currently Nauen, later kindergarten, ecological garden, health centre with doctors/therapists, perhaps later a hospice

ecological, self-managed, non-violent, spiritual, inner growth, meditation, organic diet, vegetarian diet, adult education, seminar-house, health centre with various therapy forms in development, organic gardening, organic farming, alternative energy, workshops and studios in planning, firm for office and other services, forest and meadow kindergarten starting in autumn, tantraleft-wing political understanding

☺ ( )

Our community project is witnessing the development of a long-cherished dream(space), in which the interests of individuals and the conditions for a living, social community support one another. We are committed to new forms of communal life, of dealing with nature, technology and health. In our project, all generations live together and learn from one another.
We want to live in such a way that respect for all living things and respect for diversity and variety become genuinely lived values. Areas of trust develop in which we can encounter each other in a more authentic way. When conflicts arise, we consciously seek to clarify and resolve them. Self-responsibility, truthfulness, mutual support, empathy and an eye to the well-being of the whole community become a reality in our daily lives.

No longer a castle in the air but: Lebens(t)raumJahnishausen

We also feel strongly about:

- Ecologically responsible technology
- Organic foods – an 0.6 ha organic garden supplies us with fruits and vegetables
- Healing and health – of people, the environment and nature
- Undogmatic spirituality
- Art, culture and creativity

The framework of our community is formed by the Jahnishausen manor (3.5 ha) with its historic buildings. It provides room for up to 75 persons. In order to make it the property of all community members, we have founded a co-operative.

☺ willingness to work on one's own growth; co-op investment

Lebens(t)raum Johannisthal

JT

Hartmut Glänzel | Walter-Huth-Str. - Am Rundling | 12487 Berlin
☎ +49-(0)30-681 79 85
glaenzel@t-online.de
www.lebenstraum-johannisthal.de

2004 | 7000 m² | ♀15 ♂14 | 22 | 51

- g, e, f
- all who are concerned (majority vote, aiming for consensus)
- individual financing
- Individual property and a proportional share of communal property
- none
- ecological, self-managed, non-violent, alternative energy, new technologies, ecological construction, old and young living together

☺

The (building-) community „Lebens(t)raum Johannisthal" came into existence in 2004. Most of the approximately 50 future inhabitants, who are between 1 and 63 years of age, will have moved into their flats or houses by mid 2005. These lie directly on the border of the nature reserve „Johannisthal".
However, our vision of community goes beyond the mere realization of a building project. We want to counter the typical urban isolation with a model that takes into account the fundamental human needs of individuality on the one hand and belonging to a group on the other. When moving into our living spaces, it is important to us to preserve a functioning community life while not having to do without a domain of privacy. We want to attain this through individual domains (personal flat and a small share of the garden) and through the building of a community house and a larger communally developed and animated area.
We wish for young and old to live together in tolerance of each other. We envision our community to be coined by the acceptance of different point of views and the readiness to gain and learn from one another.
We´re not fixed on a certain ideology, yet there are a few cornerstones, that have crystallized so far: no cars within the settlement, the use of alternative energy sources where possible, the use of ecologically sound materials where possible, an emphasis on healthy food, a love for the nature reserve close by and the intention to preserve it, the willingness to be politically active in local, communal proceedings.

🌐 Forum for communal living, co-housing projects in Berlin
☺ As a rule the living space is to be financed individually. Ideological prerequisite: an interest in life in community.

Lebens- und Agrarkulturelle Initiative e.V. AI

Kastanienhof | Dorfstr. 52 | 37318 Marth
☎ +49-(0)36081-60053 ✉ info@kastanienhof-marth.de
-60618 www.kastanienhof-marth.de

1994 10 ha (near Göttingen) ♀2 ♂2 6 10

g, e, f all
everyone in common (consensus) limited community financing
association, partially leased
ecological, Christian, Anthroposophic
self-sufficiency from organic farming and animal husbandry, orchard and garden, landscape care, organic building, conservation, wood collection, education, fun
ecological, self-managed, christian, anthroposophic, organic diet, adult education, occupational therapy with patients in the addiction clinic, environmental protection, self-sufficiency, organic agriculture, organic gardening, organic farming, alternative energy, ecological construction, metal workshop
☺ ()

"Sowing the future together." The Living and Agri-Cultural Initiative Kastanienhof e.V. seeks to find and realise sustainable forms of living. We are establishing an ecologically oriented farming and garden culture.
Joining the notion of progress to respect for the past, we want to link traditional crafts and simple technology with modern-day ecological awareness. The 1.5 ha

"Alex giving Berta a drink"

meadow behind the farmyard is used as grazing land for goats, a donkey, a horse and pigs. We have laid out a vegetable and herbs garden and an orchad. One of our concerns is to preserve the variety of old plant varieties and endangered breeds of farm animals. We have set up a "Fachwerk-Börse" in which used building materials can be purchased and returned and where new organic materials are sold (www.fachwerkboerse-eichsfeld.de). We have begun offering educational work in the form of seminars, school class visits and workshops. We want to network with other living and commercial communities. The farm community provides a framework for socially dedicated and supervisory tasks. An important part of our work is working with clay, wood and metal. We use these craft techniques also in the renovation of the farm. We are aware of our responsibility towards energy and raw materials as life creating and life limiting products of nature. This is why we strive for closed energy and material cycles. The farm's gate opens onto the centre of the village - a symbol for our concern to integrate our farm project into the life of Marth.

→ see also description of network "**Come Together**"

Darmstädter Liste

☺ orientation period, immediate participation in common purse, self-initiative e.g. in developing an area of activity

Lebensform Gemeinschaft

LG

Marita Bergmann und Heidi Gehring | Pappelweg 3 | 19217 Carlow

☎ +49-(0)38873-20969, -20770 b-g-seminare@t-online.de

-20948

1998 | 2 ha (near Lübeck) | ♀9 ♂7 6 22

g, e, f | 2

everyone in common (consensus) | limited community financing and individual

property of individual community members

therapists, teachers, group leaders, artists, musicians

self-managed, non-violent, inner growth, yoga, therapy: single and couple work, self-awareness groups, Reiki, firewalking; sports: TAI CHI; art: painting etc.; media: computer und recording studio

☺

We are a group of people who have come together as the result of a long and intensive process of self-awareness, during which we sensed a profound desire to form a community. We discovered, financed and built this project by ourselves. There are families, couples and individuals who live in their own separate residential unit. We have both private and common garden areas and rooms.

We meet regularly every two weeks in the common room. As needed, we communicate with each other, exchange views and experiences, clarify relationships and organisational things, or meditate, dance and sing together. To us the following are important: individual freedom, recognition and respect for individuals, as well as togetherness in love and relationships.

☺ willing to contribute, communicate, clarify; openness

Lebensgarten Steyerberg

ST

Ginsterweg 3 | 31595 Steyerberg
+49-(0)5764-2370 lebensgarten@gmx.de
-2578 www.lebensgarten.de

1985 | 4 ha (near Nienburg/ Weser) | ♀48 ♂28 | 33 | 109

e, sp., f, dutch, port., dan., swed., gaelic — 30
everyone in common (limited consensus) — individual financing
2/3 rented / leased, 1/3 common property
none
seminars, building/handicraft, various therapies and natural health care
ecological, self-managed, non-violent, spiritual, ecumenical, buddhist, esoteric/ New Age, inner growth, meditation, vegetarian diet, adult education, seminar-house, peace-work, alternative energy, ecological construction, mediation, therapies: non-traditional medicine (homeopathy, TCM, acidosis therapy according to Collier), psychotherapy, occupational therapy, family constellation, bonding therapy

☺

The Lebensgarten Steyerberg e.V. non-profit association was founded 18 years ago. The row house estate in which we live was built for armament workers in 1938. Our central themes are: tolerance and respect in our dealings with ourselves, our fellow human beings and nature, ecology in everyday life, mutual support and common decision-making processes. We live our spirituality in common on a daily basis (meditation, singing in the chapel, circle dances), we maintain neighbourly contacts and fashion our everyday life, special life phases and leisure time in common. There is a great deal which we share and just as much which distinguishes us. Community and individual growth crises bring us closer together and drive home our own responsibility. We don't have a guru. We try to make our decisions according to the consensus principle. Members can decide for themselves how they want to work on the association's tasks and goals. Our seminar enterprise passes on our own experiences and those of the seminar leaders with whom we are affiliated and also brings us some jobs. Beyond that, there is the school for understanding and mediation, natural healthcare surgeries, physical therapy and psychotherapy, a book shop, a shop for ecological construction materials, an ecological architectural and planning office, and also freelance artists and musicians. The Lebensgarten seeks to be a place which moves its residents and guests to face themselves and inspires them to join together with others.

→ see also description of networks "**GEN**" and "**Come Together**"

☺ Spend some time here several times beforehand! You have to arrange your accommodation and work yourself (we can give you some tips!) since we don't have a shared economy and our flats are largely rented out.

Lebensgemeinschaft Woldhof

WO

Woldweg 9 | 26160 Bad Zwischenahn
☎ +49-(0)441-6919908, -69001
Fax -6919908

1993 | 2 ha (near Oldenburg) | ♀2 ♂5 1 8

none

everyone in common (consensus) | limited community financing and individual

common property

ecological, non-violent, vegetarian diet

☺

After a time in which we dug a little too deep into the magician's bag of socio-ecological/spiritually dedicated communitarianism, we've reindividualised ourselves to some extent. Today, as an eight-member, occasionally fluctuating crew, we're living the charm of a relaxed and restful flat-sharing community largely free of image-based and ideological narrow-mindedness, in which a wide range of life goals, life situations, ages and temperaments co-exist and inspire one another, thriving on those nice little enriching encounters in-between. Ecological/social and self-awareness oriented thoughts live on in spite of all this at an elevated density, if no longer as a collectively self-value elevating billboard promising to cure all the world's ills on the basis of our example.
We are basically open for new recruits who can enrich our spiritual spectrum here, in fact we sometimes long for them, but that always depends a lot on our currently limited living space potential. But for nice guests we've nearly always got some to spare.
Otherwise, we live in the countryside and in genuinely pastoral surroundings in biking distance from the socially very worthwhile and appealing university town of Oldenburg (30 minutes to the city centre, 20 minutes to the university), although when the wind blows the wrong way we're in listening distance of the Autobahn.

☺ sympathy, openness to the world, wisdom

LebensGut Lübnitz e.V.

LZ

Dorfstr. 5 | 14806 Lübnitz
☎+49-(0)33841-388110 lgl@veb-leben.de
-388114 lebensgutluebnitz.dyndns.org

2002 18 ha (near Belzig) ♀8 ♂8 7 23

- sp., e, f
- everyone in common (consensus)
- limited common financing, partially common till — common property
- commitment to the issues of recognition, self-resonsibility, conflict resolution, integrity, cosensitivity
- building/remodelling, farming, food processing, creativity, energy
- ecological, self-managed, non-violent, inner growth, organic diet, adult education, free school, environmental protection, self-sufficiency, organic agriculture, organic gardening, organic farming, alternative energy, new technologies, ecological construction, handicraft: cabinetmaking, pottery, media: graphics and film

☺

We at LebensGut Lübnitz are a community under construction. In May of 2002 we bought an old estate which we are gradually renovating with the goal of developing a residential and work project. It is our intention to live together in order to highlight living alternatives. These include our "Demeter" vegetable-growing enterprise, which we are currently safeguarding by founding a CSA (community supported agriculture), and the development of an energy project using replaceable raw materials. We have a Free School on the Montessori model since 2002. Our 18 ha grounds encompass several residential and commercial buildings, barns that can be renovated, a park and fields. We want to live here together with up to 80 people who will in turn be organised, clanlike, into smaller social groups. We would be particularly pleased if the people who live here also could be employed here. For this purpose we are developing a variety of opportunities. Alongside farming and energy production there are craft opportunities (a large workshop) and the large seminar enterprise. In our area, the Fläming, the many other communities that have been founded nearby provide considerable potential for alternative offerings.
We welcome interested persons at our guest weekends. In exchange for room and board they can take part in our daily life or attend our work camps. (Photo: see "Come Together Network").

☺ approx. 6-month probationary residence, then a Yes from all and a Yes to all; 7,000 Euro credit

Lebensgut Pommritz

PR

Pommritz Nr. 1 | 02627 Hochkirch
☎ +49-(0)35939-81385
www.lebensgut.de
-83085

1993 | 70 ha (near Dresden) | ♀14 ♂12 | 16 | 42

g, e

everyone in common (consensus, majority vote) | limited community financing

everyone/individual members

educational work, organic farming, household, children, research

ecological, self-managed, non-violent, inner growth, meditation, yoga, tantra, free love, organic diet, adult education, seminar-house, environmental protection, self-sufficiency, permaculture, organic agriculture, organic gardening, organic farming, animal friendly husbandry, ecological construction, handicraft, art, humour

☺ ( )

Our human-ecological adventure has been alive and well since 1993 on a giant estate on approx. 70 ha of eastern Saxony's most fertile land. The idea came from Rudolf Bahro, the Free State of Saxony provided the real estate, and the living reality gradually grew from what started out as a small group of courageous people. Since then we have not only survived but have also experienced countless fulfilling moments of genuine living. Despite more than one critical moment, we have succeeded in withstanding and developing the whole gamut of physical and intellectual work as well as romanticism and modernism. We continue to maintain diversified ecological farming for self-sufficiency and regional distribution, a few craftspeople and planners, an educational and research centre with a learning workshop for philosophy and ethics, plenty of children and much more. Our project, which largely developed out of East German movements, is primarily concerned with human freedom. Whether a vegan or regional diet, lifelong marriage or free love, private or communal kitchens, the Church, yoga or ecology – we try to avoid ideologies and dogmas of any kind while remaining open to the varied experiences of human growth. On the first Saturday of every month we have an open house for the curious, and for those who are interested our large buildings have always provided room for new members. Our motto is: "Come out into the open, friend" (Hölderlin).

→ See also description of network "**Come Together**"
☺ good chemistry, probationary period, loan of 2,000.- Euros

Lebenshof Siboling

SI

Jörg und Julia Backsen | Siboling 2 | 83341 Kienberg
☎ +49-(0)8628-986985 ✉ e-mail@lebenshaus-im-chiemgau.de
Fax -986985

1998 | 11 ha (near Traunstein) | ♀2 ♂2 children 4 total 8

g, e | 3

one part of the group (consensus) | limited community financing

property of individual community members

Christian

organic farming and gardening, life assistance

ecological, self-managed, christian, ecumenical, organic diet, social work cf. Lebenshäuser, animal protection, environmental protection, organic agriculture, organic gardening, organic farming, animal friendly husbandry, alternative energy

☺

We live on a farm in a rural area and practice organic farming as a secondary occupation: cows, grain and gardening. We have lots of animals around us (chickens, geese, ducks, turkeys, pigs, cats, rabbits, a horse and a donkey). We have a bakery. The house is large and is full of possibilities. We are currently restoring the land in our care with a small stream and with hedges and fruit trees.
The nucleus of our community is represented by the family with 4 children (including one foster child). This "nucleus" could be expanded. We are open to people who, for whatever reason, need a community's support during a difficult phase of their lives. As a LEBENSHAUS of the LEBENSHAUS IM CHIEMGAU association (see entry in "Networks"), we can accept up to 3 persons. They live in their own room, can participate in our common meals and, if necessary, can find open-minded partners for a discussion aimed at supporting them on their path to an independent life. We have a Christian orientation and our community's guidelines are: love of God, of our fellow human beings and of nature.

Lebenshäuser, Lebenshaus im Chiemgau e.V.
☺ Christian orientation

Miravillage-Zentrum

MZ

Danzigerstr. 1 | 82131 Gauting
☎ +49-(0)89-850-8751 ✉ miravillage@mirapuri-enterprises.com
Fax -9178 www.mirapuri-enterprises.com

1970 | 1000 m² | ♀13 ♂11 children 7 total 31

g, e, it., f | 25

shared income | association

free spirit, understanding of the world as a unity of spirit and material
various professions
ecological, self-managed, anarchistic, feminist, non-violent, spiritual, chaotic, inner growth, meditation, yoga, tantra, sexuality, free love, organic diet, vegetarian diet, adult education, pedagogical, free school, seminar-house, peace-work, health and New Age seminars, animal protection, environmental protection, self-sufficiency, new technologies, various crafts, health training, various media, humour etc.

☺ ( )

Mirapuri in Italy as well as its first satellite, Miravillage in Germany, have been created for people who like Sri Aurobindo and Mira Alfassa, their ideals of human unity and spiritual consciousness progress. Mirapuri and Miravillage are environments where people can live together and work together to realise these ideals. Everyone of goodwill who likes Sri Aurobindo and Mira Alfassa and their ideals can join Mirapuri and Miravillage. There are no financial or other material obligations. If you want to live in Mirapuri or Miravillage you can do so on a private or contributing basis. That means you may buy your own house or apartment which is your property, or else you may contribute financially to the growth of the general Mirapuri property. In this case, Mirapuri and Miravillage provide accomodation and services for you during your lifetime at Mirapuri or Miravillage and the property belongs to Mirapuri or Miravillage and its future development.
Everyone works and learns on a free and independent basis. The growth and respect of individuality are understood as the basis and flowering of real communal life.
There is no institutional spiritual authority. Each individual follows his/her own spiritual evolution according to his/her aspiration and inclination.

☺ Knowledge of Sri Aurobindo and Mira Alfassa and their integral yoga, as well as good will and genuine co-operation

Mutter-Erde-Gemeinschaft

ME

Holperstr.1 | 57537 Forst-Seifen
+49-(0)2742-8251
-8251

1983 | 1 ha (near Bonn) | ♀8 ♂3 3 14

g | none
one person
individual financing | rented/leased
humanistic
spiritual orientation, care of the houses and gardens, office work, seminar activity
spiritual, vegetarian diet, adult education, pedagogical, free school, peace-work, animal protection, organic gardening

☺ ( )

The Mutter-Erde-Initiative (Mother Earth Initiative) is built on a humanistic-Christian basis and encompasses the following focal points: respect for and maintenance of the foundations of our physical existence (water, earth, air), respect for all Creation (abolition of animal experiments and the keeping of animals for slaughter), optimal education for children and youths (comprehensive general education as well as solid vocational training, our own school and/or private home schooling on a high level), maintaining the family unit (ideally a trans-generational, meaningful integration of old people), love of the Creator and his Creation. The Mutter-Erde-Gemeinschaft in Forst-Seifen has been administered by Sigrid Beckmann-Lamb since its founding in 1983. Forst-Seifen is located in the idyllic Holperbach Valley in the Betzdorf, Waldbröl and Hamm/Sieg triangle. The initiative is open to all those who wish to preserve this beautiful world and ease the suffering of others.

☺ veneration and love of the Divine and of Creation

Netzwerk Anders Leben Soest

SO

Pollhofstr. 5 | 59494 Soest

☎ +49-(0)2921-341001 — info@soestprojekt.de

-33645 — www.soestprojekt.de

1996 — 3 x 100 m² — ♀10 ♂8 3 21

g, e, it., sp. — 50%

everyone in common (consensus) — depends on flat-sharing community

rented/leased

ecological farming, organic foods shop, organic catering, architectural office, political youth work, free software

ecological, self-managed, left-wing political understanding, non-violent, organic diet, adult education, environmental protection, self-sufficiency, organic agriculture, ecological construction, humour, free software (Linux), nonviolent communication

☺

The "Anders Leben Soest" ("Living differently in Soest") network is made up of people, businesses, lifestyles and political and cultural initiatives. Our active exchange between the individual projects has led to the creation of a living network. Our goals are: creating autonomous, self-determined habitats, creatively networking them and thereby transforming and enriching society as a whole; playing a social and political role; finding new members to share our goals and ideals.
We seek to conserve resources (e.g. transportation, energy, consumption, nutrition). The network's members desire a peaceful, non-hierarchical, self-determined and open relationship. We help each other, e.g. in word and deed, financially and in joint actions.
Our network creates structures to enable communication between members.
We are not a closed network. Interested persons are welcome to get acquainted with the network and its participants. Further information is available on our website and flyers.

Here are the network's members:
WG St. Pauli +49-(0)2921-910610 | Poller-WG +49-(0)2921-341001 | Stefan Förster, Jana Kunze +49-(0)2921-3446443 | Lebensgarten (organic foods shop) +49-(0)2921-33654 | Macamato (eco-catering service) +49-(0)2921-672106

Noyana Gemeinschaft

NE

Schmerwitz 12 | 14827 Wiesenburg
+49-(0)33849-90855
-90856
mail@noyana.de
www.noyana.de

1998 | 850 m² (near Belzig) | ♀7 ♂4 | 4 | 15

g, e, f, roman., sp. | 8

everyone in common (consensus/majority) | limited community financing

rented/leased

non-dogmatically spiritual, hedonistic

Tantra seminars, coaching, food production, body work, massage, healing work, working with children, yoga

ecological, self-managed, spiritual, inner growth, meditation, yoga, tantra, sexuality, free love, organic diet, adult education, pedagogical, free school, various therapy forms, animal protection, environmental protection, self-sufficiency, sports, art, seasonal festivals, alternative economy

☺

We are a community of 11 adults and 4 children. Our main focus is on the inner growth of the individual, our mutual communication, on love and eroticism. We are striving to create a communal life which can serve as a model for other people and which entails a minimum of ideology and bureaucracy. In 2002 we moved from the Rhineland to the Fläming, near Berlin, and are on the lookout for a spacious property where we can further realise our dreams in material terms. We view ourselves as part of a regional network of interesting people and projects.
We meet once a week in our common forum. It is a kind of group-psychological communication form designed to create trust and openness. The men and the women also meet once a week, and one of the groups takes care of the children. Then there are irregular artistic actions, matinees, palavers and fun evenings. Four times a year we join together in an extra community event for 5 days.
We are in the process of creating new working opportunities in which we can develop ourselves. In the spirit of love, partnership and communal life we are seeking new paths, but always combining emotion and reason! All in all, we want to create a good life filled with joy and pleasure for ourselves and others, and we've come along way on this path.

Noyana, Netzwerk Fläming

☺ cheerful, tolerant people who want to develop themselves further. Desire for communication, psychological stability

Ökodorf Sieben Linden

38486 Poppau (Bandau)
+49-(0)39000-51235 verein@oekodorf7linden.de
-51232 www.oekodorf7linden.de

1993 44 ha (near Salzwedel, S.-Anh.) ♀28 ♂27 15 70

d, e, f, it., sp. all but 5

everyone in common (differentiated consensus model)

limited common financing/shared for subgroups

co-operative = common property

holistic, social-ecological

self-administration and self-sufficiency, communal culture, ecological building, seminars, care of guests, public relations

ecological, self-managed, anarchistic, left-wing political understanding, non-violent, spiritual, inner growth, meditation, yoga, deep ecology, organic diet, vegetarian diet, vegan diet, adult education, free school, seminar-house, peace-work, therapies (ShinTai, homeopathy, Chi Gong...), self-sufficiency, permaculture, organic agriculture, organic gardening, work horses, forestry, alternative energy, new technologies, ecological construction, straw bale building, various handicrafts, music, choire, ArtDepot

☺

In 1997 we founded a socially and ecologically oriented settlement, an "ecovillage", where eventually 300 people could live. The village represents a holistic habitat which closely integrates and harmonises different areas of life so that a positive human and ecological net balance and mutual resonance can develop.

We want to be an open and hospitable village, inspired by a communal culture where, within an ecological and self-organisational framework, a variety of lifestyles and convictions can become possible. We are striving for overall self-sufficiency in all areas of life: from nutrition, building and energy all the way to our own social, medical, educational and cultural activities. We are organising ourselves as a village community made up of smaller living communities, which exist alongside one another in a co-operative fashion in the form of a number of "neigh-

bourhoods" with a variety of life concepts (see also the →"Club99" community). We seek social and cultural exchanges with our surroundings. Together with other projects and movements we are working on the development of a societal alternative: through our own example we are demonstrating that a (more) sustainable life is possible. We criticise social deformations, point to alternatives and participate in practical acts of resistance (against Castor transports, turkey farming, the Iraq War). Until 1999 we were mainly concerned with building up communal facilities and infrastructure. We bought a large house for some 15 residents in the village of Poppau, located 1 km away. In 2000 the first two residential houses for 20 occupants were completed, followed by the first approved straw bale residential house in Germany and a wood workshop. We have just finished constructing a 3-storey strawbale-house for 18 inhabitants.

→ see also description of networks "**GEN**" and "**Come Together**"

🌍 Holon, Attac, Aufbruch „Anders besser leben"

☺ acceptance of our "vision of a holistic village", admittance to the co-operative and financial participation

ÖkoLeA

Hohensteiner Weg 3 | 15345 Klosterdorf
☎ +49-(0)3341-359390 — info@oekolea.de
Fax -309998 — www.oekolea.de

1990 — ca. 1 ha (near Strausberg) — ♀8 ♂6 — 7 — 21

- g, e, f, sp. — 9
- everyone in common (consensus) — 50% of personal income to common till
- common property
- non-dogmatically leftist
- gardening, education, household, construction
- ecological, self-managed, non-violent, organic diet, adult education, seminar-house, self-sufficiency, permaculture, organic gardening, alternative energy, new technologies, ecological construction, bakery, bookbinding (as training), art courses in training programme

☺ (✋✋)

The Ecological Living and Working Community (ÖkoLeA for short) has been in existence since the summer of 1990. We have developed a project on the outskirts of Berlin in which people live and work on a self-determined basis within a framework of ecological and social responsibility. In 1993 we bought a farm in Brandenburg which we have been restoring and expanding in an ecologically responsible manner ever since. We have a common household, cultivate an organic/educational garden and operate an educational facility, the ÖkoLeA-Bildungswerk. We have also founded the wood oven bakery "Klosterdorf Dragon Bread" as an independent commercial enterprise. The goals and rules of our community include consensus decision-making, communal property, the dismantling of patriarchal/hierarchical behaviour, a shared economy and a communal life with children.
Our group is fairly diverse, for example our ages vary from 4 to 73. We have very different professions and interests. Some of us work on the farm, other outside it. As a group we have no particular ideological or spiritual orientation, but individual members are interested in feminism, spirituality, anthroposophy, health and therapeutic work, ecological building methods, political work, Aikido, etc. We would like to grow as a commune, but interested persons must live in the trailers first. Guests who are willing to work with us in exchange for room and board are welcome to take part in our annual "encounter week" (dates available on request).

→ see also description of network "**Come Together**"
- Kommuja, Arbeitskreis Umweltbildung (workgroup environmental education) and other regional networks
- ☺ we will be happy to send a letter to interested persons

Osho Manjusha

OM

Meditations Zentrum und Kommune | Niederpöbel 27 | 01762 Schmiedeberg
☎ +49-(0)35052-224-56 info@oshomanjusha.de
-57 www.oshomanjusha.de

1986 3 ha (near Dresden) ♀20 ♂12 3 35

g, e
everyone in common (consensus) limited common financing and individual
common property
Osho movement
everyday tasks, care/construction of centre, outside work
self-managed, non-violent, leader/guru, inner growth, meditation, vegetarian diet and non-vegetarian, creativity in music, dance, performance etc., festivals and workshops, therapy: trauma work (sexual abuse), transformation and healing work; ecological construction, construction, art: photography; year-round holiday programme and guest service

The Manjusha is a place of encounter – with Osho and with oneself. Since its founding in 1987, it has passed through a number of stages both at home and abroad. Surrounded by living nature – forests, romantic stream beds, open mountain meadows and lakes – the Manjusha is located in the eastern Erz Mountains conservation area. The natural vegetation and the ancient trees of the large centre grounds on the hillside make one feel and see the energy of the Erz Mountains.
The meditation centre is a place for living and is being renovated both on the inside and the outside. Since our move to Schmiedeberg in 1999 and with our constant growth since, the centre is reorganising itself with an expanded programme for events and holiday stays. The commune has become a registered association and a co-op takes care of issues relating to living and building. We are particularly proud of the large new meditation hall. Living in a spiritual commune is a unique adventure. Like in a big family, their is always something happening. It is a pleasure for those who love it, and a challenge to those who still want to learn about it. Our resources multiply in our daily communal life – when the interaction works. Particularly in this Buddha field, whose fine-particular transformational energy constantly reshuffles established structures and rules, but we still can't do without them. It's obvious that we are all united by our

shared spiritual and healing path, enjoying profound mutual understanding and support. All communards share in our working life, depending on their abilities and possibilities. Around half of us work outside the centre, the others work in construction, in the office, in housekeeping. We live, work, learn, meditate or remain silent alone and together - the whole arc of life.

☺ financial independence, decision for consciousness work, meditation, communal life, no drugs

Pretschener Gemeinschaften

PG

Jörg Schenck | Am Landgut 6 | 15913 Märkische Heide OT Pretschen
+49-(0)35476 - 65 90 80
mail@gemeinsam-leben-und-arbeiten.de; joergschenck@web.de
www.gemeinsam-leben-und-arbeiten.de; www.pretschener-gemeinschaften.de

2005 | 20,000 m² (+50 ha, near Lübben) | ♀5 ♂6 | 6 | 17

g, dutch, e, s, isl., russ. | 9

all who are concerned (consensus)

coregroup: shared economy, others: indiv. financ. | property of all

Anthroposophy, Buddhism, Osho, Sufism, christian outlook on life

org. dyn. agriculture and animal husbandry, farm-school, school-seminars, ecological building, Rudolf-Steiner-kindergarten, Rudolf-Steiner-school, care of children and youths.

ecological, self-managed, spiritual, christian, anthroposophic, inner growth, organic diet, adult education, pedagogical, free school, environmental protection, self-sufficiency, alternative energy, humour, carpentry, art

☺ ()

Living and working. We have to admit that to keep the balance between the two is not easy in our newly started community-project.
We are in the process of renovating our community house and setting up our areas of work. Besides this, the redevelopment of the other houses needs to be planned and on top of that we also want to earn an income with what we do.
We confess that it´s not easy, but, like the Brandenburger sun, good spirits and fun are durable here.
We, a group of singles, single parents and families with children, still have more room for people with good moods and a pioneering spirit.
We want to become self-sufficient and live by our developing school-farm. Also, we are in the planning stages of a Rudolf-Steiner-school with the special character of being on a farm. The „Bauhütte" is still a small hut and the first animals have arrived.
We are building in an ecologically sound way with wood- and solar heating systems, we are farming according to bio-dynamic principles and are trying out permacultural principles. Our main field of work is with young people.
We own 3 buildings from the sixties in an own settlement a little way out of the village with about 3,000 m² of usable area, about 20,000 m² of floor space and, if

required, about 50 ha of land open to development in the coming years, belonging to our Demeter farming neigbours.

→ See also description of network "**Come Together**"

healing pedagogy and social therapy, Demeter-farming, german „Paritätischer Wohlfahrtsverband", Come-Together

☺ A readiness to live and work with children and youth and a deep interest in a spiritual life. A time of probation is needed.

Projekt Reetz

RE

Mahlsdorfer Str. 12 | 14827 Reetz
+49-(0)33849-51915
-51822

1996 — 3,500 m² (near Belzig) — ♀4 ♂4 4 12

g, e — 4

everyone in common

individual financing — property of individual community members

financial consultation, Tantra, Shinson Hapkido Schule (martial arts), new medicine (healing)

ecological, self-managed, non-violent, spiritual, inner growth, tantra, free love, organic gardening, alternative energy, new technologies, Shinson Hapkido school, art (because it's fun), healing - New Medicine

☺

Our common life is aimed at striking a balance between community and individuality. We each enjoy wide personal freedom and are entirely responsible for ourselves. Promoting everyone's interests whilst keeping with our abilities and needs in the spirit of mutual friendship and support is our common concern.
When conflicts cannot be solved alone or face-to-face, we seek to resolve them in common. Mutual understanding and empathy develop through clear, direct communication, looking and listening.
The focal points of our work are: the research and development of alternative, innovative technologies; propagation of the "New Medicine" as developed by Dr. Ryke Geerd Hamer; Tantra, body work and massage; Shinson – Hap-Ki-Do (martial arts); intellectual research and communication; the healthy cohabitation of adults and children; developing and expanding our farm.

networking in the Hoher Fläming region

☺ it's wonderful when people contribute their own experiences to our communal life

Projekt Regenwurm

RW

Rossendorf 27 | 90556 Cadolzburg

projekt.regenwurm@web.de
www.pror.de

2003 | 7 m² | ♀1 ♂1 | 2

g, e, project-internal combi-communication — 2

everyone in common (consensus) — limited community financing

property of individual community members

travel, research, gardening, ecological building, food production/processing/utilisation, education, healing, social services, house and tents, feeding earthworms, networking

ecological, self-managed, anarchistic, non-violent, spiritual, inner growth, meditation, yoga, organic diet, vegan diet oriented, adult education, peace-work, therapy: ourselves first, animal protection, environmental protection, self-sufficiency, permaculture, organic agriculture, organic gardening, animal friendly husbandry, alternative energy, new technologies, ecological construction, biking, Internet

☺ ( )

We are earthwormy [Regenwurm meens earthworm] idealists who not only love to grub around in the earth below but who also seek and find the boundless heavens above. On our voyages of discovery we soar over water and land to explore sustainable lifestyles around the world. We make contacts, expand our horizons, hone our skills, acquaint ourselves with useful techniques and above all with ourselves. In 2012 we want to found a settlement somewhere in Central Europe (definitely in Central Europe!) which will eventually develop into an eco-social healing village with several hundred inhabitants. We aren't exactly "New Agers", but we are open to anything as long as it's spiritual, creative, artistic, philosophical, playful, eccentric ... Nevertheless, we're going to work hard (but joyfully, we hope) to realise our bold ideas. We don't want to bemoan scarcity as a disadvantage, but rather use it as an evolutionary impulse. In 2012 we'll be needing 7-14 energetic people who, after careful preparation, want to manifest everybody what is our motivation for travelling around the world, working and learning. Is there a bit of the earthworm dream paired with thirst for action wriggling around in you somewhere too? Then come followus here and there!

Regenwurm-Netzwerk
☺ shared probationary period

Projektzentrum Maibacher Schweiz

MS

Hauptstraße 12 | 35510 Maibach
+49-(0)6081-443337
-443338

2003 | 2,200 m² (near Butzbach) | ♀3 ♂2 5 10

g, e, f, sp. | 2-4

everyone in common (majority vote, consensus)
limited common financing and individual
property of individual community members
seminars, courses, caring for cancer patients
ecological, self-managed, non-violent, spiritual, inner growth, meditation, yoga, vegetarian diet, seminar-house, caring for a difficult young person, alternative cancer therapy, Budwig diet, organic gardening in planning, theatre, Ayurveda, non-smokers

☺

We are a community under construction, with 3 families at the moment, who run a seminar centre together. Our project is based in a former country inn/hotel in a beautiful little town in the Taunus, approx. 45 km north of Frankfurt. The 1,500 m² of useable space provide us with many development possibilities.
The Maibach community project serves people of various age levels as a fulfilling residential, living and working space founded on the following goals:
Social/pedagogical: Setting up a protected environment for socially disadvantaged children, for young people in co-operation with the Outlaw/Greven association, and, of course, with our own children.
We provide mutual support in a human, family atmosphere as well as spiritual and material growth through inspiration and coaching. Cultural: Creating an environment which consciously integrates artistic, creative elements into daily life and which thus provides a meaningful life incorporating all human potentials. We have theatre performances and offer theatre courses.
Ecological: Environmentally friendly lifestyle through environmentally compatible waste disposal and growing organic vegetables for self-sufficiency.
Economic/material: A seminar business geared toward reinvesting in the project and which creates jobs for the community.
Health: Vegetarian, Vedic diet, meditation and yoga, smoke-free, low drug intake. Offering alternative care for cancer patients with a Budwig diet in co-operation with the "People Against Cancer" organisation.
Size: Our size goal is 10 adults plus children.
Guests are sincerely welcome; room and board in exchange for co-operation is possible by previous arrangement.

→ see also description of network "**Soshona Freundeskreis**"
ZEGG Freundeskreise
☺ work weekend, financially independent

Simhacalam Academy

IJ

ISKCON: Nava Jiyada Nrsimha Ksetra | Zielberg 20 | 94118 Jandelsbrunn
+49-(0)8583-316
-1671

1979 | 20 ha (near Waldkirchen/Passau) | ♀4 ♂8 2 14

g, e, hindi, poln., czech., hung. — 2

one part of the group (majority vote) — membership fees

property of individual community members

we belong to ISKCON

organising seminars/festivals, caring for animals, janitorial work, missionary activity, spiritual: daily (morning and evening) liturgy, singing, dancing, lectures, music, meditation

ecological, self-managed, non-violent, hierarchical, leader/guru, spiritual, inner growth, meditation, yoga, organic diet, vegetarian diet, adult education, seminar-house, peace-work, animal protection (particularly cows), environmental protection, self-sufficiency, permaculture, organic agriculture, organic gardening, organic farming, animal friendly husbandry, alternative energy, art: Indian Bhajan music, Kirtans; singing, dancing; traditional ceremonies for marriage, birth etc.

☺

We are a relatively small but very joyful commune of people who are making an earnest effort to live a modest and simple life with God at its centre. In doing so we primarily orient ourselves on the Bhagavad-Gita and the teachings of A.C. Bhaktivedanta Swami Prabhupada, the founder of ISKCON ("International Society for Krishna Consciousness"), our umbrella organisation.
Although the project was originally conceived as a monastery for Krishna monks and nuns, in recent years it has developed in such a way that all members of the commune started families and, for lack of income opportunities, migrated to the cities. This decline in our numbers presented us with new challenges in discovering how to continue to realise our ideal of a self-sufficient life. We urgently need a real farmer to take care of our fields and the cows. Our soil is very pure and fertile since it has been cultivated without chemicals for over 20 years. We also desperately need an enthusiastic caretaker. We would provide him with free room and board. Our project is now called "Simhacalam Academy" instead of its earlier name, "Nava Jiyada Nrsimha Ksetra", since we now want to transmit our extensive knowledge (Bhagavad-gita, reincarnation, Ayurveda, astrology ...) to others in seminars for the good of all people. This includes our popular Saturday "tasting programme" for our guests, complete with Bhajans, lectures and a vegetarian banquet.

→ see also description of network "**ISKCON**"

☺ vegetarian, non-smoker, no drug/medication dependency, no mentally disabled; adaptable, upright, spiritually interested

Sonnenhof

NN

Heidrun Hirt | Dedelstorfer Allee 6A | 29386 Dedelstorf
+49-(0)5832-979775 megapin.52@web.de, juliacoelho@web.de

2003 180 ha (near Hankenbüttel)

e, f

everyone in common (consensus) sales negotiations

construction, repair, garden, computing, marketing, social work, home economics

ecological, self-managed, non-violent, spiritual, inner growth, free love, organic diet, vegetarian diet, adult education, pedagogical, seminar-house, peace-work, social work: teaching workshops, holistic health approaches; animal protection, environmental protection, self-sufficiency, permaculture, organic agriculture, organic gardening, forestry, alternative energy, new technologies, ecological construction, construction, handicraft, media: information centre, networking; project: integrated energy farm

We are a community in the founding phase, i.e. we're waiting to be given title to the land. As soon as we have the grounds in Dedelsdorf, we want to start off with around 100 people. Collaborators are always heartily welcome since we've got room for several hundred people. The residential area itself is around 40 ha. The buildings are in good condition (last renovated in 1992) and can be moved into at once (former garrison).
We are looking for people of every age and with different skills. There is work in both construction and in gardening/farming. Therapists and computer/marketing people are welcome. We are open to all nationalities, religions and faiths. We want to live together in mutual respect and in respect for nature and its living beings for the good of all and everything.
In our village community there is room for businesses and service providers in the eco New Age field. The realisation of our "Integrated Energy Farm" still demands engineers and colleagues who think holistically. Our main concern is to live self-sufficiently and sustainably.

☺ 6-month probationary period, community decision, energy balancing in the form of money or labour

Sozietät Herrnhaag

HH

Ökumenische Lebensgemeinschaft der Brüdergemeinde |
63654 Büdingen-Lorbach
+49-(0)6042-9799-0 sozietaet@herrnhaag.de
-12

1982 2,000 m² (near Büdingen) ♀2 ♂2 2 6

g, e 1

everyone in common (consensus) limited community financing

rented/leased

ecumenical

open house for people in various life situations

christian

☺ ( )

Sozietät Herrenhaag is a partnership of Christians from different backgrounds. It is especially linked to the Herrnhuter Brethren. The house is lived in by families and singles who organise their communal daily lives on a foundation of Christian faith and who practice a peaceable co-existence with their respective peculiarities, viewpoints and traditions. Right now four adults and two children form the permanent house community, and three families reinforce the group as external members.
The Sozietät keeps its house open to guests. The invitation to participate in the Sozietät's daily life is addressed to people who find pleasure in a communal life and/or who seek help and orientation for the management of their own lives. Guests who take advantage of the Sozietät's offer for a mutually pre-determined period of time are considered to be responsible members of the house community and are expected to contribute their own abilities. Several times each year we organise working weekends for wood gathering, fruit harvesting and construction work.

☺ must be Christians

SSK - Sozialistische Selbsthilfe Köln

SY

Salierring 37 | 51063 Köln
+49-(0)221-213175 ssk_salierring@web.de
-249325 www.sozialistischeselbsthilfe.de

1997 250 m² ♀3 ♂9 1 13

everyone in common (consensus) shared income

rented/leased

collecting, refurbishing, selling used furniture, second-hand items, clothing etc.

ecological, self-managed, left-wing political understanding, chaotic, vegetarian diet, vegan diet, social work: migration work; alternative energy

☺ (hands)

The SSK Sozialistische Selbsthilfe Köln ("Socialist Self-Help of Cologne") is a living and working community in which people of various classes and age groups have joined together and where they finance their living expenses and their political work through the sale of used furniture, second-hand articles etc.
Each SSK member is paid the same amount of money and at regular meetings the daily work is distributed, the financial details of the common purse are discussed and whatever problems have cropped up in the meantime are ironed out. A year and a half ago we expanded our sales activity and opened a "second-hand café" - this means that alongside the clothing shop in the courtyard of the house at Salierring 41, in which large furniture, clothing, shoes, and fabrics are offered for sale, people can dig around at their leisure in books, records, household effects, and rummage in the second-hand store at Salierring 37.
To a small extent we also produce works of art made from cast-off materials, for example mobiles made from surplus wood and paper, lampshades made of wire and resistors, collages made of old magazines, and other things as well. Beyond that, we sell garden soil, packed into sacks which the SSK group in the Oberberg area produces in its compost bin.

SSK-Netzwerk
☺ interest in communal life and work, volunteerism

SSM - Sozialistische Selbshilfe Köln-Mülheim

SZ

Düsseldorfer Str. 74 | 51063 Köln
+49-(0)221-6403152 — info@ssm-koeln.org
-6403198 — www.ssm-koeln.org

1979 — 1,600 m² — ♀6 ♂14 3 23

g — 20

everyone in common (majority vote, consensus when possible)

shared economy — rented/leased

New Work

clearing flats, moving, second hand shop, hall rental, renovation, institute for New Work, project development

self-managed, left-wing political understanding, mentally/psychologically handicapped persons, self-sufficiency, construction

☺ (hands)

The systemic crisis of the labour society and the growing social marginalisation it entails demand that we seek new paths. In "New Work" people only devote part of their working time to the market. They earn the other part of their financial needs jointly through individual work. They build their own living space, they do craft work, they engage in farming and gardening, they salvage used items and gather knowledge. The various initiatives help and support one another. Work no longer merely refers to activities for which one can receive money on the market, but rather to all activities which are important to the community. Creating living space, cooking, carrying out relocations, launching projects, assisting children, writing a leaflet - at the "Socialist Self-Help Mülheim" (SSM) these are all forms of work, whereby the mentally disabled, homeless people and other marginalised persons all have their place. Everyone can contribute, no one is to old, to weak, to handicapped. "New Work" excludes no one. Instead, it combines the strengths of individuals and balances out their weaknesses. While in some cases it may be less productive than specialised firms, overall it is more effective since, for example, it renders asylums and traffic jams, social work and job creation measures projects superfluous.

☺ people of good will

Stallkultur e.V. SK

Dorfstraße 38, 39, 40 | 29416 Sallenthin-Jeggeleben

☎ +49-(0)39009-50431, -90917 oder -90107 www.stallkultur.de

1998 2 ha (near Salzwedel) ♀3 ♂6 7 16

g, e nearly all

me (in consensus, forward-looking, responsible and empathetic)

limited common financing, no expenditures association

freedom

kids, kitchen, compost toilet

ecological, self-managed, anarchistic, left-wing political understanding, non-violent, hierarchical, spiritual, chaotic, inner growth, meditation, yoga, organic diet, free school, seminar-house, therapy, self-sufficiency, permaculture, organic gardening, forestry, ecological construction, handicrafts: clay building, cabinetmaking; sports: trampoline, boule; art: music, poetry & prose, humus

☺

It was a morning like every other. At first, everything was possible, Knolli the plant acted differently with the others yesterday, there was plenty of gold in the sun, and the day was still young. "Where shall I grow today?" So there she stood, green and free, at the place where heaven and earth touch. "Who am I and what do the others matter?" she asked the dwarf Knowitall, and he said: "Knolli! That's enough of that! You aren't what you were anymore, so become what you want!" "Good idea!!" Knolli realised that she had seen plants that blossomed in all colours and sang songs, and she could smile innocently too. Fantastic!

And she also knew wise old plants who sometimes seemed pretty overwhelming, but they stayed put and even had a special kind of humour. Suddenly Knolli recognised how funny truth can be and told everyone: "I am what I can and I'll do what I want." She was so enlightened that she got hungry and nibbled on a couple of minerals.

So she grew and got round and happy with herself and everyone else, and now she's ripe for the salad bowl.

And the moor-owl of the story is that life's a yummy morning glory.

loose contact to communities in Kaulitz (DUB), Zierau, →Hof Erdenlicht, Liesten, Badel, →Groß Chüden, Klein Gartz, →Sieben Linden

accept group structure

Stamm der Likatier

SF

Magnusplatz 6 | 87629 Füssen
+49-(0)8362-38993 stamm-der-likatier@likatien.com
-6418 www.likatien.de

1974 65 ha ♀62 ♂63 55 180

g

everyone in common (consensus) limited community financing and individual

tribal property

neo-tribal movement, community movement, bio-regionalism, deep ecology

a number of service businesses, retail/crafts businesses, farming/forestry, gardening

ecological, self-managed, tribal chieftain, spiritual, esoteric/New Age, inner growth, sexuality, organic diet, vegetarian diet, adult education, holistic medicine, environmental protection, self-sufficiency, permaculture, organic agriculture, organic gardening, forestry, alternative energy, new technologies, ecological construction, renovation, house remodelling, matriarchy, ability to love

In our view, tribes and communities are the basis of understanding and genuine human dynamism, and in our opinion they alone are in a position to create a genuinely life-supporting culture.
One of our central goals is the development of an autonomous tribal culture harmonising its relationship to itself and to the world on the basis of a spiritual world view and a numinous-intrinsic and external realisation of the world (healing); which creates culture-specific communication opportunities (e.g. its own language); and which examines adequate opportunities for dynamic development and makes it possible to live them. We also concern ourselves with dreams, trances, relationships, eroticism, power, aggression, therapy forms, nutrition, education, questioning morality and taboos, philosophers, revolutionising lifestyles etc. We are linked to neither religious nor political institutions, ideologies or traditions. Each week we hold separate women's and men's meetings. We are striving for increasing autarky in all areas. At the same time we seek intensive co-operation and friendship with other communities and tribes. We also consider our involvement with our own roots and visions to be important. On a global scale we view our activity as a small contribution towards a total way out of a misguided path of humankind and towards a total way into a new future for humanity. The community's members are active in their own businesses which earn the financial basis of the total community. At the same time we are active in a number of very different economic areas, in which on the one hand we try to make sure that we cover our own needs and, on the other, that we remain as crisis-resistant as possible. The tribe's members own 47 houses and operate various businesses, as for example publishing houses,

a printing shop, an advertising agency, retail shops, a seminar operation, a trade fair organising business, a real estate office, mail-order businesses, a doctor's surgery, a law office, a software company, a natural health practitioners' school and correspondence school. We are currently beginning work in farming, forestry and gardening. Everyone who would like to get to know us is sincerely welcome. We are looking for new members.

→See also description of networks "**GEN**" and "**Come Together**"
Neue-Stämme-Bewegung (New Tribes Movement)
none

Therapeutische Lern- und Lebens-Gemeinschaft

LR

Hp (M) Raimar Ocken | Görschstr. 12 | 13187 Berlin
+49-(0)30-4413916, -4413917

1997 ♀15 ♂5 7 27

- g, e, f, russ.
- individual financing
- holistic worldview (psyche, soma, environment), holistic physio-psychotherapy, (learning) to live together
- public relations (lectures, workshops), environmental work, organic foods shop co-operative, support of people with learning disabilities
- ecological, leader/guru, inner growth, adult education, therapy

Using the "Hp (M) Raimar Ocken Lebensschule" or "school of life", a non-medical practitioner's school in Berlin-Prenzlauer Berg, as a starting point, the "Therapeutische Großfamilie" ("Therapeutic Extended Family") has been developing since 1997. Since then, we have continually revised our community concept and have been calling ourselves the "Therapeutic Learning Community Hp (M) Raimar Ocken" since 2002.
We live in Berlin-Pankow in 1-3 person households located in each others neighbourhood in normal apartment blocks. Most of us work as employees or self-employed persons in the social/medical field. We have three regular community events per week in which the members can participate.
Common leisure activities are co-ordinated at one of these meetings. We are interested in social developments, take a critical stance toward natural science, eat all-organic food and in regard to clothing, furniture, dyes etc. we prefer natural materials. We feel a need to explore our "spiritual life" and both conceive and experiment with new approaches toward living differently.
In order to preserve our culture as much as possible and to help our new members find their place with us, we require them to undertake a one-year introductory course. It demands a fee. Further information can be found in our brochure "Anders leben (leben)" ("living differently"), which is available free of charge.

1-year course: "Introduction to psycho-somato-ecology"

Traumschule

Dorfstraße 78A | 29416 Riebau
☎+49-(0)39037-958993
-958994

2003 3 ha (near Salzwedel/Gorleben) 8

- g, e
- chaotic, seeking shared economy
- still individual property, purchase planned
- anarchistic, children's rights
- crafts, construction, political action, everything is doable
- self-managed, anarchistic, left-wing political understanding, chaotic, vegan diet/containers, no pedagogy, no school, instead: children's rights, animal rights, handicrafts: metal-working, cabinetmaking, bike repair, electrical work..., sports: riding Giganto bike trailers

☺

Since July of 2003 we have been reviving a former border garrison and outbuildings in the Altmark and are currently in the process of purchasing a beautiful but dilapidated train station building along with a neighbouring lot. We want to create a place where everyone can develop him/herself equally, responsibly and freely – regardless of age, gender, skills and economic usefulness. We do not want to suppress feelings and love and become intellectually numb (which is pretty much standard in this society). Children have rights of their own. People of all ages should live and learn where and how they want.
We are building what we need with natural materials and cast-off items. Living in a responsible way, which means not supporting the unjust economic system. Revealing excess by welcoming what other people would call worthless junk.
We don't just want to develop an alternative, but stage resistance. A library, info shop, educational play centre, cuddle cave, playroom, gym, mattress room, labyrinth, metal shop, joinery shop, sewing workshop, sports hall, blacksmith shop, bicycle workshop, darkroom, plenty of storage space for used material of all kinds, an electric workshop and much more will be individually and creatively developed and combine with nature to make the Dream School a place of learning for young and old.
A children's house is planned in which grownups – actually, grown-ins and grown-outs – will not have the last word. We still need lots of children to help generate Kid Power in this (school)free place.

☺ open to: children's rights, politics, resistance; self-responsible

Trauringja - Forsthaus Triesch

TA

Triesch 3 | 36214 Nentershausen
☎ +49-(0)6627-915593
forsthaustriesch@yahoo.de
www.forsthaustriesch.de

1981 | 1 ha (near Bebra) | ♀3 ♂5 2 10

e, f, it., sp., g | 5

everyone in common (consensus) | limited community financing

rented/leased

individual, lively

children, gardening, kitchen, health food shop

ecological, self-managed, non-violent, spiritual, inner growth, organic diet, vegetarian diet, peace-work, environmental protection, organic gardening, ecological construction, handicrafts: indoor renovation, wagon building and others, art: theatre group, music; healing workshops: Reiki, Chakra healing, intuitive massage, craniosacral, long-distance healing, meditative jogging; healing meetings

☺ ()

Our community has changed strongly in the past few years. We almost exhausted ourselves in discussions. The discussions masked the fact that the readiness to really share money and love was not yet present, where sharing is understood as a free giving from the heart and not something that happens under pressure from the group. Before we talked a lot about "community", individuals could hide behind that concept. When we meet today, every person comes from their own free will and stands responsible for themselves.
Sadly, we have lost the land on which we had been planting our organic vegetables (1.8 ha) and have been confronted with the land laws of the earth, also with the logic of money as an innocent strategy of inequality and injustice, where the truth is a logic of destruction and of the North.

- Our living houses are worth taking a look at: www.naturbauten.com
- From May to September we stage our healing meeting "Mal wieder 'Sein'". You can come anytime, join us for a few days and celebrate the sun, nature and the joy of living with us. www.forshaustriesch.de
- The "Food for All People" run takes place throughout the year – a nature mandala! The day when no one in our world community is hungry will be the day when peace on earth will begin.

Netzkraft Bewegung, Peace & Dignity

☺ the future of the site is uncertain, otherwise: living space must be brought along, self-support, four-week probationary period

ufafabrik e.V.

UF

Internationales Kultur Zentrum | Viktoriastr. 10-18 | 12105 Berlin
+49-(0)30-75503-0 info@ufafabrik.de
-110 www.ufafabrik.de

1976 18, 000m² ♀12 ♂12 6 30

d, e 21

everyone in common (consensus) individual financing

rented/leased

none

culture, bakery, guest house, workshops, courses, seminars for all age levels

self-managed, non-violent, inner growth, humour, adult education, neighbourhood self-help centre, alternative energy, new technologies, ecological construction, Dojo for Asian sports and meditation, school for African and Brazilian percussion, dance school, children's circus school, culture centre, events, world music, stage

☺

This comprehensive cultural, working and living project on the 18,000 m² grounds of the former UFA film processing laboratories has been in existence since 1979. The theatre operation, the "International Kulturcentrum ufaFabrik", maintains two stages year-round, an open-air summer stage, organises guest performances and its own in-house productions with artists from Berlin and from around the world.
There is a guesthouse, a neighbourhood selfhelp centre with extensive workshop programme for young and old, a children's farm, an organic bakery, an organic foods shop, the Café Olé with a summer garden, the centre's own UFA Circus, the circus school and the Terra Brasilis samba band. Extensive ecological projects ranging from roof greening to solar energy systems have been realised over a period of 25 years and can be viewed in an exhibit and in seminars.
The heart and driving force of the UfaFabrik is the commune, which is made up of ca. 50 people who live and work on the grounds. In this way the various working areas are linked together and can complement one another. Important decisions are made in consensus at a plenary meeting of all residents.
The ufaFabrik is an active member of various cultural, social and ecological networks. It enjoys international recognition as a sustainable example for quality of life and contribution in an urban area.

☺ long-term acquaintance; friendship, sympathy, shared understanding of work and life

Umweltzentrum Ökohof Auterwitz e.V.

OA

c/o Frank Ende | Auterwitz 13 | 04720 Zschaitz-Ottewig
☎ +49-(0)34325-20200 info@auterwitz.de
-20507 www.auterwitz.de

1991 2.5 ha (near Döbeln) ♀4 ♂3 7 14

g 6

everyone in common (majority vote) individual financing

association and property of individual members

none

environmental training/education, traditional crafts, animal friendly husbandry, landscape care, ecological building, maintaining village strucures and traditions, public work, guests

ecological, self-managed, left-wing political understanding, adult education, pedagogical, seminar-house, classic homeopathy, phytotherapy, environmental protection, self-sufficiency, organic gardening, animal friendly husbandry, alternative energy, new technologies, ecological construction, cheese making, clay building, joinery, wool processing, herb processing, herb garden, holiday events and project days for children, museum

☺

Our association was founded in 1991 with the goal of developing a solidarity-based living and working community in a rural area. We have comprehensively renovated the 4 old 4-square farm buildings and have reconstructed them using traditional clay building techniques. They house flats, seminar rooms, goat cheese-dairy, a spinning and weaving studio, a project room, offices, a modern kitchen with a dining room and rooms for up to 40 guests. Furthermore, the village includes a culture barn, a consultation centre, a museum and a baking house. We see our main areas in nature conservation and landscape preservation. Among other things, we sponsor job-creation measures in environmental training and education and in the promotion of ecological farming. We have been sponsoring the Voluntary Ecological Year in Saxony since 1993. In the village we organise many events throughout the year to which we welcome numerous guests. We are endeavouring to develop closed cycles and are attempting self-sufficiency in certain areas. In addition, we are doing our best to preserve old and threatened breeds of domesticated animals. We use alternative energies, e.g. in the form of thermal heating and a wood chip system. Our waste water is purified in a reed bed system. You can join us by accepting our articles of association and after a majority vote at our member's assembly. A sustaining membership is also possible. We also welcome helpers and co-workers in the various activities our village offers. Furthermore, seasonal help is always welcome in our vegetable and herb gardens.

☺ agreement with association principles, joining solidarity-based village community, ecological orientation

Verein zur Förderung ganzheitlicher Lebensweise und Kulturpflege

LK

Zschachenmühle | Zschachenmühle 1 | 07368 Remptendorf
+49-(0)36652-28027 zschachenmuehle@t-online.de
-28029 www.oshostadt.de, www.zschachenmuehle.de

1979 12 ha (near Lobenstein) ♀6 ♂8 14

g, e 10-14

all concerned persons together/part of the group (consensus — because those who do not bow to consensus, mostly leave)

varies property of individual community members

OSHO as teaching and presence are central, i.e. an effort for the greatest possible consciousness

construction/garden, cooking, hospitality, office, film, meditation, creativity

ecological, self-managed, anarchistic, non-violent, leader/guru, spiritual, esoteric/New Age, chaotic, inner growth, meditation, yoga, tantra, sexuality, organic diet, vegetarian diet, peace-work, therapy, animal protection, environmental protection, self-sufficiency, organic agriculture, organic gardening, alternative energy, construction, handicraft, art, media

☺ ()

On the initiative of the Association for the Promotion of a Holistic Lifestyle and Cultural Preservation, a group of friends settled down in the Zschachen Mill (an old sawmill, which was later used as a fireman's home and then by the East German army after the war) in 1995 in order to construct an alternative (in all senses of the term) living and working community. This includes the creation of various businesses – e.g. the Siddhartha Crystal Co. (therapeutic stones and minerals), a mail-order book company, workshops, museums and a seminar centre. A café, 5 more workshops, a new residential section with 8 rooms, baths and heating, a 160 m² meditation room, a large multi-use building, a sauna and the remodelling of a grain silo as a children's playhouse are in the planning or construction phase. There is plenty of interesting construction and development work. Pioneers are very welcome.
We do most of the work ourselves. When needed, we ask outside experts for advice. Each of us is responsible for one or more work areas. But that does not mean that he/she has to do all the work him/herself, but rather that he/she assumes responsibility and delegates tasks to other community members. We are open to all people who are ready to assume responsibility for themselves and for the vision of constructing an Osho town.

world-wide movement oriented on OSHO

☺ we are an OSHO commune, but not all members of the society view OSHO as their master

Villa Locomuna

VL

Kölnische Str. 183 | 34119 Kassel

+49-(0)561-920094920 info@gemeinsam-leben-eg.de

-920094959 www.gemeinsam-leben-eg.de

2000 3015 m² ♀10 ♂10 10 30

e, f, sp.

everyone in common (consensus)

test phase: limited common financing/shared economy common property

office, practice

ecological, self-managed, left-wing political understanding, feminist, non-violent, inner growth

We are a living community of some 20 adults and 10 children living in the centre of Kassel.

In the autumn of 2000 our group coalesced around the issue of interpersonal communication: We meet on a weekly basis to discuss matters on a personal, emotional level, and also come together every 1-2 weeks at a plenum to talk over practical and organisational topics and decisions. We also use other communication approaches, particularly non violent communication. Our goals are to treat each other more gently, mutual support in our personal development, a constructive attitude in regard to our different needs and characters, the facilitation and support of the consensus process, and preventing and handling conflicts.

We are experimenting with variations on the notion of a solidarity-based economy; the guidelines we follow are the need principle, a social balance between various ways of earning money, and valuing unpaid work.

We are experimenting with alternative lifestyle and relationship forms beyond the closed nuclear family and exclusive 2-person relationships. We give our children the opportunity to absorb a variety of social contacts with each other and also with adults, regardless of their biological relationship. We are trying to overcome traditional gender roles on a practical basis. A sustainable lifestyle is important to us.

Most of us work outside, while some are self-employed within the community.

Every day we sit down to a shared evening meal.

Kommunefond

☺ participation in forum and plenum, assuming responsibility, purchasing a co-op stake

Villa Magdalena

MG

Frauen/Lesben/Kunst/Werk/Statt | Bernstorffstr.160a | 22767 Hamburg

+49-(0)40-4303570 www.internetfrauen.w4w.de/villa

1989 ♀5 5

g, e, f

everyone in common (majority vote) limited common financing

rented/leased

silk-screen printing, book printing, photo, exhibits, events
self-managed, feminist, printing workshop, photography

Once upon a time, "the villa" was an auto garage and was slated for demolition. A handful of women had a better idea and finally made it happen: in 1989 it was given to the Verein Magdalena K. e.V. to use (and renovate!). The house soon became the "Villa Magdalena" with the declared purpose of "artistic and craft autonomy for women".
Since then a great many women have come and gone, have lived and worked here, argued and laughed, created art or just had fun, developed, discussed, or simply sat in the garden and enjoyed the sun. Much has changed, much hasn't, but one thing has stayed the same: Villa Magdalena is a SpaceDream (or the other way around) open to all women who can or want to make something out of it. With 107 m² the workshop is the villa's heart and we always welcome women who can bring even more life into it. We provide a partially furnished room with an optional flat-sharing connection for up to 3 months for artists who would like to develop an idea and would like to take advantage of the project's space, time and atmosphere.

☺ artistic interest, interest in workshop use

Vindorf

VN

Vindorf 3 | 21368 Boitze
☎ +49-(0)-5851-6024-00 vindorf@t-online.de
-21 www.vindorf.de

1998 2 ha + 5 ha forest (near Lüneburg) ♀3 ♂4 7

e, sp., f 0,4 employments
everyone in common (consensus)
limited common financing, co-op structures common property
none
vegetable garden, workshop, room and space for new areas
ecological, self-managed, left-wing political understanding, non-violent, self-sufficiency, organic gardening, ecological construction, chickens and ducks

On our farm in Vindorf we want to put our ideas of living and working together into action.
We founded our farm community some 5 years ago as an ecological and social project. Since then we have been learning how to plaster walls with clay and paint them with curd paint, how to save head lettuce from snails and how to cut asparagus, how to tile bathrooms and build garden ponds without PVC-foil. We are learning how 7 people in a residential project arrive at decisions that everyone is satisfied with, we celebrate festivals and stare into the campfire at night, and we beat drums and sing. We are teaching each other how baby chicks are raised, how to exasperate nuclear waste transports, what to watch out for with electrical toggle switches and how leather shorts are sewn. We are discovering how important a fire brigade ball and a communal room are and much more...

On the farm there is a large dwelling house, an old cow barn (which today, sadly, is only lived in by swallows), and a barn which we have remodelled into a woodworking shop. We largely supply our own needs from our organic vegetable garden. We have some cow "friends" on the adjacent meadow and we also have a stretch of forest some distance away where we gather our firewood. We still have plenty of free space(s) for people with ideas similar to our own...

Wagendorf Karow

KA

Pankgräfin e.V. | Pankgrafenstr. 12d | 13125 Berlin
☎ +49-(0)30-47471622
-47471622

1993 | 8 ha | 20

e, sp. | 1

everyone in common, part of the group (majority vote, consensus)

individual financing | rented/leased

none

development, environmental education in the summer

self-managed, environmental protection

☺

The community has not sent a current selfdescription.

☺ 6-month trial period, no more dogs, ideally people who want to get involved

Wassermühle Eime GbR

EI

Steffi Kroll | Mühlenstraße 12-14 | 31036 Eime
☎ +49-(0)5182-960192 steff-e-mail@freenet.de
-960801

1994 | 2 ha (near Hildesheim) | ♀4 ♂3 6 13

g, e, f, sp. | 3

everyone in common (consensus, representatives)

limited common financing (building fund) | common property

Anthroposophy, authenticity and tolerance

fruit/vegetable garden, child-care, animal husbandry, hay fields, maintenance/repair/caring for property, food co-op, fluit-building

ecological, self-managed, left-wing political understanding, non-violent, spiritual, chaotic, anthroposophic, inner growth, organic diet, organic gardening, organic farming, animal friendly husbandry, forestry, alternative energy water, sun, (wind), ecological construction, handicrafts: self-acquired skills for maintaining buildings and grounds, other: food co-op „In the House"; cultural events, humour

☺

We currently live in an old water mill as a single with three families whose members are between 2 and 42 years old. Each party lives in a flat (one will probably become vacant in the summer of 2004), plus there are a variety of remodelling opportunities. We live together with 2 donkeys, some sheep, chickens, ducks, bees, rabbits, cats, moles, bats, mice, frogs, cranes, kingfishers, butterflies... A stream with a water fall snakes through the spacious grounds, ideal for bathing and well-suited for power generation.
Once a week we come together for our "situation report". Our current issues include the balance between the community, "house and farm" and individual needs; the future financing of our project through private loans if possible ... Our old idealistic motto "We'll all share each other's burden" is progressively giving way to "Welcome to reality": By getting involved in group processes where no one knows in advance what will happen – and things can get pretty heated sometimes – our communal life remains exciting, (bio)dynamic, often too strenuous, definitely never boring, extremely lively, and increasingly relaxed, laid back, funnier. Plus, we're always open to new ideas. And when we can't handle things ourselves, or when we think it's a good idea, we ask for outside help (CommunityBuilding, organisational offices, supervision).
Our reality also includes common meals whenever possible or when it makes daily life easier; summer building weeks where we all join forces and take a swing at the most urgent building site on the property; winter wood-gathering actions; donkey excursions on Sundays; our annual summer fest; cultural events in the former grain silo etc.

☺ 1 year probationary living to get to know each other; joy and interest in communal life, growing, working

Zar Nekla Die Zweite

ZN

Zarnekla 19 | 17121 Düvier

☎ +49-(0)39998-10487 od. (0)39993-76944 zar.nekla.2@lapsus-gil.de

www.coforum.de/index.php4?ZarNekla

1998 18.5 ha (near Greifswald) ♀2 ♂2 2 6

e, f all

everyone in common (consensus) limited common financing and individual

the building is private, otherwise association property

aimed in the right direction

main life and secondary life

ecological, non-violent, yoga, organic diet, vegetarian diet, adult education, free school, social work: taking old folks over the street, therapy: particularly after accidents, environmental protection, self-sufficiency, organic gardening, forestry, ecological construction, sports: peasant Olympics, art: open, media: www.Coforum.de

☺

Zarnekla - endless sky, forest, pasture, sheep, moor, hedges, garden, fairground, solar shower, caravans, barn, farmyard, house. The doors are open.

In the large sun room in the barn one's eyes drift freely to the edge of the forest. Several times a year it is filled with happy voices and music, and the floor boards bend beneath the dancers. Activity room, rooms for guests.
Usually it is quiet: the birds chirp, the frogs croak, the sunlight is audible, the cat purrs. The essence of this place is: to be alive.
We move in the alternative currents of life, toeing the narrow line between the inner and outer world. We shape our lives, realise our dreams. Since 2003 we've been doing it in Hohenbüssow too, some 40 km further on – in the alternative village community there we are helping to develop the autonomous and community-friendly property on the edge of the village.
We want to provide impulses, we want to convey experiences and knowledge in areas that are important to us: healing, self-sufficiency, living in tune with nature, ecological building, handicraft, social criticism... we have a lot of interesting literature on all this. We want to create a framework for healing in an all-encompassing sense. We offer what we have to give. We view ourselves as a networking node in the region.
We live on a vegetarian basis and with a compost toilet, without a refrigerator, television etc.
The Rakow and Sternfeld train station are nearby, guests can arrange to be picked up.
Clay construction week(end)s, endless tree planting, children's playground, yoga courses/private lessons...

Netzkraftbewegung, Erdenbürger
☺ ecos, veggies, non-druggies, non-doggies, awards for good knowledge

ZEGG - Zentrum für experimentelle Gesellschaftsgestaltung

ZE

Rosa-Luxemburg-Str. 89 | 14806 Belzig
☎ +49-(0)33841-595-10 empfang@zegg.de
-595-12 www.zegg.de

1991 15 ha (near Berlin) ♀41 ♂33 13 87

e, f, sp., dutch, greek 25
everyone in common (consensus) limited common financing and individual
Zegg GmbH
non-violent, inner and outer peace work
seminars and guest accommodations, grounds care + construction, gardening, several independent businesses
ecological, self-managed, non-violent, spiritual, inner growth, meditation, sexuality, free love, organic diet, vegetarian diet, adult education, seminar-house, peacework, environmental protection, organic gardening, forestry, alternative energy, ecological construction, sports: Tao Sport Belzig - Ultra Marathon; art: painting, sculptures, pottery, music, choir, multimedia performances, painting, sculptures, media: newsletter, homepage

☺

Culture at the ZEGG summer camp, Germany

ZEGG was founded by an initiative group on 15 ha of land 80 km south-west of Berlin in 1991. Its goal was to establish an international conference and research centre which would develop new models for a socially and ecologically sustainable life. Since then, ZEGG has also developed into a vibrant cultural centre, a regional meeting place and a networking centre for communities and dedicated persons seeking new solutions in politics, ecology and social life. The community of 90 adults and children has passed through various transformations: what began as a relatively homogeneous pioneer community has turned into a network of various initiatives, spiritual and political groups, firms, artists and political mavericks, all of whom share the quest for new models for love and sexuality and the realisation of inner and outer peace. The centre includes a large organic garden, forest land, the campus as meeting place, a children's house, a guest house, group meeting rooms, bars, pool, workshops, media rooms, an artist's studio and several commercial buildings.

Our wide-ranging yearly programme provides information on our seminar offerings and large-scale conferences (Easter, Pentecost, summer camp, New Year's Eve).

→ See also description of network "**GEN**"

Meiga

☺ 5-week community course, probationary year, 2,300.- Euro stake in corporation and 4,000.- Euros credit

Zeitlos e.V.

ZL

Kieler Str. 650 | 22527 Hamburg

☎ +49-(0)40-57197716

1996 | 420 m² | ♀4 ♂3 | 2 | 9

g, e, f, it., indon., port.

everyone in common (consensus) | limited common financing and individual

rented / leased

various professions, students, welfare recipients

ecological, self-managed, left-wing political understanding, non-violent, environmental protection, ecological construction, football

☺

We, the Timeless ones (zeitlos means timless), live in an old farmhouse on the outskirts of Hamburg, but we're not exactly rural. We bought this farmhouse, the Langelohhof, almost 10 years ago and have repaired and restored it ourselves as ecologically as possible.
We have gone through many processes since then. Many people have lived here, and only two of the original residents are still at it. Many further processes still await us, particularly in regard to the development of our "still rural surroundings", where another residential project is about to be built in the immediate vicinity.

☺ Willingness to participate and live together in project, 2,300.- Euro co-op stake per person

Zentrum PrinzHöfte

PH

Simmershauserstr. 1 | 27243 Prinzhöfte
☎ +49-(0)4244-644 — kontakt@zentrum-prinzhoefte.de
Fax -2767 — www.zentrum-prinzhoefte.de

1982 | 1.5 ha (near Bremen) | ♀7 ♂6 7 20

g, e — 6

limited common financing — association

Freinet pedagogy, permaculture

kindergarten, conference centre, permaculture, architecture, landscaping, wilderness school

ecological, self-managed, organic diet, adult education, pedagogical, free school, seminar-house, self-sufficiency, permaculture, organic gardening, animal friendly husbandry, ecological construction, landscaping, cultural café

☺ ()

Prinzhöfte is not a "classic commune" but rather an old farm in the possession of an association. Communal life is not the association's goal but is merely the form of association life we are practising at the moment.
Instead, our centre's purpose is to be an idea incubator for projects in the fields of ecology and pedagogy, specifically permaculture and Freinet pedagogy on a systematic basis.
Many of the people living in Prinzhöfte also work here – in the kindergarten, in the attached school (primary and middle school), in the architectural office, in the wilderness school, in landscaping, at the conference centre. Others live here and work outside. There are also people who live elsewhere but work here with us. A colourful mix.
Since we consider ourselves to be undogmatic and have no "narrow" goals as an association, the project is always in transition.
We always welcome new contacts, including those with people who do not want to move into a project but "only" want to work with us on a practical basis. As we always say: everyone can decide for him/self how closely or distantly he/she wants to work with the project.

Great Britain/Northern Ireland

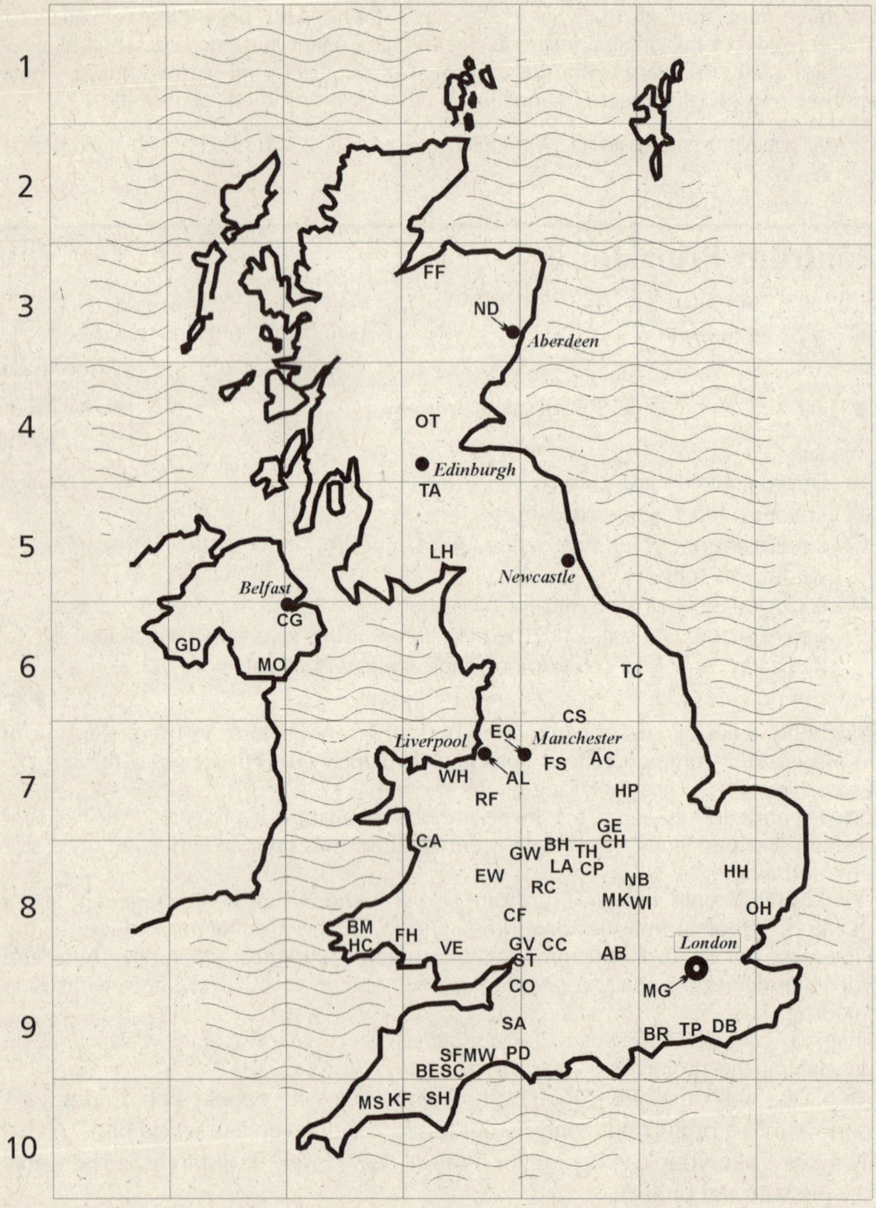

AB	The Abbey *E8*	KF	Keveral Farm Community *C10*
AC	Ashram Community Trust *E7*	LA	Lee Abbey Household Community *E8*
AL	L'Arche Liverpool *D7*	LH	Laurieston Hall *D5*
BE	BeechHill Community *D9*	MG	Mornington Grove *F9*
BH	Birchwood Hall *E8*	MK	Camphill Milton Keynes Community *E8*
BM	Brithdir Mawr *C8*	MO	Camphill Comm. Mourne Grange *B6*
BR	L'Arche Bognor Regis *F9*	MS	The Monkey Sanctuary *C10*
CA	C.A.T.: Centre f. Alternat. Technol. *D7*	MW	Monkton Wyld Court *D9*
CC	The Cohousing Company Ltd. *E8*	NB	The Neighbours Community *E8*
CF	Canon From Court Community *D8*	ND	Newton Dee Village Community *D3*
CG	Camphill Community Glencraig *C6*	OH	Old Hall Community *G8*
CH	Corani Housing and Land Co-op *E7*	OT	Ochil Tower School *D4*
CO	Cherry Orchards Camphill Com. *E9*	PD	Pilsdon Community *D9*
CP	Coventry Peace House *E8*	RC	Community for Reconciliation *E8*
CS	Cornerstone Housing Co-op *E6*	RF	Redfield Community *D7*
DB	Darvell Bruderhof *F9*	SA	Shekinashram *D9*
EQ	Equinox Housing Co-op *E7*	SC	Steward Community Woodland *D9*
EW	Earthworm Housing Co-op *D8*	SF	Stentwood Farm *D9*
FF	The Findhorn Foundation *D3*	SH	South Hams Holistic Education Community *D10*
FH	Fox Housing Cooperative *D8*	ST	Stepping Stone Housing Co-op *E8*
FS	Fireside Housing Co-op *E7*	TA	Talamh Housing Co-op *D5*
GD	ISKCON: Govindadwipa Dhama *B6*	TC	The Croft Community *E6*
GE	Grooby Ecohamlet *E7*	TH	Torch Housing Co-op *E8*
GV	Grange Village *E8*	TP	Two Piers Brigthon *F9*
GW	Gwerin Housing Association *E8*	VE	Vegan Enterprises *D8*
HC	Heartwood Community *C8*	WH	Welhealth Co-op *D7*
HH	Hengrave Hall *F8*	WI	The Well at Willen *F8*
HP	The Hockerton Housing Project *E7*		

Anarres

c/o Blackcurrent | 24 St.Michaels Ave | Northampton NN1 4JQ
☎ +44-(0)845 458 8259 blackcurent@lineone.net

f, g, it., bulg., port., span.
all who are concerned (consensus)
ecological
ecological, self-managed, feminist, non-violent, adult education,peace-work, environmental protection, self-sufficiency, organic gardening, alternative energy, ecological construction, organic food

☺

At the time of writing, we do not yet have any land but we are intending to buy some during the summer of 2005 to form an ecovillage. So please write to us or look at our website for current information.

We are intending to:
- Live from the land, eventually growing all our own food and material
- Use ecological building techniques
- Demonstrate that people can exist happily and healthily without degrading the environment
- Develop an extensive natural woodland

Anarres will have the following rules which everyone living in the village agrees to live by:
- No sale of produce – plants, minerals, water from the land.
- No pets or livestock
- No motor vehicles within the village
- No toxic chemicals
- One third of land to be kept wild and undisturbed
- All growing to be done vegan organically

The first community to live in the village is 'Peace and Plenty'. We welcome other communities and individuals/couples to come and live in the village who believe that the earth's resources should not be owned, sold or bartered, but are for the inhabitants of a locality to use in an environmentally sensitive way.

☺ sign up to basic rules, probationary period, that we enjoy your company

Ashram Community Trust

AC

178 Abbeyfield Road | Sheffield S4 7AY
☎ +44-(0)114-2436688
✉ ashramcommunity@hotmail.com
Fax -2447278
www.ashram.org.uk

1967

? e
12 part-time or volunteers
all who are concerned (consensus)
property of trust
ecumenical
inner city projects, eco projects
self-managed, spiritual. christian, ecumenical, vegetarian diet, adult education, peace-work, social work: community projects

☺

Ashram Community began in 1967, with the intention of developing committed urban communities, which would develop appropriate new forms of Christian community related to urban needs. There are at present two inner-city community houses in Sheffield and one in Parkfield, Stockton-on-Tees. Meanwhile, Ashram developed its community presence in terms of shops and residences. The first of these, the Ashram Centre and New Roots Shop (wholefoods, fruit & veg, Traidcraft) was opened in 1987. The second, the Burngreave Ashram and New Roots Shop was opened in 2001. It is a complex of shop, residence, public meeting rooms, offices and basement, plus being the base for various community groups. It is hoped that this model of volunteer-served shop plus local community base plus residence will develop elseshere. The shop/ house in the Parkfield inner-city area of Stockton-on-Tees is on this model. The common life of Ashram Community is inspired by the radical styles of Jesus and the earliest Christians. The Community sustains this through regional Branches, half-yearly Weekends and half-yearly Community General Meetings, plus Retreats, Holidays, Walks and other occasions.

☺ christian

Beech Hill Community

Beech Hill House | Morchard Bishop | Crediton, Devon EX17 6RF
☎ +44-(0)1363-877228 beechhill@ukonline.co.uk
-877587 web.onetel.net.uk/~beechhill

1983 2.8 ha (near Exeter) ♀7 ♂5 1 13

e none
all who are concerned (consensus) limited common financing
owned by co-op, rented and owned by private leaseholders
ecological
gardening, maintenance, arts & crafts, recycling, community compost scheme
ecological, self-managed, organic diet, organic gardening

☺

We live in a large country house in the rolling Devon hills. Accomodation is both rented and leasehold in the converted outbuildings and in the mainhouse. We grow our own organic fruit and vegetables. We have a paddock with three sheep and chickens, an orchard, a walled garden, swimming pool and compost toilet.
Together we run a course centre and spend the income on community projects. We share responsibility for our home and the land on which we live. We eat together in the evenings and celebrate birthdays and other events together.
We participate in th wider community through various events including community open days and our community composting scheme. Individuals earn their income in the outside world in journalism, education, mechanics, complimentory health, recycling and alternative ceremonies. Some work from home.
We are a diverse group of people who try and live more sustainably together. We enjoy visitors and volunteers by prior arrangement. We even enjoy a good laugh sometimes.

☺ none

Birchwood Hall

BH

Storridge | Malvern | Worcestershire WR13 5EZ

paddymcc@netcomuk.co.uk

www.diggersanddreamers.org.uk/pnppage.htm

1971 3.6 ha (near Malvern) ♀9 ♂8 3 20

e none

everyone in common (consensus) limited community financing / common till

common property

green, left, feminist

external work

ecological, self-managed, left-wing political understanding, feminist, non-violent, organic gardening, volleyball, various media

Birchwood Hall is a Housing Coop with two houses (Mainhouse & Coachhouse), set in 3.6 ha of garden. Each house is operated separately with a shared budget for maintenance etc. There is the Large & Victorian Mainhouse with lots of space, therefore lots of potential maintenance, cleaning and play value. But no bevy of Victorian servants to keep the brass polished! Individuals have their own rooms or share with a partner. Communal rooms include: kitchen, sitting room, TV room etc. Difficult house to heat and be energy efficient but we're trying!
Our older children go to local schools. Some of us have grown up offspring who lived here and now visit. We have a range of full and part time, in a variety of jobs such as: photographer, architect, cleaner, teacher, civil servant, plus 2 people on "sabbatical" at the moment. We think we live here for ethical and practical reasons. We like each other and enjoy sharing the house (most of the time!). Our joint politics are leftish, greenish and feminist, with enough variation for some rowdy teatime arguments! We hope we're fun people to live with! We eat together in the evening, taking it in turns to cook, trying to accommodate likes and dislikes. We're mostly vegetarians with occasional meat extravaganza! We take turns to shop for food etc. Estimating the amounts of silver, red and blue top milk we need each day is one of lifes' more difficult tasks!! We do clean and maintain the house sometimes, but we don't operate a 3 line whip saying we must all clean toilets today! Meetings are once a week, alternating business and community meetings, with a whole co-op meeting every 2 months. We don't have many defined expectations of each other but trust that everyone will add to the community and pull their weight in some way. The Coachhouse is divided into 3 living areas with a degree of communality. Anybody's Barn is a small residential centre for outside groups, set up as a separate charity. The garden, beautiful and wooded, a struggle to maintain! The vegetable garden is fairly productive but not self-sufficient.

☺ green, left, feminist

Brithdir Mawr

BM

Cilgwyn Road, Newport | Pembrokeshire SA42 0QJ
+44-(0)1239-820164 www.brithdirmawr.com

1994 30 ha (near St. Davids) ♀4 ♂3 4 11

e, welsh, f, it., sp., dan. nearly all earn their money outside
everyone in common (consensus) limited community financing
ecology, simplicity
garden, coppicing, farm animals, alternative technology, dancing
ecological, self-managed, chaotic, inner growth, organic diet, vegetarian diet, vegan diet, environmental protection, self-sufficiency, permaculture, organic gardening, organic farming, animal friendly husbandry, alternative energy, ecological construction, rural handicraft, „greenwood skills"

Brithdir Mawr is a land-based community endeavouring to live as sustainably and simply as possible. We grow most of our own organic vegetables; chickens and ducks provide eggs and our motley crew of goats provide milk. Our power needs are met entirely by renewable resources, horse power or shared cars. We welcome volunteers for a week at a time to share our work, in return for food and a bed. Please email a brief introductory letter with some idea of your availability and skills.

☺ interest in resource-conserving construction. Enthusiasm and tolerance. Be financially solvent.

C.A.T.: Centre for Alternative Technology

CA

Llwyngwern Quarry | 5Y20 9AZ Machynlleth
+44-(0)1654-702400 info@cat.org.uk
-702782 www.cat.org.uk

1974 3.2 ha (near Machynlleth) ♀8 ♂4 1 13

e, welsh 11
everyone in common (consensus) limited community financing
other

- ecological, pragmatic
- educational/environmental work
- ecological, self-managed, organic diet, vegetarian diet, vegan diet, environmental protection, organic gardening, alternative energy, ecological construction, humour

☺ ( )

Our community is a constituent part of the Centre for Alternative Technology which promotes and implements renewable energy, ecological building, energy efficiency, sustainable sewage treatment, permaculture and organic growing.
We twelve residents are all CAT volunteers or staff and their families. We live in either low-energy timber framed homes or eco-renovated slate quarry workers' cottages.
We are self-sufficient in drinking water filtration and reed bed sewage treatment. Our electricity is sourced from on-site wind, hydro and solar generation or „green electricity" import/export.
We have 4 communal meals a week, organise fire-wood, organic food & laundry collectively to save money, reduce our environmental impact and learn from each other. On recent community work days we have built a compost-loo, eco-renovated a house, planted fruit trees and improved our fire-wood sheds. Decision making is achieved at regular community meetings, and is almost entirely by consensus.
The CAT visitor centre (excluding our homes) is open to day-visitors all year round. We also host short-term and long-term volunteers. Applications for volunteerships should be made by post or email with CV to Rick Dance since we have a waiting list.

Environmental action by C.A.T. (photo: Hildur Jackson)

- ECOLINK, UK EVN
- ☺ Open only to employees of CAT

Camphill Community Glencraig

CG

Craigavad | Holywood, Co. Down BT18 0DB
+44-(0)1232-423396
-428199
office@glencraig.org.uk

1954 | 40 (near Belfast) | ♀80 ♂80 40 200

e | all

everyone in common (discussion and agreement)
limited common financing/common purse — Foundation
Anthroposophic
care and education of children /adults with learning disabilities
ecological, self-managed, non-violent, spiritual, christian, esoteric/New Age, anthroposophic, inner growth, meditation, organic diet, adult education, pedagogical, seminar-house, mentally/psychologically handicapped persons, physically handicapped persons, various forms of therapy, self-sufficiency, organic agriculture, organic gardening, organic farming, animal friendly husbandry, forestry, alternative energy, pottery, weaving, bakery, candle-making, wood, music, theatre, art

☺

Camphill Community Glencraig was founded in order to live and work with children and adults in need of special care. In 1954 a group of parents and friends, inspired by the work of Dr. König, at Camphill near Aberdeen, in Scotland, wished to establish a similar place in Northern Ireland. They acquired Glencraig, a beautiful estate of 100 acres, sloping down to the shore of Belfast Lough. In its woods, fields and parklands are 19 houses, a school and workshops, with the farm at its heart. There is further farm land near Helen's Bay.

→ See also description of network "**Camphill**"
☺ willingness to accept demands. Work is voluntary, financing occurs through community

Camphill Community Mourne Grange

MO

169 Newry Road | Kilkeel | Co. Down BT34 4EX
☎ +44-(0)28-41760128 — info@mournegrange.org
Fax -41765372 — www.mournegrange.org

1971 — 45 ha (near Newry) — ♀50 ♂57 — 26 — 133

e, g, japanese, poln., dutch — all
everyone in common (consensus) — shared economy
Camphill Trust
Anthroposophian
farm work, handicrafts, baking, laundry, household
ecological, self-managed, non-violent, christian, esoteric/New Age, anthroposophic, inner growth, organic diet, adult education, mentally/psychologically handicapped persons, various therapy forms, biodynamic farming, organic gardening, organic farming, animal friendly husbandry, weaving, pottery, woodworking

☺

Mourne Grange is a Camphill Village Community of 130 people where adults with learning difficulties live and work together with co-workers and their families.
Set in a beautiful location in the Mourne Mountains, we have a large biodynamic farm and garden, which we work on to supply the community with our own pro-

duce. We also have a bakery, a food processing workshop, a laundry, pottery woodwork shop, weavery and a coffee and craft shop.
We have a large hall, which is a centre for our social and cultural life. We are Christian and non-denominational and we celebrate the Christian festivals of the year. Mourne Grange is based on the idea of mutual care where there is interdependence among all members of the community. We welcome volunteers from many different parts of the world for short and longer periods of time.

→ See also description of network "**Camphill**"
☺ being open-minded

Camphill Milton Keynes Community

MK

Japonica Lane V10 Brickhill Street | Japonica Lane, Willen Park South |
Milton Keynes MK15 9JY
☎ +44-(0)908-235707 office@camphillmk.ndirect.co.uk
Fax -235505

1980 | 4 ha | 70

e | all

one part of the group (consensus) | shared income

common property

Rudolf Steiner

gardening, baking, weaving, café, refurbishing tools

☺

Camphill Milton Keynes is a residential working Community providing a meaningful life for adults with learning difficulties. 45 residents live together with staff and their families in eight separate households, forming a community of over 70 people.
Daily life is arranged around the various households, each of which has its own character based on a common routine. Meals are taken together and household tasks are shared. Workshops include two vegetable and fruit gardens, food processing, bakery, a café that is open to the public, a weavery and a workshop that refurbishes tools that are then donated to developing countries.
Cultural life within our own community is varied and we have a regular programme of artistic and therapeutic activities. As in every Camphill centre, the Christian festivals play an important part in our lives throughout the year and are shared by those of quite different cultural backgrounds.
Future plans and developments: 2003 should see the completion of the final phase of the Willen project – a hall/theatre with seating for approximately 200. The hall is designed not only to meet our own needs but also to forge stronger links with the wider community.
We welcome long-term members and one-year volunteers.

→ See also description of network "**Camphill**"
☺ desire to live and work with adults with learning disabilities

Canon Frome Court Community

CF

Canon Frome Court | Ledbury | Herefordshire HR8 2TD
+44-(0)870-7650711 membership@canonfromecourt.org.uk
www.canonfromecourt.org.uk

1979 16 ha (near Hereford) ♀15 ♂13 19 47

e none

all who are concerned (consensus) limited common financing

property of all

none

farm, maintenance of buildings and estate

organic diet, organic agriculture, organic gardening, organic farming, animal friendly husbandry

Canon Frome Court is a Georgian manor house and stable block set in 40 acres of rural Herefordshire skirted by the River Frome.
We are a community of 47, ranging in age from 0 to early 70s. We do not have a common philosophy or political stance. The farm is the main focus of community life.
We farm our land cooperatively and organically (as far as possible) to produce a considerable proportion of our food, including a good deal of our own meat. Our stock includes cattle, sheep, goats, chickens and bees. We have a walled kitchen garden of about 2 acres growing vegetables and soft fruits, two polytunnels, one large greenhouse (and a smaller one), and an
orchard. Our arable land provides wheat for our flour, potatoes, further vegetables and animal fodder. Dogs are generally discouraged, mainly because of the live-stock.
Other communal activities include supper on Saturday nights (Pot Luck), trips out, as well as celebrations - Bonfire Night, Christmas, Easter, the Summer Party, sol-stice celebrations, children's birthdays - and the agricultural rituals of haymaking, harvesting, potato-lifting, fruit-picking...
Working together and independently on communal tasks and being concerned foreach other are essentially what ‚community' means to us. It's never boring!

☺ to visit according to our membership process

Cherry Orchards Camphill Community

CO

Canford Lane, Westbury-on-Trym | Bristol BS9 3PE
+44-(0)117-9503183
-9593665

1975 8 ha ♀7 ♂6 13

20

everyone in common (consensus) shared income

charitable trust

free individuality, Anthroposophy
therapeutic community, organic garden
ecological, self-managed, non-violent, spiritual, christian, anthroposophic, inner growth, organic diet, vegetarian diet, vegan diet, adult education, mentally/psychologically handicapped persons, therapy: garden, art, conversation, language and theatre), environmental protection, organic agriculture, organic gardening, animal friendly husbandry, farmers' market, candle making, no TV

We are a registered care home on a small estate within the boundaries of the city of Bristol. Twenty acres of fields and garden slope down the river Trym and are bounded by woodland creating a peaceful rural setting within an urban context. The village of Westbury is within walking distance and there is a convenient public transport service to the centre. Two houses of different character form a warm setting where staff (called "co-workers") and residents live together. The size of each house community varies between eight and twelve people. Each person living in one of the house communities is expected to make a contribution to the regular domestic activities of cooking and cleaning, and shares in all aspects of daily life. The close relationship of trust and involvement built between co-workers and residents ensures that support and understanding are there consistently. Living and working on the land forms an important part of activity in Cherry Orchards. The organic produce grown is the basis of the healthy diet we believe necessary to support the therapeutic life as a whole, and surplus is sold at the local farmer's market. Cherry Orchards also offers a range of craft workshops, artistic activity and therapy supervised by experienced co-workers. The daily programme of each resident is made by them so that individual interest can be balanced with the experience of group interaction in a variety of ways.
Cherry Orchards is a community offering people who have experienced mental health difficulties a safe, residential therapeutic environment.

→ See also description of network "**Camphill**"
☺ desire to work with mentally disabled people

Community for Reconciliation

RC

Chadwich Manor Estate | Bromsgrove, Worcester B61 0RA
☎ +44-(0)562-710231
cfrenquiry@aol.com
Fax -710278

1986 — 2 ha (near Bromsgrove) — ♀3 ♂1 4

e
none
part of the group decides in vote
individual financing
the community
Christians working and praying for peace and reconciliation
conferences, retreats, support work in Rumania, Croatia, Kenya
christian, peace-work

The community started as a network community of Christians committed to praying and working for peace and reconciliation. The intention to find a residential base for the work was realised in 1986 with the purchase of Barnes Close. Here in the beautiful Worcestershire countryside just 20 km south of Birmingham a small residential community runs a conference centre which in addition to welcoming guests is the focus for our work on peace and justice issues in the United Kingdom as well as our links with Rumania, Croatia and East Africa. We run our own programme of retreats, conferences, seminars, holidays, children's activities and youth house-parties as well as welcoming both groups who come for their own programme and individuals on private retreats. The community receives international volunteers for periods of 3 to 12 months at a time, whilst here the volunteers receive board, lodging, English tutoring and pocket money in return for assisting in the domestic work of the conference centre and grounds, alongside residential and non-residential staff and volunteers. The community is ecumenical and in addition to residential members and local staff and volunteers has over three hundred members across the British Isles and some beyond its shores.

→ See also description of network "**Church & Peace**"

NACCAN

☺ after invitation, please check website

Corani Housing and Land Co-op Ltd.

CH

Some People in Leicester | 10-12, Bartholomew Street | Leicester

☎ +44-(0)116-2545436

info@corani.org

-2555727

1978 | 2 houses | ♀2 ♂3 1 6

e

none

everyone in common (consensus)

limited common financing

common property

co-operative

co-operative life

left-wing political understanding, organic diet, organic gardening

☺

We have two generous adjoining terraced houses, workshop spaces and cellars. We eat together most evenings, and make decisions by consensus.
Things some or all of us like to do are: walking, growing vegetables, wood craft folk, drama club, watching films, teaching, plumbing, promoting devolved government, participating in a residents association, promoting sustainability.
We aim to take control of our lives, consume less resources & energy, to be open to different needs and to be involved in the wider co-operative scene.
We are a 25 year old co-operative totally owned by us, the members. Capital is not essential. For further information do get in touch with us!

SPIL, Radical Routes

☺ willingness to co-operate

Cornerstone Housing Co-op

CS

16, Sholebroke Avenue, Chapeltown | Leeds LS7 3HB
☎ +44-(0)1132629365
-(0)1132629365
cornerstone@ukf.net
www.cornerstone.ukf.net

1993 | 2 houses á 0.2 ha (near Leeds) | ♀6 ♂7 13

e, f, welsh | 2

all who are concerned (consensus) | limited common financing

housing co-operative

no

(eco) direct action

ecological, self-managed, anarchistic, vegetarian diet, vegan diet, animal protection, environmental protection, organic gardening

☺ ( )

Cornerstone has two large shambolic Victorian houses in Chapeltown, an ethnically diverse and run-down part of Leeds, Yorkshire (slowly being gentrified, though). Both houses need a lot of maintenance, but have large gardens front and back, where the odd co-op member does their best to create beautiful and productive landscapes. Each house has space for seven members. Both houses have office space and computer facilities, enabling us to run campaigns, produce newsletters, do websites, etc.
There is also a printing company (Footprint Worker's Co-op), which operates from the cellars of both houses.

Radical Routes

☺ ecologically aware, socially active

Coventry Peace House

CP

311 Stoney Stanton Road | Coventry CV 6 5DS
☎ +44-(0)2476663031
covpeace@gn.apc.org
www.covpeacehouse.org.uk

1999 | 320 m² (near Coventry) | ♀2 ♂1 2 5

2

everyone in common (consensus) | limited community financing

co-operative

peace and environment

refugee support, working with people on the margins of society

ecological, self-managed, left-wing political understanding, non-violent, vegetarian diet, peace-work, social work: working with people on the margins of society, environmental protection, organic gardening

☺

Coventry Peace House is based near the centre of Coventry. It consists of a row of 6 terraced houses. One house is lived in by refugees, and the remaining 5 are being converted into a community resource and housing co-op.
The main ethos is to live simple green lifestyles and to work actively for peace. We currently run projects for asylum seekers based in Coventry, and for disengaged young people. We will soon open a bike workshop, where we will be recycling bikes.
We are members of the Radical Routes network of co-ops, which means that we have made a commitment to work for radical social change.
Coventry peace house needs new members. If you like the idea of living in a co-op and want to work towards peace in any way, then we want to hear from you.

Radical Routes
participation in active peace work and a simple ecological lifestyle

Darvell Bruderhof

DB

Brightling Road | Robertsbridge TN32 5DR
+44-(0)1580-883300
contact@bruderhof.com
-883317
www.darvellbruderhof.co.uk

1920
120 ha (near Hastings)

g, e
everyone in common (consensus)
shared economy (shared income and capital)
association
early Christian brotherhood - communism
christian, peace-work

The Bruderhof is a counter-cultural network of people around the world who are building a new society where there is no money, no unemployment, no bosses, no weapons, no prisons, no retirement and no nursing homes — where war, divorce and abortion are no longer needed. Members abandon careers, pool their possessions and earnings, and commit to one another for life. They are living proof that people from different classes, various religious (and nonreligious) backgrounds and warring nationalities can live together in harmony as brothers and sisters.

→ See also description of networks "**Bruderhof-Communities**" and "**Church & Peace**"
NACCAN

Earthworm Housing Co-op

EW

Wheatstone | Leinwardine, nr. Craven Arms | Shrops SY7 0LH
+44-(0)1547-540461

1989 · 7 ha (near Hereford) · ♀3 ♂3 · 4 · 10

e, f, sp. · none paid
everyone in common (consensus) · individual financing
housing co-operative
conservation
garden & land work, building renovation
ecological, self-managed, yoga, vegetarian diet, vegan diet, adult education, pedagogical, animal protection, environmental protection, permaculture, organic agriculture, organic gardening, forestry, ecological construction, basket weaving, manufacturing willow furniture, closeness

☺ ( )

The Earthworm Housing Co-op has been living and working in Wheatstone since 1989. It has 7 ha of fertile land in a lovely valley with a big old house and outbuildings. We are endeavouring to reduce the consumption of products connected to the exploitation of animals, human beings and the environment. Our common meals are vegan. We welcome children and support home schooling. We employ permaculture and forest garden growing methods and have planted many trees. There is a large vegetable garden. We hope to earn money with this someday. We want to use alternative energy sources, to recycle as much rubbish as possible and use compost toilets. Our living conditions are still very simple as the house was very dilapidated. Our efforts to create more comfort and energy efficiency often depend on the availability of funds. Our well-appointed camping kitchen can be used for camping groups, workshops and other assemblies. We organise regular events such as permaculture courses and green meetings. We supply programmes on request. We are open to new members who are genuinely interested in the areas described above. We have special visiting times for these guests.

Radical Routes
☺ pay rent, provisional membership, contributing to work and food

Equinox Housing Co-op

EQ

161, Hamilton Road, Longsight | Manchester M13 0PQ
+44-(0)161-2489224 · mail@eqnx.co.uk
-2244648 · www.eqnx.co.uk

1995 · 0.02 ha · ♀4 ♂3 · 7

e · none
all who are concerned (consensus) · limited common financing
common property
none

ecological, self-managed, anarchistic, buddhist, taoist, esoteric/New Age, chaotic, organic diet, vegan diet, environmental protection, other

Equinox is a housing co-operative within the Radical Routes network. It is an inner city multiracial area with a small garden. Members are involved in diverse activities relating to social change, peace, animal rights and ecological campaigning. We also funktion as a resource and social centre for local social change groups. We do not accept visitors and are not looking for new members.

Radical Routes
none

Fireside Housing Co-op

FS

55-61 Melrose Road | Sheffield S3 9DN
+44-(0)114-2760630 simonlimb@burngreave.net

1995

♀6 ♂3 5 14

e, sp., g, f

7

everyone in common (consensus)

limited commom financing

common property

none

living and self-sufficiency

ecological, self-managed, non-violent, vegetarian diet, organic gardening, alternative energy, ecological construction

Fireside is situated in the inner city of Sheffield. We are very lucky to live in an area where there is plenty of green space, our four adjacent terraced houses back onto a lovely old cemetery and there's an adventure playground at the end of the road. We share a large garden, in which there is plenty of space for the children from the co-op and their friends to play, space to grow our organic veg and ample space for fires and parties too. We have a wind generator and a solar panel which we use as a display at local festivals. We are interested in renewable energies on a national scale as well as small design projects at home and are currently advancing plans to install photovoltaic and grey water recycling systems. Each house is run as a separate household, so we have a lot of personal space. We do however eat communally on a regular basis, particularly when having a workday on the houses or gardens.

Radical Routes
none

Fox Housing Cooperative

FH

Werndolau | Golden Grove | Gelli Aur SA32 8NE
+44-(0)1558-668798 roger@werndolau.fsnet.co.uk
-668088

1998 28 ha (near Swansea) ♀6 ♂5 1 12

e, f, g, welsh all
one part of the group (consensus) limited community financing
property of the co-operative
ecological
organic vegetable delivery scheme, school at home
ecological, self-managed, anarchistic (in the true sense), left-wing political understanding, feminist, non-violent, spiritual, inner growth, meditation, yoga, organic diet, vegetarian diet, vegan diet, adult education, free school, peace-work, one-world development, animal protection, environmental protection, self-sufficiency, permaculture, organic agriculture, organic farming, alternative energy, ecological construction, construction, wood crafts, art: sculptures, media: writing articles, celebrating seasonal festivals, humour

Fox is a small community that lives on a 70 acre farm in rural West Wales. We grow organic vegetables and fruit and run a delivery scheme from here, so we welcome help, both long and short-term, to do this work. All members work some of the time on the farm, as we are all committed to doing practical things to bring about a better world. We also home educate our beautiful children. As well as working on the farm, our members are involved in personal development and/or a spiritual practice, and we join together to celebrate Nature's seasons. We support freedom from addiction and so choose to live without wing drugs, i.e. smoking, cannabis, coffeine, processed sugar, TV etc. So despite having a busy delivery scheme here, this is a stable and calm (most of the time!) place to live, which seems to suit families especially. Self-responsibility, humour, openness and kindness are always much appreciated in visitors and volunteers.

Radical Routes
non-consumerist, low impact, vegetarian/predominantly vegan, spiritual/meditative practice

Grange Village

GV

The Grange, Newnham | Gloucestershire GL14 1JH
+44-(0)594-516246 grangeoffice@breathmail.net
-516969

1965 13 ha (near Gloucester) ♀30 ♂30 20 80

e all
everyone in common (consensus) shared economy

common property
Christian/anthroposophic
house, garden, pottery, woodwork, basketry, bakery
ecological, self-managed, non-violent, spiritual, christian, anthroposophic, inner growth, organic agriculture, organic gardening, organic farming, pottery, basket weaving, wood workshop

The Grange is a community of people, many of whom have learning difficulties, living together in an atmosphere of mutual care and responsibility. There are about 80 people living in the village and households vary from 6 to 13. Each household lives as a family. Villagers, co-workers and their children share the daily joys and sorrows of family life. A large variety of workshops and work-areas ensure that everyone has the possibility to contribute to the needs of the whole community through their work and according to their abilities. The workshops produce high quality goods, which are sold on the open market. Outdoor work is provided from the small holding of 33 acres, we have a farm and vegetable garden which meet a good portion of the needs of the village. Concern for the environment is a vital issue and the land is treated according to biodynamic principles. We have a natural reed bed system for treating our sewerage. The social and cultural life is lively and varied. It thrives on the active preparation for the Christian festivals and offers a wide range of possibilities for individual participation whether it be in drama, singing or music.

→ See also description of network "**Camphill**"
☺ openness and interest in our lifestyle

Grooby Ecohamlet

GE

Lawn Hill | 57 Markfield Road | Groby LE6 0FL
+44-(0)116-2876728 alisonc@stayfree.co.uk, alison@groby.com

1996 0.5 ha (near Leicester) ♀1

e, f, sp.
everyone in common (consensus) the one member
spiritual, people care, earth care, fair shares
permaculture, local networking
ecological, self-managed, spiritual, inner growth, organic diet, environmental protection, self-sufficiency, permaculture, organic gardening, animal friendly husbandry

My old cottage and garden is the start of Grooby Ecohamlet, designed to show the large village of Groby that it is possible to live with a small ecological footprint and be reasonably normal. 1/3rd acre, permaculture vegetables, fruits, herbs, flowers, and soon hens. Working towards solar water heating, planning grey water use etc. Friendly help needed, plus some heavy gardening.

EVNUK
☺ Experience of living in communities & applying permaculture

Gwerin Housing Association

GW

PO Box 9121 | West Midlands, Birmingham B13 8AU
☎+44-(0)121-2561303 gwerin@ironmanrecords.co.uk

1980 ♀5 ♂8 3 16

e, japanese, czech
everyone in common (consensus) individual financing
consensus, co-operative

☺

Started in 1979 and located 10 minutes walk from Stourbridge town centre, Gwerin is a co-operative of five houses, four of which are part of a Victorian terrace. These large houses are shared between members of the association. Each House is run differently, according to the individuals who live there. We have weekly meetings where the membership comes together to discuss the running of the association and a financial budget produced by rents. We are a mixture of individuals, and as a community have no particular ideological focus. Every aspect of the association is open to scrutiny by the members who, in turn, volunteer their skills to ensure that the rules of the constitution are tempered by the day-to-day reality of life in the community. Over the past 23 years Gwerin has evolved into an intentional community encouraging freedom and responsibility within a supportive and co-operative community environment. If you would like more information and details about how to apply to live in Gwerin, send a self-addressed envelope with a brief letter and some more information about yourself.

Heartwood Community

HC

Blaen Y Wern | Llangyndeyrne, Kidwelly | Carmarthen SA17
hippiesontour@yahoo.com

1997 14 ha (near Swansea) ♀2 ♂3 1 6

e, welsh, it. all 1 day per week
everyone in common (consensus) limited community financing
common property
garden
ecological, self-managed, meditation, yoga, organic diet, vegetarian diet, vegan diet, therapy: counselling, environmental protection, permaculture, organic agriculture, organic gardening, forestry, alternative energy, ecological construction, handicrafts: basket weaving, greenwood handicrafts, music, communication, sustaining relationships

☺

We are a Permaculture-based Housing Co-op based in South Wales where we have 35 acres of land, including pasture, wetland, streams and woodland. Since we came here in 2000 we have created new living space in one of our barns, built raised beds, acquired a polytunnel, made a herb garden and started a vegetable garden. Recently we have installed a solar thermal unit on the house and have put

in a Rayburn for heat in the winter. Future plans to make us more eco-friendly include the possibility of getting a wind turbine. We have also planted a coppice of ash, hazel and sweet chestnut, which is now 2 years old and some of the ash is bigger than us! We are planting another 6 acres of deciduous trees this winter.
There are currently 5 adults and one child living here and we would like more people to join us. We would like to create enough independent space for about 8 adults and their children. In addition to the barn we have planning permission for a self-built extension to the farmhouse.
We would also like to develop some land-based business here, a small willow growing and craft business already exists, and future plans might include growing vegetables or running courses and workshops. Our practise of Permaculture and sustainability includes maintaining sustainable relationships with each other as well as with the land we live on. This forms the basis of our community.

🌍 UK ECO Village network

☺ vegan and/or vegetarian diet, 1 common workday per week, sharing cooking and cleaning

Hengrave Hall

HH

Hengrave Community of Reconciliation I Bury St. Edmunds, Suffolk P28 6LZ
☎ +44-(0)1284-701561 ✉ co-ordinator@hengravehallcentre.org.uk
-702950 💻 www.hengravehallcentre.org.uk/

1974 17,6 ha ♀7 ♂6 13

all

everyone in common (consensus)

ecumenical

seminars, household, garden

christian, ecumenical, seminar-house, environmental protection

☺

We are an international Christian community of lay and religious volunteers committed to carrying out Christ's work of reconciliation by living its spirit among ourselves, by welcoming guests to our home, Hengrave Hall, and by working in partnership with other educational organisations.
Surrounded by 44 acres of fields, trees and a lake, Hengrave Hall is a 16th century manor that functions as a retreat and conference centre. On the estate, we also have a youth centre, a converted barn, and a camping area. Every day, we gather together for prayer and our work includes gardening, housekeeping, serving meals, washing dishes, setting tables, and making sure our guests feel welcome and are comfortable. Inspired by a sense of reconciliation, we welcome volunteers of different ages and backgrounds, from all parts of the world.

☺ desire to participate in community's Christian ethic

ISKCON: Govindadwipa Dhama

GD

Upperlough Erne | Derrylin | Co. Fermanagh BT92 9GN
+44-(0)2867721512 Lotus108@eircom.net
www.krishnaisland.net

1984 8.8 ac (near Enniskillen) ♀4 ♂6 10

one person (president considers everyone's opinion) donations, tours
ISKCON
Krishna
visitors centre
feminist, spiritual, yoga, vegetarian diet

Govindadwipa Dhama is the home of a Hare Krishna rural community. It's a very beautiful and picturesque island on a lake, and is situated in a nature reserve. The island has thick natural woodlands and a variety of flora and fauna. At the centre of the island is a temple. Ceremonies of chanting, music and meditation begin every morning at 4:30 a.m. The „aroti“ ceremony has been practised in Hindu temples for millenia.
Ten people live permanently on the island and there are guest-rooms for visitors. Guided tours are offered for day visitors in the summer. The tours are approved and supported by the Northen Ireland Tourist Board.
The temple is also the main place of pilgrimmage for Hindus in Ireland, and many visitors from all over the island of Ireland. The project has been featured on national TV and in newspapers dozens of times over the past 20 years.

→ See also description of network "**ISKCON**"
☺ no meat, no intoxication, no illicit sex, no gambling

Keveral Farm Community

KF

Keveral Farm | Looe, Cornwall PL13 1PA
+44-(0)1503-250135, -250215 oak@keveral.org; keveral@hotmail.com, billkit@dircon.co.uk
www.keveral.org

1973 12 ha (near Plymouth) ♀6 ♂9 7 22

sp., e 10
everyone in common (consensus, nearly always works; majority vote)
limited common financng and individual common property
ecological, sustainable
permaculture, organic farming
ecological, self-managed, permaculture, organic agriculture, organic gardening, forestry

Keveral Farm is a community 15 minutes walk from the sea in south-east Cornwall. We have a housing co-operative that owns and manages the house, and a worker's co-operative that manages the land. The 12 ha of land consists of vegetable plots, polytunnels, pasture, orchard and woodland, and is organic. We have a camping area that is open to holidaying visitors. We also take working visitors. We run a two-week Permaculture Design Course every August.

Radical Routes

L'Arche Bognor Regis

BR

Bradbury House | 51A, Aldwick Road | West Sussex P021 2NJ
+44-(0)1248-63426 bognor@larche.org.uk
-40383 www.larche.org.uk

1978 0,4 ha ♀20 ♂20 40

- e
- one part of the group (consensus)
- shared economy (shared income and capital) community
- Christian
- mentally disabled, garden and workshops
- spiritual, christian, ecumenical, mentally/psychologically handicapped persons

☺ ( )

L'Arche Bognor Regis is a community of about 40 people, of which 16 are people with learning disabilities. We are part of the International Federation of L'Arche Communities.
We have three residential houses, a workshop (including weaving, rug making, candle making, dance and drama) and a garden project (which also includes hens, a wood workshop and pottery).
We welcome people from all over the world who are keen to live and work with people with learning disabilities for a minimum of a year. We currently have people from 10 different countries ranging from 25 to 64 years old. We are a Christian Community, but accept people from all faiths and none. We are located by the sea in one of the sunniest towns in England.
Our aim is to have fun and to live as a Christian Community in which each person grows in love, maturity and creativity.

→ See also description of network "**Arche following Jean Vanier**"
☺ the desire to work with people with learning disabilities

L'Arche Liverpool

AL

The Ark Workshops | Lockerby Rd | Liverpool L7 OHG
☎ +44-(0)151-2600422 ✉ liverpool@larche.org.uk
Fax -2632260 www.larche.org.uk/liverpool/

1976 | 6 houses & workshop | ♀30 ♂30 60

- everyone in common and/or part of the group
- shared economy (shared income and capital) — rented/leased
- ecumenical, Christian
- to create a home, and share it with people with learning disabilities
- non-violent, christian, ecumenical, mentally/psychologically handicapped persons, physically handicapped persons, organic gardening, weaving, candlemaking, printing ☺

L'Arche means ‚the Ark' and began in France in 1964, when Jean Vanier said ‚yes' to God's call to share his life with two men with learning disabilities. From this call grew an international federation of communities where people with learning disabilities and assistants share daily life through living, working and praying together, rediscovering the depth of the Gospel and the love of God for each one of us. The L'Arche Liverpool Community opened its first house in 1976. Four more community houses have since opened, along with a house of prayer and a flat for more independent supported living. A workshop, the Ark, is the focus for craft, horticultural and therapy projects and a work experience scheme with local employers. Older members enjoy activities geared towards a slower pace of life, while a shop sells handicrafts. The community presently provides home and work to 23 people with learning disabilities, and a similar number of residential assistants (others work at the Ark), while the Ark also welcomes ten more people with learning disabilities who live locally. We often have vacancies for assistants, mainly in the community houses. We normally ask applicants to make a commitment of a year.

→ See also description of network "**Arche following Jean Vanier**"
☺ desire to live and work with people with learning disabilities

Laurieston Hall

LH

Castle Douglas | Dumfries & Galloway | Kirkcudbrightshire DG7 2NB
✉ everybody@lauriestonhall.demon.co.uk

1972 | 62 ha (near Dumfries) | ♀11 ♂9 8 28

- e, f, swed., g, czech. — the half
- everyone in common (consensus) — limited community financing
- common property
- none
- conference centre, farm, woodland management

self-managed, self-sufficiency, therapy: sauna, card games, conventional gardening, animal friendly husbandry, forestry, alternative energy, ecological construction, handicrafts: felt-making, woodworking, jewellry making, photography, volleyball

Laurieston Hall Housing Co-op is 20 adults and 8 children. About half of us live in the main house, mostly in small groups sharing one of three communal kitchens and half live in cottages or caravans. Each adult pays rent to the housing co-op and is domestically and economically independent. We enjoy a high degree of co-operation and caring. Much of what we eat is home-produced: there's a large fruit and vegetable garden, a small shop for bought-in food, and a restaurant service, which is a worker co-op providing income earning work for some residents. We also have cows, calves, hens, bees and sometimes pigs and sheep (three-quarters of us eat meat). Our heating is all from woodstoves and we have our own hydro-electric scheme which (when it rains, which is often) provides all the lighting, most of the other power and a lot of the hot water in the house. We use as little electricity as possible from the main grid. Part of what we call "Workshare" (2-3 days each week) is taking a share of responsibility by being on "committees". Additionally everyone is expected to attend the weekly meetings, to go on a wood-collecting trip each week, and to take part in "Maintenance Weeks" each year. Visitors to the community are invited to join in the building maintenance, gardening, land work and domestic work on Maintenance Weeks - the times when we function as one big group. Except for personal guests, we're not able to invite people to stay at other times. We're not actively seeking new members, so it will usually be left to people who are interested in joining us to discuss the possibility with friends they make among residents during Maintenance Weeks.

Lee Abbey Household Community

LA

121 Albert Road | Birmingham, Aston B6 5ND

1988 ♀3 ♂1 4

e

all

everyone in common (consensus)

shared income

Lee Abbey Fellowship

promoting the unity of God's Church

teaching, counselling, management, administration

christian, peace-work, local social work, counselling, prayer

We are a small ecumenical Christian community of adults, part of the Lee Abbey Fellowship, committed to living and working in a multi-faith, multi-racial area. Our Victorian terraced house has four single and one double bedroom, a community lounge, kitchen and bathroom all upstairs. Downstairs has facilities which can be used by others in the neighbourhood for committee meetings, quiet days etc., with a pleasant garden. We meet together for daily worship and prayer, share the use of the community car. We try to reach decisions by consensus, and are committed to spending time together, supporting, encouraging and listening to each other. We do paid and voluntary work, spend time with local folk, offer hospitality, and share our faith as and when appropriate. Each of us is an active member of a local Christian fellowship or church, and we want to deepen our faith. We offer a supportive, reflective, prayerful environment in which to experience life in the inner city. Enquiries by post welcome.

Lee Abbey, NACCAN
see text

Monkton Wyld Court

MW

Charmouth | Bridport DT 6 DQ
+44-(0)1297-560342
-560395
info@monktonwyldcourt.org
www.monktonwyldcourt.org

1982 | 4.4 ha (near Exeter) | ♀6 ♂6 2 14

e
everyone in common (consensus) | common till
Trust
education and sustainability
conference centre, gardening, livestock, kindergarten
ecological, self-managed, non-violent, inner growth, meditation, yoga, organic diet, vegetarian diet, vegan diet, adult education, seminar-house, environmental protection, permaculture, organic gardening, conventional gardening, animal friendly husbandry, ecological construction, anthroposophic kindergarten

Monkton Wyld Court is an educational charity run by a resident community of about a dozen adults, plus children and animals. The 11-acre grounds include a 15-bedroom Victorian rectory, a converted stable block and other outbuildings, a large organic vegetable garden, terraced lawns, fields, woods and stream. Facilities include a library, meditation hut, art hut, pottery, workshop, healing room and piano room.

Living at Monkton is a full-time commitment. Each morning we meet together to talk and plan the day. Cooking, cleaning, milking the cows, etc is organised by rota, but each resident is also responsible for specific areas of work, from gardening to admin. We generate income through a programme of educational courses and other events, and also run a kindergarten for the local community.

Our weekly community meetings alternate between „business“ meetings, where we make decisions by consensus, and „communication“ meetings, where we address (inter)personal issues. We are committed to making continual improvements to our levels of ecological sustainability, and usefulness to the wider community as an educational resource.

We welcome volunteers to work with us for one week initially. Volunteers often return for longer visits, and sometimes end up living here.

none

Mornington Grove

MG

13 Mornington Grove | London E3 4NS
☎+44-(0)181-9804534

1982 ♀6 ♂3 3 12

e, sp., roman., g — none
everyone in common (consensus) — individual financing
common property
green, leftist, feminist (but that's not a main focus)
local theatre, social change, psychotherapy, multicultural consciousness, refugees
self-managed, left-wing political understanding, feminist, non-violent, vegetarian diet

☺

We are a group of singles, couples and families who live together as a community. We have no common project but work outside. We follow the principle of consensus decision-making and come together every two weeks for joint organisational or private meetings. We eat vegetarian food and our current members are interested in: local theatre, pantomime, psychotherapy, feminism, social change, refugee studies and multiculturalism. We are homo- and heterosexual.

☺ men with an ecological consciousness and practical skills

Newton Dee Village Community

ND

Bieldside | Aberdeen AB15 9DX
☎+44-(0)224-868701
-867007

1960 72 ha (near Aberdeen) 200

e — none
all permanent members
shared economy (shared income and capital) — Camphill Trust
anthroposophical, Christian
living and working with adults with learnig disabilites
ecological, spiritual, christian, anthroposophic, mentally/psychologically handicapped persons, organic agriculture, organic gardening, organic farming, animal friendly husbandry, alternative energy, metal and wood handicrafts, toy workshop, art and creativity, humour, bakery, café, health foods shop

☺

Newton Dee Village is one of 70 Camphill communities around the world. We are a semi-rural community of around 200 people, 93 of whom are adults with learning disabilities. Our striving is based on Anthroposophy and Christianity. We live and work together in 21 households, on a 170 acre estate. The products of our village workshops include dolls, toys, metal work, bakery and confectionery goods. In addition we have a café, gift shop and organic grocery store, also two farms and gardens which are run using bio-dynamic methods. We receive no salaries and our needs are met by the community. We are open to new members as space is available.

→ See also description of network "**Camphill**"
☺ openness

Ochil Tower School

OT

140 High Street | Auchterarder PH3 1AD
+44-(0)1764-62416
-662416
info@ochiltowerschool.org.uk
www.ochiltowerschool.org.uk

1972 8 ac ♀20 ♂20 40 60

40

some members decide (consensus) shared income

foundation

Camphill, Anthroposophy, community

care and education of children with special needs

self-managed, spiritual, christian, anthroposophic, inner growth, organic diet, vegetarian diet, adult education, pedagogical, social work with children with special needs, therapy: art, games, music, eurythmics, organic gardening

☺

Ochil Tower is a small independent residential special school with 28 residential and 12 day places. Ochil Tower offers care and education to children and young people with a wide range of special needs. The school was established as a Camphill School.
The aim of life in Ochil Tower is to provide a stable, secure and supportive environment where the children can relax, feel at home and learn to live with others in a mutually beneficial way. A number of children need one to one care, but as a rule, the children live in small groups of two or three, cared for by a carer under the guidance of the houseparent. Co-workers, children and young people live in an extended family setting, where all aspects of domestic life are shared. The houses are organised in such a way that they can provide a homely, familiar environment in which each child, depending on individual needs and abilities, can gradually acquire the social and personal skills necessary for him/her to grow into meaningful adulthood.
As a residential school and Camphill Community, Ochil Tower offers an educational provision embracing all aspects of life. Educational practice is fostered in house and class, by both care and teaching co-workers, as part of an integrated holistic approach.

→ See also description of network "**Camphill**"
☺ desire to work with children with special needs

Old Hall Community

OH

Rectory Hill | East Bergholt, Colchester | Essex C07 6TG
+44-(0)1206-298045, -298294 old_hall@btopenworld.com
-299043 www.diggersanddreamers.org.uk/pnppage.htm

1974 30 ha (near Suffolk) ♀19 ♂24 16 59

e, g, f, sp. all
everyone in common (consensus) limited community financing and individual
house association
ecological, egalitarian
organic growing, self-sufficient farming and animal husbandry
ecological, self-managed, left-wing political understanding, feminist, non-violent, esoteric/New Age, inner growth, organic diet, self-sufficiency, organic agriculture, organic gardening, organic farming, animal friendly husbandry, alternative energy, ecological construction, wood, thatch

Old Hall has been a working community for thirty years. We are the custodians of 75 acres of farmland that has never been contaminated by chemical or genetic pollutants. Unless the British army did things with DDT during ist WW2 occupation. But that was sixty years ago. We farm our land organically, produce our own flour, make our own bread, and grow a whole range of exotic vegetables. We don't mind looking after animals and so we have cows, sheep, pigs, chickens and geese. The cows are milked by hand morning and evening. Butter and cheese are made in the dairy. We have members who manage the pigs and the chickens also. We cook meat. Despite the dependence upon animals a large number of us are vegetarian and some are vegans. Vegetarians and vegans therefore have a liberal attitude otherwise they cannot bring it on themselves to live here. We eat collectively twice a day and food is prepared in our big kitchen. There is always a vegetarian and a vegan option on the menu. Everyone is a cook at sometime. Everyone is also a washer-upper at sometime. We have a socialist ethos. To live here you must commit ideologically and financially and do a minimum of fifteen hours community work a week. Visit http://www.diggersanddreamers.org.uk for updates.

☺ capital needed, must match gender and age "quota"

Pilsdon Community

PD

Pilsdon Manor | Bridport | Bridport DT6 5NZ
+44-(0)1308-868308 pilsdon@lineone.net
-868161 website.lineone.net/~pilsdon

1958 4.8 ha (near Bridport, Bristol) ♀8 ♂25 2 35

all
core group / caretaker (consensus) shared income
charitable Trust

Christian, ecumenical, welcome all faiths and none
farm, garden, household, building, maintenance, pottery, art, music, crafts
self-managed, non-violent, christian, ecumenical, inner growth, conventional agriculture, organic gardening, social work: assistance to homeless people, mentally disabled, recovering from addictive disorders etc.

☺ (✋✋)

We seek to provide an environment where people can rebuild their lives after experiencing a crisis, whether sudden or progressive. We also welcome people who wish to find a time to reflect on their lives before making a change in direction, or just want time out to live as part of a Community. It is not necessary to have a specific reason or illness to come here. Most people who come and stay here find that with time, the routine and friendships developed, they can move on to live more independent lives; or discover that living in community is the way of life for them. This can take as long as seems mutually appropriate, whether months or years. Stays are usually between 6 months and two years, with people staying as long as 20 years. Responsibility for the running of the Community is carried out by 6 to 8 resident, unpaid Community Members (there are no paid staff). Everyone who stays, guest, visitor, wayfarer, volunteer or community member participates fully in our life and some may find the Christian foundation of the Community an assistance, though there is no religious requirement for guests. People of all races, cultures and faiths are welcome.

☺ willing to contribute to community, no alcohol, no drugs, spiritual searching

Redfield Community

RF

Buckingham Road | Winslow | Buckinghamshire MK18 3LZ
☎+44-(0)1296-713661 ✉info@redfieldcommunity.org.uk
Fax -714988 www.redfieldcommunity.org.uk

1978 7 ha (near Aylesbury, Milton Keynes) ♀11 ♂8 10 29

e, g none
all decide in consensus
individual/limited common financing Housing Co-operative
environmental and ecological focus
property maintenance, food production, living together
ecological, self-managed, non-violent, environmental protection, permaculture, organic gardening, animal friendly husbandry, alternative energy, ecological construction, football, volleyball, humour

☺ (✋✋)

We are a community living together in a large country house in Buckinghamshire. The buildings are situated in within an area of 7 ha with gardens, fields, newly planted and older trees. Redfield was established in 1978 and has developed progressively towards closer community. We live together as a single household, eat together and share the work. We try to be self-reliant producing our own fruit, vegetables and meat using organic techniques. We make decisions through consensus at our weekly meeting. One meeting a month has no agenda and offers the possibility to examine and celebrate different aspects of our communal lives. Spending so much time together places many private and common demands on us. Coping with them can be worthwhile and inspiring. We have found that the result of this way of life is just as great and positive as the effort we put into it.

Shekinashram

SA

Dod Lane | Glastonbury, Somerset BA6 8BZ
☎ +44 (0)1458 832 300
info@shekinashram.org
www.shekinashram.org

2003 kleines Haus mit Garten (near Glastonbury) ♀4 ♂1 5

e all

everyone in common (consensus) property of one community member

working on self-realisation, more conscious non-violent lifestyle

seminars, food preparation cleaning, garden work, office work

ecological, self-managed, non-violent, spiritual, inner growth, meditation, yoga, organic diet, vegan diet, therapy: Reiki, massage, permaculture, organic agriculture, organic gardening, alternative energy, raw foods

☺

The Shekinashram is a newly formed spiritual community based at the foot of Chalice Hill, in Glastonbury. There are currently 5 permanent residents at the ashram. Essentially the vision of the Shekinashram expresses a way of life that is both totally conscious and effortlessly selfless, which deeply honours the One in all its miraculous forms. We aim to provide spaciousness and facilities where all who are drawn to join us are made welcome.
We have chosen to live by a set of principles, in a way that is peaceful, self-responsible and conscious. This environment is naturally conducive to the development of spiritual practice and is intended to genuinely reflect freedom of Being. We promote an abundant and sustainable lifestyle, enjoy an organic vegan raw food diet, meditate, practice yoga and sing devotional songs together. A commitment to living Self-Realisation and a willingness to enter into profound relationships underpins our being together.
We have a group room for hire, and are able to accommodate up to 10 guests at residential workshops. We also have bed and breakfast accommodation available for short and longer term paying guests, and a growing programme of events, workshops, and retreats.

are interested in networks but not yet a member

☺ have to fit our vision, personal application required, have to say YES to a whole range of things

South Hams Holistic Education Community
SH

10a Riverside | Totnes TQ9
+44-(0)1803-868744

2001 | ~3 ha (near Totnes) | ♀5 ♂6 3 14

e, f

everyone in common (consensus) | limited community financing

common property

eco-spiritual, holistic education for the entire world

ecological, self-managed, non-violent, spiritual, meditation, organic diet, vegetarian diet, adult education, seminar-house, peace-work, one-world development, physically handicapped persons, holistic and spiritual non-traditional medicine, environmental protection, self-sufficiency, permaculture, organic agriculture, organic gardening, forestry, alternative energy, ecological construction, pottery, architecture and landscape design, construction and furniture trades, art.

☺ ()

We are a small group of families & individuals needing to live our own ideals of eco-spiritual relationships with each other, with nature around us & with the cosmos. Another combined desire is to pass on our skills and experience to others outside in a holistic, mutually participative way.
To achieve this we have planned a wide range of courses, seminars, workshops & holistic holidays. We are buying a large country house with outbuildings & land in the South Hams rural region to become a centre for these broadly holistic educational & natural health activities.
The working core want to live in eco-homes clustered around the main house for guests, studios, meeting rooms, dining room and kitchens, sauna, meditation room, library etc.
Our legal structure enables us ownership of all our land & property. Homes can be sold to fresh members after a certain time, but not the land they occupy. It is a registered not-for-profit benefit of the Community Society in which each member has only a single £1 nominal share certificate irrespective of their financial investment, and each has a vote in decision making. An elected committee does all paperwork, but other members can voluntarily help sometimes to relieve stress! Visitors are welcome and new residential members are too if they have savings or capital. Non-residing members can use the centre for their workshops or practice.

Network of Light

☺ ideally some capital or skills needed by the community

Stentwood Farm

SF

c/o Jonathan Stagg | Dunkeswell, Honiton | Devon EX14 0RW
+44-(0)1823-681155 community@stentwoodfarm.co.uk
www.stentwoodfarm.co.uk

1995 1.6 ha (near Exeter) ♀8 ♂7 15 30

e, f, g all
everyone in common (consensus) shared economy (shared income and capital)
common property
naturalness
bread-baking
spiritual

We exist as a light in the darkness of a corrupt world, a demonstration of God's Kingdom on the earth, as a witness of the resurrection of His Son, in which we find hope of eternal life. We see corruption in our own hearts and want to be free of it, so we are learning to judge ourselves and come back to the way we were created to be. We were thankful to give up our old rotten life and all our possessions and vain pursuits to be part to this new life. To us, community is not some idyllic lifestyle that's easy to live, it's a refiner's fire where all the daily circumstances of living together expose the hidden motives of our heart, so we may learn to be vulnerable, to share our heart with one another and be personal. In this lies the greatest healing. The little farm where we live needs just as much restoration as we do, which keeps us all very busy along with baking our organic bread, which we sell at local markets. You are always welcome.

→See also description of network "**Communities of the Twelve Tribes**"
☺ willingness to join in current projects

Stepping Stones Housing Co-operative

ST

Highbury Farm | Redbrook | Monmouth NP25 4LX
+44-(0)1600-713942 highburyfarm@hotmail.com
www.highburyfarm.freeserve.co.uk

1999 11.2 ha (near Bristol) ♀3 ♂2 5 10

e all (voluntary)
all who are concerned (consensus) limited common financing
property of all
conservation (grassland & forestry), hosting camps and gatherings
ecological, self-managed, anarchistic, non-violent, organic diet, vegetarian diet, vegan diet, organic gardening, animal friendly husbandry, forestry, alternative energy

Stepping Stones Housing Co-op was formed in 1999 with the intention of providing secure, ecologically friendly housing to its members in a rural setting where people could live in a non hierarchical community. Highbury Farm is a 30 acre smallholding with a large farmhouse, extensive outbuildings, mobile homes and the possibility of low impact structures. The land comprises mainly of pasture, which has greater conservation than agricultural value, though we have an historic, productive orchard and space for vegetable production. We also host camps and gatherings in our fields. We are situated above the incredibly beautiful Wye Valley, surrounded by woodland nature reserves, but are not isolated from local amenities and are integrated into the local community. At the moment we are trying to grow at a sustainable rate to form a stable, committed community of about 10 adults. We aim to be child-friendly, and to give consideration to their needs. Accommodation is in the main house, in caravans or vehicles, but a variety of other options can be explored. You are welcome to visit, but please arrange this beforehand. We ask for a small contribution towards food and bills. Arrival by public transport is encouraged.

Radical Routes

☺ Committed to social justice, ecological, vegetarian.

Steward Community Woodland

SC

Affinity Woodland Workers Co-op | Moretonhampstead |
Newton Abbot, Devon TQ13 8SD

☎ +44-(0)1647-440233

affinity@stewardwood.org

www.stewardwood.org

2000 — 12.5 ha (near Exeter) — ♀3 ♂4 4 11

e — 7

all who are concerned (consensus) — limited common financing

property of all

ecological

gardening, woodland managment, home education, eco-build, running courses, outreach, renewable energy

ecological, self-managed, anarchistic, non-violent, inner growth, meditation, organic diet, vegan diet, adult education, free school, peace-work, therapy: Massage, Reiki; animal protection, environmental protection, permaculture, organic agriculture, organic gardening, forestry, alternative energy, ecological construction, humour, crafts: basketry, green woodworking, childrens crafts; media: website

☺ ( )

We are a cooperative of people living and working together in a mixed woodland by Dartmoor. We are running a permaculture project to demonstrate the value of integrating conservation woodland management (such as coppicing and broadleaf planting) with organic growing, traditional skills and crafts, and positive-impact sustainable living.

We are living in bender-style and timber frame dwellings, which include the communal Longhouse and Kitchen. We have a micro hydro scheme and solar panels to generate electricity, from which we run lighting, computers and even an electric chainsaw. There are communal vehicles run, where possible, on bio-fuels.
We spend our time gardening, coppicing, conifer felling and native tree planting, maintaining and improving our dwellings and infrastructure, home education, running courses, on outreach, and on working for social change. We have a large veg growing area and young forest garden. We are a vegan community and so do not have any livestock. We have been granted planning permission for five years to live here and continue the project. We welcome visitors (please contact us first to arrange this) - we ask for a small contribution towards food and board. Finally, our lively website contains our latest news and events alongside ‚how to' guides, a photo gallery and more.

→ See also description of network "**GEN**"
☺ Ecological and vegan philosophy.

Talamh Housing Co-op

TA

Birkhill House | Coalburn ML11 0NJ
☎ +44-(0)1555-820400
talamh@lineone.net
website.lineone.net/~talamh

1993 | 20 ha (near Hamilton) | ♀4 ♂6 2 12

e | 12

everyone in common (consensus) | limited community financing

common property

ecological

environmental education, social integration

ecological, self-managed, non-violent, chaotic, vegetarian diet, peace-work, physically handicapped persons, environmental protection, self-sufficiency, permaculture, organic agriculture, organic gardening, alternative energy, new technologies, ecological construction

☺

Talamh Housing co-op is a rural community consisting of 50 acres of land, a 17th century farmhouse, a cottage and outbuildings containing workshops, venue space and an office/community resource centre. We are made up of 10 adults, 2 kids, cats, dogs, chickens, and horses. Since its founding in 1993, it has added a large pond and 10,000 native broadleaf and evergreen trees to the land, along with ever expanding organic gardens, orchards, and polytunnels. Our land is surrounded by motorway and opencast mine development in an unemployment blackspot. We exist as a challenge, an alternative, and hopefully an example to mainstream capitalist ideals and lifestyles, through living, working, and learning co-operatively how to live sustainably, in balance with nature, not in conflict. Current projects include the completion of our micro-hydro power system. We are continuing our work with our environmental educational charity „Talamh Life Centre", providing work for 2 full-time employees. This entails the repair and conversion of our outbuildings into a visitor centre. The sustainable boundaries project involves hedge-laying, fencing, and much more, such as managing a 2 ha plum orchard and 30 acres of mixed woodland as an outside project. We welcome visitors during our working weeks, or through the willing workers on organic farms network, or at our parties where we can laugh and dance together.

Radical Routes

☺ desire to work toward sustainability

The Abbey

AB

The Green Sutton Courtenay | Abingdon OX 14 4AF

☎ +44-(0)1235-847401 admin@theabbeysc.demon.co.uk

-847608 www.theabbey.uk.com

1980 1.6 ha (near Oxford) ♀3 ♂3 6

e all

everyone together/part of the group (in a circle, with space and silence)

trust

holistic spirituality, universal Christian root, open to all faiths and those with no faith

education and retreat centre

self-managed, spiritual, christian, ecumenical, buddhist, taoist, esoteric/New Age, chaotic, inner growth, meditation, vegetarian diet, organic gardening

☺

The Abbey is a beautiful and historic 13th century house. It is set round a peaceful courtyard, surrounded by informal gardens. It is a place which encourages the growth of a holistic spiritual life. This requires nourishing our relationships with the divine, our true selves, the earth and the world-wide community. Our own community seeks to be inclusive: we welcome all who are searching, whether or not they find themselves within a particular faith. The source and inspiration of the ongoing work here has been the ecumenical Christian tradition. The emphasis is on the mystical expression of this tradition, which draws us to interfaith exploration and the incarnating of a universal vision.

☺ spiritual seeking outlook, willingness to be open and inclusive

The Cohousing Company Ltd. CC

Springhill Cohousing Community | Frankleigh House |
Bradford on Avon BA15 2PB

info@cohouses.net
www.cohouses.net

2000 1 ha ♀28 ♂21 30 79

e, f sp., hebrew
ecological, self-managed, organic diet, vegetarian diet, organic gardening, alternative energy, ecological construction

☺

This will be the first (new build) Cohousing Community in the U.K. Located on our car-free grounds, we've got private houses and a large community house in which we meet every evening for dinner (ecological, vegetarian). Solar panels, strong thermal insulation and log cabins are additional features.

☺ purchasing a share

The Croft Community TC

Highfield Road, Old Malton | North Yorkshire YO17 7EY
+44-(0)653-694323
-694323

1976 2.4 ha (near York) ♀26 ♂26 17 69

e, g 52
everyone in common (consensus) shared income
Camphill Village Trust
Anthroposophy
Café, bookshop, papery, weaving, household/cooking, garden
ecological, spiritual, christian, anthroposophic, organic diet, vegetarian diet, adult education, mentally/psychologically handicapped persons, physically handicapped persons, social work, therapy, biodynamic gardening, art, humour

☺

Like other Camphill Communities, we also dedicate ourselves to working together with people with special needs. We have a large biodynamic garden, a café and bookshop, a woodworking and weaving workshop. Our houses lie scattered around a small and friendly market town. We maintain good relationships with the local population; all in all we are supported and accepted. We see our role as a vanguard in the development of gentler and more humane forms of co-existence.

→ See also description of network "**Camphill**"
☺ the desire to work with adults with special needs

The Findhorn Foundation

FF

The Park | Findhorn | Moray IV36
+44-(0)1309-690311 enquiries@findhorn.org
-691301 www.findhorn.org

1962 10 ha (near Inverness) ♀200 ♂170 80 450

e 60

everyone in common (consensus) individual financing

varies

Eco-village Ltd, and New Findhorn Directions

spiritual, non-confessional

education, gardening, kitchen, renovation

ecological, self-managed, non-violent, spiritual, inner growth, meditation, organic diet, vegetarian diet, adult education, peace-work, physically handicapped persons, non-traditional healing, self-sufficiency, organic gardening, organic farming, forestry, alternative energy, new technologies, ecological construction, handicrafts, art

☺

The Findhorn Foundation has been known internationally since 1962 for its experiments with new models for holistic and sustainable living. Today it is at the heart of the largest intentional community in the UK and the centre of this rapidly developing Eco-Village Project. Started in a caravan park in the Northeast of Scotland, the Findhorn Foundation is now a major centre of adult education conducting programmes for more than 4,000 residential visitors a year from over 50 countries. Co-operation and co-creation with nature has always been a major aspect of the Foundation's work and from its earliest days it became well known for its beautiful gardens grown in adverse conditions on the sand dunes of the Findhorn peninsula. Since 1981 the Findhorn Foundation has been involved in the development of the Eco-Village Project as a natural continuation of its work with nature. A number of other organisations within the community work in partnership with the Foundation to help make the Eco-Village Project a reality. The Community is comprised of approximately 400 individuals who live and work in this rural area of Scotland. They come from over 40 countries to join the experiment in discovering what is necessary for joyful, sustainable living. The built environment is gradually growing to reflect shared ecological values.

→ See also description of network "**GEN**"

UNESCO

☺ individual financing for 1 year, then membership

The Hockerton Housing Project

HP

The Watershed, Gables Drive | Southwell NG25

+44-(0)1636 816902 hhp@hockerton.demon.co.uk

www.hockerton.demon.co.uk

1995 8 ha (near Nottingham) ♀4 ♂5 11 20

e, it. all between part time and full time

everyone in common (consensus) limited community financing and individual

leased, rented, partly owned by one community family

environment

organic food growing, communal management of utilities/facilities, eco-consulting, demonstration visits, talks

ecological, self-managed, free love, organic diet, environmental protection, self-sufficiency, permaculture, organic agriculture, alternative energy, new technologies, ecological construction, sports: volleyball; art: spontaneous art projects

The Hockerton Housing Project (HHP) is the UK's first earth sheltered, self-sufficient ecological housing development. Project members live a holistic way of life in harmony with the environment, in which all ecological impacts have been considered and accounted for. The residents of the five houses generate their own clean energy, harvest their own water and recycle waste materials causing no pollution or CO_2 emissions. Their houses are amongst the most energy efficient, purpose built dwellings in Europe. They aim to produce as much food on site and meet as many of their needs for work from the site and project.
Working guests are welcome - only via WWOOFing!

The Monkey Sanctuary

MS

Looe, Cornwall PL13 1NZ

+44-(0)1503-262532 info@monkeysanctuary.org

-262532 www.monkeysanctuary.org

1964 15 ha (near Plymouth) ♀6 ♂5 11

e

everyone in common (majority vote) shared income

co-operative

animal protection

caring for monkeys, environmental education

ecological, self-managed, vegetarian diet, vegan diet, adult education, animal protection, environmental protection, self-sufficiency, permaculture, organic gardening, alternative energy

The Monkey Sanctuary at Murrayton, near Looe, has become a refuge for monkeys who have been rescued from the isolation of life as pets. We make every effort to provide the monkeys with a stimulating and interesting environment and they now live on an expansive compound with an outdoor enclosure and heated rooms. The caretakers live as a community in Murrayton House and provide these unbelievable creatures with round-the-clock care.

The Neighbours Community

NB

140-148 Ardington Road | Northampton NN1 5LT
☎+44-(0)1604-633918 rog@fish.co.uk

1984 | 0,4 ha, 5 Reihenhäuser | ♀5 ♂4 6 15

e, some g/f — none
all who are concerned (consensus) — limited common financing
some owner-occupied, some rented
ecumenical
we are a „community of households"
self-managed, spiritual, christian, ecumenical, vegetarian diet, peace-work, one-world development, mentally/psychologically handicapped persons, conventional gardening, crafts, art

☺ ()

Founded in 1984, The Neighbours Community is a community of households. Fifteen people, some single, some married, some children. Each household lives in one of five adjacent terrace houses with a common meeting room and a large garden. We are ecumenical Christians (Anglican, Catholic, Quaker), pray together every day and share some meals each week. Our stated purpose is „to develop a community life which enables us to explore and share our faith and care for others according to the gospel". We arrange creativity mornings and quiet days and offer hospitality to visiting groups. We have a contemplative eucharist each month and a Taize prayer. We lead diverse lives, some in paid work, some voluntary, and we try to support each other, and to visit friends, in our different journeys and callings.

Touching Place
☺ christian

The Well at Willen

The Well | Newport Road, Willen | Milton Keynes, Buckinghamshire MK15 9AA
☎+44-(0)1908-242190 community@thewellatwillen.org.uk
-242187 www.thewellatwillen.org.uk

1997 | 1.2 ha (near Milton Keynes) | ♀3 ♂4 2 9

e, some g, f, it. — all on part time basis
all who are concerned (consensus) — limited common financing
rented
ideological, ecumenical and interfaith, some peace work

- spiritual program & ecological interest as well as working; offering hospitality to homeless
- ecological, self-managed, non-violent, spiritual, christian, ecumenical, peace-work, social work: asylum seekers, refugees & homeless, respite care / retreats, organic gardening, art: music, some drama, clay & art work; other: workshops on various themes relating to our spiritual program

☺

The Well at Willen is a comunity of single people, couples and families from different faith communities, attempting to live a contemporary expression of religious life through our values of spirituality, hospitality, inclusivity, peace and justice and sustainability. Both in Milton Keynes and in partnership with our local and global communities.
We are people who want to devote our lives to the service of that which we call God, through service to others, by offering all who come to The Well the opportunity to discover healing and wholeness and develop gifts they may not have been aware of.
We are committed to valuing and supporting others and ourselves equally, within a spirit of honesty, love, reconciliation and compassion and by reflection, discussion and action, to encourage ways of renewing human community.

- Chistian communities
- ☺ financial and ideological

Torch Housing Co-op

TH

10 Richmond Road | Hockley, Birmingham | East-Mercia B18 5NB
+44-(0)121-5544256/-5513161 jantorch@aol.com
-5153524

1993 | 2 houses, 2 gardens | ♀3 ♂7 10

- e, f, g, greek, sp. — none
- everyone in common (consensus) — individual financing
- common property
- anarchism, vegetarian, vegan living and working
- environmental, refugee and asylum work etc.
- ecological, self-managed, anarchistic, left-wing political understanding, feminist, non-violent, buddhist, esoteric/New Age, chaotic, anthroposophic, inner growth, meditation, organic diet, humour, vegetarian diet, vegan diet, adult education, peace-work, one-world development, social work, art and other therapies, animal protection, environmental protection, organic gardening, new technologies, ecological construction, construction, walking, biking, painting, drawing, media, music, cinema, parties...

☺ ()

Torch Housing Co-op is a houseshare community of two houses of 7 men, 3 women, a dog and a cat in the Hockley, Lozells and Handsworth areas of inner-city North-West Birmingham. We live within 2 minutes walk of each house and each other

Both houses have gardens. One house has a community room for use by the local community around us. We collectively own the properties and we run them as individual self-financing households. We have popular parties, make our own music and make cuppies and go out for baltis, gigs and the pub occasionally. We believe in getting along with each other as friends and enjoying each other's company. We are always advertising for and recruiting new Co-op members. We always welcome working visitors by prior arrangement.

Radical Routes
getting along with other people, sense of humour

Two Piers Brigthon

TP

The Secretary | 14 Oriental Place | Brighton BM2 2AD
+44-(0)1273-739779
info@twopiers.co-op.org
www.twopiers.co-op.org

1979 | 80 beds | ♀36 ♂40 4 80

e | all
everyone in common (majority vote) | shared income
common property
safe and affordable living
maintaining homes and nurturing community identity
self-managed, non-violent

We are a self-managed registered social landlord, a Housing Co-Operative. We communally own the Properties. We pay rent to ourselves.

Confederation of Co-operative Housing
willingness to participate in the management of the Co-op

Vegan Enterprises

VE

c/o 31 Caerau Road | Caerau, Maesteg CF34 0PB
+44-(0)1656-739813
-739813

1988 | 4 houses & stores | ♂1 1

e | 1
everyone in common
individual financing
healing this crazy world
developing our property
ecological, self-managed, anarchistic, non-violent, organic diet, vegan diet, adult education, free school, peace-work, one-world development, environmental protection, self-sufficiency, organic agriculture, organic gardening, forestry, alternative energy, new technologies, ecological construction

☺ (hands)

From the age of 12, when I read the Age of Reason by Thomas Paine and reached my own age of reason, I have been trying to understand the world with a view to changing it for the better. I am now 55 and still struggling with the greatest task anyone could set himself.
No one person can change the world very much, alone, but anyone can try. Anyone can take the problems seriously and search for solutions that others might benefit from. We can all look at the solutions others come up with and see if we can do better.
Plenty of ideas have been tried, with qualified success, or dismal failure, and we just have to keep trying till we get it right. Money, and the lack of money, are equally big problems. We cannot abolish money, but we can collectivise to buy land to grow our own organic fruits and vegetables, and trees for future fuel to replace fossil fuels, and just to give us access to the countryside where we can connect with the earth.
We can promote true representative democracy, locally, nationally and globally, with the every-candidate-gets-elected strategy. No losers, all of us winners. Please!

the Vegan Community Project
☺ non-smokers, no drugs, reason

Welhealth Co-operative

WH

c/o Diggers & Dreamers | BCM Edge | London WC1N 3XX
+44-7980-158661 & +44-1490-420074 frank_bowman@yahoo.co.uk

1992 10.8 ha on 2 farms (near Bangor/Ruthin) ♀2 ♂2 4

e, span., welsh none

all who are concerned (consensus) limited common financing

One farm is co-operatively owned, the other is promised into the co-operative.

The circle. Green. Down shifting diggers & sharing roles and permanent culture. No gender roles.

Permanent culture and agriculture for a completely sharing world - no starvation.

ecological, self-managed, anarchistic, left-wing political understanding, feminist, non-violent, organic diet, vegan diet, adult education, peace-work, social work: give & take free cycling for a sharing; therapy: stress free world; environmental protection, self-sufficiency, permaculture, organic agriculture, organic gardening, organic farming, forestry, alternative energy, new technologies, ecological construction, construction, humour: play, comedy, happiness! Crafts: high quality, art, in our work it's not work, it's play! Sport: is for „competitives", not us! Art; other: renewable energy, getting everything for free. Sharing agapé love. Worship is for „competitives" bowing down to the hierarchy!

☺ (hands)

WelhEALTH Share the World.
We share the vision of Mahatma Ghandi. Mahatma Ghandi had a vision of a new world order of:
„innumerable, self sufficient villages, Gardens of Eden, where would dwell highly intelligent folk whom none could deceive or exploit. The villages would develop in ever widening circles, never in ascending order. Life will not be a pyramid with an apex sustained by the bottom but an oceanic circle."
Welhealth, as an organisation provides the use of free land to grow free food and free fuel, also free initial renewable energy equipment, free initial energy efficiency materials also free initial building materials of quality and longevity in order to obtain from that land their material physical needs for food, warmth and shelter, and water all for FREE, no charge, no rent, as a birthright, for solely people who are not „free riders" - who are sharers, who are committed:
to make decisions by consensus, who are working to get out of the competitive success oriented money, exchange, wage slave system and into the free moneyless co-operative sharing system of „give and take" doing permaculture and forest gardening, and are vegan thus extending humane sharing and non-exploitation of the other animal species.

🌍 Radical Routes, Vegan Organic Network
☺ vegan, income limit, focus on self sufficiency, sharing, no exchange, ethical green.

"Luckily, the children keep reminding us
of what's really important in life:
climbing trees, playing in the grass, swimming in the lake."
(Forest kindergarten at Ökodorf Sieben Linden)

Hungary

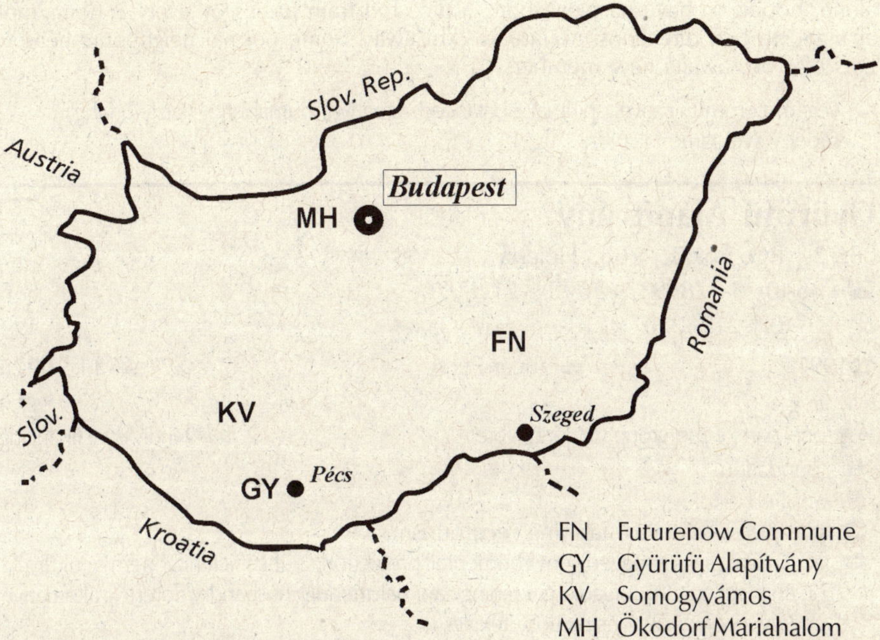

FN Futurenow Commune
GY Gyürüfü Alapítvány
KV Somogyvámos
MH Ökodorf Máriahalom

Futurenow Commune

FN

c/o Toma Sik | PF 18/541 Konyaszeki tanya 410 | 6640 Congràd
☎ +36-(0)705266031 siktoma@freemail.hu

23 ha (near Congràd) ♂1 1

hungar., esper., e, hebrew — all

everyone in common (consensus) — shared economy

Toma (for now)

vegan, humanistic, natural

self-sufficiency, social activities in the outside world in the struggle for human rights

ecological, self-managed, anarchistic, left-wing political understanding, feminist, non-violent, sexuality, free love, organic diet, vegan diet, peace-work, one-world development, therapy: naturopathy, animal protection, environmental protection, self-sufficiency, permaculture, organic agriculture, organic gardening, forestry, alternative energy, ecological construction, intercultural, world-cultural, money-free

☺

Modest and simple pleasant life is the basic element. Real sustainability is the aim. To be happy with ourselves and a good example to others. At the moment Toma is cleaning, constructing, pruning, planting, and eating sweet fruits from the garden - alone, hoping to have partners soon. A nice red train passes by every 2 hours (not at night) in two directions. Mainroad 2km away. Some normal neighbours nearby. Lots of work awaits new members.

☺ vegan, communicative, spiritually balanced, creative, humanistic, hardworking, money welcome

Gyürüfü Alapítvány

GY

086/2 | P.O. Box 3 | 7683 Helesfa
☎ +36-(0)73-378593, +36-(0)1-2128026
Fax +36-(0)1-2128026

1991 (near Pécs) ♀7 ♂7 11 25

e, g 9

one part of the group (majority vote) individual financing

foundation

applied ecology

computer sciences, farming, ecotourism

ecological, self-managed, environmental protection, self-sufficiency, permaculture, organic agriculture, organic gardening, animal friendly husbandry, forestry, alternative energy, ecological construction, textiles

☺

Gyürüfü is an emerging full-fledged ecovillage based on the Permaculture principle and other methods of ecological planning. It is designed for a 1100 ha outstanding watershed partly owned by the Gyürüfü Foundation. The rest is either privately owned land or state forest. The village was started from scratch, no road, no electricity, no infrastructure were present in a formerly populated area which was abandoned during the Communist era. The community has set up a master plan for the area which contains the main rules for activities as well as including housing, transport, agriculture, water management and forestation goals. Building permits have been [granted] for family houses and agricultural facilities since 1996. Available land is held in common, officially owned by the Gyürüfü Foundation and the municipality of Ibafa, respectively. Plots are sold to the house owners. Upon completion, the village might not hold more than 300 permanent residents as determined by the ecological carrying capacity of the area. Appropriate building technologies include mud bricks, rammed earth buildings, composting toilets, reed bed systems and rainwater harvesting as well as a host of other methods. Gyürüfü might well be the first ecovillage where ecological constraints are integrated into the state administration in form of the master plan, the nature conservation requirements and other resolutions of the cognisant authorities. Beside 10 residential houses, the village accommodates a community house, a camping area and several businesses, a goat farm, an integrated agroforestry project, a wool processing unit, a horse riding facility, an information technology company and a translation service, the latter two based on the Internet. Plans for the future include a village school, a forestation project, an aquaculture pond and other water management schemes.

→ See also description of network "**GEN**"

☺ Newcomers shall be able to build their own houses and provide themselves with a livelihood

Ökodorf Máriahalom

MH

Szechènyi 51 | 2527 Mariahalom

☎ +36-(0)33481102

geza@biofalu.hu

www.biofalu.hu

2000 | 50 ha (near Piliscsaba) | ♀1 ♂1 4 6

e

1

only one family lives here at the moment

property of individual community members

none

building ecological houses, wood ovens, vegetables

ecological, self-managed, organic diet, environmental protection, self-sufficiency, permaculture, organic agriculture, organic gardening, animal friendly husbandry, alternative energy, new technologies, ecological construction

☺

Our Ecovillage is eco but not village yet, since only 1 family is living here at the moment. In the past years the founder of the ecovillage has built several ecological houses, but these are rented out for normal housing purposes. The first few years of use showed that they are good places to live. The experimental phase is over. This year we shall sell them.

In the meantime, these experiments have led us to build more radical ecological houses. So in the phase 2 we have built a house, which is used by the founder of the ecovillage, and another house and a community house is in the construction process. Permaculture principals have been added. These new houses are designed for a more natural way of life (passive solar, timber frame, light clay, strawbale, masonry wood stove, dry toilet,...).

→ See also description of network "**GEN**"

Hungarian Ecovillage Network

☺ environmentally-friendly attitude towards life

Somogyvámos

KV

Krisna-Völgy | Fö u. 38. | 8699 Somogyvámos
+36-(0)85-340-185 new.vraja-dhama@pamho-net
-189 www.krisnavolgy.hu

1992 200 ha (near Kaposvar) ♀70 ♂90 12 172

hungar., g, e 95%
one part of the group (majority vote) limited community financing
common property
spiritual and religious focus
education, Vedic culture, ecological farming
ecological, self-managed, non-violent, hierarchical, leader/guru, spiritual, inner growth, meditation, yoga, vegetarian diet, adult education, seminar-house, peace-work, social work (distributing food), animal protection, environmental protection, self-sufficiency, organic agriculture, organic gardening, organic farming, animal friendly husbandry, forestry, alternative energy, ecological construction, construction, bakery, pottery, candle workshop, art, dance, painting, Indian music, non-violence, media: magazine, therapies currently developing, Krishna consciousness

☺ ()

Some 20 km from the Plattensee, in beautiful surroundings on the outskirts of the community of Somogyvámos, lies the Krishna Valley with a surface area of 200 ha. The goal of this institution, unique in all of Europe, is to realise and present a natural lifestyle in physical-mental harmony. It is based on the holy scriptures of India, the Vedas, in the translation of A.C. Bhaktivedanta Swami Prabhupada, the founder of the International Society for Krishna Consciousness and the bearer of Vedic culture. In the approximately 1,500 m² building, which is richly decorated with murals and reliefs, visitors can attend the traditional temple ceremonies. The guesthouse and campground await holidaymakers and persons seeking relaxation in surroundings rich in natural beauty, whether for a week or for a longer holiday stay.
Besides the rural life, the farm is also a site of cultural development. Krishna Valley festivals, music and theatre events, as well as colourful Indian celebrations take place regularly. Numerous attractions and specialities await our welcome visitors year-round.

→ See also description of network "**ISKCON**"

☺ religious, no meat, no drugs, no "illegal" sex, no loafing

Ireland

AA Aisling Aran
AD L'Arche Dublin
AK L'Arche Kilkenny
DF Camphill Village Community Duffcarrig

Aisling Aran

AA

An Charraig | Mainistir, Inis Mor | Co. Galway, Aran Islands
☎+353-(0)99-61245 aismag@iol.ie, info@aislingmagazine.com
-61245 www.aislingmagazine.com

1985 0.8 ha (near Galway) ♀3 ♂3 4 10

e, gaelic
everyone in common (consensus) limited community financing
Celtic spirituality, green politics, feminist, ecumenical
self-sufficiency, publishing of holistic magazine, pilgrimage/study groups
ecological, self-managed, left-wing political understanding, feminist, non-violent, spiritual, christian, ecumenical, inner growth, meditation, organic diet, vegetarian diet, adult education, pedagogical, seminar-house, one-world development, therapy, environmental protection, self-sufficiency, permaculture, organic agriculture, organic gardening, organic farming, alternative energy, ecological construction, handicraft, media

☺

We are a small group of people who run two centres on the island of Inis Mor. The first, Killeany Lodge, is a centre for education focussing on Celtic spirituality, holistic lifestyle and Gaelic culture. The second, An Charraig, is a spiritual centre where a small group of people have created a lifestyle based on Celtic spirituality, ecological living, and justice. This centre receives guests and volunteers, publishes a holistic magazine, hosts groups and pilgrimages, leads Celtic rituals and lives self-sufficiently.

☺ only guests and volunteers, no permanent residents

Camphill Village Community Duffcarrig

DF

Duffcarig, Gorey | Co. Wexford
☎+353-(0)55-25911 | duffcarrig@camphill.ie
Fax -25910 | www.camphill.ie

1972 | 24 ha (near Gorey) | ♀35 ♂35 | 15 | 85

- e
- everyone in common (consensus) | shared economy
- common property
- Anthroposophic, Christian
- living/working with disabled people in farm, garden, state and craft work (weaving, pottery, basketry), home care (laundry and cooking)
- ecological, self-managed, non-violent, spiritual, christian, anthroposophic, organic diet, adult education, mentally/psychologically handicapped persons, physically handicapped persons, eurythmics, massage, hydrotherapy, environmental protection, organic agriculture, handicraft: basket weaving, weaving, pottery; painting; sports: biking, swimming

☺

Duffcarrig was the first Camphill Community to be established in the Republic of Ireland. Founded in 1972, the village has grown to include seven households and is home to about 90 people, about half of whom are in need of special care. The members of a household live as a family of from eight to 16 people, creating social awareness and mutual support in their daily lifes. Tasks and responsibilities are shared according to individual ability and are fostered by encouraging the willingness to help. Some people work on the farm or in the garden, while others work as hand-weavers, potters or basket-makers. Others help with the cooking and in the laundry. All work situations are designed to be creative, useful. Orderliness, rhythm and a beautiful end product, which can be used in the community or sold, give a feeling of satisfaction and dignity to all involved. Work often needs to be in a one to one situation to give some individuals the chance to master the challenges of their lives. Those beyond retirement age are being integrated in the cultural and domestic life, which is of central importance to the village community. Where needed, more specialized care is provided for our ageing population.
Among recent projects are the renovation of a house in the nearby village of Ballymoney, which will in the future provide a home outside of the community, for a more independent group of people. Furthermore, surrounded by holiday homes,

Ballymoney House offers itself to host a coffee-shop as well.

→ See also description of network "**Camphill**"
☺ interest in living and working in a community with handicapped adults and want to stay only for a longer period

L'Arche Dublin

AD

Baidin | 8 Warrenhouse Road | Baldoyle, Dublin 13
☎ +353-(0)1839-4356, -4362 dublin@larche.ie
-5897

1993 — 2 houses — ♀7 ♂6 13 26

everyone in common (consensus) — limited community financing
common property
Christian
caring for/living with people with learning disabilities (mental handicap)
spiritual, christian, ecumenical, mentally/psychologically handicapped persons, physically handicapped persons

☺

L'Arche Dublin is a small community of two homes, situated in Baldoyle, a suburb of Dublin. It is part of the world-wide L'Arche-Federation (of Jean Vanier), communities dedicated to providing a home for people with learning disabilities (mental handicaps) in a family-type setting, where assistants and people with learning disabilities live together and help each other to grow. The first home, Seolta, which was opened in 1996, is built on land donated by the Christian Brothers. It is home for 4 people with learning disabilities and 4 assistants. The community purchased a second house in 1999, called Leoithne, which is home to two people with learning disabilities and 3 assistants. It is planning to extend that house in order to welcome 4 more people.

→ See also description of network "**Arche following Jean Vanier**"

L'Arche Kilkenny

AK

Cluan Aoibhinn | Fair Green Lane | Callan, Co. Kilkenny
☎ +353-(0)56-7725628
-7725946

1978 — 1.2 ha (near Kilkenny) — ♀12 ♂10 22

e
one part of the group (consensus) — individual financing
property of L'Arche
Christian, ecumenical
gardening, printing, weaving, candle manufacture

⇏ ecological, spiritual, christian, ecumenical, mentally/psychologically handicapped persons, organic agriculture, organic gardening, handicraft: weaving, candle making, printing; art therapy

☺ ✋✋

This Arche community strongly remembers the Arche community in Dublin - read their descripton for more info.

→ See also description of network "**Arche following Jean Vanier**"
☺ a desire to live and work with handicapped people

"It is how we apply our talents that makes them so valuable"

Italy

AA Ananda Assisi
AC Az. Agr. Acquasanta
AF Arcobaleno Fiammeggiante
AR Associazione Archeus
BG La Comune di Bagnaia
CB Cooperativa di Bordo
CC Case Caro Carrubo
CH Associazione Arca Italia
CL Comunella Casagatti
EG Villaggio Ecologico Granara
EP Rainbow Eco Peace Village
ES Villaggio Ecologico Solidale
EU Upacchi Ecovillaggio
FD Federazione di Damanhur
HL Hairakhandi Love Center
IC Il Casale
IF ISKCON Firenze
IN Inspira
MF Mirapuri-Friedensstadt
ND Nomadelfia
OM Osho Miasto
PE Il Popolo Elfico della Valle dei Burroni
TS Associazione Culturale Torri Superiore
UP Utopiaggia
VV Comunità Coop. Villaggio Verde

Ananda Assisi

AA

C.P. 48 | 06088 Santa Maria degli Angeli (PG)
+39-0742-81-3620 info@ananda.it
-3536 www.ananda.it

1987 5.5 ha (near Assisi) ♀45 ♂35 3 83

g, e, it. nearly all

everyone in common (consensus) shared income

partially common property, partially rented / leased

living according to the teachings of Paramhansa Yogananda

hospitality, courses on spiritual issues, gardening, sale of spiritual articles and music, translations into I, G, E

spiritual, esoteric/New Age, inner growth, meditation, yoga, vegetarian diet

☺ ( )

Ananda Assisi is part of an international network of spiritual communities and retreats founded by Swami Kriyananda, a direct disciple of Paramhansa Yogananda, in 1968. At the moment some 80 community members live here, dedicating themselves to a spiritual search in accordance with the teachings of self-fulfilment. In our community, spiritual values are placed above economic values - co-operation counts more than competition. The community's members come from 12 nations. We have 75 beds for guests and a factory which supports the community financially through the production and sale of yoga, meditation, and health-related products. We are striving to create an environment in which spiritual development and the happiness of the individual stand centre-stage. We regularly meditate together and try - in accordance with Yogananda's teachings - to lead a "simple life of high ideals" in which we support one another in our search for God. Our main area of work is the guest centre through which we endeavour to help truth seekers to grow spiritually and find their way to God (Please ask for our twice-yearly programme pamphlet).

Since the possibilities for working and living within our guest retreat are limited, our community sees itself as a kind of "training centre for spirituality in everyday life" for others who want to live in or found a co-operative, spiritual community. At the moment 16 persons live outside and independently of the retreat. That is also the direction we want to take in the development of a larger spiritual Yogananda Community.

☺ several-months admission programme, participation in guest programme, must already be or else become a disciple of Yogananda

Arcobaleno Fiammeggiante

AF

Bioregione PARTENOPEA | Vico S. Pietro a Majella 6,C.P. 82 | 80138 Napoli
+39-08145-5026
-5026

1986 — 150 m²

- it., e
- everyone in common (unanimous) — limited common financing
- rented/leased
- ecumenical spirituality, vegetarianism and bioregionalism, anarcho-spirituality, Rainbow Family
- vegetarian-macrobiotic restaurant, organic foods shop, specialised bookshop, seminars
- ecological, anarchistic, non-violent, spiritual, ecumenical, inner growth, meditation, yoga, organic diet, vegetarian diet, vegan diet, macrobiotic diet, peace-work, one-world development, animal protection, environmental protection, organic agriculture, organic gardening, art, communication

OM NAMO NARAYANAYA! The Flaming Rainbow (Arcobaleno Fiammeggiante) has reorganised its headquarters, founded in Naples in 1986. Now a group is concerned with the vegetarian-vegan-macrobiotic restaurant, the organic foods store and the specialised book shop; another group of association members is involved in organising and conducting projects, courses and seminars on natural, spiritual and psycho-physical techniques (body work). One group has been organising the "Music Laboratory" for peace mantras since 2002, with which it takes part in various local and national events. It also organises the annual Mantra Rock Festival for Peace in the Hearts and on the Earth.
Gino Sansone (0039-08154 69636) focuses people interested in the realisation of an ecological and spiritual village in the spirit of the Age of Aquarius on this magic earth of the sirens. May all beings of this earth be happy! OM SHANTI SHANTI SHANTI !

☺ ecumenical spirituality, love of Mother Earth

Associazione Arca Italia

CH

Il Chicco | Via Ancona, 1 | 00043 Ciampino, Roma
+39-06796-2104 — arcachicco@libero.it
-2104 — www.larche-europesud.org

1981 — (near Rom)

- 15
- part of the group (consensus)

Christian community
living and working with people with learning disabilities
christian, mentally/psychologically handicapped persons

As a member of the International L'Arche Federation, the community of Il Chicco di Ciampino is dedicated to the assistance of mentally and physically handicapped adults and children. L'Arche is a living and working environment where people with disabilities can grow as well as discover both a meaning to their lives and new hope. L'Arche is also a therapeutic and educational environment where people with disabilities receive the professional help they need in order to regain their health and their psychological balance, and where they can gain what is necessary to develop their capacities. L'Arche is organised in small structures called "hearths" which are organised on the family level and which are places of communal existence where voluntary assistants and people with disabilities share lodging, meals, and services. L'Arche's special therapeutic approach is based on the idea of "living together". In order to make this happen, our volunteers dedicate a period of their lives (six months, a year, several years, their entire lives) which they share with people with disabilities during different moments of the day.

☺ communal spirit and desire to serve disabled people

Associazione Archeus

AR

Via Berta n.7 | 36010 Laghi (VI)
☎ +39-0444-961812

3 ha ♀4 ♂4 5 13

f, it.
one part of the group
individual financing
property of individual community members
ecological, anthroposophic, organic diet, vegetarian diet, free school, seminar-house, one-world development, „terapia naturale", environmental protection, homeodynamic organic agriculture, organic farming, forestry, alternative energy, ecological construction

Laghi, with its approx. 100 inhabitants and an area of 22 km², is the smallest municipality in the Veneto. As a result of the industrial lunacy of the past 50 years, it has been gradually depopulated. We now want to resettle the area and rebuild it as an ecovillage. There are no production facilities there, nor is any industrial activity planned. The current population is largely old and unmotivated, but still full of hope for a new life. The region is alpine and uncontaminated (it could become a nature preserve) with great potential for environmental tourism and several hiking paths which can be revived and upgraded.
The idea behind our project is development and repopulation in the spirit of Rudolf Steiner's ideas on the spread of the "free individuality". It is in this spirit that everyone should be given the opportunity to develop, cultivate and pass on his or

her own talents within an environment characterised by nature, practical activities, social relations, thoughts and culture, thus contributing to the development of a truly human community in a harmonious way. The skills of every free, self-trusting and autonomous individual can contribute to the development of free communities – places of peace, democracy, tolerance and diverse culture, with spaces dedicated to the constant development of learning for life.

→ See also description of network "**RIVE**"

Associazione Culturale Torri Superiore

TS

Via Torri Superiore 5 | 18039 Ventimiglia (IM)
+39-0184-215504, -215290 info@torri-superiore.org
-215914 www.torri-superiore.org

1989 2.3 ha (near Ventimiglia) ♀6 ♂5 5 16

it., e, f, g 6

everyone in common (consensus for residents, majority in assoc. Votes)

limited common financing common property and/or individual property

Vision of an ecologically friendly way of life

ecotourism, education, ecovillage training, restoring medieval village

ecological, self-managed, organic diet, adult education, seminar-house, permaculture, organic agriculture, ecological construction, construction, creative: pottery, natural soap manufacturing, networking, volunteer programmes

☺

Torri Superiore is a medieval village (8th century) that has been progressively restored and reinhabitated over the last ten years by a community of Italians and Germans. The village is made of 160 rooms, all built in local stone and lime, which still feature the traditional arches and vaults.
The Cultural Association that has been developing the project since 1989 also includes non-residents and owns about 50 % of the village, while the other 50 % is individually owned by the members. Only members of the association are entitled to buy property in Torri Superiore.
The restoration of the buildings respects the original character of the beautiful hamlet while using ecological materials and appropriate technologies wherever possible. The main aim of the community is to create a supportive environment for its residents while respecting and protecting nature. The co-operative company runs an educational centre teaching sustainability, hands-on training and ecotourism. Courses are organised mostly in the summer and range from permaculture design to facilitation, consensus decision-making, ecovillage creation, pottery and creative cuisine. Organic agriculture activities focus mainly on olive oil production and vegetables gardens to supply the community centre.
The proximity to the beautiful river and the sea, the easily accessible walks on the surrounding mountains and the mild climate make Torri Superiore an attractive guest-house for year-round visits by ecologically sensitive people who appreciate the informal, friendly style of the group. Advance booking requested.

→ See also description of networks "**RIVE**" and "**GEN**"
ARCI
☺ 1-6 month probationary period, independent financing

Az. Agr. Acquasanta

AC

loc. Malagronda 104 | 06062 Citta della Pieve (PG)
+39-0578-294099 info@terrediacquasanta.it
+39-178 2728 112 www.terrediacquasanta.it

1997 4.5 ha (near Chiusi) ♀2 ♂1 1 4

e 1

everyone in common (consensus) individual financing, shared income

property of individual community members

permaculture

growing olives, saffron and vegetables; seminar programme; hospitality

ecological, self-managed, non-violent, inner growth, organic diet, vegetarian diet, free school, seminar-house, peace-work, animal protection, environmental protection, self-sufficiency, permaculture, organic agriculture, organic gardening, organic farming, art of living

We are an "accordion community" with 4 permanent residents plus Wwoofers, friends and parents, who sometimes come and help out for a few weeks, sometimes for a few months. We live in an ancient stone farmhouse, hidden deep in nature, with olive trees, bushes and macchia as far as the eye can see. We open our house for people who yearn to spend some time experiencing contact with nature while respecting all life forms and natural resources. Together we share responsibility, work, the use of all facilities, and enjoyable moments. We have a natural spring for our drinking water and a garden that covers our basic needs. We apply the principles and ethics of permaculture, which help us care for the earth and its people. As far as our food supply is concerned, we are largely self-sufficient. We only buy products which do not exploit labour and we also disseminate counter-culture information. We will keep at it until Acquasanta becomes an ecological oasis for body and spirit. We receive guests who are conscious of what respect for nature and a responsible use of its resources mean, who integrate themselves into our lifestyle and who respect and share the daily tasks and jobs which must be done.

→ See also description of network "**RIVE**"

Case Caro Carrubo

CC

c/o Nunzio Taranto | Via dei Platani, 12 | 97013 Comiso (RG)
☎ +39-339 3154580 Handy — www.carocarrubo.org
+39-0932 723688

1992 — 4 ha (near Comiso) — ♀2 ♂1 — 3

g, e, it., fin. — all

everyone in common (consensus) — property of individual community members

agriculture, re-structuring, crafts, guests, local/international contacts

ecological, self-managed, non-violent, inner growth, organic diet, vegetarian diet, seminar-house, peace-work, cultural exchange, environmental protection, self-sufficiency, organic agriculture, organic gardening, alternative energy, processing and direct marketing of agricultural products, arts & crafts

☺

Case Caro Carrubo (English: "the houses of the beloved carob tree") is located on a small hill of the Monti Iblei, a mountain chain in the south of the island of Sicily. The property encompasses 4 ha of land with old country houses. This place is intended to provide a concrete alternative to the continuous depopulation and devaluation of Sicily's rural areas. Our lifestyle is: living simply on the land and honouring the riches of earth and nature. Our projects and activities include care for the land (farming and organic gardening), harvest processing, artistic work, managing the guest house, cultural exchange, and personal growth within the community. We want to become a community of 4-5 persons, even if we are still struggling with financial and space problems. Our guest house provides 5 beds for people who would like to spend their holidays with us. We can provide room and board for up to 2 persons who would like to live and work with us for a longer or shorter period of time.

Modell Wasserburg c.V.
☺ trial period and interest

Comunella Casagatti

CL

Strada di Fungaia 3 | 53035 Monteriggioni (SI)
+39-0577317003, 3339598632 casagatti@interfree.it

5 ha (near Siena) ♀3 ♂2 2 8

e, it., sp.
everyone in common (consensus) limited common financing
rented/leased
libertarian, anti-authoritarian
garden, chickens
ecological, self-managed, anarchistic, spiritual, chaotic, vegetarian diet (some), seminar-house, self-sufficiency, organic gardening, ceramics, juggling, festivals, children, political discourse, concerts, encounter

An association heading toward a communal life (have sent no further description).

→ See also description of network "**RIVE**"
CIR
no fascists, „fattoni" or freeloaders

Comunità Coop. Villaggio Verde

VV

Villaggio Verde Comunità Acquariana | loc. S. Germano, snc | 28010 Cavallirio (NO)
+39-(0)163-80447 info@villaggioverde.org
www.villaggioverde.org

1982 9 ha (near Navara) ♀8 ♂8 5 21

e, f, it., japanese 6
one part of the group (majority vote)
individual financing, co-op, non-profit assoc. community
Aquarian Movement
course/conference programme, farm holidays, horseback riding, organic farming
leader/guru, spiritual, ecumenical, inner growth, massage, Shiatus, Reiki, organic agriculture, animal friendly husbandry

Villaggio Verde ("The Green Village") was created in the 1980s by our spiritual leader, Bernardino del Boca, who vanished in 2001. He conceived it as a centre to develop a consciousness for the New Era, as an experiment for a life oriented on the values of the Age of Aquarius in the search for harmony with oneself, with others and with nature. This project intends to create a village which will be as self-sufficient and ecologically sustainable as possible. It will be formed around autonomous, family-based nuclei with many shared places, moments and possibilities. There will be neither political prescriptions nor a dominant religion passing out rigid

laws: everyone is free to participate in communal activities according to one's own needs and inclinations.
So far, only part of this plan has been realised, namely 12 dwellings situated around a small lake. The residents are members of a co-operative which owns the dwellings, the common building and the land (9 ha, 3 of which are under cultivation; the rest is forest). There are 10 family nuclei in which one of the spouses usually works outside the community; a large part of the work is undertaken by volunteers.
The residents and numerous sympathisers have formed the association "Friends of the Green Village" which supports a wide variety of activities such as organic agriculture, a guest house and canteen, horseback excursions, environmental education and wide-ranging seminar and conference offerings on a variety of topics, extending from agriculture to organic construction all the way to spirituality. The project also foresees the establishment of a library which will archive 15,000 books and magazines collected by Professor Boca along with his literary and artistic works.

→ See also description of network "**RIVE**"
- CONACREIS (Italian associaton of communities exploring ethics, inner world and spirituality)
- ☺ no hard drugs or alcohol abuse; respect for internal regulations; pay rent or purchase residency rights

Cooperativa di Bordo

CB

Karma Dechen Yangtse Ling | 28841 Viganella (VB)
☎ +39-0324-56101 bordo@bordo.org
-56139 www.bordo.org

1982 | 4.25 ha (near Domodossola) | ♀4 ♂5 1 10

- g, e, it.
- everyone in common (majority vote, consensus) — limited common financing
- co-operative
- Tibetan-Buddhist (Karma Kagyü)
- Dharma course, other courses, construction of village
- buddhist, Karma Kagyü Centre, mental training

☺

The community (made up of Swiss, Germans, and Austrians) lives in the 400 year old Italian hillside village of Bordo. After having been left unoccupied and overgrown for some thirty years, it has been restored continually since 1982. Other Germans, Swiss, etc. have settled in further villages in the area. Bordo is located in Piemont, twenty minutes by car from Domodossola and about 40 minutes from Lago Maggiore, near the Swiss border in the beautiful Antrona Valley. The village can only be reached via a footpath - the nearest village and road are some fifteen minutes away. Bulky items are transported by cable-lift.
Bordo is a centre for Tibetan Buddhism with a retreat house and is visited each year by many lamas and meditation teachers. In the guest house with its group room and kitchen a variety of courses are taught and holiday guests are received as well. There are communal facilities such as the temple/meditation room, library, kitchen

and dining room, workshops, sauna, and baths. The children attend the regional schools. The village still offers considerable potential and there are several houses which can be restored for the use of families, couples, and singles.

☺ trial period, interest/openness for Buddhism, contribution to personal support in B.

Federazione di Damanhur

FD

Via Pramarzo 3 | 10080 Baldissero Canavese (TO)
+39-0124-512226 federation@damanhur.org
-512371 www.damanhur.org

1975 450 ha (near Turin) ♀264 ♂200 138 602

it., e, g, japanese 75%

we have a complex system of democratic bodies/organisms

individual and limited common financing common property

we are a combination of communities and ecovillages with a developing social and political structure

ecological, self-managed, spiritual, esoteric/New Age, inner growth, meditation, adult education, free school, seminar-house, peace-work, social work, therapy, self-sufficiency, organic agriculture, organic gardening, organic farming, forestry, alternative energy, new technologies, ecological construction

☺

Founded in the early 1970's, the Federation of Damanhur in Italy is now an internationally renowned center for spiritual, artistic and social research. Damanhur is an eco-society, a federation of communities and eco-villages with a continuously evolving social and political structure.
The aims of Damanhur are: the freedom and re-awakening of the Human Being as a divine, spiritual and material principle; the creation of a self-sustaining model of life based on ethical principles of good communal living and love; harmonic integration and co-operation with all the Forces linked to the evolution of Humankind. Damanhur numbers 44 small communities, each one built around approximately 20 people. Approximately 400 other supporters live nearby and participate regularly in its activities. They are contributing to the creation of a new social model based upon solidarity, volunteering, a respect for the environment and the sharing of ethical and spiritual values. Damanhur has centres in Italy, Europe and Japan and maintains contact with spiritual groups worldwide.
The Federation has internal schools for boys and girls up to 13 years of age, a daily paper, a publishing house, a Constitution and a University open to researchers from all over the world.

→ See also description of network "**GEN**"

☺ desire to be a protagonist of the New Millennium, exploring it with joy, humor and a touch of magic

Hairakhandi Love Center

HL

Vocabolo Villarosa, Localita Corniole | 06026 Pietralunga (PG)
☎+39-075-933074 info@babajicenter.net
-933074 www.babajicenter.net

1993 30 ha (near Cagli) ♀3 ♂3 5 11

it., e, f, sp. 3

part of the group (consensus) individual financing

property of individual community members

spiritual path, Babaji-Ashram, meditation, ecology

healing, yoga, meditation, garden, crafts, medicinal herbs

ecological, leader/guru, spiritual, inner growth, meditation, yoga, tantra, organic diet, vegetarian diet, Reiki, crystals, emotional work, massage, phytotherapy, organic agriculture, organic gardening, animal friendly husbandry, art

☺

This centre, immersed in the wild nature of Burano in the Appenine Mountains of Umbria and the Marches, is dedicated to BABAJI, our spiritual master, and is working for the reawakening of consciousness, in the name of the one supreme being, God, who resides in the centre of our consciousness, "the heart".
Harmony is created in the union of our soul with the mind, the heart, the body. Karma Yoga (yoga in action). Our work in this centre manifests itself in taking care of "human beings" on the various levels at which their disenchantment with themselves manifests itself in the spiritual, physical, mental, emotional, and energetic body.
A DAY IN OUR LIVES: Each morning we celebrate worship in the temple dedicated to BABAJI, with devotional songs, prayers spoken with the ardour of the heart, and we also worship in the temple dedicated to HAIRAKHANDI, the divine mother, where we practice the ancient Vedic rituals which our master has left to us, like the purification of different bodies. The message left by BABAJI is TRUTH, SIMPLICITY, LOVE.
We continue with: work performed with joy; hours dedicated to building maintenance, painting, cooking and cultivating the earth; hours dedicated to the various seminars, instruction in harmonisation, yoga, healing, shamanism, dance, contact with angels and working on one's own emotions; hours dedicated to caring for people; hours dedicated to listening to one's self, in the temple of fire, in the woods, on the banks of the river, or in the peace of your own room.
When all of our attention is placed outside of ourselves – in singing, working, caring, eating, sleeping – we produce joy and beauty. Joy carries you directly into the divine womb. The first step is to recognise the beauty in ourselves, the Divine. The second step is to support this beauty, so that, in the passage of days, love may purify our dark side, our fears, our resistance and our adopted behaviours.

☺ shared intentions, desire for individual growth, spiritual awareness

Hare Krishna Temple

IF

Villa Vrindavana | Via Scopeti 108 | 50026 San Casciano Val di Pesa (Firenze)
+39-055-820054 rkcfi@radiokrishna.com
+39-055-828470 www.radiokrishna.com

1979 100 ha (near Firenze) ♀7 ♂5 12

it, e, russ. nearly all
one part of the group (majority vote) limited common financing
common property
Hare Krishna Community
religious services, self-awareness through Bhakti Yoga
ecological, self-managed, non-violent, spiritual, meditation, yoga, animal protection, conventional agriculture, conventional gardening

This is the greater Hare Krishna Temple in Europe, about 4500 square meters built over 100 ha of land. The community is open to all serious researchers of spiritual experiences through meditation, yoga practice and free service to God. Following the simple way of Bhakti-Yoga, it is possible to develop our personal relationship with the Lord and reap all benefits, such as peace of mind and complete happiness. Everyone is welcome, we await you. Hare Krishna!

→See also description of network "**ISKCON**"

Il Casale

IC

Azienda Agricola Biologica | 53026 Pienza (Siena)
+39-0578-755109 podereilcasale@libero.it
-755109

1991 61 ha (near Pienza (SI)) ♀1 ♂2 5 8

e, g, f, it. 4
everyone in common (consensus) shared income
common property
none
farming, gardening, livestock, milk, reproductive work (kitchen, cleaning...), educational work (school groups)
ecological, self-managed, organic diet, environmental protection, organic agriculture, organic gardening, organic farming, animal friendly husbandry, forestry, alternative energy, ecological construction

The project was founded in 1991 and is being realised by a group of people who live near the Il Casale farm. They are engaged in reconstructing the house according to ecological principles (water treatment system, an energy-efficient water heating system, thermal insulation in the walls and under the roof, organic paints and varnishes). They collect rain water, compost organic wastes, and all agricultural work is performed according to biological principles, which represents the Casale's main activity. The farm is the property of the Association of the Friends of the Il Casale Farm, while the actual administration is carried out by the group which resides on the farm and which is responsible for the project's decisions and activities.

Today Il Casale is a place of rural hospitality and offers facilities for campers year-round, both for tents and recreational vehicles. In co-operation with the farm holidays movement, Il Casale also accepts guests who are willing to exchange their physical work for room and board. Our main interest is the propagation of the ideas of organic farm holidays. The farm is open for visitors all the time, and also for persons who would like to purchase our natural products, such as wine, oil, honey, cheese and pasta.

In the near future we intend to consolidate our activities with the goal of using new energy-saving systems. Our project subscribes to the philosophy of villages integrated into the city in order to promote both responsibility towards the countryside and the communal life.

Il Popolo Elfico della Valle dei Burroni

PE

Mario Cecchi | Montevettolini | 51010 Pistoia

1980 | 200 ha (near Pistoia) | ♀60 ♂80 | 60 | 200

g, e, sp. — all

- everyone in common (consensus)
- shared economy for all, individual financing
- leased, shared and individual property
- see text
- farming and forestry, animal husbandry, crafts
- ecological, self-managed, anarchistic, left-wing political understanding, feminist, non-violent, organic diet, peace-work, phytotherapy, Reiki, animal protection, environmental protection, self-sufficiency, permaculture, organic agriculture, organic gardening, organic farming, forestry, alternative energy, ecological construction, handicrafts, theatre, dance, street art

☺ (✋✋)

We are a group of approx. 200 people who live in houses and abandoned villages lying scattered across the Apennines of Pistoia at an altitude of between 800 and 1,000 m. Since we largely live off of our own products, our chief activities centre around farming and animal husbandry for our own needs. Those who provide for the village's provisions and growth are supported by the common till; special private expenses are covered by the respective individual. Our income derives either from gifts or from the profits from our pizzeria, which we take with us to festivals and other events, and to which we are all called upon to contribute. We are an open community in which each house and/or village has its own character and whose self-administration is inviolate, unless the entire valley council is called together. It has the right to make final decisions in difficult conflicts. Our common denominator is the sacredness of the earth and deep ecology. Aside from that, everyone can follow his/her own political, spiritual or religious inclinations. We have neither bosses nor dogmas.

→See also description of network "**RIVE**"
☺ none

Inspira

IN

Località Pignano 6 | 56048 Volterra (PI)
☎+39-05883-5032 bcazac@tin.it
-5120

1999 140 ha (near Volterra (Pisa)) ♀8 ♂6 4 18

e, f, it., sp., dutch 9

everyone in common (consensus) limited common financing

property of a friend living abroad

guests, seminars/workshops, retreats, farming, animals, garden, forest

ecological, self-managed, non-violent, hierarchical, spiritual, inner growth, meditation, organic diet, vegetarian diet, adult education, peace-work, environmental protection, permaculture, organic agriculture, organic gardening, organic farming, forestry, alternative energy, new technologies, ecological construction, sports, art, Montessori

☺

We are a group of friends, 14 adults and 4 children. We live in Pignano, a beautiful little town surrounded by 140 ha of forests and fields, far out in the countryside near Volterra (Pisa). It was all acquired by a friend and benefactor in 2000 with the idea of supporting our project and then, from time to time, coming back to visit a warm, hospitable and familiar place. Above all, we want to create a place of joyfulness, empathy and friendship. Our project is dedicated to the following:
Achieving a high level of self-sufficiency in regard to food and energy with great attention to environmental protection; developing hospitable structures for courses, retreats, conferences, seminars, workshops, voluntary work assignments; supporting individual creativity; maintaining spiritual practises.
In order to achieve these goals, we have selected the planning methods of permaculture, whose ethical, analytical and practical principles we find deeply satisfying.

→See also description of network "**RIVE**"
☺ 1-year probationary period; agreement with our interests and our visions; chemistry has to work

La Comune di Bagnaia

BG

Via Bagnaia 37 | 53018 Sovicille (SI)
+39-0577-311014, -311051
lacomune.bagnaia@libero.it
-311014

1979 | 80 ha (near Siena) | ♀7 ♂12 6 25

e, f, it., port. — 6

everyone in common (consensus) — shared economy

common property

social-political awareness, solidarity

organic farming, external work (largely in education), environmental, pacifist, political and cultural involvement

ecological, self-managed, left-wing political understanding, equality of women, non-violent, inner growth, yoga, organic diet, peace-work, environmental protection, self-sufficiency, organic agriculture, organic gardening, organic farming, forestry, alternative energy, construction, basket weaving, joinery, sculpture, painting, dance, singing, festivals, spectacles, good cooking

„La comune di Bagnaia" has existed for over 20 years. At the moment 25 people are living together and sharing their economy, work and ideals. We believe in sustainability and we aim at self-sufficiency, our organic farm produces wine, olive oil, cereals, honey and vegetables. We also have woods and livestock. Some members have external jobs while others are full time farmers. Individual interests and concerns are resources and provide stimulation for group activities. Our commune is non-authoritarian. Solidarity, mutual comprehension, social awareness and environmental concern characterise our daily experience. All decisions are made by consensus in weekly meetings. Visitors are welcome after prior arrangement. We live about 10 km outside of Siena in one of Italy's most beautiful areas.

→See also description of networks "**RIVE**" and "**GEN**"

CONACREIS, CIR

☺ interest in communal life, shared economy and autonomy, trial period of 1 year

Mirapuri-Friedensstadt

MF

Via Monte Faló 8 | 28010 Mirapuri/Coiromonte (Prov. NO)
+39-0322-999009 mirapuri@mirapuri-enterprises.com
-999129 www.mirapuri-enterprises.com

1970 500 m² (near Stresa) ♀13 ♂11 7 31

g, e, it., f 25

shared income association

free spirit, understanding of the world as the unity of spirit and matter

various professions

ecological, self-managed, anarchistic, feminist, non-violent, spiritual, chaotic, inner growth, meditation, yoga, tantra, sexuality, free love, organic diet, vegetarian diet, adult education, pedagogical, free school, seminar-house, peace-work, health and New Age seminars, World Peace Meetings, animal protection, environmental protection, self-sufficiency, organic agriculture, conventional agriculture, organic gardening, conventional gardening, forestry, alternative energy, new technologies, ecological construction, construction, various handicrafts, health training, music and all types of art, various media, humour etc.

☺ ()

Mirapuri in Italy as well as its first satellite, Miravillage in Germany, have been created for people who like Sri Aurobindo and Mira Alfassa and their ideals of human unity and spiritual consciousness progress.
Mirapuri and Miravillage are environments where people can live and work together to realise these ideals. Everyone of goodwill who likes Sri Aurobindo and Mira Alfassa and their ideals can join Mirapuri and Miravillage.
There are no financial or other material obligations. If you want to live in Mirapuri or Miravillage you can do so on a private or contributing basis. That means you may buy your own house or apartment, which is your property, or you may contribute financially to the growth of the general Mirapuri property. In this case, Mirapuri and Miravillage provide accomodation and services for you during your lifetime at Mirapuri or Miravillage and the property belongs to Mirapuri or Miravillage and its future development.
Everyone works and learns on a free and independent basis. The growth and respect of individuality is understood as the basis and flowering of real communal life. There is no institutional spiritual authority. Each individual follows his/her own spiritual evolution according to his/her aspirations and inclinations. There are no financial or other obligations.

Mirapuri

☺ knowledge of Sri Aurobindo and Mira Alfassa and their integral yoga, as well as good will and genuine co-operation

Nomadelfia

ND

C.P.176 | 58041 Grosseto (GR)
+39-0564-338243 visitatori@nomadelfia.it
-338233 www.nomadelfia.it

1931 380 ha (near Grosseto) ♀100 ♂100 120 320

e, it. all
everyone in common (unanimous) common till
common property (foundation)
Catholic faith
farming, book printing, construction, TV
early Christian education, self-sufficiency, own school

"Nomadelfia" means: Fraternity is our law. Nomadelfia is a small "people" consisting of Catholics who live according to the model of Early Christian communities. Our community consists of more than 50 families who have already given a home to more than 5,000 orphaned children. The families do not live for themselves, but rather in "family groups" of 4 to 5 families. They have a common dining room, kitchen and workshops in a central building, while each family has its personal rooms in its own separate cottage. In Nomadeflia everyone works in the community; heavy and repetitive work, including seasonal work, is dealt with by organising all the members. There is neither money nor private property. All those who reside in the community work without pay: Everything belongs to everyone. We have our own schools, which are operated by the parents. Our children attend school up to the age of 18, after which - as with students attending private schools - they are examined by a state commission. We also organise our own direct democracy on an internal basis. All members participate through an assembly in the passing of laws, in making important decisions, and in the filling of constitutional positions. In the eyes of the Catholic Church we are a parish, in the eyes of the Italian state we are an association.

☺ practitioners of the Catholic faith, working independently of others/superiors, at least 21 years old

Osho Miasto

OM

S. Gorgio | 53010 Frosini (SI)

+39-0577-960124 oshomiasto@oshomiasto.it

-960213 www.oshomiasto.it

1980 130 ha (near Siena) ♀18 ♂18 36

g, e, it. some

one part of the group (consensus) common property

we are Osho followers

meditation, therapy groups and training, meditation camps, everything aimed at personal and spiritual growth

ecological, self-managed, non-violent, spiritual, inner growth, meditation, organic diet, vegetarian diet, therapy, organic gardening

Istituto Osho Miasto is one of the few existing Osho Communes in Europe. It is a commune for meditation, personal, and spiritual growth. Each year we organize some 460 therapy groups, workshops and meditation seminars for approx. 5,500 participants.
Furthermore, we are a community of Osho followers/disciples who live here as an experimental laboratory. The structure and form of the commune is constantly changing. 3 meditations are held daily – Osho Dynamic Meditation, Osho Kundalini Meditation & White Robe – Evening Meditation Meeting. The meditations are largely free for members. An annual association membership fee of Euro 18.00 is requested.

links to other Osho centres

training as well as independent accommodation, pursuit of higher aims

Rainbow Eco Peace Village

EP

Earth Foundation | Via Cheggio | 28030 Viganella (NO)

+39-0324-56030 cheggio@libero.it

-56030 chegg.blogspot.com

1986 10 ha (near Domodossola) ♀12 ♂15 12 39

d, e, it. 50%

all who are concerned in common or part of the group (majority vote, consensus)

limited common financing and individual

property of all or individuals

Rainbow Family of living light

ecological building, gardens, fields, seminars

ecological, spiritual, buddhist, esoteric/New Age, inner growth, meditation, yoga, vegetarian diet, vegan diet, macrobiotic diet, adult education, peace-work, one-world development, permaculture, organic gardening, alternative energy, new technologies, skiing, outdoor, sculpture, peace art

☺ (✋✋)

Cheggio is a small mountain village in Piemonte in the Italian Alps. It can be only reached after a 15-minute walk. In 1986 we acquired the first houses and a few years later we founded the „Rainbow Peace Projects" non-profit association. Today more than 30 people usually live here between spring and autumn. The residents have not created a structured organisation so that new arrivals have to find the place that suits them best on their own.
There is a small guest house and every year we offer courses, consultations, events and festivals. (Kontakt: Bhakti, Tel. +39-032456308)
The Earth Foundation was founded for the purpose of constructing and operating a peace and ecological institute in Cheggio. The Cheggio village community is linked with the neighbouring village of Bordo and its Buddhist community, and also with the neighbouring village of Zonca, in which a place of peace, tolerance, the acceptance of others and a simple life is being developed.
Important: Visitors are always welcome in all these projects. However, we request minimal and adequate personal mountaineering equipment and a certain amount of sweat equity. Please contact us by phone or writing.

Rainbow Peace Projects
☺ families with children, participation in house property, membership fee, vegetarians

Upacchi Ecovillaggio

EU

Upacchi | 52031 Anghiari (AR)
+39-0575749-323, +39-03358015799 ndupacchi@yahoo.it
-330

1990 | 60 ha (near Arezzo) | ♀14 ♂12 18 44

it, d | 25
everyone in common (majority vote) | individual financing
property of individual community members
none
agriculture
ecological, organic diet, adult education, therapy: Tantra, trance dance, feminist therapy, communication, environmental protection, self-sufficiency, permaculture, organic agriculture, organic gardening, organic farming, animal friendly husbandry, forestry, alternative energy, new technologies, ecological construction, construction, handicraft: stove building, bio-electrics, clay building, heating systems; otherwise: environmental education, children-friendly, democratic

☺ ✋✋

The history of the Upacchi ecovillage began in 1990 with the founding of a farming co-op. Over the next few years we found buyers for the 16 old, partially ruined stone houses which, over several years, have largely been renovated according to ecological building principles - at individual expense and partially through individual work. During this time, many Upacchians have gained considerable expertise in building biology, clay building, heating systems, bio-electrical engineering and organic gardening. In the latter field they have been advised by experienced locals who have been glad to share the profound understanding of nature they have acquired through tradition and observation. About half the village's residents come from various regions of Italy, the rest is German (-speaking). The people didn't know each other beforehand. Following a turbulent phase of the community, the co-op was dissolved in 2000, the land was partially privatised, partially sold, and the infrastructure was transferred to a community of owners. Since then, some of the residents have been seeking new paths toward communal living in order to prevent a withdrawal into the isolation of the nuclear family, whereas others are satisfied with things as they are. Over time a series of common activities have stabilised themselves: men's and women's evenings, yoga, volleyball, hikes, a sweat lodge and regular celebrations. We have erected a community house. We are happy to pass our experiences and knowledge on to others, but we ask potential visitors to contact us first.

→See also description of network "**RIVE**" and "**GEN**"

Legambiente

☺ no ideology; necessary is a lot of money to buy a house, for up to 2 persons, renting is also a possibility

Utopiaggia

UP

Eugen e Susanne | Villa Piaggia 21 | 05010 Montegabbione (TR)

+39-0763-837020 beatrixe@tin.it

-837020

1982 100 ha (near Perugia) ♀9 ♂7 3 19

d, e, it. 4.5

everyone in common (consensus) limited common financing

common property

none

sheep, cheese making, pottery workshop, dyeing workshop, olive production

ecological, self-managed, left-wing political understanding, organic agriculture, organic gardening, organic farming, animal friendly husbandry, forestry, handicrafts

☺

On a large piece of land in the hills south of Lago Trasimeno in Central Italy, we rear sheep and try to cultivate olives. We meet a small part of our needs through self-sufficiency. We finance our daily needs from a common purse. Some gainful employment takes place on the grounds themselves (lambs, sheep cheese, dyed silk, ceramics, guests), others outside (environmental consultation, restoration of houses, school). The 19 members living in the compound are between 40 and 60 years old; our young people are preparing to move on. We are looking for new members who ideally should be older than our children and younger than us. Members and visitors who would like to live with us for an extended period are welcome, but they must contact us beforehand. Important decisions are made by the plenary meeting on a consensus basis. In recent years we have increasingly focused our activities on the region: we run a small café for the local area, work with the community council in developing an environmental education centre and organise conferences on new rural development models. In the future we want to work more intensively with groups on our property.

→See also description of network "**RIVE**"

☺ 1 probationary year, membership contribution is set by agreement

Villaggio Ecologico Granara

EG

via Granara 38 | 43050 Valmozzola (PR)
☎+39-0525-67251 granara@alekos.org
-67600 www.alekos.org/granara

1993 95 ha (near Parma) ♀2 ♂3 5

- g, e, f, sp.
- entire community (consensus) individual financing
- property of individual community members
- alternative (solar) technology, seminars of Sario Genere, environmental education, theatre
- ecological, self-managed, anarchistic, left-wing political understanding, non-violent, chaotic, inner growth, yoga, sexuality, organic diet, adult education, pedagogical, seminar-house, peace-work, one-world development, SCI, environmental protection, organic agriculture, organic gardening, organic farming, forestry, alternative energy, new technologies, ecological construction, construction, handicraft, sports, theatre

The village of Granara is located at an elevation of 630 m on the slopes of the Appenines within the municipality of Valmozzola (PR), which lies in the Toscana-Emiglia region. The project's intention is to create a place where it is possible to realise and network projects dedicated to adapted technology, organic farming, environmental education, organic architecture, health and theatre. In the village there are both people who live here and people who live in the town, but who have also renovated a house here and are implementing joint projects through which they are endeavouring to integrate town and country: connecting production with daily experience, 2 fields which are otherwise normally separate, and revealing the existing relationships that exist between natural resources, energy consumption and human resources.
The village's structure is characterised by residential nuclei (families and a commune) and by areas in which our communal life takes place. All members of the village community make common decisions according to the principles of direct democracy on issues affecting the entire group, while within the nucleus an absolute decision-making autonomy prevails which nevertheless takes the general rules into consideration. Granara's guests are received by the individual nuclei depending on their capacity. We ask all visitors to call us up beforehand and, if need be, let us know if they are going to bring dogs.

Villaggio Ecologico Solidale

ES

Fraz. Monterosso 126 | 60045 Sassoferrato (AN)
+39-0348-5114842, -0732-974225 ecosolidale@tiscalinet.it
web.tiscali.it/ecosolidale/, www.sostenibile.org

1998 300 m² (near Urbino) ♀3 ♂1 1 5

e, it. none

everyone in common (consensus) limited common financing

rented/leased

garden, communication seminars

ecological, self-managed, non-violent, inner growth, organic diet, vegetarian diet, permaculture, organic gardening, ecological construction, frugal and sustainable life

☺

We are a group of 5 to 20 people who, since 1998, have been endeavouring to realise a village for the discovery and exploration of a simple and sustainable lifestyle. During this time we have decided to concentrate on developing and imparting the communicative skills which we view as essential for a healthy group life: learning to listen to others; to live and co-operate with people who are different from oneself; to make decisions through participation and consensus; also to be able to live with conflicts without turning them into "wars"; bringing our own emotions and feelings to the surface. We have studied other ecological village communities (Arche, ACF, ZEGG etc.) and have organised events with them through which we have grown and tried out their methods: information circles, emotion workshops, the ZEGG forum. This work has moved us greatly, and we want to continue it in the spirit of our growth, which will never really end, and carry on this voyage of discovery with others.
Today, 5 of us live on the land in a large house with a garden, in a place where the sun shines all day long. Around us there is an excellent area for camping. All who are interested and who would like to support us are welcome to join us. Room and board provided.

→See also description of network "**RIVE**"

☺ transparency, participating in quest for new sustainable lifestyles

Netherlands

AD Adidam Holland
DV De Vlierhof
EE Stichting Emmaus Eindhoven
EL Stichting ELIM
FM Franciscaans Milieuproject
GO De Ark Gemeenschap Gouda
GW Gemeenschappelijk Wonen Project
HC Humaniversity
HO Hobbitstee
LA Stichting Emmaus Langeweg
LI Centraal Wonen Lismortel
WO De Wonne

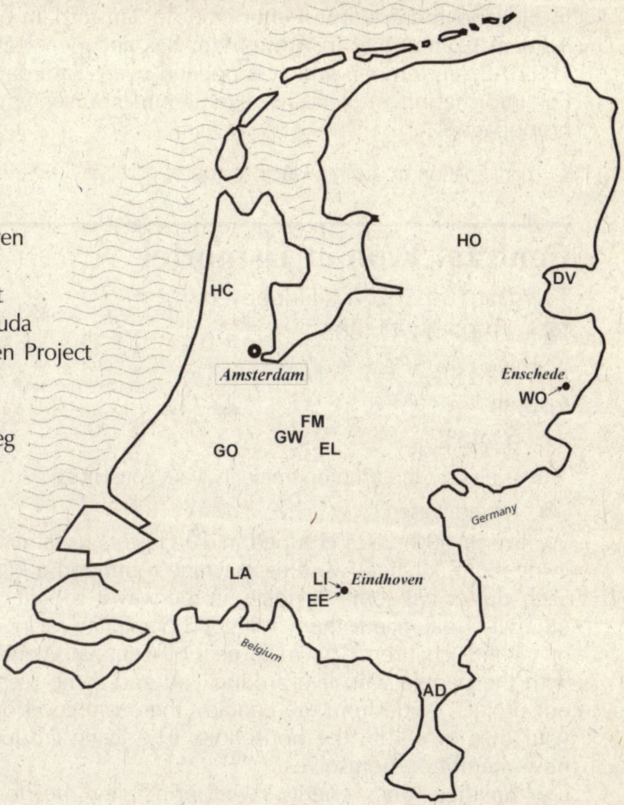

Adidam Holland

AD

Annendaalderweg 10 | 6105 AT Maria Hoop
☎ +31-(0)20-4681442
adidam_amsterdam@adidam.org
www.adidam.nl

1983 | 9 ha (near Echt, Roermond) | ♀14 ♂13 | 6 | 33

g, e, dutch — 8
everyone in common (majority vote) — individual financing
common property
the Path of Adidam
a dedicated life in community
non-violent, hierarchical, leader/guru, spiritual, esoteric/New Age, meditation, yoga, vegetarian diet, adult education

☺ ( )

Adidam Holland is part of the European Adidam Community Network.
In Holland there is one community in Amsterdam and one in Maria Hoop. The Adidam Community in Amsterdam has an open learning centre (Oosterpark 39, 1092 AL Amsterdam) which is opened every Saturday from 1 to 4 p.m.
For information on retreats, events and courses you can call us up or visit our homepage.

☺ participation in an introductory course

Centraal Wonen Lismortel

LI

Tourslaan18 | 5627 KX Eindhoven

☎ +31-(0)40-2424808 | info@cwl.antenna.nl | www.cwl.lvcw.nl

1983 | 3 ha | ♀43 ♂34 | 35 | 112

dutch, e, g | 5 or 7

everyone in common (majority vote/consensus) | individual financing

rented/leased

We live in 60 houses grouped in 10 clusters (6 family houses with a common hall, living room, kitchen, washing machine room and a big garden around each cluster). Each cluster has some flexibility in the way it is built, so that houses can be split or otherwise rearanged: there is a good possibility for people living on their own, with or without children. The main goal of Centraal Wonen is to mantain good contact with the people who live around you and some responsibility for each other and our project. Aside from the contacts there is a good opportunity to live privately on your own or within the household. The living groups (the ‚clusters‘) choose their new members themselves.
Our buildings obey energy-saving principles: the houses are more insulated than ‚normal', the first ten years of earth warmth was used to heat the houses.
15 people share three cars in an organisation, several other cars are also shared.
We buy our organic food from a mobile food shop that comes by once a week and from an organic farmer.
Some of the other activities in the project are: a paint club, a ‚walking club', our own computer network.
Centraal Wonen Lismortel has a community building for social (a weekly bar-evening and weekly coffee hours, parties) and other activities (paint and yoga courses, etc).

→See also description of network "**LVCW**"
☺ should support our form of community life

De Ark Gemeenschap Gouda

GO

(Arche Netherlands) | Wethouder Venteweg 224 | 2805 JV Gouda

☎ +31-(0)182-54-8024 — ark.gouda@planet.nl

-8122 — home.planet.nl/~Ark.Gouda/

1994 — ♀5 ♂7 12

dutch — 10

one part of the group (consensus) — association

ecumenical

communal life/work for people with and without mental disabilities

spiritual, christian, ecumenical, mentally/psychologically handicapped persons

☺

Coming together to live and work with people with learning disabilities in a simple way.
The Arche communities are places which offer a way of life that is neither competitive nor dependent on material success and intellectual achievement.
They are places that heal rather than divide. Founded by Jean Vanier in France in 1964, the Arche communities quickly spread throughout the world.
Our community is a community of faith. It is ecumenical. Assistants share their lives with our core members for a certain period of time.
We do not see ourselves as „staff" who work in shifts and „look after the residents". We live in community, sharing our lives together with each person.

De Wonne

WO

Noorderhagen 25 | 7511 EK Enschede

☎ +31-(0)53-4318787 — d.smeijers@alumnus.twente.nl

www.wonne.nl

1979 — 0.4 ha — ♀14 ♂15 12 41

dutch, e, arab., g — 20

everyone in common (majority vote)

shared economy (shared income and capital) — rented/leased

ecumenical, shared property

hospitality, becoming one family, recycling, reflection

left-wing political understanding, non-violent, christian, ecumenical, meditation, social work, environmental protection, organic gardening, animal friendly husbandry

☺

"De Wonne" was founded in 1979 out of the desire to demonstrate and express faith in Jesus of Nazareth and to follow the principles of the Franciscans. Our goals are to live and pray together, to share and celebrate and keep the house open for others, especially needy persons with all kinds of problems: marriage problems, people released from psychiatric institutions; people whose commitment to psychiatric institutions can still be prevented, refugees, asylum-seekers; above all people who need to distance themselves from something or someplace, or for other reasons: people like you and me. The community is open for those who would like to spend a longer or shorter period of time with us and share responsibility. We also try to assume responsibility in the parish. Thanks to the "Handje Twee" second-hand store, the community largely supports itself. "De Wonne" rents a monastery in the centre of the city of Enschede and has also founded two new communities in the neighbouring towns of Almelo and Glanerburg (on the border to Germany).

☺ (Jewish-)Christian tradition

Emmaus Langeweg

LA

Kloosterlaan 6 | 4772 RA Langeweg
☎ +31-(0)168-324524 info@emmaus-langeweg.nl
+31 (0)168 336011 www.emmaus-langeweg.nl

(near Breda) ♀3 ♂7 1 11

dutch, e all
one part of the group (mostly consensus) shared income
foundation
support and second-hand shop

☺

Once more! These words are symbolic for the activities of Emmaus in Langeweg. Emmaus houses people who are in trouble, especially the homeless. Emmaus gives them the opportunity to rebuild their lives. Meanwhile Emmaus gives chances to idealistic people to put their ideas into practise. Finally, Emmaus combats the economy of excessive consumption and returns value to discarded objects. Emmaus collects cast off goods and sells them. In this way, Emmaus is financially independent. Part of the income is donated to projects, both in the Third World or nearby. The community in Langeweg houses about 10 persons. All community members work in the second-hand shop, collecting, sorting and selling goods. They attend to the housekeeping together. Community members receive food and board, insurance, pocket money, travel expenses and items from the shop. Aside from them there are over 25 volunteers and some salaried employees. Emmaus Langeweg is situated in a former monastery in a small village in the south of the Netherlands. A stay in the community gives you the chance to put your ideas into practise and discover your talents. We want to live, work and share together. We choose solidarity.

→See also description of network "**Emmaus**"

☺ enthusiasm for common work working and living, probationary period required

Franciscaans Milieuproject

FM

Stoutenburgerlaan 5 | 3835 PB Stoutenburg
+31-(0)33-4945500
www.stoutenburg.nl
-4325522

1991 | 11 ha (near Amersfoort) | ♀4 ♂2 6

e, g | all

everyone in consensus

shared income | rented/leased

Franciscan, ecological, ecumenical

gardening, household, conference centre

ecological, self-managed, non-violent, christian, ecumenical, vegetarian diet, seminar-house, permaculture, organic agriculture, organic gardening, forestry

We are an ecumenical religious community with an emphasis on the relationship of human beings to other living beings. We orient ourselves on the life of St. Francis of Assisi and are part of the broader Franciscan movement in Holland. In our daily routine there are set times for meditation, work, communal and private life. In order to pay our rent and other expenses we maintain a small conference house. We work in our organic garden and manage the house in a consistently environmentally friendly manner. We are dependent on the help of volunteers. They share our life. We organise various events in the area of human beings and the environment, ranging from ecological suppers to several weeks of activities and meditation.

Franciscans

☺ Christian/Franciscan background, health

Gemeenschappelijk Wonen Project

GW

c/o Bewonersvereniging | Bedumerschans 2 | 3432 TC Nieuwegein
+31-(0)30-6060985
wiscie@gwwebsite.com
www.pen.nl/gw/

1983 | 2 ha (near Nieuwegein) | ♀70 ♂70 10 150

dutch

everyone in common (majority vote) | limited community financing

rented/leased

parties, films, spiritual actions

left-wing political understanding, non-violent

The GW project is a small community in the middle of a residential area of Nieuwegein. There are 20 houses which are inhabited by groups of 3 to 8 people. Additionally, there are a few individual apartments. Living in a group means sharing

bathrooms and toilets, the kitchen and of course the living room. Each group member has his or her private room, some even have two rooms.
The age of the members of this community may vary between 20 to 40 years. Most of them are employed outside the project. There are communal project-facilities like a pub and ballroom, a small pub serving food and a second-hand shop. Volunteers organized in different committees see to arrangements concerning the pub, the admittance of new group members, the organisation of parties and the running of the second-hand shop. Apart from this, some residents organise individual activities for their fellow community members such as creative courses, evening festivities or sports tournaments. Community representatives meet in a 5 person executive committee. All decisions concerning the project are made in consensus with all residents.

Hobbitstee

HO

Van Zijlweg 3 | 8351 H.W. Wapserveen/Drente
☎ +31-(0)521-321087, -321324 hobbitstee@wxs.nl, hobbitherberg@ddh.nl
-321089 www.leefgemeenschapdehobbitstee.nl

1969 | 3.5 ha (near Zwolle) | ♀4 ♂4 3 11

e, g, sp. | 2

everyone in common (consensus) | individual financing

Foundation

crafts, candle-factory, organic garden

ecological, self-managed, left-wing political understanding, non-violent, spiritual, inner growth, organic diet, vegetarian diet, peace-work, animal protection, environmental protection, organic agriculture, organic gardening, forestry, alternative energy

☺ ( )

The community "Hobbitstee" has already been in existence for over 30 years. The desire to change society, to stimulate personal growth, to get rid of the bourgeois mentality were important aims for the founders in the late sixties. Times change, just as people and their social environment change. But the primal ideals of seeking love, harmony, simplicity are still the drives, the wells from which the present inhabitants draw their energy to form and reform daily community life and our relations toward society. Aside from the promotion of organic/biological agriculture and the handicrafts candle-factory, the issues we embrace are non-violent conflict resolution and the receiving of guests in various forms. That is what gives us a kind of right to exist. The hope or wish to become a larger community in this country of utmost individualism is no longer among us. And it may be better that way. We can still direct our energy, as a core group, at the topics we find important. Together with short- or long-term guests, therapy-groups, environmental and peace-organisations, we'll resist the world-wide devastating religion of the so-called free market. The right to exist - that's what binds all groups and communities working for positive social change together on the threshold of the 21st Century.

Union of Solidarity
☺ own income

Humaniversity

HC

Dr. Wiardi Beckmanlaan 4 | 1931 BW Egmond aan Zee
+31-(0)72-5064114 info@humaniversity.nl
-5061844 www.humaniversity.nl

1978 3 ha (near Alkmaar) ♀20 ♂25 1 46

e, g all

one part of the group (higher consciousness, meritocracy) shared income

rented/leased

Osho, therapy, addiction therapy, spirituality

therapy, therapist training, administration, garden, household

self-managed, non-violent, hierarchical, spiritual, inner growth, meditation, yoga, tantra, sexuality, free love, vegetarian diet, adult education, pedagogical, free school, peace-work, physically handicapped persons, Humaniversity therapy, organic gardening, construction, handicrafts, martial arts, music studio

☺

If you have never done the "Tourist Programme", you've missed a great opportunity to find out what your potential is and how to become more deeply fulfilled. The Tourist Programme is probably the most powerful and fastest process of personal transformation.
The Humaniversity, which offers this original group, is an international community where personal growth, treatment of people in crisis and therapist training are happening simultaneously. Its style is highly innovative and its therapists are passionate rather than detached. Psychology students, spiritual seekers, housewives, unemployed labourers, businessmen, addicts, teachers – they are all in the same basic program, learning how to relate to others in a healthy way and how to be themselves.
The Humaniversity is a social awareness school where you can get an emotional education. It sees the main causes of human misery in isolation and in the suppression of one's true feelings. Authentic friendship is therefore considered to be the highest goal a human being can achieve.
The technique of the Zen and Sufi masters and all major psychological schools are used to make this the most exciting learning experience in your life. You will emerge from it emotionally purified, powerful, aware and with a new purpose in life.

☺ participate in therapeutic programme

Stichting ELIM

EL

Bergweg 7 | 3941 RA Doorn

+31-(0)343-417064 info@elim.nl

-415355 www.elim.nl

1975 1 ha ♀2 ♂3 2 7

dutch, e 5

everyone in common (consensus) shared economy (shared income and capital)

Foundation

Protestant/Christian

design, missionary work, church, parish contacts

self-managed, christian

The Elim community provides for their own livelihood through full-time and part-time jobs, and consists right now of 5 adults and 2 children. Most of the income comes from the running of a technical illustration and design bureau. Community members live with a common purse, from which all costs are paid: rent, cars, holidays, pocket money, etc. The evangelical Elim church emerged in 1985 from the community's circle of friends. This church has 3 meetings each week. We try, both in the community and in the church, to live with God in our everyday life. In addition, there are ongoing contacts with Christians in Third World countries – mainly India- both with western missionaries and native believers. Eight years ago, Elim initiated a community movement of what has grown to become 35 Dutch communities. There is a magazine, a study course and an annual conference. We hope that the way we lead our lives will help people discover that it is possible to live in peace and happiness through the life-giving and transforming power of Jesus Christ, our Lord and Saviour. Come and visit us!

Christian Community Network

Stichting Emmaus Eindhoven

EE

Genneperweg 11 | 5654 AG Eindhoven

+31-(0)40-2527527 emmaus@dse.nl

-2515767 www.dse.nl/emmaus

1977 0,5 ha ♀5 ♂5 2 12

15

one part of the group (consensus) individual financing

rented/leased

all religions, particularly Christian

About 15 people of various ages, nationalities, cultures and religions live together in our community. Four of them are permanent members, the others are on their way through to a place where they are accepted as they are.

At work the community consists of the resident members plus an average number of 20 volunteers: regular assistants, but also refugees who live elsewhere in town and are looking for temporary work, unemployed people, trainees and others. Emmaus does not receive any subsidy and does not apply for it either. The recycling business brings in enough to cover our livelihood and rent. We don't hoard money in a bank account. About half the annual revenues are granted to charities which try to improve the lot of people who are less fortunate than we are. We also comply with requests from social institutions to give material aid to people as needed.

→See also description of network "**Emmaus**"
☺ willingness to live together with refugees

Vlierhof

DV

Kleverstrasse 115 | 47533 Kleve-Keeken | Deutschland
☎ +49(0)2821 970242, +31(0)5539 1430 info@vlierhof.nl
+49(0)2821 970244 www.vlierhof.nl

2002 — 3 ha (near Kleve) — ♀1 ♂3 4

- dutch, g, e — all
- everyone in common (consensus) — limited community financing
- common property
- non-violent, holistic, spiritual (to be present in the moment - Satsang
- community development, hospitality for similar organisations, working the land, workshops, redeveloping the grounds with ecological construction
- ecological, self-managed, left-wing political understanding, non-violent, spiritual, esoteric/New Age, chaotic, inner growth, meditation, free love, organic diet, vegetarian diet, adult education, pedagogical, peace-work, one-world development, animal protection, environmental protection, self-sufficiency, permaculture, organic agriculture, organic gardening, alternative energy, ecological construction, construction, handicrafts: straw bale building, earth buildings, carpentry work, art: printing, communication techniques: forum, talking stick discussions

☺

The community is situated in Germany, 2 km from the Dutch border on about 3 ha of land in an area of great natural beauty, a couple of hundred metres from the River Rhine. The farm is 18 km from the Dutch university city of Nijmegen, and 5 km from the German city of Kleve.
On this land stands a monumental farmhouse consisting of 3 large buildings with a total floor area of about 2,000 m². We will also build all kinds of experimental buildings made of straw, earth and other materials that the land provides us.
We believe that our society is in trouble, and we experiment to create a better world where people accept each other just as they are, were there is peace and freedom, and were there is no room for hypocrisy and violence.
Our aim is to establish a community of some 15 people. We hope that most of these people will find their livelihood in the community. Our emphasis is that we

have frequent guests who come to us to experience community and to learn from what we are doing.
At the moment our principal aim is to form a community where there is trust and where we are transparent to each other. We work together by working on the land and building more living quarters in the farmhouse. We also build experimental cottages of various types on the land.
We welcome and invite anybody who wants to get to know us or to work with us as volunteers.

→See also description of network "**Vereniging Ecodorp**"
☺ Must be willing and able to care for oneself; should support our ideas; be open to a new lifestyle

No community can survive (except as an ideological fossil)
if it separates from the social Framework to which it belongs.
It draws its real justification from the service
which it gives to this social whole."

(Donald Waters)

Norway

HG Handnesgarden
JL Jøssåsen Landsby
SB Solborg
VL Vidaråsen Landsby

Handnesgarden

HG

8724 Saura

+47-(0)75057397

1986 | 200 ha (near Mo, Rana) | ♀4 ♂4 8

norweg., e — all

one part of the group (consensus) — individual financing

one family

ecological farming

organic farming and animal husbandry, horses, ecological tourism

ecological, organic diet, adult education, pedagogical, animal protection, self-sufficiency, organic agriculture, organic gardening, organic farming, animal friendly husbandry, forestry, new technologies

Handnesgarden is an organic farm on a small island near the Arctic Circle. We are two families running the farm, and there are several people staying here for shorter or longer periods. We keep about 75 cattle, 50 sheep, 10 horses, hens and bees and grow vegetables for the market. We are mostly self-sufficient with food and try to use as much horsepower as possible. Our goal now is to develop eco-tourism on the farm. We are open to new members who want to share a hard-working life with a small income. We're particularly looking for people with interest and skills in ecological construction or manufacturing meat products. We offer different kinds of education in a self-sufficient lifestyle, organic farming, gardening, outdoor life, and training and keeping horses in a natural way.

Handnesgarden in winter

Jøssåsen Landsby

JL

7550 Hommelvik
+47-(0)7397-9940, -9950
landsby@online.no
-8840
www.camphill.no/jossasen

1978 | 46 ha | ♀25 ♂25 | 3 | 53

e, g, dutch, norw. — all
everyone in common (majority vote) — shared income
common property
anthroposophy
working with people with special needs
ecological, christian, anthroposophic, seminar-house, mentally/psychologically handicapped persons, social work, organic agriculture, organic gardening, organic farming, forestry, alternative energy, new technologies, ecological construction

The community has not sent a current selfdescription.

→See also description of network "**Camphill**"
☺ open to Anthroposophy

Solborg

SB

3520 Jevnaker
+47-(0)32132480
solborg@camphill.no
-(0)32132020
home.no.net/solborg

1975 | 75 ha (near Hønevoss) | ♀30 ♂16 | 6 | 52

norw., e, g — all adults
everyone in common (consensus) — varies
foundation
Anthroposophy
animal husbandry, garden, forest, baking, weavery, housekeeping, woodworking

Solborg Camphill Village in Norway has a bio-dynamic farm, extensive vegetable gardens, a bakery, a weavery, and a large forest for timber and firewood.
Most of us live in large extended families, co-workers (long term people with their families, and young temporary volunteers) and villagers (mentally handicapped or otherwise in need of help), sharing our lives, our meals, our living rooms and bathrooms. There may be as many as fifteen people gathered round the dining table every day. Each house has its own budget, and is run more or less autonomously by a couple of responsible co-workers. In the morning and the afternoon everyone goes to work, in a variety of workplaces. Each person contributes to the running of the village according to their capability. Within this sphere no money

changes hands, and work is seen to be something that is freely given within the fellowship.
Solborg is in southern Norway, an hour from Oslo, on the edge of an extensive wilderness area. Within the village we have a Steiner school with over 100 pupils. We are open for volunteers and long term co-workers who would be interested in sharing their lives with us.

→ See also description of network "**Camphill**"
☺ enjoying work, health, happy

Vidaråsen Landsby

VL

3158 Andebu
☎ +47-(0)33444100 — vidaraasen@camphill.no
Fax -(0)33444101 — www.camphill.no/vidaraasen

1966 — 40 ha (near Tønsberg) — ♀69 ♂51 — 40 — 160

norw., e, g — all
one part of the group (majority decision/consensus)
shared economy (shared income and capital) — Camphill Trust of Norway
anthroposophy
ecological, self-managed, spiritual, christian, anthroposophic, adult education, pedagogical, mentally/psychologically handicapped persons, massage, eurythmics, organic agriculture, organic gardening, organic farming, animal friendly husbandry, forestry, alternative energy, ecological construction, construction, handicraft, music, singing, theatre, no TV.

Vidaråsen Landsby is a community of 150 people founded in 1966 to provide living and working accommodations for people with mental handicaps. It is the largest of seven Camphill Communities in Norway. Vidaråsen has developed steadily through the years and is now a thriving village comprising a bio-dynamic farm, garden, dairy, herb workshop, food processing, pottery, weavery, concrete workshop, wood workshop a nursing home and a rich cultural life.
Living with those with mental handicaps is regarded not as a job, but as a way of life with the unique deeply human qualities they bring underpinning all aspects of community life and challenging so-called co-workers to develop there own potential. Each receives according to their needs irrespective of status or workload.
Vidaråsen, like all Camphill communities, is based on anthroposophy and a celebration of the Christian festivals but people from all backgrounds and cultures are welcome. The village is set in wooded hills near the coast and is one and a half hours drive south of Oslo. Television is not encouraged and the use of alcohol and drugs are prohibited. Co-workers are usually required to stay for at least 12 months although short-term working visits in the summer months are welcome. All visits must be pre-arranged.

→ See also description of network "**Camphill**"
☺ dedication to working with mentally disabled adults

Portugal

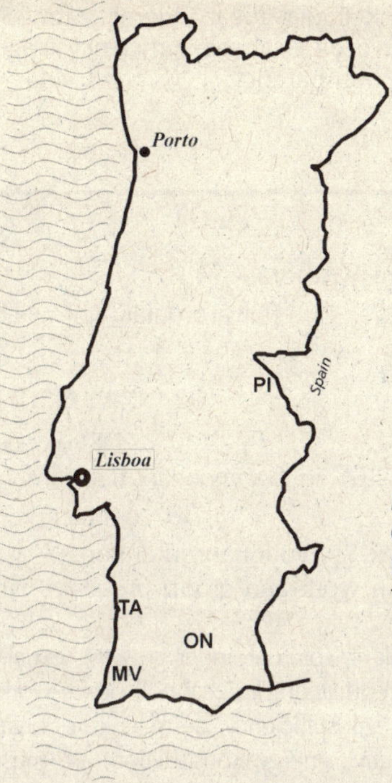

MV Community in planning MOINHO VELHO
ON O Ninho
PI P.I.F.R.S.
TA Tamera

Community in planning MOINHO VELHO

MV

M. Schwarz, J. Otterwell7630 Reliquias
+351-939328460

2003 — ca. 1 ha (near Odemira) — ♀2 ♂2 — 4

g, e, port.

yet nobody

everyone in common (majority vote)

limited community financing

rented/leased

buddhism

ecology, peace work

ecological, self-managed, left-wing political understanding, non-violent, spiritual, ecumenical, buddhist, inner growth, meditation, organic diet, vegetarian diet, peace-work, physically handicapped persons, animal protection, environmental protection, self-sufficiency, organic gardening, construction, humour, handicraft: building shelters out of wood

☺

We are looking for people to help found a community in Portugal – people who view LOVE, Inner Peace and self-knowledge as their path. Creativity and self-initiative are desired. Various faith orientations would like to live in harmony with animals and Mother Earth.

We are living with a small Portuguese family at Reliquias (near Odemira, ca. 35 km from the sea) on our own. We are striving for ecological self-sufficiency (vegetarian). Free love within the framework of group transparency.
YOU ARE HEARTILY WELCOME!

☺ none

O Ninho

ON

Alvaro Maia | Rua Alvez Redol 45 | 2845 Pairas / Amora
+351-938629476 alvaromaia@hotmail.com
-212268909

2004 | 70 ha (near Almodôvar) | ♀3 ♂4 1 8

e, g, f, sp., port. | yet nobody

everyone in common (consensus, consensus -10% in less important decisions)

limited common financing | common property

free spirituality, no dogmas, no hierarchies, revolutionary intentions

farming for self-sufficiency, communication work and group processes, art, autodidactic school and warm hearts

ecological, self-managed, anarchistic, non-violent, spiritual, inner growth, sexuality, free love, organic diet, vegetarian diet, adult education, free school, peace-work, animal protection, environmental protection, self-sufficiency, permaculture, organic agriculture, organic gardening, forestry, alternative energy, construction, art: music, constructions, astrology, philosophy and humanity

☺

We're a starting community in the south-east of Portugal, intending to develop a warmer, more peaceful and human new culture. Basic lines:

- This project is for people who seriously want to free their spirits from psychological patterns which block life energy: dogmas, fears, dependencies, ideologies,...
- Only for people who build up a warm and loving relationship to everybody.
- Another aim is to become more and more ecological and to use less and less destructive techniques.
- Sharing expenses and income. No exploitation.
- Everybody works the same minimal amount of time (with generous flexibility) and everybody does communal work.
- We don't sell alcohol. Cigarettes and drugs only out of the village.
- Absolutely no hierarchy, gurus or ideologies.
- Job rotation (knowledge transfer; no power positions or privileges)
- No killing of animals.
- Self-sufficiency in alimentation (organic agriculture and permaculture).
- Individual rooms.

We'll create a space for free spirit, creativity and integral development of each person's potencial; without teachers. We'll also try to influence the outside society through the spread and liberation of life forces and love.

☺ people who are open to an intensive process of freeing themselves from fear, dependencies and cultural or psychological patterns

P.I.F.R.S.

PI

Ap. 111 | 7320-999 Castelo de Vide
☎+351-245-992419

1990 | 22 ha (near Portalegre) | ♀2 ♂3 7 12

g, e, port. | all

one, if consensus doesn't function; otherwise all (consensus)

rented/leased, one part bought

vegetarian raw foods, Christian (naturally)

self-sufficiency, book publication, making music, teaching children/adults

ecological, self-managed, hierarchical, christian, vegetarian diet raw, adult education, pedagogical, free school, peace-work, mentally/psychologically handicapped persons, social work: back to the roots; environmental protection, self-sufficiency, permaculture, organic agriculture, organic gardening, organic farming, animal friendly husbandry, forestry, alternative energy, new technologies, ecological construction, handicrafts: various old trades; art: mainly music making; media: writing and marketing books

☺

The P.I. System and/or overall project is intended to provide more and more people with opportunities for meaningful, natural activities and participation, and thus to help realise the gradual transformation of our so-called "civilised" society into a free and natural one. It provides all the necessary practical knowledge for such a transformation and is able to eradicate all currently circulating erroneous ideologies, misconceptions, barriers... More information on this can be found in the voluminous writings of Reinhold Schweikert. The Paradise Island Family in Castelo de Vide will be changing its staff with an eye to establishing new projects (Brazil, Germany).

Interdis

☺ many conditions, can be found in our programme/literature

Tamera

TA

Herdade Monte Cerro | Monte do Cerro | 7630 Colos
☎+351-283-635306 | tamera@mail.telepac.pt
-635374 | www.tamera.org

1995 | 134 ha (near Odemira) | ♀35 ♂25 10 70

g, e, port. | all

everyone in common (consensus) | limited community financing

property of individual community members

none

gardening, reforestation, horse farm, children's project and own school, political networking, craftsmanship in building infrastructure, youth project, computer

⚙ self-managed, non-violent, spiritual, sexuality, free love, vegetarian diet, vegan diet, peace-work, organic gardening, alternative energy, construction, carpentry, bricklaying, joinery, electrical work, water supply, planned artists' colony

☺ (✋✋)

Tamera is a project for a future worth living, situated in southern Portugal. It was founded by Sabine Lichtenfels and Dieter Duhm and sees itself as a base for the development of a global peace force. The research work deals with new ways of healing humans and nature. Its aim is to create a non-violent cultural model for a couple of hundred people and the development of a "healing biotope". A healing biotope is a life community of people, animals and plants whose life forces complement each other and which are no longer blocked by violence or fear. In the field of human interaction, charity of one's neighbour, honesty in relationships, truth in love and transparency in the community, above all the dismantling of leadership cults through the assumption of individual responsibility are central. At the moment some 70 permanent staff are living and working in Tamera. During the summer months many friends and guests help construct the compound. Projects such as the "Global Learning Youth School" and the "Place for Children" are now being developed. Other projects, e.g. the "Institute for Global Peace Work", the "Mirja" school for the training of young peace workers and the "Horse Farm" are already in place.
Tamera seeks support and co-operation with other dedicated peace workers and future-oriented communities. They are always welcome from May to the end of October, but we request that you contact us by telephone or e-mail in advance.

→See also description of network "**GEN**"

☺ attendance at a basic/community course, agreement with main goals of research project

Setting up a tent in front of the guest house in Tamera

Spain

AY Argayall
DT Sunseed Desert Technology
EF Ecoforest
EL Equi-Libre
EP El Pardal
IR Comunidad de Irún
JA Jardines de Acuario
LK Lakabe
MV Matavenero y Poibueno
PE Ermita del Padre Eterno
PO Aldea de Pano
SE La Semilla
VA Cooperativa Vall D'Angel

Aldea de Pano

PO

Kurt Fridez | 22438 Pano (Huesca)

☎ +34-974-347000 panofridez@yahoo.es

1996 280 ha (near Barbastro) ♀2 ♂5 7

sp., e, catalan, g, port., f 3

one person (consensus) individual financing

property of individual community members

reconstruction, infrastructure, help in hostel

ecological, non-violent, spiritual, organic gardening, forestry, alternative energy, ecological construction, music

☺

The hamlet of Pano has been inhabited again since 1991 and is located at the foot of the Huesca Pyrenees. It belongs to Graus (13 km to the south) and is located near the famous Buddhist temple of Panillo. A simple hostel, naturally produced whole-grain bread, marmelade and other products provide us with a small income. Together we are making a sincere effort to achieve cooperation on an integrated balance of the environment, nature and development.
We are looking for people who

- choose this lifestyle out of conviction
- bring with them joy, endurance, energy and ideas for creative, constructive work and who are not afraid of a certain amount of hard labour
- want to contribute their own qualities and experience
- experience their environment as their own world and behave in a corresponding manner
- consider such values as respect, openness, tolerance and the acceptance of the private sphere important
- feel responsible for their personal behaviour

☺ no drugs, no smoking, Spanish language skills

Argayall

AY

„Place of Light" | Valle Gran Rey | 38870 La Gomera / Canary Islands
☎ +34-922-805704,-697008 — info@argayall.com
Fax -805704, -697008 — www.argayall.com

1986 — 1.5 ha (near Valle Gran Rey) — ♀12 ♂8 1 21

g, e, sp. — all

one part of the group (consensus)

members' investments, hotel and seminar operation — common property

open spirituality

kitchen, laundry, rooms, gardens, technology & maintenance, plantation, reception, administration

self-managed, spiritual, inner growth, meditation, yoga, tantra, organic diet, vegetarian diet, seminar-house, therapy: rebalancing, Esalen massage, Shiatsu, sound massage; natural health: acupuncture & homeopathy; organic gardening

☺

Argayall lies on a narrow bay, surrounded by cliffs, directly on the Atlantic Ocean on the Canary Island of La Gomera. Since 1983 an old finca in the middle of a fruit tree plantation has been a living space for our approx. twenty member community, which one can picture as a circle made up of three progressively larger circles. The central circle represents the core community: twelve people who call this place their home, who organise the hotel and seminar operation (our economic basis) and who share the process of their personal spiritual growth with one another.
The next circle expands into the living community, often called the "crew". It encompasses those persons (eight to ten people) who are only with us for a limited

time and who help out in the kitchen, garden, on the plantation, in the office, the laundry or with the caretakers. Besides room and board, they above all are given the opportunity to gain personal experience.
The third circle draws the alternating holiday and seminar guests (25 to 30 people) into the community. They meditate, eat and celebrate with us, and treat themselves to (body-) therapy sessions.
We see ourselves as an openly spiritual community, in which everyone is "on their way" - some of us direct our gaze inwardly with a master, some without one. We see meditation as an aid to this and integrate it into our everyday lives.
Beyond the necessary qualifications in their respective fields, people who would like to work with us in the crew for a while should above all have experience with self-responsibility, and bring with them team spirit, flexibility and a certain degree of composure.

→See also description of network "**GEN**" and "**Come Together**"
☺ qualification for free positions in our hotel and seminar operation

Comunidad de Irún

IR

Caserío Barraca, Barrio Ventas 88 | 20305 Irún, Guipúzcoa
☎+34-943-632316

1995 (near San Sebastian) varying

g, e, f, sp. — all who are able

council (consensus) — dependent on situation

housebuilding, trade, bakery...

non-violent, spiritual, adult education, seminar-house, peace-work, medicine: happy hearts!, organic agriculture, organic gardening, various handicrafts, art, „Freepapers"

☺

Seeking love, peace and a society without strife... Most of us didn't expect that Yahshua, known as Jesus, would be the way. The community life that we saw wasn't like anything we had experienced or heard of before. Many of us came from alternative lifestyles. We've lived in Spain since 1995. Before that we lived together with our friends from other countries in a little village in France. We grew and swarmed just like bees forming new hives, but we haven't broken up. The story of our tribe is wonderful.
Many people visit us, some live with us for a time. Some even decide to follow our same way of life. Our community is dynamic, continually developing, and full of activity. We educate our children, we have little cottage industries and we celebrate together. Artistic activities are very important to us. We prefer to deal with organic products, ecological materials and alternative energy. We love Creation and the Creator with all our hearts. To live according to your conscience is a freedom that is not easy to enjoy in today's world. As human beings created in the image of the Creator we have the right to love and trust. Shalom.
At the moment we've got a few communities in the Basque Provinces and in Catalonia. We are looking forward to visitors.

Contact address:
Communidad de San Sebastian | Paseo de Ulia 375 | San Sebastian | 20014 San Sebastian | Tel: +34-943580029"

→See also description of network "**Communities of the Twelve Tribes**"
☺ sincerity; we love the Gospel but are independent of the Christian Church

Comunidad Walden

no postal address, contact only via e-mail: waldencm@wanadoo.es
perso.wanadoo.es/waldencm

1996 | 95 m² | ♀1 ♂2 2 5

sp., port., e
everyone in common (consensus) | shared income
common property
personal, interpersonal and cultural development
renovation, education, reflection
ecological, self-managed, non-violent, inner growth, vegan diet, humour

☺

Our reason to be is personal, interpersonal and cultural development, allowing primary prevention of social and ecological problems. Critical to this aim is the application of scientific psychology, with an integrative, yet neither mentalistic nor spiritualistic approach, as well as regarding ecology as a basic criterion for our behavior. According to our preventive concept of health, as well as to vital ecological reasons, we choose vegan nutrition.
Members self-determine their behaviour by their own commitment to the community's principles. We have a non-political, non-religious, non-dogmatic approach. We emphasize reflection, good communication and coherence.
We share our income, and we all participate in basic tasks and in decision making through collaborative consensus.
We practice communal education. Our social structure is based on true friendship and not on family. We defend monogamy and respect pertinent individual privacy. In order to preserve our identity as a culture, we keep an aware position in our outer contacts.
If you are interested in this specific community, read our homepage carefully. There you'll also find our e-mail address.
Potential members can visit us once a deep written communication has made clear that they can come to see this community as the crucial option for their lives.

☺ thorough postal contact before visit

Cooperativa Vall D'Angel

VA

Mas Den Miguelito | 12170 Sant Mateu, Castellón
+34-946-471073

1998 | 130 ha (near San Mateo) | ♀4 ♂4 | 8

cast., e, f, g — all

everyone who is concerned in common (majority vote)

own capital, subsidies

belief in personal growth

rural tourism, organic agricultur, permaculture, health (therapy), eco-construction, courses in organic gardening

ecological, non-violent, spiritual, inner growth, meditation, yoga, organic diet, vegetarian diet, one-world development, therapy, environmental protection, permaculture, forestry, alternative energy, ecological construction

The community has not sent a current selfdescription.

☺ of economic and ideologic type

Ecoforest

EF

Apdo 29 | Coin 29100 Malaga
+34-678 014 534
info@ecoforest.org
www.ecoforest.org

2000 | 1.1 ha (near Coín, province Malaga) | ♀1 ♂2 | 3 (saisonal 10-15)

e, sp.

part of the group (permanent residents)

non-profit association

vegan, raw foods, ecological spirituality, self-sufficiency

earth, plants, building

ecological, self-managed, inner growth, organic diet, vegan raw foods, adult education, environmental protection, permaculture, organic gardening, permaculture seminars

Ecoforest is a vegan raw food community and a non-profit organisation providing education about living and working in a natural, sustainable and healthy way. People live and learn here in a simple and sustainable environment, that is special to both visitors and residents for ecological, health and spiritual reasons. It is a beacon of positivity and has changed many people's lives by providing inspiration, education and support.

We are living in tents, domes, caravans etc. before deciding on locations for more permanent dwellings. We are rebuilding the main house, and planting vegetables

and fruit trees to establish a multi-levelled edible eco-system. We also host 2-4 two week permaculture design certificate courses here each year.
We intend to demonstrate that food can be produced by families, communities and farmers, all around the world, without destruction of the natural environment - thus making people more economically self-reliant and offering a positive alternative to globalisation trends. We welcome help in this work - and donations to acquire more land/property for this purpose, whilst running the project as a charity. No drugs, alcohol, smoking and no pets - Yes, vegan raw food, and nature! Visitors must phone or email before visiting.

☺ 6,000.- Euro investment, eating vegan and raw, living simple and ecological

El Pardal

EP

Lista de correos | 23300 Villacarrillo-Jaén
☎ +34-9-53128171 (20-22 h) ecopardal@yahoo.es

1981 | 27 ha (near Villacarrillo) | ♀2 ♂2 3 7

g, e, sp., f
everyone in common (consensus) — limited community financing
property of individual community members
all people are brothers in spirit and should work and learn to help each another
self-sufficiency: chickens, milk sheep, goats, fruit, vegetable garden, reforestation, improvement and beautification of site
ecological, self-managed, non-violent, spiritual, christian, inner growth, meditation, yoga, organic diet, vegetarian diet, pedagogical, social work: working with home children in preparation, depth massage, spiritual focussing, natural health care, environmental protection, self-sufficiency, permaculture, organic gardening, organic farming, animal friendly husbandry, alternative energy, new technologies, ecological construction, handicraft: working on house with natural stone and wood, furniture etc., art: several instruments available, humour

☺

El Pardal is located in Spain's largest nature reserve just below a mountain peak at an altitude of 1,470 m (what a view!!), 130 km northeast of Granada. Our nearest neighbour lives 1 hour away. We have a large organic vegetable garden, many fruit trees, pasture land for milk-giving sheep, milk goats (around 20 altogether) and two horses, chickens and ducks, 2 dogs. There are four natural springs on the estate. One part of the land is being reforested according to permaculture principles, another part has been left to nature. We use both solar and wind energy; water energy will soon follow. The community's principle goal is to promote an ecological consciousness, as much self-sufficiency as possible and the development of the personality. We employ natural health care in many forms, from healing herbs, acupressure and reflex zones, depth massage and inner work, to yoga and meditation in order to support the self-discovery and healing process. We always have from 3 to 12 helpers from all over the world staying with us. Middle and long-term working guests, including those with children, as well as eco vacationers and new members are welcome – call us in the evening!

☺ good will and mutual understanding

Equi-Libre

EL

Apdo. 15 | 43570 Santa Bárbara, Tarragona
☎+34-977-261159

1989 | 2.5 ha (near Amposta) | ♀1 | 1

sp., e, g, catalan. | 15-35 within a year

evolution

general development, evolution

ecological, self-managed, non-violent, spiritual, esoteric/New Age, chaotic, inner growth, organic diet, vegetarian diet, pedagogical, peace-work, one-world development, animal protection, environmental protection, organic agriculture, animal friendly husbandry, ecological construction, construction, horses

☺

Equi-Libre started in 1989 searching for a natural alternative lifestyle, building a house by myself on a small piece of land (between the Ebro delta and the mountains), it has grown to 2.5 ha of land with varying landscapes. We are rebuilding an ex-rabbit farm (living and common rooms, workshops, stables etc.). There is (still!) plenty to do.
We have room to live, work and grow together; for people (particularly horse-lovers!) who would like to give of themselves and realise dreams and utopias together. (Which isn't easy, but not impossible.)

☺ trial period, mutual accord

Ermita del Padre Eterno

PE

Apdo. 118 | 18400 Orgiva (Granada)
☎+34-958 347136

1997 | 5 ha (near Orgiva) | ♀2 ♂4 2 8

e, f, sp. | 2

everyone in common (consensus) | limited common financing

common property

desire for shared life with us, the earth and the pilgrims

ecological, spiritual, organic diet, vegetarian diet, free school, seminar-house, organic agriculture, agrotourism

☺

One day we went into the mountains to live together. We threw our money together and bought this abandoned piece of land with its ruins of impenetrable stone and the remains of an ancient hermitage. Yes, and so ... emerged an obliga-

tion to take care of it. We decided to move some stones to their places, to shower each corner of this universe with water and our visions, to plant new trees, work, observe, learn... and ultimately keep ourselves alive!
We live as a group - a hard, funny and indescribable challenge. Some of those who were here at the beginning have gone other ways. Others on their way have come here to stay, not to mention the countless and delightful visitors whom the wind brings and takes away!
We are dedicated to a life in community, with self-sufficiency, respect for nature, human understanding, a motherly spirit that comes from the heart, and healthy nutrition for body and soul...

☺ balanced relationship between residential expectations, work and financial contribution; desire for shared life with us, the earth and the pilgrims

Jardines de Acuario

JA

Apdo. 40 | 30850 Totana (Murcia)
+34-619096514, -968 487227
eliaslopez@eresmas.com, sylvathor@yahoo.es

2001 — 20 ha (near Totana/Murcia) — ♀1 ♂2 4 7

e, f, sp. — 2

everyone in common (majority vote/consensus)

limited common financing and individual — common property

ecology and contact with nature

ecological farming, rural tourism, renovating old buildings, permaculture

ecological, spiritual, inner growth, meditation, seminar-house, animal protection, environmental protection, permaculture, organic agriculture, forestry, alternative energy, new technologies, ecological construction

☺

In the spring of 1998 some utopia fans sowed the first seeds and watered them with the kindness and enthusiasm of the moment. The Aquarius Gardens project (jardines de acuario) joined in, appearing with the suggestion that we support one another in living and realising our petty wearinesses and spectacular sunrises. We look forward to seeing how these seeds will sprout, develop charming branches, spread their fragrances, attract the moths with their songs of praise, how the sun and moon will wink at us etc ... And we shall follow this wonderfully enchanted wave, growing with our project, which will transform us into a mighty forest in which we shall learn to co-operate with one another. Intertwined with the earth, we seek full assimilation in this beautiful area, which is located in the heart of the Sierra Espuña National Park in Totana (Murcia).
We invite you to share with us in growing with our emotions and joining our paths of light, peace and hope.

Red Íberica de ecoaldeas

☺ supporting a life project and the means to realise it

La Semilla

SE

el realillo-bolonia | 11380 Tarifa (cádiz)
+34-956 236 753 grahola@yahoo.es

1997 12.5 ha (near Tarifa) ca. 5

sp., e, it. all

everyone in common (consensus) limited community financing

property of individual community members

permaculture, sale of organic foods

ecological, non-violent, organic diet, environmental protection, permaculture, alternative energy, ecological construction

☺

The La Semilla project developed with the goal of rediscovering a more natural lifestyle better suited to our needs. Working together, respect for natural cycles and energy saving are our most important principles. Permaculture is the theory which comes closest to our ideals.

We have build a kitchen/living room which we use as a common room, as a workplace for baking bread and, on the weekend, as a vegetarian restaurant. An additional, newly built hall is available for workshops, conferences and festivals. We are not linked to the public energy network and use a wind-powered generator, a photo-voltaic system and a generator for our needs. We heat water with a solar power system. In order to save water, we use home-made dry toilets and a reed bed system. We eat seasonal products from our own garden and from the La Verde co-operative. But at the moment the restoration of our farm has priority.

We are interested in environmental education with children and in projects in concert with organisations working with young people who are exposed to discrimination. We meet weekly for decision-making and co-ordination. You can visit us on Saturdays or Sundays, or else write to us if you would like to stay longer. At the moment we are interested in volunteers who can help perform the project's tasks.

☺ admission requirements

Lakabe

LK

Valle de Arce, Aoiz | 31438 Nafarroa - Euskadi
+34-948-392002
-392002

1980 | 550 ha (near Pamplona (Navarra)) | ♀8 ♂13 | 8 | 29

eusquera, catalan, f — all

weekly meeting (consensus) — shared economy (shared income and capital)

occupants

non-violent action, political activity in region

farming, organic bakery, organic animal husbandry, village reconstruction, self-sufficiency, „amorro energetico"

ecological, self-managed, anarchistic, left-wing political understanding, feminist, non-violent, environmental protection, self-sufficiency, permaculture, organic agriculture, organic farming, alternative energy, ecological construction

Lakabe is a village that was occupied in 1980. It developed from the antimilitarist movement. Its goal is to put philosophical principles of active non-violence into practise. We foresee the development of a small society based on various social parameters such as equality, justice, anti-patriarchy, feminism… Thus from the very first moment, Lakabe witnessed the development of a community. Decisions are made at the assembly, the earth and the livestock are treated on an ecological basis, the forest and the surroundings are cared for. We are conducting experiments with alternative energy forms. At the moment we are self-sufficient and use sunlight as well as water and wind power (along with a generator for emergencies). We bake ecological full-grain bread for our own needs and to earn money for our village. We have rebuilt ten houses and the church with stone and wood according to organic construction principles and in the traditional style of the region.
We have 17 children. Most of them were born here in the natural way; today they are between 6 and 22 years old. We ran an alternative school for a number of years, but soon decided that the children should attend conventional institutions; several are studying renewable energies and forestry at the university or are completing their A-levels. Nine of them participate in the plenary meeting.
We have a shared economy; all resources belong to everybody. There is no private land. We remain an occupied village but the government of Navarra is not particularly interested in resolving this issue. We are celebrating our 25th anniversary this spring and want to write a history of our first 25 years.

Red Ibérica de Ecoaldeas

☺ consent to the following: 1 year trial period, consensus principle, life in a rural commune

Matavenero y Poibueno

MV

Pueblo Ecologico Europeo | lista de correos | 24300 Bembibre, Leon
+34-987-693216 (7.30-8.30 pm)
-693216 (10-12 am)

1989 | 3,000 ha (near Bembibre) | ♀12 ♂15 | 15 | 42

g, sp., e | 5

everyone in common (consensus) | limited common financing and individual

restored and administered as official community

organic gardening, wood gathering, preserving village centre, pedagogy, hospitality

ecological, self-managed, anarchistic, chaotic, inner growth, organic diet, pedagogical, free school, environmental protection, self-sufficiency (lots of sweet chestnuts), permaculture, organic agriculture, organic gardening, organic farming, alternative energy, ecological construction, drums, jewellry, wood, sewing, sports: pushing wheelbarrows up the hill and just the fact of living here!; music, painting, dance; international

Matavenero and Poibueno are two sister villages at an altitude of ca. 1,000 m in the mountains of north-western Spain. Before our first "pioneers" arrived in 1989 the villages had been abandoned and completely unused for over 20 years, making them ideal for our purposes. From the beginning there was no resistance whatsoever against our settlement on the part of the neighbouring villages and the former owners. Following a fire, a core of four buildings survived, which we repaired for the community's infrastructure (bakery, school, shop, alcohol-free bar, communal workshop, meeting and banquet hall, guest space). Settlement began in tepees and tents, then we built huts and wooden houses. The number of inhabitants grew to 100 people from around 10 countries. It later declined and is now on the rise once more. The basic idea - partially influenced by the Rainbow Movement - is ecological living and working close to and in harmony with nature - close to and in co-operation with like-minded people - as well as the development of our own pedagogy. We try to make the necessary decisions in the weekly council on a consensus basis. For the past

eight or so years we have been formally recognised as a village with our own mayor. We fund community projects such as the water system etc. from our shared purse. At the moment (12/03) there's a co-op store, a school with a Spanish teacher, professional musicians, a political group, plus dairy cows in Poibueno. Long-term guests are welcome. It's hard to earn money here and only a minimalist economy is possible (survival). To some extent we're a tribal culture.
The village can only be reached on foot or on horseback. We generate electricity with solar collectors and a small wind turbine. We largely supply ourselves with vegetables from our own organic gardens. Thanks to birth-experienced women and men, more than 35 children have been born here. We practice alternative medicine as much as possible (homeopathy, herbs, Bach flower remedies, raw vegetables and fruits, etc.).
The best time to visit us is between May and September – but the not very cold winter is interesting too. Spanish skills are desirable, as is financial independence.

Red Íberica de ecoaldeas
☺ at least a one-year stay + co-operation + acceptance by the council

Sunseed Desert Technology

DT

Apdo. 9 | 04270 Sorbas, Almeria
☎+34-950-525770
sunseedspain@arrakis.es
www.sunseed.org.uk

1986 | 31 ha (near Almeria) | ♀6 ♂3 9

e, sp. | 15-35

one part of the group (manager has last word, otherwise consensus)
individual financing
sustainable living
ecological, organic diet, vegetarian diet, vegan diet, self-sufficiency, permaculture, organic gardening, alternative energy, ecological construction, construction

☺ ()

Sunseed Desert Technology is the Spanish Project of The Sunseed Trust (GB). We live as a community of up to 30 people, 9 full-time staff members (1 of whom is voluntary) and short and long-term volunteers who stay for 2 weeks to one year and make a financial contribution of 69 - 137 Euros per week to cover their food and accommodation (the amount depends on time of year and length of stay).
Sunseed Desert Technology aims to develop, demonstrate and communicate accessible, low-tech methods of living sustainably in a semi arid environment. We therefore live in as sustainable a method as possible, growing much of our own food, composting, reusing and recycling our waste as far as possible and making full use of solar energy and other appropriate technology. As part of our work we carry out low-tech research in areas such as appropriate technology and dryland growing. Volunteers are welcome throughout the year and work in all our departments. All members of the community share in the cooking and cleaning duties. For more information on joining us, please see our website or contact us.

☺ weekly donation for room and board

Sweden

- BB ISKCON: The Bhaktivedanta Book Trust
- FS Foreningen Staffansgården
- KB Kadesh-biyqah
- KF Kvarn-Folket
- LN Libuse Nastrom
- RB Rydebacke By
- ST Stiftelsen Stjärnsund
- VB Villa Billebro
- VH Vita Hästen

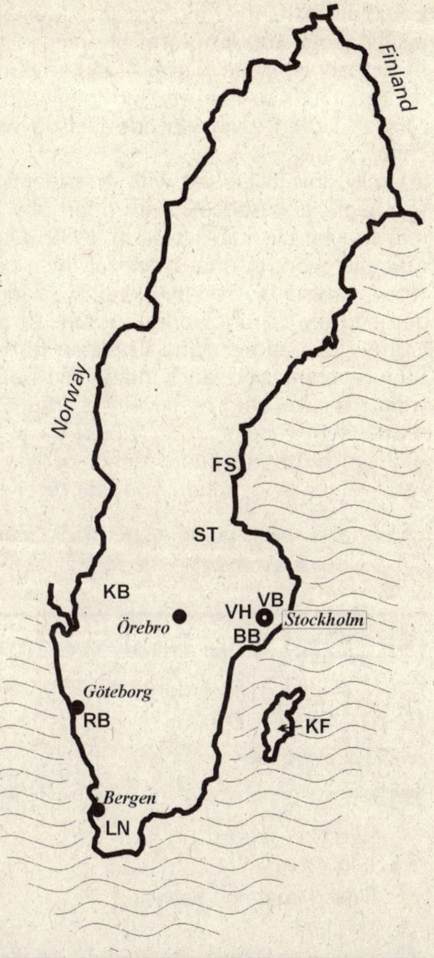

Foreningen Staffansgården

FS

Furugatan 1 | 82060 Delsbo

☎ +46-(0)653-16850

-10968

1974 | 28 ha (near Hudiksvall) | ♀40 ♂30 70

e

50+25

part of group or leadership group (consensus)

individual financing

foundation

anthroposophy

disabled people

anthroposophic

☺

Camphill Staffansgården is a living-working community with mentally handicapped adults about 300 km north of Stockholm.
It consists of three places: Staffansgården in Delsbo with 11 handicapped residents, ca. 10 co-workers and their resp. children,
Mickelsgarden 2 km outside Delsbo with 9 residents, c. 8 co-workers and their children and
a family-unit in Delsbo with 4 residents, 3 co-workers and their children.
Our work is based on Anthroposophy and the ideas of the Camphill impulse as initiated by Dr. Karl König in 1939. During the week all co-workers, interns and residents work in one or two of the workshops or in one of the houses. Our main work consists of woodworking, weaving, the bakery, the farm, the vegetable garden and the candle workshop. One of the important aspects in our community life is the celebration of the Christian festivals. On Saturday evenings we conduct a Bible evening and on Sundays we hold a special morning assembly, sometimes with a service held by a visiting priest from the Christian Community.
All new co-workers are accepted for a 12-month trial period. During this time the stay can be terminated if either party wishes.
As a volunteer or intern you will receive free room, board and pocket money.

→See also description of network "**Camphill**"
☺ work or internship, no ideology

ISKCON: The Bhaktivedanta Book Trust

BB

Korsnäs Gard | 14792 Grödinge
☎ +46-(0)8-53029800 — bmd@com.bbt.se
Fax -53025062 — www.harekrishna.se

1976 — 2 ha (near Tumba) — ♀13 ♂15 — 1 — 29

swed., e, russ., g
ISKCON
limited common financing
spiritual
book publishing, multimedia production, gardening
ecological, non-violent, spiritual, esoteric/New Age, inner growth, meditation, yoga, organic diet, vegetarian diet, seminar-house, animal protection, environmental protection, self-sufficiency, organic agriculture, organic gardening, animal friendly husbandry, design, painting, film

☺

The community in Korsnäs Gård is located ca. 30km south of Stockholm in a beautiful natural setting, overlooking a large lake and extensive forests.
The community was started in 1976 by a group of spiritual practitioners with the aim to facilitate themselves, as well as everyone interested in leading a spiritually oriented life, in their meditation and worship. Since then renunciates as well as families have inhabited it. Later the north-European division of the Bhaktivedanta Book Trust, the world's largest publisher of India's spiritual classics, made their headquarters in Korsnäs Gård, producing books in more than 43 languages, as well

as CDs and multimedia presentations.
Since the beginning days the members of the community have maintained their spiritual values and have increased the intensity of the mode of worship they are following. All the members lead a purely vegetarian and drug-free life.

→See also description of network "**ISKCON**"
☺ vegetarian, drug-free, acceptance of all rules, co-operation in the community

Kadesh-biyqah

KB

Box 120 | 67123 Arvika
nccg@nccg.org
www.nccg.org/kadesh.html

1997 4 ha (near Arvika) ♀6 ♂4 4 14

norw., swed., e
all
one part of the group (consensus)
limited community financing
property of Chavurat Bekorot Community
Christians with Hebrew roots
web design, media production, publishing, conferences, market garden
non-violent, hierarchical, spiritual, christian, adult education, pedagogical, free school, seminar-house, social work: orphan assistance in the Third World

☺

Kadesh-biyqah is an embryo teaching and conference centre of the Chavurat Bekorot (Community of the Firstborn) for international visitors, principally pastors and other trainee leaders and their families from the New Covenant Church of God (NCCG). Its leadership consists of three men and three women. It is convenient to Oslo and Göteborg Airports. It is also the main production centre for printed and electronic media materials (New Covenant Press) for use in the mission field as well as a centre for raising funds for orphanages in India and Africa. Our goal is to be partially self-sustaining through market gardening, web design and other projects. Children are homeschooled in three languages (Swedish, Norwegian and English) to a high standard and enjoy good ITC resources together with a library of over 7,000 multi-lingual books. Kadesh-biyqah is a caring community and welcomes young and old, our most senior resident being 90. Permanent membership is conditional upon being debt-free, adherence to high moral, ethical and spiritual standards and is reviewed annually. The land and buildings are owned by the community and are leased to members as a stewardship. Visitors must be recommended by an NCCG Pastor and receive an invitation.

Emerging international Network
☺ Membership in the Chavurat Bekorot Community

KVARN-FOLKET

KF

Stiftelsen Väderkvarnen | 62016 Ljugarn
+46-(0)498-491308

1980 3 ha (near Visby) ♀2 ♂2

swed., e all
all who are concerned (consensus) limited common financing
Foundation
vegan, nature-free-spiritual love
Eco-Construction, organic gardening
ecological, self-managed, anarchistic, left-wing political understanding, feminist, non-violent, spiritual, buddhist, inner growth, meditation, yoga, tantra, sexuality, free love, organic diet, vegetarian diet, vegan diet, peace-work, one-world development, animal protection, environmental protection, self-sufficiency, organic gardening, animal friendly husbandry, alternative energy, ecological construction, humour

Stiftelsen Väderkvarnen is a foundation which started as a summer community about 20 years ago. Some close friends were living together in an old five-floor building with 8 corners and with a window in the 4 cardinal points. The house was used as a windmill for about hundred years. In 1990 the foundation bought another windmill on the westcoast for a new summer-community. People in the community have changed many times in these 20 years and started up new families in other places. The founder and the committee wanted to start something new in 2000 with the name "Living Love Family" in a new house on an island. The old windmill will be donated to the local monument preservation associations. So the Foundation has bought a 200-year-old stonehouse in the countryside of the island of Gotland south-east of the Swedish mainland. It has been empty for 5 years and needs a lot of love and good spirits again. Gotland has the sunniest days of all Sweden, the town Visby is the biggest medieval town in Northern Europe. Gotland is also very clean with very little pollution, friendly people and sheep. The house is going to be fixed, cleaned and repaired, so in summer 2004 people can move in. We hopefully find out together, that peace, love and understanding are the most important things in communitylife. Welcome!

Kollektivkontakten Sweden
vegetarian, no drugs, peace minded, self-sufficient, living love

Libuse Nastrom

LN

V. Storgata 11C | 29338 Olofstrom

2001

swed., g
„Gaia", „Ecosophy", solidarity, openness

ecological, spiritual, ecumenical, inner growth, organic diet, vegetarian diet (no fanaticism), adult education, free school, seminar-house, peace-work, one-world development, acupressure, massage, Tai Chi, Chi Gong, self-sufficiency, permaculture, organic agriculture, organic gardening, organic farming (hemp as a useful plant), animal friendly husbandry, forestry, alternative energy, new technologies, ecological construction, sports: no resource-gobblers like golf or racing, dance; interaction with the world outside the community.

☺

Since the 1970s I have been trying to live with people on an ecological basis, and I recently got to know two young people with identical dreams who know other people in turn... We met frequently to discuss our ideas about the ecovillage, the relationships we should have with the outside world etc., and about what we could do to come closer to a good, green world for all. It's a funny thing that we agreed on everything, even though I'm 82 and they were only around 20. We're looking for some land near Lund where some other interested persons are currently studying. Land is expensive in Sweden; we are going to try to get it subsidised by the EU or someone else. We'd like to have community-owned land on which people can build their own houses. We would like to work with labour-saving techniques (permaculure), have time for thorough decision-making, and also do something for old and young people who don't "belong" anywhere. (Libuse Nastrom)

☺ ecological, interested persons with money would be very welcome...

Rydebacke By

RB

Ryde Backe | 43064 Hällingsjö
+46-(0)30143325
piers.byford@telia.com
www.rydebacke.nu

1997 — 3.4 ha (near Göteborg) — ♀8 ♂7 — 21 — 36

swed., e, g, fin. — none

everyone in common (usually consensus, also majority vote)

individual financing

holistic world view, assuming responsibility for the world both locally and globally

few common activities at the moment, e.g.: politics, economics, construction

ecological, self-managed, left-wing political understanding, organic gardening, organic farming, alternative energy, ecological construction

☺

Rydebacke By is a small "eco-village" taking shape in a rural setting ca. 40 km south east of Gothenburg (Göteborg). The project is made up of around 10 families, working together to create an alternative lifestyle based on ecological principles. So far, 4 family houses and a building with four living quarters have been built, with each family owning their own plot and being responsible for building their own house. The project has good contacts with local tradesmen and work groups are

formed when needed. In total there are 13 residential building plots. In addition, there are plots for a community building and small business units as well as land for allotments and domestic animals. The community building and a sheep/hen house are currently at the planning stage.
The village is sited on a little forest clad hill overlooking forest tarns. Close by is a larger freshwater lake (perfect for swimming or canoeing) and an organic farm "Gunnagård". About 3 km away is the "centre" of Ubbhult where there is a junior school, nursery schools, village hall and chapel.
The village is as much a social project as a collection of buildings. Early co-operation laid the basis of relationships and ways of working together that live on in the village today. One goal has been to seek knowledge and understanding of both ecological and social structures while, wherever possible, planning, building and managing the village ourselves.

☺ no official conditions

Stiftelsen Stjärnsund

ST

Bruksallén 16 | 77071 Stjärnsund
☎ +46-(0)225-80001
fridhempost@hotmail.com
-80005
www.frid.nu

1984

♀12 ♂5 2 19

e

17

one part of the group (consensus)

limited community financing

the community

kitchen and gardening, renovation

ecological, non-violent, spiritual, meditation, vegetarian diet, massage, therapy, organic gardening, animal friendly husbandry

☺

Stiftelsen Stjärnsund is a centre for spiritual development and for bringing a holistic view of life into reality. We, the Foundation's members, believe that the growing consciousness of humanity will bring about new patterns of society where spiritual values can be integrated with culture and science. Stiftelsen Stjärnsund was started in 1984 and was inspired by the Findhorn Foundation in Northern Scotland. Our foundation is a non-profit organisation and is completely independent of political and religious organisations. We have no leader, spiritual or worldly, but all activity occurs in co-operation and through personal responsibilities.
Our retreat centre is a large red-painted timber building from around 1890. Here we have a large kitchen, library, dining room, meditation room along with a shop where we sell books, biodynamic food and some health products. We offer courses throughout the year but a majority of these are during the summer months. However, there are other activities at Fridhem even when there are no courses. Members of the Foundation as well as other people living in the village meet in the evenings to practise different kinds of dances, to sing, attend lectures etc. Fridhem is also open for exhibitions.
We have a large garden, where we cultivate vegetables for our own use.

Villa Billebro

VB

Höglidsv. 28A | 13550 Tyresö
+46-(0)8-7127850 info@billebro.se
-6400875 www.billebro.se

1995 | 1000 m² (near Stockholm) | ♀2 ♂3 2 7

e, swed. | 1-2
varies (majority vote) | individual financing
one member
love, joy, spirituality, transformation, meditation, dance, fun and games
art, dance, meditation
ecological, self-managed, non-violent, spiritual, taoist, inner growth, meditation, yoga, tantra, sexuality, organic diet, vegetarian diet, vegan diet, macrobiotic diet, seminar-house, voice dialogue, alternative energy, ecological construction, sports, art, humour

☺

We are a small community which dreams of love, freedom and passion. We work within society, long for transformation and dare to transform ourselves a little every day. We get a lot of help from "landmark education" – see: www.landmarkeducation.com.
Kent Billebro, founder and owner, has a small firm which rents out sound and light equipment and works as a disc jockey. Paul Atkinson lived in Findhorn for 10 years, Tony Bingefors does a lot of Falun Gong. Kent is in love with Emma (as of 12/03 = the editor), has 2 kids and only lives here part-time. Paul is a fantastic painter and musician. At the moment we've got room for 2 more persons. Kent likes to dance and sometimes we stage therapeutic dance parties in our house.

Vita Hästen

VH

Ringarstigen 3 | 16858 Bromma

1970 | 350 m² | ♀6 ♂4 10

swed., e | none
everyone in common (majority vote / consensus)
limited common financing | foundation
vegetarian, non-violent, equality
social life
ecological, self-managed, feminist, non-violent, inner growth, meditation, free love, vegetarian diet, peace-work, one-world development, animal protection, environmental protection, humour, art, great parties

☺

The Name of our Community is Världshuset Vita Hästen, which means „The White Horse Inn". It was created in 1970 by the poet Jarl Hammarberg. The house is

located northwest of Stockholm in a residential district 30 minutes from the city centre.
There are 10 persons living here and the average age at the moment is 28.5. Our cats Källa and Baba are as much members of the community as we are (except that they don't clean, aside from themselves).
We have different interests and ways of making a living, but the wish to live together in an environmental friendly way links us together.

☺ open lifestyle, creativity, tolerance...

„Many communities get into problems because they don't rate playing as high as working." (Patch Adams, doctor, clown and founder of a community in the USA)

Switzerland

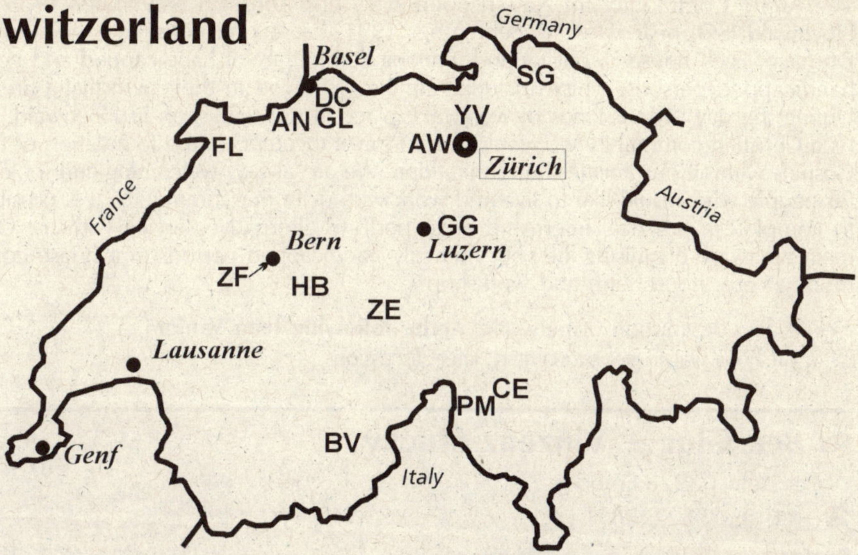

AN Arche im Nauen
AW Hof allne wind
BV Bea Glur + Vinzenz Stucky
CE CES - Fondazione per la rinascita di Chiesso
DC Communauté Don Camillo
FL Bergerie de Froidevaux
GL Projektgruppe GLOBI
HB Humanus-Haus Beitenwil
PM Genossenschaft Pianta Monda
SG Schloss Glarisegg
YV Yamagishi Vereinigung für glückliches Zusammenleben
ZE Zentrum der Einheit
ZF Zaffaraya

Arche im Nauen

AN

Oberdorfstr. 9, Postfach 34 | 4146 Hochwald

+41-(0)61-7514933 imnauen@arche-helvetia.ch

-7539334 www.arche-helvetia.ch

1985 (near Basel) ♀12 ♂11 6 29

g 90%

everyone together/some decisions made by assoc. (majority vote)

individual financing and state subsidies

partially rented, partially association property

Catholic, ecumenical

living and working together in house communities (incl. assisting "mentally disabled" residents)

spiritual, christian, ecumenical, inner growth, pedagogical, mentally/psychologically handicapped persons

☺

The Arche Community Im Nauen opened its first house in November 1985 in Hochwald (SO) near Basel. In September 1991 the second house was opened in Dornach. Each house is a living and working community of handicapped and non-handicapped persons, which includes families who live in their own living areas. During the day various kinds of work take place in our workshop in Hochwald.
As a Christian community we would like to travel together on the foundation of the Gospels with all our abilities and limitations. We are always welcoming and looking for people who would like to live and work with us in our community. It is possible to complete a practical internship or to perform alternative service with us. Our main areas are organising life with mentally handicapped persons in a house community, care, household, and workshop.

→See also description of network "**Arche following Jean Vanier**"
☺ a previous visit to get acquainted, later discussions

Bea Glur + Vinzenz Stucky

BV

Walkerstein | 3926 Embd
☎+41-(0)279522958

1999 — 10 ha (near Brig) — ♀1 ♂1 — 2 — 4

g, e, it., f — all
everyone in common
in planning — property of individual community members
closeness to simplicity (nature religion)
working on the land and on the farm (milk, goats), gathering wild herbs and berries,
ecological, self-managed, feminist, spiritual, chaotic, inner growth, meditation, yoga, sexuality, organic diet, peace-work, environmental protection, self-sufficiency, organic gardening, organic farming, alternative energy, construction, handicraft: leather, furs, cloth, feathers, stone, wool, wood, dyes, sports: haymaking + irrigation, looking for goats

☺

We live in the Wallis Mountains (Switzerland) on a wild, precipitous piece of land at ca. 1,200 m above sea level. For several years we have been building and renovating a small mountain farm. We keep 20 milk goats, two donkeys, chickens, three dogs and cats. We process the goat milk into cheese, yoghurt and curd. We also keep a large garden and gather many wild herbs and berries. We consume these products ourselves and also sell part of them. In addition, we rent a remodelled grain barn out to holiday guests. We also engage in arts and crafts, turning leather, cloth, furs, wood, stone etc. into a wide range of articles. We also want to offer workshops and donkey trekking in the future.
Bea, Vinzenz, Resa (8) and Joshua (11) are our hard core here on the Walkerstein. People come by throughout the year and both work and stay with us for different lengths of time. Although we lead a relatively hard life in order to follow the rhythm of the seasons, we think it is important to cultivate spiritual growth as well. Closely linked to Mother Earth and the elements, with respect for life and growth,

with knowledge of the transitory nature of all things, we trust in the elemental forces and enjoy the here and now.
We dream of expanding the hard core of the family living here in order to share responsibility and to take full advantage of all the possibilities this lovely place has to offer. So that we can become strong as a small community and provide our children with a place to live and grow. People who have the time and the inclination to come stay and work with us for a time are sincerely welcome.

Verein Bergheimat, freies Netzwerk wurzeliger Wilder

motivated people whose heart is where they are, and who work together to create a new living space

Bergerie de Froidevaux

FL

2887 Soubey
+41-(0)329551253

1989 | 60 ha (near Delemont) | ♀2 ♂6 | 8

f, g | 4

everyone in common (consensus) | shared income

common property

we are people who work: spiritually, with the earth and with animals

agriculture, sheep meadow, gardening, tanning, forest, house construction, household

ecological, self-managed, feminist, non-violent, spiritual, anthroposophic, free love, organic diet, social work, animal protection, environmental protection, self-sufficiency, permaculture, organic agriculture, organic farming

The shepherds of Froidevaux are a community in a remote village in the Swiss Jura, not far from the French border. We operate an organic farm which includes a meadow with sheep and cows, a large garden, cereals, a tannery and a forest. We share all the work among ourselves according to our individual abilities. Please contact us by telephone.

discuss on the spot

CES - Fondazione per la rinascita di Chiesso

CE

6747 Chironico (Ticino)
+41-(0)91-8651414
info@cesnet.ch
www.cesnet.ch

1972 | 10 ha (near Bellinzona) | ♀3 ♂3 6

g, it, e, f | 6

everyone in common (consensus) | limited community financing

partially leased, partially Fondazione (foundation)

social competence, agreement with community's goals

farming, gardening, construction, landscape conservation

ecological, self-managed, left-wing political understanding, organic diet, adult education, seminar-house, group work, environmental protection, self-sufficiency, organic agriculture, organic gardening, organic farming, forestry, alternative energy, ecological construction, construction

CES is a formerly abandoned mountain village on a high plateau in northern Tessin (1,450 m above sea level). Together with four other "montes" it forms part of the community of Chironico in the Val Leventina. Ces is located far from the chaos of traffic and can only be reached on foot, two hours uphill. Already on the way up one encounters a varied landscape. In Ces itself the naturally cultivated plateau with its waterfall, moor areas and rare flowers strikes the eye. Since Ces is located in a no hunting zone, we can also observe wild animals. Ces consists of some 25 houses and barns, some of them in ruins and others rebuilt, as well as a chapel. One third of the houses belong to us, the self-administered "Foundation for the Reconstruction of Ces". For over 20 years we have been dedicating ourselves as a collective to the preservation of the village and its surroundings in their original form and to the accessibility of Ces for alternative communal forms of living and working. In the wintertime Ces is quiet, in the summer it is busy: that is when we cultivate our organic garden, care for our animals, cut the hay and just talk; in the village renovation work goes on; we play and discuss. We consciously live simply, do without many forms of mechanisation, and work with our hands. Since we want to live as independently as possible, we produce our own electricity (with a small hydroelectric plant and a solar energy system) and support ourselves - as far as possible - from our own products from our organic gardens. Ces is remote but not isolated: it is intended to reach out to the rest of the world and demonstrate alternatives. We are visited each year by a large circle of friends and guests from many countries. Our conference house "Veridirum" is available for small groups (up to 25 persons), and the stone house "Ti an Dour" is available for small groups and families (up to 8 persons). If you would like to visit us or work together with us, please let us know beforehand by telephone.

☺ ecological consciousness and social competence

Communauté Don Camillo

DC

Montmirail | 2075 Thielle-Wavre
☎ +41-(0)32-7569000 — info@doncamillo.ch
-7569001 — www.doncamillo.ch

1977 — 24 ha (near Neuchâtel) — ♀12 ♂11 — 28 — 51

g, f — approx. 10

everyone together, part of the group (majority vote, consensus)

shared income — rented/leased, building rights contract

ecumenical/Christian

large guest house, renovation, farming

christian, ecumenical, adult education, seminar-house, one-world development, social work: accommodating people in life crises, animal friendly husbandry, construction, democratic administrative form, liturgy of the hours

☺

The Don Camillo Community was founded in Basel in 1977. The original idea was a lifestyle closely oriented on the Gospels. We borrowed the name Don Camillo from the novels of Giovanni Guareschi – his main character lives in constant loving conflict with the communist mayor, Peppone. A friendly Christ, who patiently answers Camillo, helps him to endure feuds, joys and defeats with generous helpings of humour. We have also had the experience that an occasional dose of humour can help us through the ups and downs of communal life. The heart of our communitarian life lies in our "liturgy of the hours". We organise it on the Benedictine model. We share our income and take joint responsibility for our communitarian projects. We have also developed a democratic structure.
We run a large guest house in Montmirail near Neuchâtel. We offer retreats, seminars and courses and make the house available to groups with their own programmes. In addition, we provide room for around 10 people who are looking for a sheltered place to live for a certain time.
Our main concern in Montmirail is providing an oasis for people passing through. Some 20 adults live here as individuals and as families. Another community family lives in Basel. Our association belongs to the Evangelical-Reformed Church of Neuchâtel and Basel.

☺ desire to follow Jesus

Genossenschaft Pianta Monda

PM

Pianted | 6692 Menzonio (Ticino)

info@piantamonda.ch
www.piantamonda.ch

1993 | 4.5 ha (near Locarno) | ♀2 ♂4 6

g, e, it., f, sp. | 3

everyone in common (majority vote) | rented/leased, co-operative

goal: living in harmony with Creation

gardening, building, wood-cutting, tree-clearing, hay-making, caring for guests, living together

ecological, self-managed, non-violent, spiritual, inner growth, organic diet, one-world development, environmental protection, self-sufficiency, organic agriculture, organic gardening, alternative energy, new technologies, ecological construction, construction, agritourism, simple life, few drugs, little consumption, autocultural, holistic

☺

The politically and confessionally independent co-operative of Pianta Monda has been in existence since 1993. This ecovillage in the Tessin, located at an altitude of 840 m above sea level, is a place of encounter free of stress and excess. It is just 20 minutes by foot from Menzonio in the Maggia Valley. Five team members and many younger and older short-term visitors from all over the world work around 30 hours per week in exchange for free room and board.

We grow organic vegetables, herbs, berries and fruit on 20 terraces; several stone houses were/are being refurbished ecologically for residents and soft tourism. Our main goals are reviving an abandoned piece of earth and trying to practice life's essential values on a daily basis while cultivating an ecological attitude toward the earth, animals and our fellow human beings. In addition, we are concerned with a simple life, solar energy, working with our hands and self-sufficiency. We are endeavouring to develop an organic farm on the approx. 5 ha of land with its precipitous, often overgrown meadows, surrounded by chestnut forests.

☺ 3-week probationary period

Pianta Monda

Hof allne wind

AW

Bemerberg | 8903 Birmensdorf
☎+41-(0)1-7371547 info@hofallnewind.ch
+41-(0)1-7371771 www.hofallnewind.ch

1993 12 ha (near Zürich) ♀3 ♂6 2 11

g, e, several all

everyone in common (majority vote, consensus, final word to owner)

individual financing, same wages for everyone

property of individual community members

create unity within variety, realise a social life where everyone can be happy and satisfied

vegetable gardening, animal care, mountain pasture with cheese production, kitchen, weekly market, woodcutting, construction

ecological, left-wing political understanding, non-violent, organic diet, animal protection, environmental protection, self-sufficiency, permaculture, organic agriculture, organic gardening, organic farming, forestry, alternative energy, ecological construction

☺

The Hof allne wind is located on a mountain (Bemerberg) in a remote rural hamlet where most of the residents live in huts, campers and trailers. We all eat together in the communal kitchen (common room). The project's goal is to develop a living community of people, animals and plants, a place where these life forces can complement one another and whose resources from farming, dairy and forestry – but also from animal husbandry and fruit, herb and vegetable gardening – provide the foundation for a community's livelihood. We produce our goods according to state organic farming guidelines and directly market our products – alongside a constantly growing body of regular customers – in Zürich and the surrounding area. Our goals are:

- Finding a harmony between the lives of humans, animals and plants
- Following new paths in the area of communal life, love and child-rearing
- Developing ecological and autonomous survival skills
- Creating unity within variety
- Testing and imparting spiritual and practical knowledge
- Realising a social life in which everyone can be happy and satisfied.

Having combined our efforts, we are endeavouring to achieve these goals and implement these ideas.

☺ willingness to lead a simple life

Humanus-Haus Beitenwil

HB

Postfach 55 | 3113 Rubigen
☎ +41-(0)31-8381111 info@humanus-haus.ch
-8397579 www.humanus-haus.ch

1973 13 ha (near Bern) ♀70 ♂60 20 150

g, e, f, ... 60

all members and/or part of group (consensus)

Federal Social Security Agency foundation

anthroposophy

caring for people with a mental disability

ecological, spiritual, anthroposophic, inner growth, organic diet, adult education, pedagogical, mentally/psychologically handicapped persons, physically handicapped persons, therapy: painting, music, language, eurythmics, massage; environmental protection, self-sufficiency, organic agriculture, organic gardening, organic farming, animal friendly husbandry, forestry, alternative energy, handicraft: wood, weaving, candle-making, instrument building, herb workshop; humour

☺

The community has not sent a current selfdescription.

→See also description of network "**Camphill**"

☺ training in social fields

Project Group Kommune*

GL

Karin Oetterli/Peter Portmann | Kulmackerweg 8 | 4450 Sissach
☎ +41-(0)61-9718815 info@kommune.ch
www.kommune.ch

2003 (near Basel) ♀10 ♂10 3 23

g, e, f, port., russ.

everyone in common (consensus)

none

☺

Since early 2003 the Kommune* project group has been meeting for monthly discussions and further activities, bringing us closer together and fostering trust. All of us have had the dream of „living together differently" for a long time. Now realisation „threatens". We are ready and before we've even found a place to live together we have already begun cutting our previous security nets.
By now, we have drafted a statue of principles. We are inspired by the ideas of existing political-social communities and are fascinated by the fact that utopian communes already have a very long tradition - we don't have to reinvent the wheel. We seek a self-determined, concious life on the margins of economic and

social compulsions, but with the intention of making a passive or active impact on them. We can't wait to find out what's possible in Switzerland!
Those of you who are interested in this project and/or would like to contact us for any reason are welcome to do so by e-mail, letter or phone. In addition, in February 2004 we have published our project's concrete outlines and we also document our development process under the given web address.

Netzwerk Gemeinschaftsleben
none

Schloss Glarisegg

SG

Schloss Glarisegg | 8266 Steckborn/Bodensee
+41-(0)52-77021-88 info@schloss-glarisegg.ch
-90 www.schloss-glarisegg.ch

2003 5 ha (near Konstanz/Zürich) ♀11 ♂7 10 28

g, e, f, swed. 12
everyone in common
combined individual and shared economy corporation
respect, daily spirituality, direct communication
therapy centre, free school, seminar centre, art and culture laboratory, construction, hospitality
ecological, non-violent, spiritual, inner growth, meditation, organic diet, vegetarian diet, adult education, pedagogical, peace-work, various therapy forms, partially self-sufficiency, organic agriculture, organic gardening, alternative energy, new technologies, ecological construction, handicraft, sports, art, digital media

At Glarisegg Castle, a growing 20-member living and working community is developing a centre for encounter, healing, art and learning. A seminar centre, a school, a therapy centre and an art laboratory are being networked into a single unit. Transformation and consciousness in everyday life and creating space for growth into one's great inner potential take centre stage, without a religious or confessional basis.
Alongside the previously mentioned areas, we are planning workshops for instrument building, electricity, metal, wood, pottery making, plus a wellness centre, a castle shop and an Internet shop.
We are planning to open the centre in April 2004. However, starting in January 2003 guests have the opportunity to get acquainted with the project and its participants.
Particularly since the sale of the castle in October 2003, working guests are more than welcome. They receive a 15 Euro per day discount in exchange for construction help (integrating building biology and geomancy), helping with events etc. combined with the opportunity to take part in our daily life and our daily offerings. The five large houses with 52,000 m² of land, located in close proximity to the

forest and the Swiss shores of Lake Constance, are the property of Schloss Glarisegg AG, which was founded by the living and working community (you can take part in the project by buying shares).
Aside from holiday making and attendance at our many seminars, people of all ages can take time off at Glarisegg Castle and, if needed, take advantage of professional therapy over periods ranging from one week to four months. Glarisegg Castle offers an excellent vegetarian cuisine with controlled organic foods and works closely with two nearby biodynamic Demeter farms.

☺ at least 6 months experience before admission and other conditions

Yamagishi Vereinigung für glückliches Zusammenleben

YV

Yamagishihof | Schneitbergstrasse | 8523 Hagenbuch
☎ +41-(0)76 588 1044, -(0)52 364 1528 — info@yamagishi.ch
Fax -(0)52 364 1629 — www.yamagishi.ch

1983 — 25 (near Winterthur) — ♀5 ♂5 — 7 — 17

g, japanese — all
everyone in common (through Kensan) — shared income
common property
none
sales, farm work
self-managed, non-violent, inner growth, seminar-house, peace-work, animal protection, environmental protection, conventional agriculture, animal friendly husbandry, new technologies, Tokkoh, the Yamagishi Seminar

☺

The name: Yamagishi, Miozo, a peasant from Japan who died in 1960, made a close study of (human) nature.
Our goal: "A stable world community which makes it possible for everyone, including our children, to be happy." Is there anything more worth living for?
Starting from the fact that all beings and all existence are inextricably linked with one another – I flourish when everything else flourishes – this principle equally applies to marriage, the family, the workplace... And with the knowledge that every person in this world wants to live in peace and satisfaction, Yamagishi developed a model for society, a guide on "how to construct the world revolution".
We believe that the happiness of all people begins in each of our everyday lives and only each small individual like you and me can make it happen. This has been practised with Kensan for over 40 years in the 80 Yamagishi villages around the world. There are no bosses or gurus, there are no rights or responsibilities. Instead, everyone does what he can and when he wants. Everything is free, as in nature. A pleasant life. Let us build such a society together. We believe we have found a practical, viable path and heartily invite you to join us. Kensan is a "scientific" method of study designed to make optimal use of human intelligence and free it of its own delusions. Kensan leads us to act out our true human nature. This is prac-

tised in the Tokkoh, the time-honoured seminar without teachers, theories or dogma. It is highly recommended for people in communities.

→See also description of network "**Yamagishi**"

☺ desire to help build a happy society and participate in the Tokkoh, the Yamagishi seminar

Zaffaraya

Park & Ride Neufeld | 3000 Bern 26

zaffaraya@zaffaraya.ch
www.zaffaraya.ch

ZF

1985 | 1 ha (near Bern) | ♀12 ♂12 3 27

g, f, e | 10%

everyone in common (consensus) | limited community financing

Autobahn-Terrain (canton + state)

human rights, living inexpensively and free

crafts, cultural matters, university studies

ecological, self-managed, left-wing political understanding, non-violent, chaotic, animal protection, environmental protection, conventional gardening, ecological construction, construction, social work: very expensive in CH and hardly any more old flats available; art: music, circus

The community has not sent a current selfdescription.

☺ desire to work with us (building, discussing), not just live on the cheap!

"Well, you can make this community idea pretty complicated… After all, we sit together all day too!"

Zentrum der Einheit

ZE

Schweibenalp | 3855 Brienz
+41-(0)33-9512001 info@schweibenalp.ch
-9514409 www.schweibenalp.ch.

1982 20 ha (near Interlaken, Bern) ♀4 ♂4 8

g, e, f 7

one part of the group (advisory board: non-community residents)

pocket money, room and board, social benefits

Foundation for the Development of Truth, Simplicity and Love

open to all spiritual orientations

household, kitchen, reception, outer area, garden, temple service (Vedic temple, Christian chapel, Buddhist meditation room)

non-violent, spiritual, ecumenical, inner growth, meditation, vegetarian diet, seminar-house, peace-work

The "Zentrum der Einheit" (Centre of Unity) was founded on the recommendation of the Indian teacher Sri Haidakhan Baba in 1982 and offers space for the praxis of all spiritual orientations. This means that we have been working for more than 20 years on an interreligious mission aimed at promoting understanding and tolerance between religions and cultures.
The community, which lives all year-round on the Schweibenalp, runs the centre according to the principle of a spirituality practised in everyday life. The residents live and work together and lead a spiritual life in a holistic sense, with regular meditation and prayer times. Mutual respect, community spirit and the willingness be flexible and get involved with new ideas and traditions are part of our daily routine.
The Schweibenalp is a place of transformation, energy, silence and simplicity. We live and work with the goal of making life more natural, simpler and thus more liveable and treating each other with greater truthfulness and love. In this spirit, we welcome guests and new residents who wish to take part in this experiment as part of our community. Guests staying longer than 6 weeks receive free room and board.

Holon

interest and flexibility, spiritual praxis

Countries placed on a common map:

BG Basisgemeinde Galiläa
EG Ecovillage Grishino
ER Ecotopia Romania Association
ET Ecovillage Tiberkul
GK Green Kibbutz Samar
KL Kibbutz Lotan
NE Neve Shalom
OS Osho Shangri La
PL PermaLot
RI Viscri startet e.V. im Kreis Brasov
TB Familie vom Taubenberg
TK Tchamla Kingdom
TT Tal der Träume
ZO Community of fra Francesco

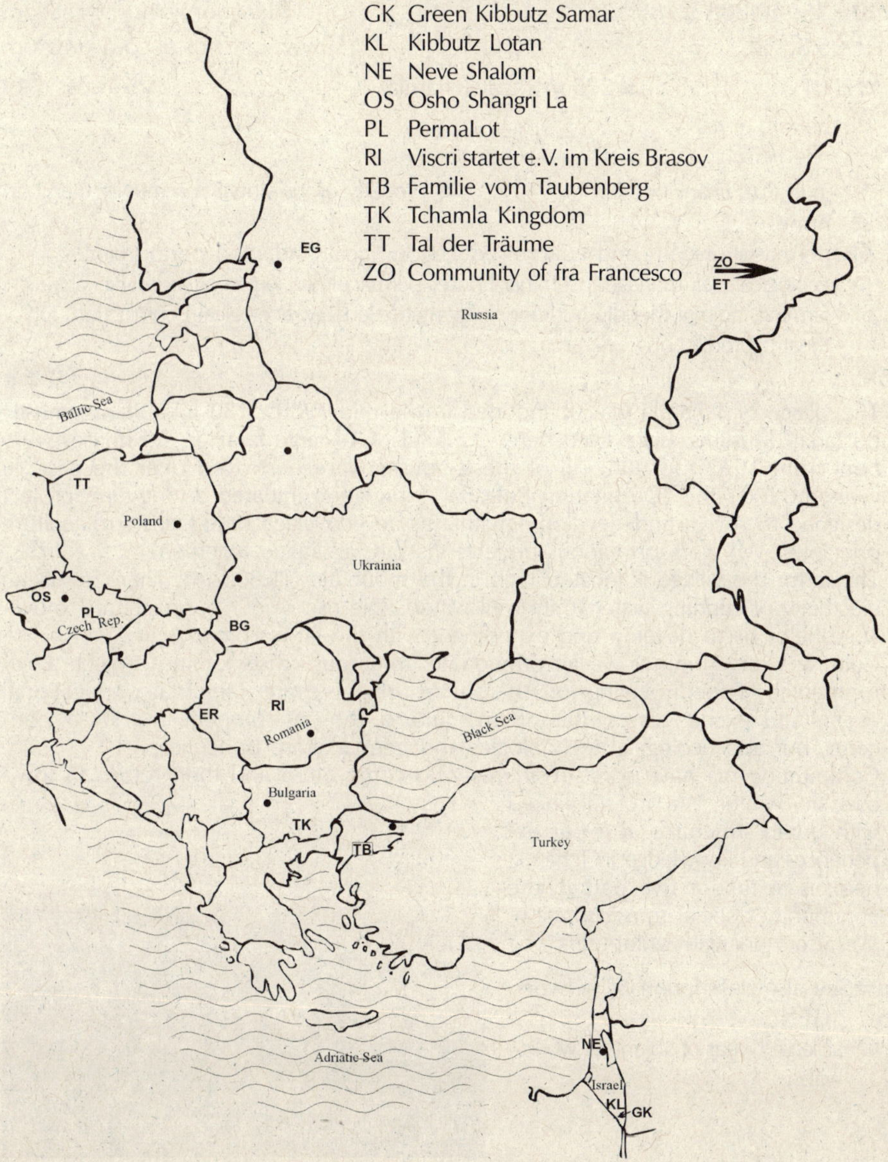

Bulgaria

Tchamla Kingdom

TK

Mugla Village | Smoljan municipality
+359-(0)888-95 88 32
kingdom@art-hostel.com
-95 88 32
www.art-hostel.com/kingdom

2001 275 m² (near Tchamla) ♀5 ♂4 9

- bulgar., e, russ.
- one person
- individual financing — property of individual community members
- none
- permaculture, art and culture, education, locally adapted performances
- ecological, self-managed, seminar-house, permaculture, organic gardening, organic farming, animal friendly husbandry, alternative energy, ecological construction, art: theatre productions

The village of Tchamla was abandoned in the mid-1980s. 180 inhabitants, mostly Bulgarian Muslims, once lived here - a total of 14 large families. 30 houses were built from 1912 to 1984. All of these houses were destroyed over the past 16 years. In 2001 the "Destination Bulgaria" foundation initiated a long-term project designed to revive and develop Tchamla as an ecovillage based on permaculture principles. We work on various projects that are all linked together.

The farm: the village is located high in the mountains (1,800 m). There is still no electricity or running water (only well water). The use of our permaculture knowledge helps us to develop and experiment with the farm's productivity.

Culture: every summer we accommodate numerous artists for the project "Environmentally Friendly Living for Artists". We organise many seminars, educational events and exchanges combining art, culture, the environment and social concerns, but also ecological technologies and permaculture principles.

Community: we have some residents who come often and then return to town over the winter. We are still linked with urban structures. But our experiences and knowledge in Tchamla help us to take active part in the community's social transformation. We also work with volunteers.

→See also description of network "**GEN**"

☺ at least 1 year of voluntary work with us

Czech Republic

Osho Shangri La

OS

Meditation Center | Lazany 49 | 36452 Zlutice

+420-(0)353-395310 shangri.la@sannyas-on.net

-395310 shangrila.sannyas-on.net, www.familyconstellation.org

1995 1.8 ha (near Karlsbad) ♀4 ♂5 1 10

czech, e, g 5

one part of the group (consensus)

individual and limited common financing

property of individual community members

Osho

gardening, cooking

ecological, self-managed, spiritual, meditation, vegetarian diet, seminar-house, therapy, organic gardening, new technologies

The Shangri La OMC is a place of lively togetherness for people who love silence and untouched nature. The centre is located in a wide, wild, silent and natural landscape near Carlsbad in the Czech Republic, 50 km from the German border. There are daily meditations and a wide range of offers for meditation and therapy. Our spiritual leader is Osho.

Osho

meditation experience and/or interest in meditation / Osho

PermaLot

PL

Svojanov 3 | 78325 Bouzov

+420-(0)585-152010 permalot@permalot.org

+420-585-152010 www.permalot.org

2000 10 ha (near Olomouc) ♀2 ♂2 4

e, dan. 4

everyone in common (consensus) limited community financing

common property

holistic cultivation of the land according to permaculture principles

organising and conducting camps

ecological, self-managed, inner growth, yoga, free love, organic diet, vegetarian diet, adult education, environmental protection, self-sufficiency, permaculture, organic agriculture, organic gardening, organic farming, alternative energy, new technologies, ecological construction, camping opportunities for seminars, courses...

PermaLot is a small ecovillage initiative with big plans!
Since we intend to grow to around 20 people, we have acquired a large piece of beautiful land and are now pioneers, preparing the place for the future; this includes cutting and planting 100s of trees and bushes according to permaculture design, creating jobs and accommodation for the people to come. We have created a teepee campsite where we run various courses typically for young people, but please have a look at our homepage for all the details.
The basic intention of this little write-up is to make sure that you stay away if you're yet another curious person coming to steal our most precious resources: Time and Energy! - Especially if you're not (as usual!) balancing the rip-off with a suitable amount of another precious resource: Cash!
Should you, however, be a complete workaholic, well-balanced and pleasant to be around, then please do come by, but contact us beforehand! – And keep your dogs and drugs at home ;o)
Our vision for the future is to create a small community, based on a high degree of social contact, working locally and living relatively simply, predominantly off the grid. In other words: We're working on re-establishing the village's local sustainability.

→ See also description of network "**GEN**"

☺ pleasant people; people who are financially and psychologically independent; also see homepage

Israel

Green Kibbutz Samar

GK

88815 M.P. Hevel Eilot
☎ +972-(0)8-6356-711
-758

1976 | 280 ha (near Eilat) | ♀46 ♂42 | 115 | 203

hebrew, sp., f, e — approx. 50
everyone in common (majority vote, consensus) — shared income
common property
none
organic date production, peat, dairy cows, computer-supported agriculture, health food shop, aquaculture
ecological, self-managed, anarchistic, organic agriculture, organic farming, new technologies, construction and others

Kibbutz Samar is a people-owned collective enterprise. It is also our home. Together we farm some 700 acres in the Arava Desert. We are located 20 minutes north of Eilat on the Red Sea. Founded in 1976, Samar is home to 40 families, with a total population of about 200. The Kibbutz's main business activities involve agriculture, specifically the production of milk, the Ardag fish farm in Eilat, the production of turfgrass, as well as the cultivation of our organic dates. In addition we run the SoomSoom health food store in Eilat, design and build computerised control devices for agriculture systems, and operate the Desert Studies Center which offers highly informed guided tours in Israel, Jordan and Egypt.
We are democratically run, believe in the worth of each individual and rely upon our own labour to produce our sustenance. We share many of the means of living to meet transportation, food and laundry needs. This makes our community more ecologically benevolent. We see the preservation of the environment, especially the desert in which we live, as of the highest imperative. Our work - in this case, our organic dates - certainly reflects this approach.

Kibbutz

Kibbutz Lotan

KL

88855 D.N. Chevel Eilot
+972-(0)7-635-6888, -6935 lotan-office@lotan.ardom.co.il
-6827 www.birdingisrael.com/KibbutzLotan

1983 500 Dunan (near Eilat) ♀25 ♂25 60 110

e, hebrew, sp., russ., g, f 30

everyone in common (majority vote)

shared economy (shared income and capital) common property

reform Judaism

dairy, tourism, ecology

ecological, self-managed, left-wing political understanding, non-violent, hierarchical, environmental protection, organic agriculture, conventional agriculture, ecological construction

Kibbutz Lotan, founded in 1983, is located in the Southern Arava desert, 55km North of the city of Eilat. Population varies - about 140. There are 50 members with 60 children. In addition there are 20 rent paying residents and a varying number of volunteers and youth groups. Half the adult members are native born Israelis and half come from other countries - mainly from the English speaking world.
The Lotan economy is based on a dairy barn (275 head), date plantation, tourism, and partnerships with other kibbutzim in field crops and maritime agriculture. Almost half of our members work outside the kibbutz, in the regional services or the city of Eilat. Their income is pooled into the kibbutz economy.
Among Israeli kibbutzim, Kibbutz Lotan is unique by virtue of its triple identity.
1. Kibbutz Lotan is a collective kibbutz and belongs to the collective stream of the kibbutz movement (currently, a majority of kibbutzim are partially or wholly privatized).
2. Kibbutz Lotan belongs to the Israel Movement for Progressive Judaism - Reform movement. Our approach to Judaism is liberal, creative, egalitarian, and non-coercive.
3. Kibbutz Lotan strives to relate to the fragile desert ecosystem in its daily life and development plans and is part of GEN. In Israel, we are pioneers in the use of waste materials in alternative building.
For further information, we invite you to surf for a virtual visit.

→ See also description of network "**GEN**"

Kibbutz movement

☺ Jewish, ages 25-35

Neve Shalom

NE

Wahat al Salam | 99761 D.N. Shimshon
☎ +972-(0)29915621 www.nswas.com
-(0)29911072

1970 20 ha (near Ramle/ Ramallah) ♀50 ♂50 100 200

arab., hebrew 50
everyone in common (majority vote) individual financing
particular attention to Palestinian-Israeli relations
education of children, Israeli-Palestinian encounters
left-wing political understanding, adult education, pedagogical, peace-work

☺

Neve Shalom~Wahat al-Salam (NSWAS) is a village in Israel of Jews and Palestinian Arabs of Israeli citizenship. Situated equidistant from Jerusalem and Tel Aviv-Jaffa, NSWAS was founded in the early 1970s on land originally leased from the adjacent Latrun Monastery. By 2003, almost 50 families had come to live in the village, with an equal number of Jews and Arabs. Eventually the village will include about 140 homes.
The members of NSWAS are demonstrating the possibility of coexistence between Jews and Palestinians by developing a community based on mutual acceptance, respect and cooperation. Democratically governed and owned by its members, the community is not affiliated with any political party or movement. NSWAS gives practical expression to its vision through various branches:
- The bilingual, binational schooling with equal participation by Jews and Palestinians in administration and teaching and the use of both Hebrew and Arabic in teaching...;
- the School for Peace (SFP), engaging in encounter work between Arabs and Jews and informed by the vision awareness of the participants towards the conflict and their role in it;
- the pluralistic spiritual centre "Doumia~Sakinah", attempting to tap into the spiritual resources available within our cultures and religious traditions;
- hospitality/the hotel as a base for people touring Israel and/or participating in programs.

☺ Israeli citizen

Poland

Tal der Träume (Valley of Dreams)

Brzezinka | 78552 Kluczewo
+48-6644-524 eschenquell@yahoo.de
-524

200 ha (near Stettin)

g, poln., e
everyone in common (consensus) property of individual community members
holistic
building, shaping, realising visions, later: receiving summer guests
there's room and opportunity for everything here

What we have are 200 ha of wild and free landscape located 250 km north-east of Berlin in Pomerania (Poland), sufficient investment funds and some pretty cool visions. We want to live our shared, archetypal dreams together within the framework of an unconventional holiday (and perhaps more): living in caves and playing Stone Age; setting up a circle of tepees on the rolling plains and surrounding it with a herd of 100 horses; travelling over the prairie hills in covered wagons and gypsy caravans; steering a canoe between the reeds of a large swamp; living in tree houses with rope ladders and suspension bridges; erecting a reed-roofed pile village over the waters of a shallow bay of our lake; building a Viking village and sailing over Drazig Lake in long ships; linking the woven willow structures into a great water/land palace/labyrinth; spending the night of the summer solstice dancing, drumming and singing inside a giant stone circle…; sharing leaves, flowers, roots and fruits together at the communal table following a long day at work in a giant, chaotic permaculture garden; shaping matter in the image of the soul in workshops; entering a magical circle and climbing into the depths, integrating them, transforming them… and simply enjoying the breathtaking beauty of nature in the Dramburg landscape park.

The overall concept is based on low luxury and soft adventure tourism, supported by experimental archaeology and cultural exploration. We would like to link it with undogmatic, free, versatile and balanced healing, liberation, growth and transformation in the eco, psycho, spiri, socio and polit fields. Everything is still possible (including the project's basic shape and ways to participate) since the project is just getting started…

This project should not be totally commercialised, although it should provide its direct participants with a certain income.

Romania

Ecotopia Romania Association

ER

ERA | sat Stanciova 129 | 307347 Stanciova
+40-(0)256-330359 comunitate@yahoogroups.com
ecotopia.ngo.ro

2000 2500 m² (near Temeswar) ♀2 ♂3 1 6

roman., e, f, g, esper. none
everyone in common (consensus) limited community financing
common property (community house) and private houses
none
gardening, renovation (clay building), youth work
ecological, self-managed, chaotic, adult education, seminar-house, environmental protection, self-sufficiency, permaculture, organic gardening, ecological construction, handicraft: building stone ovens, clay building

☺ ( )

We are a small ecovillage initiative originating in the Rumanian environmental youth movement. Inspired by the staging of a large environmental youth camp (Ecotopia 1999 – EYFA), we are now trying to establish our "permanent Ecotopia" in Stanciova. We have bought a small three-sided farm in Stanciova, a very remote town located 35 km from Temeswar. We are renovating it and are also gradually repairing the old town hall, which currently houses the primary school and the village pub, and operate an informal youth centre there. Beyond that, we are experimenting with food self-sufficiency.
Some of our group's members bought and renovated their own houses in Stanciova last year, but now interest in common activities is back on the rise. Visitors are always welcome after previous notice. Once we get to know each other, long-term internships may be possible within the framework of the European Volunteer Service.

→ See also description of network "**GEN-Europe**"
EYFA, Ruralnet
☺ interest in a simple life and self-sufficiency; willingness to learn Rumanian and live in a traditional, i.e. often conservative Rumanian village; a certain openness and tolerance toward cultural differences

Viscri / Brasov

RI

c/o Riese | Viscri Nr. 57 | 507039 Judetul Brasov
+40-(0)724-570992 www.viscri.de

1996 (near Sighisoara) ♀3 ♂3 2 8

g, rom. all

everyone in common (consensus) individual financing, some donations

property of individual community members

Christian-ecumenical-spiritual

supervision of children from difficult social situations, operation of a soup kitchen, development of self-help projects

ecological, self-managed, non-violent, spiritual, christian, ecumenical, adult education, pedagogical, free school, peace-work, mentally/psychologically handicapped persons, social work, organic gardening, humour, lots of music

☺ ()

In 1996 we – Maria, our daughter Dorothee and I, Harald – moved to the tiny village of Viscri (Deutsch-Weisskirch) in the middle of Rumania near the Carpathians. The village has 450 inhabitants and is located off the main road. We simply wanted to live here, grow organic food and enjoy the peace and quiet. Also in 1996, without any connection to us, Anne and Roman arrived in Viscri and settled down. They wished to transform one of the many empty houses into a beautiful guest house and to invite people from the West in order to get to know the country's untouched wild beauty. We fell more and more under the spell of the great poverty here – and became increasingly involved in helping the people in the village, in many ways and with combined forces. That brought Tina and Ronni to us. They had their first child in August of 2003.
Over the years we have initiated and developed a great deal, letting much of it run of its own accord: the special school, the soup kitchen, the tutoring programme, a health station, the necessary organisation for 150 women and girls who knit socks, a spinning mill, a café – and finally, we (Maria and Harald) care for 7 children at our house every day.
Perhaps we will turn into a true community. Those who wish to visit us definitely must contact us beforehand. We want to exchange wishes and ideas beforehand, to the extent this is possible. We can't provide anyone with free room and board. Otherwise: come see us, there's plenty to do.

☺ early contact, willingness to put up with very humble conditions, largely self-financed

Russia

Community of fra Francesco

ZO

Kontaktadresse: Damien Gangloff | Belvoir | 05100 Puy St. Pierre | Frankreich

core.asso@free.fr

core.asso.free.fr

2002 2500 m² (near Sargatskoie/ Omsk)

f, e, it., russ. depending on season 1-15

part of the group (C.OR.E. organisation council)

individual financing property of individual community members

we are ecumenical Christians of various confessions

protection of flora and fauna, local development (fruit trees), ecological sensitivity, reception

ecological, non-violent, spiritual, christian, ecumenical, organic diet, adult education, pedagogical, seminar-house, peace-work, one-world development, animal protection, environmental protection, organic gardening, alternative energy, ecological construction

☺

Some members of the C.OR.E. (Christian Organisation for Ecology, exists in France and Russia) are creating a centre for ecology and local development in Orlovka, a village with 120 inhabitants in Western Siberia (without running water). We have a house there that we are reconstructing on ecological principles. Everyone who wants to spend a few days or years with us (that's possible) becomes part of the community. It is made up of C.OR.E members, people who briefly stop by, the volunteers – everyone who is here for different periods of time.
We take part in regional initiatives to protect nature. In Orlovka, we develop activities which help provide the local population with work, particularly young people (environmental activities): we are currently financing the planting of 500 fruit trees. What's important for us is: being active in God's Creation – both people and nature – without separating the environment from social concerns.
We are teaching ourselves to take a brotherly/sisterly view toward all things – seeing animals, plants and minerals as God's creations (which is quite a challenge when it comes to the mosquitoes) and taking a gentle attitude toward them all. We invite everyone to work with us as a volunteer.

☺ members live according to Christian values, fairly simply (in material terms) and love nature

Ecovillage Grishino

EG

P.O. BOX 32 | P/O Soginitsy, Podporozskii rayon | 187743 Leningradskaya oblast
+7-(0)812-1150413 vasudeva@mail.spb.org, grishino@e-mail.ru
-5940696 www.grishino.ecology.net.ru

1993 9000 m² (near Podporozhye) ♀4 ♂6 2 12

russ., e all

one part of the group (consensus) limited community financing

property of individual community members

spiritual workshops, garden, construction

ecological, self-managed, non-violent, spiritual, inner growth, meditation, organic diet, vegetarian diet, seminar-house, peace-work, environmental protection, organic agriculture, organic gardening

In the northwest of Russia, in the historic village of Grishino (300 km northeast of St. Petersburg), at the confluence of two rivers, we have lived in and built up an ecological village for over ten years. We came here from different cities to live on the land in harmony with each other and with Nature. We all have different world-conceptions, but we are learning to accept each other and to co-create our community in common.

Twelve of us live in Grishino all year round. We have several traditional Russian-style community and private houses. We grow what we eat in our vegetable gardens, and gather lots of herbs from a large meadow of wildflowers. Our ecovillage is surrounded by natural forests, where we gather berries and mushrooms, and in which there live many kinds of wild birds and animals, like beavers, moose, bears, hares, foxes, wolves, wildcats and many others. We are starting a project on ecological forest management.

We aim to continue the cultural traditions of our ancestors, learning the folk arts, their songs and dances, woodcraft, ceramics and village architecture; and we are endeavouring to create a family school for our children. Each summer we hold seminars for adults and children where one can participate in the spiritual life and work of our community and merge with the spirit of Russian nature.

Ecovillage Tiberkul

ET

c/o Ökopolis e.V | Lasker-Schüler-Str. 3 | 50829 Köln
☎ ++49-(0)711-833629 (deutsch)
info@vissarion.info
www.vissarion.info

1992 — 100 km² (near Abakan/Südsibirien) — ♀2100 ♂1400 — 1000
5000

- bulgarian, g, e, rus, several others — all
- all who are concerned (consensus)
- individual & common financing, giving and sharing
- 30 villages: leased and/or common property depending on the village.
- spiritual-christian
- handicraft, art, fruit, vegetable, farming, horses, construction, schools
- ecological, self-managed, non-violent, leader/guru, spiritual, christian, inner growth, organic diet, vegan diet, adult education, free school, self-sufficiency, organic agriculture, organic gardening, alternative energy, new technologies, ecological construction, all traditional crafts, art: music, dancing, singing, painting, pottery, sculpture, architecture; other: horses, bees, clothmaking, soyproducts, bee-keeping

☺

The ecological-spiritual community Ecopolis Tiberkul was founded in 1992 by the spiritual teacher Vissarion. Today we are some 5,000 people who live in about 50 taiga villages 150 kilometres east of Abakan (airport and Trans-Siberian Railway), which is on about the same degree of latitude as Northern Germany.
The region we have settled in is an ecologically unspoiled part of the taiga. We draw our drinking water from rivers and wells. Usually each family lives in their own house, simply and close to nature. Every house has a large garden, big enough to allow living from our own crops. During the hot months in summer from May to September with temperatures often higher than 40°C every family grows their own supply of food for the whole year.
Our diet is vegetarian but we aim towards a vegan diet, if the individual feels ready for that. Drugs including alcohol and tobacco are not consumed.
In winter temperatures drop to -30°C but the dry coldness is much easier to bear especially as the sun is shining almost every day. We then devote ourselves to handicrafts, arts and crafts, music, dance, theatre. Throughout the year we celebrate colourful festivals.
Everybody gives and receives loving support from the community according to their needs and requirements. We build our houses, schools and churches together, assist each other in tilling the ground, and in some villages also woodcutting for the winter is done together.
Love towards others is of greatest importance. The members of our community are willing to investigate their thoughts and perceptions and practise careful relationships. We often meet to communicate and to clear up difficulties and disagreements, thus developing the art of living together.
In this way it is possible for thousands of people to form a steadily growing community here, that will continue to exist and not break down in quarrels. We regard it of

special importance that our children grow up healthily, we encourage their imagination and creativity and encourage them to treat each other lovingly.
In our everyday work we do not only try to carry out everything with loving care, but also in a beautiful and artistic way, which can be seen in all the buildings which we construct together. Concerning economy we are trying to substitute a system of giving and receiving in place of the monetary system, as in a big family. We are trying to achieve: production by handicraft of everything needed for living, self-sufficiency without use of money, to give everything as a present without expecting anything in return (which is already put into practice in many fields), money transactions and exchange dealings with outsiders only, minimal purchasing of products, considerate treatment of the environment, minimal use of machines. We work with horses for transport and agriculture and want to further enhance the use of alternative technologies.
Not far from Lake Tiberkul a prototype settlement is being created, which is intended to exist self-sufficiently some day.
Vissarion still inspires and advises the community and lives here with his wife and six children. There is a German support society called Ökopolis e.V., which supplies extensive information on www.vissarion.info (in German) and will assist in organising travel to the community. Everybody is invited to come and see.

☺ spiritual-christian orientation

Turkey

Familie vom Taubenberg

TB

Catharina Hinrichs | Mesut Dayanak, Güvercintepe | 10940 Avsa adasi, Erdek
+90-2668963392, +49-(0)7681-4936476 peter.jesse@gmx.de

1986 4 ha (near Istanbul) ♀1 ♂2 2 5

g, e, turkish all

one part of the group (consensus) limited common financing

property of individual community members

„We are part of the earth" speech of Chief Seattle

garden, island life, hotel, self-sufficiency, restoring an antique oaken ship (with an eye to a later round-the-world journey), partially raw foods

self-managed, self-sufficiency, island life, own ship, hospitality, some raw foods, simple life

☺

We live on a hill called "Taubenberg" ("Dove Hill") on the island of Avsa in the Sea of Marmara (between Europe and Asia), which has not yet been discovered by the international tourism industry. Our property is 5 minutes from the sea by foot. Since we have lots of room, we would like to become a larger community - we are currently managing our property as a family of 5. It would be desirable if the people joining us would be interested in the sea since we own our own antique ship (but that's not a requirement).

The people coming to us should be open to the Mediterranean mentality and not be fanatical, because we are searching for a centre in everything. In any case, the property is set up in such a way that we rent out space during the summer months. Otherwise, our goal is to lead as simple and self-sufficient a life as possible with several families or 10-15 people. We want to view ourselves as part of our Mother Earth and desire a simple, respectful life in harmony with her, whereby raw foods also play a certain role.

The "Taubenberg" is a very special corner of the world, created by us on our own. An infertile granite hill has been transformed into a little green oasis, a genuine paradise. After endless, gruelling hand labour, it is now covered with 250 trees of different kinds. We created everything we could using rustic building traditions, which gives the whole property its special atmosphere. On our "Taubenberg" we can share in the experience that, with love and patience, the impossible can happen … Everything is ready. All we need now are the right people to fill it with life.

☺ should not be fanatical, should like Mediterranean mentality

Ukraine

Basisgemeinde Galiläa

BG

c/o Bernd Pietruck | Ul. Schkilna 4 | 47643 Dibschtsche
☎+380-3547-26171
+380-3547-26171

1996 | 350 ha (near Kosova) | ♀3 ♂2 1 6

g, ukrain., rus. — all

everyone in common (consensus) — shared economy (shared income and capital)

rented/leased

we are Christians and orient ourselves on the Bible (Sermon on the Mount)

farming, household

non-violent, christian, ecumenical, organic agriculture, organic farming

☺

(Developed from the Basisgemeinde Wulfshagenerhütten)
Our association with the Ukraine began in 1991, first with encounters, reciprocal visits, aid shipments and medical assistance. In 1995 a Ukrainian family decided to set up a formal relationship with the Basisgemeinde. This decision moved the Basisgemeinde to send one of its families to the Ukraine. Today, 5 of our members live in Dibschtsche, a small village in the western Ukraine, and form a community of their own. Their daily life is largely dominated by farming (approx. 350 ha of land, animal husbandry), which they attend to together with the Ukrainian family. We orient ourselves on the Bible and are inspired by the life of the first Christians (cf. Acts 2:42 ff). For us, the Sermon on the Mount is the main guidepost. Jesus's non-violence is our model, and our communal life provides us with plenty of opportunities to practice love, to continue taking the path to reconciliation, to perceive our own violence and to let ourselves be transformed.
Most of the people around us belong to the Greek-Catholic Church, a form of Orthodox faith. Our relationships bring us into contact with their faith and vice versa: we experience the world-wide Church in daily life, in small things, in practical things. And we also experience East and West in small things and in our concrete daily lives. This closeness is both a challenge and an opportunity.

larger unit together with Basisgemeinde Prenzlauer Berg (Berlin)

☺ willingness to get completely involved in our life

Addresses from the 2000/2001 edition

In this appendix you will find addresses of communities which were published in the 2000/2001 edition but which did not respond to our repeated requests for updated information for the 2005 edition. We do not know why they did not respond and we have no indications that these communities no longer exist or that their addresses are incorrect. Should you stumble across other address data during your own search for community, please let us know (e.g. on the reply form). Thanks!

The addresses have been listed alphabetically according to country and name. Explanations of the symbols and abbreviations used here can be found in the legend on page 414. Except for the country signature, the addresses are listed the way they would appear on an envelope, whereby the vertical beam (|) indicates the start of a new line. Please don't forget to include the country's name at the bottom of the address.

Austria

Emmausgemeinschaft St. Pölten

A Herzogenburger Str. 48-50 | 3100 St. Pölten
☎ +43-(0)2742-31990-105

Gärtnerhof-Siedlung

A Hochwaldstr. 37 | 2230 Gänserndorf
☎ +43 (0)2282-70289 -702898

Belgium

L'Arche Communauté de Namur

B Rue de Bruxelles, 62B | BBE-5000 Namur
☎ +32-(0)8122-1322 -3457 namur@larche.be
www.larche.be/namur/index.html

Denmark

Andelsforeningen Kirkebakken

DK Kirkebakken 80 | 8330 Beder
☎ +45-(0)2612 8023 marianne@filmkompagniet.dk

Christiania

DK Nyt Forum | Bådsmansstraede 43 | 1407 Copenhagen K
+45-(0)-32956507 -32956507 nytforum@christiania.org
www.christiania.org

Ibsgaarden, Bofaellesskabet

DK Ibsgaarden 62 | 4000 Roskilde
+45-(0)46323820 ib@ibsgaarden.dk www.ibsgaarden.dk/

Finland

Tapolan Kyläyhteisö

SF Raikkolantie 40 | 16350 Niinikosi
+358-(0)18-882450 -8824528 tapolan@kolumbus.fi

France

Association Bouddhiste Zen-Kwan um

F Centre Parisien | 35, Rue de Lyon | 75012 Paris
+33-(0)144870770

Collectif de la valette
la vieille valette

F Association Résonances | Hameau de la Vieille Valette | 30160 Robiac-Rochesadoule
+33-(0)4-66 25 32 62, -66 60 07 89 collectif.valette@free.fr
collectif.valette.free.fr

CRISE

F 23340 Faux-la-Montagne
+33-(0)5556-9363 -9702

L'Espérance

F L'Arche de Pierrefonds | 1, Rue du Bourg | 60350 Pierrefonds
+33-(0)344428788 -(0)344428788

L'Olivier

F 30 rue de la Noé | 35170 Bruz
+33-(0)2995-27274 -71136

Le Levain

F 1 Pl. St Clément, B.P. 10733 | 60207 Compiègne cedex 2
+33-(0)344-862503 -209983

Germany

Alte Feuerwache

D Kultur Wohnen Vreiraum e.V. | Dorfstr. 61 | 99441 Kromsdorf
☎ +49-(0)3643-418251

Ashram Ananda Ma

D Bretzenheimerstr. 92-94 | 55545 Bad Kreuznach
☎ +49-(0)671-36090 -8459109 anandateam@net-art.de
www.net-art.de/anandateam

Biolandhof Warmuth

D Dorfstr.30 | 97618 Junkershausen
☎ +49-(0)9762-6273 -931294

Das Nest

D Postfach 46 | 18249 Boitin
☎ +49-(0)38450-30614 / -30624 -30613

Emmaus

D Alpener Str. 40 | 47665 Sonsbeck
☎ +49-(0)2838-96446 -96478

Trailer life in the autumn

Genova Wohnbaugenossenschaft

D Vauban e.G. | Merzhauser Straße 170/37 | 79100 Freiburg
+49-(0)761-407767 -4098811 genova.vauban@t-online.de

Gruppe Laufdorf des Laurentiuskonvents

D Ringstr.21 | 35641 Schöffengrund 2
+49-(0)6445-5560 -92051

Hofgemeinschaft Ebenau

D Im Dorfe 3 | 99826 Ebenau
+49-(0)36926-99511

Hofgemeinschaft Hof Nr.10

D 07407 Mötzelbach
+49-(0)36742-60744

Im Ökohof

D Gnevsdorfer Weg | 19395 Hof Retzow
+49-(0)38737-3040 -30414 oekowellness@plawe.de
www.oekowellness.de

LACOMA e.V.

D Dorfstr. 12 | 03053 Cottbus-Lakoma
+49-(0)355-862300 Lacoma@Lacoma.de www.lacoma.de

Land in Sicht - Prowo gGmbH

D Wendtshof 4 | 17291 Carmzow-Wallmow
+49-(0)39862-2145 -5009 land.sicht@t-online.de
www.land-sicht.de

Laurentiusgruppe Bosenholz

D Bosenholz 11 | 33154 Salzkotten

Lichtblick COOP

D Oberer Dorfweg 13 | 88299 Leutkirch
+49-(0)7567-1425 -1280

Vereinigte Varben WaWaVox

D Kastanienallee 77 | 10435 Berlin
+49-(0)30-4494330 -44358787
www.k77.org

Great Britain/Northern Ireland

Botton Village

UK Danby, Whitby | North Yorkshire YO21 2NJ
☎+44-(0)1287-661288 Fax -660888 ✉botton@camphill.org.uk

Camphill Community Clanabogan

UK 15 Drudgeon Road | Clanabogan | Omagh BT78 1TJ
☎+44-(0)662-256111, -256100 Fax -256114
✉camphill@btconnect.com

Camphill: Rudolf Steiner-Schools

UK Central Office, Murtle House | Bieldside | Aberdeen AB15 9EP
☎+44-(0)1224-867935 Fax -868420 ✉b.porter@crss.org.uk
💻www.camphillschools.org.uk

Camphill: The Hatch

UK St. John's House | Kington Lane, Thornbury | Bristol, Avon BS12 1NA
☎+44-(0)1454-413010

Cornerstone Housing Co-op

UK 16, Sholebroke Avenue, Chapeltown | LS7 3HB Leeds
☎+44-(0)1132629365 Fax -(0)1132629365 ✉cornerstone@ukf.net
💻www.cornerstone.ukf.net

Delrow College and Rehabilitation Centre

UK Hilfield Lane, Aldenham | Watford, Herts WD2 8DJ
☎+44-(0)1923-856006 Fax -858035 ✉email@delrow.newnet.co.uk

Equinox Housing Co-op

UK 161, Hamilton Road, Longsight | M13 0PQ Manchester
☎+44-(0)161-2489224 Fax -2244648 ✉mail@eqnx.co.uk
💻www.eqnx.co.uk

Govanbank Barn

UK West Lothian, Scotland FK1 1AA

Grimstone Community

UK Grimstone Manor | Horrabridge | Yelverton PL20 7QY
☎+44-(0)1822-854358 Fax -852318
✉enquiries@grimstonemanor.co.uk 💻www.grimstonemanor.co.uk

L'Arche Edinburgh

UK 132 Constitution Street | Leith, Edinburgh EH6 6HJ
☎+44-(0)131-5533478 Fax -5543236 ✉edinburgh@larche.org.uk
💻www.larche.org.uk

L'Arche Kent

UK Little Ewell | Barfrestone
+44-(0)1304-830930 -832393 kent@larche.org.uk
www.larche.org.uk, www.larchekent.fsnet.co.uk

Larchfield Community

UK Stokesley Road, Hemlington | Middlesbrough, Cleveland TS8 9DY
+44-(0)642-593688 -595 778

Losang Dragpa Buddhist Centre

UK Dobroyd Castle, Pexwood Road | Todmorden, West Yorkshire OL14 7JJ
+44-(0)1706-812247 -818901 info@losangdragpa.com
www.losangdragpa.com

Manjushri Institute

UK Conishead Priory | Ulverston / Cumbria LA12 9QQ
+44-(0)229-549029 info@manjushri.org.uk
www.manjushri.org.uk

New Creation Christian Community

UK Nether Heyford | Northampton NN7 3LB
+44-(0)1327-349991 -349997 nccc@jesus.org.uk
www.jesus.org.uk/nccc

Orchard Leigh Farm Community

UK Bath House, Eastington, Stonehouse | Gloucestersire GL10 3AY
+44-(0)1453-823811 -823811

Pilgrims Hall

UK Ongar Road | Brentwood, Essex CM15 9SA
+44-(0)277-72206

Postlip Hall

UK Winchcombe | Cheltenham, Gloucestershire GL54 5AQ
+44-(0)1242-602237 sandymcmillan@careersolutions.co.uk

Simeon Care for the Elderly

UK Cairnlee Road, Bieldside | Aberdeen AB15 9BN
+44-(0)224-862415 -862415

Simon Community of Ireland

UK St. Andrew's Hous | 28-30 Exchequer Street | Dublin 2
+44-(0)1-6711606 -6711098 simon@simoncommunity.com
www.simoncommunity.com

Templehill Community
UK Auchinblae, Laurencekirk | Kincardineshire AB30 1UJ
+44-(0)1561-320230 -320283

The Hive Housing Co-op
UK c/o 17-21 Chapel St | Bradford, West Yorkshire B15 DT
+44-(0)1274-745002 the_hive_coop@yahoo.com

The Neighbours Community
UK 140-148 Ardington Road | NN1 5LT Northampton
+44-(0)1604-633918 rog@fish.co.uk

Iceland

The Snaefellsas Community
IS Brekkubae, Hellnar | 356 Snaefellsbaer
+354-(0435-6810, -6820 -6801 gudrun@hellnar.is
www.hellnar.is

Ireland

Camphill Community Ballybay
IRL Corraskea | Robb Farm | Ballybay, Co. Monaghan
+44-(0)42-9741-939 -359 ballybay@camphill.ie
www.camphill.ie

Camphill Community Dunshane
IRL Dunshane House | Brannockstown, Near Naas | Co. Kildare
+353-(0)45-483628 -483833 dunshane@camphill.ie
www.camphill.ie

Camphill Community Thomastown
IRL Jerpoint Barn | Thomastown, Co. Kilkenny
+353-(0)56-24844, -54132 -54286 jerpoint@camphill.ie
www.camphill.ie

L'Arche Cork
IRL Le Ceile | Togher, Cork 4
+353-(0)2131-8880 -8883

The Bridge Camphill Community
IRL Main Street | Kilcullen, Co. Kildare
+353-(0)45-481597 -481519 thebridge@camphill.ie
www.camphill.ie

Italy

Comunità della Guedrara

I Baconi, 1 | 41029 Sestola (MO)
+39-0536-61062

Cooperativa Dulcamara

I Via Tolara di Sopra 78 | 40064 Sttefonti (BO)
+39-051-796643 -6511630

I Cavalieri del Sole

I Podere Monte Sabatino | S. Maria di Lignano | 06081 Assisi (PG)
+39-075802424 -075802424

Instituto Lama T. Kapha

I 56040 Pomaia (Pi)
+39-050-685654 -768 iltk@sirius.pisa.it

Libera Universita di Alcatraz

I Alcatraz - Localitá santa Cristina | 06020 Gubbio (PG)
+39-075-92299-38, -39 -92287-14 info@alcatraz.it
www.alcatraz.it

Passalmonte

I Campagna 52 | 06065 Passignano S/T (PG)
+39-075-826563

Solaria - Center for Alternative Energy,Permaculture and Environment

I Centro su Energie rinnovabili, Ambiente e Permacoltura | Casella Postale | 18037 Pigna
+39-0328-4817529 paea@libero.it

Netherlands

De Weyst

NL Pater Petrusstraat 21 | 5423 SV Handel
+31-(0)492-322509 -322509

Effeta-Gemeenschap

NL Goirkestraat 69 | 5046 GE Tilburg
+31-(0)13-5437877

Emmaus De Bilt

NL Burg. de Withstraat 16 | 3732 EK De Bilt
+31-(0)30-2210513 Emmausdebilt@hetnet.nl

Het Arendsnest

NL Lindenhoorst | Hoofdstraat 260 | 3972 LL Driebergen-Rijsenburg
☎+31-(0)343-517549

Stichting De Refter

NL Rijksstraatweg 37 | 6574 AC Ubbergen
☎+31-(0)243235259

Wilhelmina Hospital terrein

NL WH Grounds Foundation | Helmerstraat | 1054 CX Amsterdam Oud-West
☎+31-(0)20-6168966

Woongroep H.U.G.O.

NL Heel't Gedoe Oecologisch | Hugo de Grootstraat 10 | 2518 ED ,s-Gravenhage/Den Haag
☎+31-(0)70-3467362 Fax -3625820

Poland

Dobrowka Community

PL Dobrowka 30 | 21-132 Kamionka
☎+48-(0)81-8527876

Russia

Camphill Village Svetlana

RUS Alexina Village, Volchov | 187439 Leningrad County
☎+7-(0)812-6338760

Kitezh Children's Ecovillage Community

RUS Kaluzhskaya oblast | 249650 Baryatinsky
☎+7-(0)8454-23224 ✉kitezh@kaluga.ru ; ecoliza@rmplc.co.uk
www.civilsoc.org/nisorgs/russwest/kitezh.htm

National Community „Aleskam"

RUS Loudmila Ignatenko | 60 Let Oktyabra Str. 1, Ap. 17 | 416300 Radzdolny Settlement, Kamchatka
☎+7-041531-97140 Fax -97140 ✉yupik@elrus.kamchatka.su

Zapovednoye

RUS Tver region, Nelidovsky district, p/o Zapovednik | 172513 Nelidovo District, Tver Region
☎+7-(0)8266 22416 ✉okovfors@mail.ru

Spain

Colectivo Manzanares

E 42315 Peralejo de los Escluderos (Soria)
☎ +34-(0)975186426

Els Isards

E Saleta del Mas | 17403 St. Hilary Sacalm, Girona
☎ +34-972-868842

Rambla Alascar

E 18813 Cuevas del Campo, Granada
☎ +34-696347655

Sweden

Bostadskollektivet

S Örgryte g:a Prästgård | Prästgårdsgatan 44 | 41271 Göteborg
☎ +46-(0)31-831034 -7730260 prastgarden@telia.com
w1.317.telia.com/~u31733998/

Gullbackens Lantrasgård

S Box 3757 | 90314 Umeå
☎ +46-(0)103359358 gullbacken@hotmail.com

Järna-Almviks Gård

S (Hare Krishna Center) | 15395 Järna
☎ +46-(0)8551-52050

Kursgarden Lindsberg

S Lindsberg 10, (Pl. 4795) | 79191 Falun
☎ +46-(0)23-43030

Mickelsgården

S Lund 2905 | 82060 Delsbo
☎ +46-(0)653-16982/ -10917

Rumpans Fritidsby

S Pråmviken 9500 | 86296 Njurunda
☎ +46-(0)60-36280 -36469 anders.nyquist@ebox.tninet.se
www.crosswinds.net/~ecovillage/ekoby.htm#

Smeden

S Korgebogvägen 67 | 55308 Jönköping
☎ +46-(0)36185979 -(0)36164211 pia_larsson@swipnet.se
www.crosswinds.net/~ecovillage/eindex.htm

Switzerland

Association Epidaure

CH Essertfallon | 2886 Epiquerez
☎+41-(0)32-9551337 ass.epidaure@freesurf.ch

Kulturfabrik

CH Zürcherstr. 42 | 8620 Wetzikon
☎+41-(0)1-9322525 -9326525 info@kulturfabrik.ch
www.kulturfabrik.ch

La Corolle

CH 26, Chemin d'Ecogia | 1290 Versoix, Genève
☎+41-(0)22-7555182 -7792918

La Grotte

CH Communauté de l'Arche | Av. Jean-Gambach 28 | 1700 Fribourg
☎+41-(0)26323-1585 -1435 lagrotte@arche-helvetia.ch
www.arche-helvetia.ch

Via Felsenau

CH Spinnereiweg 17 | 3004 Bern
☎+41-(0)31-34856-20 -21 wbg.viafelsenau@bluewin.ch

This community just sent us this Identikit picture... or maybe it's a network of different life forms?

Networks of communities and ecovillages

Texts and research by Martin Stengel

This chapter presents networks whose members are either exclusively (e.g. Camphill) or predominantly (e.g. Come Together) communities and ecovillages, or else which represent a major target group for communities and ecovillages (e.g. GEN). The descriptions derive either from the networks and their administrative organs themselves, or else they have been assembled from informational material which they sent to us for this purpose. For individual smaller networks we have published the addresses of all their member communities/ecovillages to the extent that we have received them from the networks' central offices. For all networks we list the member communities, which are listed in full in the directory. And many networks publish a complete list of addresses for their member communities all over the world.

After each network description you will find addresses:

Boldface addresses are the network's official contact address, while normally printed addresses are members of this network. The official contact addresses are sometimes also a community or an ecovillage, sometimes just an office.

The addresses have been listed alphabetically according to country and name. **An arrow** (→) before an address means that this group is listed in more detail elsewhere, usually in the data section, and the name behind the arrow can be found in the index. Explanations of the symbols and abbreviations used here can be found in the legend on p. 414. Except for the country signature, the addresses are listed the way they would appear on an envelope, whereby a vertical beam (|) indicates the start of a new line. Please don't forget to include the country's name at the bottom of the address. The country abbreviations (A-Z) are explained on p. 415.

Adidam

The members of the Adidam community in Europe live cooperatively together in small groups in England, Germany and the Netherlands. These communities are part of a larger network of communities that, together, form the world-wide gathering of devotees of the Divine World-Teacher, Adi Da Samraj.

Over the past 33 years, Adi Da Samraj and his followers have developed a very specific and practical life path: the path of the heart, or Adidam, which is lived and practised by his followers in their communities.

"The linked, co-operative (and thus genuinely religious) community has a fundamentally liberating function… Free men and women must create a sacred refuge or a human sanctuary for their own growth – and not isolated from one another but only in committed cultural and communal co-operation." Adi Da Samraj – from an essay in the book Eleutherios (The Only Truth That Sets The Heart Free).

His followers in the Adidam Communities know that through their lifestyles they not only support their own spiritual growth, but also focus Adi Da Samraj's love and his delightful being, effectively transmitting it into the world for the benefit of all living things.

Adidam Holland

NL Annendaalderweg 10 | 6105 AT Maria Hoop
☎+31-(0)20-4681442 ✉adidam_amsterdam@adidam.org
🖳www.adidam.nl

→Adidam Center&Bookstore (D)

Adidam London Community

UK PO Box 20013 | London
☎+44-(0)845 3301008 ✉london@aboutadidam.org

Arche following Jean Vanier

The first Jean Vanier Arche Community was founded by Jean Vanier in the Roman Catholic tradition in France in 1964. His fundamental conviction was that all persons, independent of their gifts or their personal limits, share a common human nature. In Arche Communities mentally handicapped persons live together with non-handicapped "assistants", share their daily worries and joys, and form a Christian community in the spirit of the Gospels and of joy. The communities want to make it possible for their members to take advantage of appropriate educational, employment and therapeutic activities supporting their sense of dignity, their growth and their development, and which simultaneously support them in their endeavours to become more independent. Each handicapped member finds an activity fitting to his or her needs within the framework of work assistance centres, occupational workshops or gardens, through which the development of new abilities and self-confidence are encouraged. The Arche thus hopes to make the special gifts of people with mental disabilities visible. Communal living takes place in groups of from six to eight mentally handicapped women and men and four to six assistants. These households are integrated into towns or villages, and each member has his or her own room. Cooking, eating, house work, birthday parties etc. all take place in common. The Arche Movement offers people from all countries the opportunity to participate as assistants in its communities. Potential members must be at least eighteen years old and be willing to commit themselves for one year. They must further send a written application to the community of their choice and be able to speak the national language of the community well. After a probationary month the common year can be confirmed. Assistants receive room and board, social benefits and pocket money. They work in the households, contribute to pedagogical projects for the handicapped people, participate in group life, as well as in the financial administration. They also participate in the workshops and the work centres. The helpers learn among other things how to establish a relationship with the handicapped people in the form of friendships or simply through assisting them in their daily lives.

Today there are more than 120 Arche Communities according to Jean Vannier on all continents.

Bureau Administratif L'Arche Belgique

B **Francois Gaystraat, 276 | 1150 Bruxelles**
☎+32-(0)2-771 7954 🖷-779 1829 ✉info@larche.be
💻www.larche.be

Arche Deutschland

D **Erik Thouet | Klosterhof 3 | 88255 Baindt**
✉arche.thouet@gmx.net 💻www.arche-deutschland.de

Arche Dänemark

DK **Niels Steensens Hus | Nygade 4a | 3000 Helsingør**
☎+45-(0)49-21 21 39 🖷-20 11 76 ✉jhviid@get2net.dk
💻hjem.get2net.dk/jhviid

Arche Spanien: El Rusc

E **Veïnat de Sant Ponç 12 | 08490 Tordera**
☎+34-(0)93 764 01-50 🖷-50 ✉associacioelrusc@wanadoo.es
💻www.larche-europesud.org

Bureau l'Arche en France

F **39-41, rue Olivier de Serres | 75015 Paris**
☎+33-(0)145 32-23 74 🖷-45 41 ✉arche.en.france@wanadoo.fr

Federation Internationale des Communautes de l'Arche

F **L'Arche Internationale | 10, rue Fenoux | 75015 Paris**
☎+33-(0)-153 68 08 00 🖷-142 50 07 16
✉international@larche.org

Office l'Arche United Kingdom

UK **10 Briggate | Silsden, Keighley | BD20 9JT West Yorkshire**
☎+44-(0)1535-656186 🖷-656426 ✉info@larche.org.uk
💻www.larche.org.uk

Associazione Arca Italia

I **Il Chicco | Via Ancona, 1 | 00043 Ciampino, Roma**
☎+39-06796-2104 🖷-2104 ✉arcachicco@libero.it
💻www.larche-europesud.org

Office l'Arche Irland

IRL l'Arche Belfast | 563, Ormeau Road | Belfast BT7 3JA
☎+353-(0)5677 25 283 ✉admin@larche.ie 🖳www.larche.ie

De Ark Gemeenschap Gouda

NL (Arche Niederlande) | Wethouder Venteweg 224 | 2805 JV Gouda
☎+31-(0)182-54-8024 🖷-8122 ✉ark.gouda@planet.nl
🖳home.planet.nl/~Ark.Gouda/

L'Arche Sledziejowice

PL (Arche Polen) | Sledziejowice 83 | 32020 Wieliczka
☎+48-(0)12 882-851 🖷-470 ✉region@larche.org.pl
🖳www.larche.org.pl

Skupnost Barka

SLO Arche Slowenien | Zbilje 66 | 1215 Medvode
☎+386-(0)1361-3617 🖷-3617 ✉barka.skup@guest.arnes.si
🖳www.larche-europesud.org

→De Ark Gemeenschap Antwerpen (B)

→De Ark Gemeenschap Moerkerke (B)

→L'Arche Communauté de Bierges, a.s.b.l. (B)

→Arche im Nauen (CH)

→Arche Tecklenburg (D)

→L'Arche à Cognac (F)

→Le Moulin de l'Auro (F)

→Le Sénevé (F)

→Les Trois Fontaines (F)

→L'Arche Bognor Regis (UK)

→L'Arche Liverpool (UK)

→L'Arche Dublin (IRL)

→L'Arche Kilkenny (IRL)

Bruderhof Communities

The network of Bruderhof Communities represents an international movement of more than 2,500 men, women and children who live together without private property in eleven Bruderhof settlements in Germany, England, Australia and the USA. We are very ordinary people and come from a wide range of cultural, religious and professional backgrounds. The first Bruderhof was founded in 1920 in Sannerz (Hessen/Germany) by Dr Eberhard Arnold, an influential theologian and publisher.

We subscribe to the Apostolic Confession of Faith and view Jesus Christ as the source and head of our lives. The teachings of Jesus in the New Testament, particularly the Sermon on the Mount, play a central role. We are committed to nonviolence, love of neighbour and enemy, and fidelity in marriage. The communal life of the early Christians as described in the Book of Acts is our model. At the same time, we recognise God's presence in all people who strive for a new social order based on peace and justice.

The common table – "We work, celebrate, laugh and walk together our whole lives long through thick"

Loyalty to God and to one another is the foundation stone upon which our family and community life are built.

We mainly earn our livelihood through the manufacture and sale of kindergarten materials as well as tools for people with disabilities. We share this money through a common purse. Everything in our lives should be an expression of mutual love. Thus our work is not separate from our lives but is performed out of joy in service to one another.

Bruderhofhaus Sannerz

D Lindenstr. 13 | 36391 Sinntal-Sannerz
☎ +49-(0)6664-402498 ✉ contact@bruderhof.com
💻 www.sannerzbruderhof.de

Beech Grove Bruderhof

UK Sandwich Road | CT15 4HH Nonington
☎ +44-(0)1304-842980 📠 -841923 ✉ contact@bruderhof.com
💻 www.beechgrovebruderhof.co.uk

→ Darvell Bruderhof (UK)

Camphill

Camphill was established to work with those in need of special care and continues to provide today for the educational and social needs of people with a diverse range of disabilities. From the outset, the intention has been to do this work not as a "job" in the usual sense of the word but as a "way of life", where cultural and human values are as important as those of the work place.

The essence of Camphill is to provide a way of life where children, young people and adults diagnosed with autistic disorders, Down's syndrome, genetic disorders, epilepsy, brain damage, behavioural problems or other developmental difficulties can live together with co-workers and helpers in a mutually supportive environment. Each Camphill community, whatever its main task, takes full responsibility for the land which it administers. Land stewardship is normally based on biodynamic (organic) methods using organic composting techniques, natural fertilisers and preparations to bring about a healthy, balanced and enriched soil life. Nearly all communities have their own garden and many have larger areas of cultivated land. Camphill communities endeavour to provide food that is free from artificial additives. When supplies from home production are insufficient, they are supplemented as far as possible from other organic sources. In Camphill, the ideal is that of a community life based on Christian values where, according to ability, each person contributes what he or she can towards the well-being of his or her fellows. This ideal is approached in many ways from community to community to reflect the age, needs and abilities of those who live there. People come to Camphill at different stages of their lives and for many different reasons. As a result, a wide variety of Camphill communities has been established to provide education, training and social therapy. The world-wide Camphill Movement comprises more than 5,000 people living in over 90 centres in 21 different countries, providing for over 1,700 Adults and Children. The contact addresses for the individual communities are currently available on the Internet under http://www.camphill.org.uk

Association of Camphill Communities in the British Isles

UK **Gawain House | 56 Welham Road | YO17 9DP Norton, North Yorkshire**
☎+44-(0)1653-694197 🖷-600001 ✉info@camphill.org.uk
💻www.camphill.org.uk

Camphill Scotland

UK **Murtle House | Bieldside | AB15 9EP Aberdeen**
☎+44-(0)1224-867685 🖷-867659
✉facilitator@camphillscotland.org.uk

→Humanus-Haus Beitenwil (CH)

→Camphill Dorfgemeinschaft Hausenhof (D)

Camphill Schulgemeinschaft und Hof Brachenreuthe

D 88662 Überlingen

☎ +49-(0)7551-80070 📠-800750 ✉info@brachenreuthe.de 💻www.brachenreuthe.de

Lebensgemeinschaft Alt Schönow

D Alt Schönow 5 | 14165 Berlin (Zehlendorf)

☎ +49-(0)30-84571890 📠-84571899 ✉info@camphill-alt-schoenow.de 💻www.camphill-alt-schoenow.de

→Sylvia-Koti (SF)

→Camphill Community Glencraig (UK)

→Camphill Community Mourne Grange (UK)

→Camphill Milton Keynes Community (UK)

→Cherry Orchards Camphill Community (UK)

→Grange Village (UK)

→Newton Dee Village Community (UK)

→Ochil Tower School (UK)

→The Croft Community (UK)

→Camphill Village Community Duffcarrig (IRL)

→Jøssåsen Landsby (N)

→Solborg (N)

→Vidaråsen Landsby (N)

→Foreningen Staffansgården (S)

Church and Peace

is a European network of Christian communities, intentional communities, parishes, peace organisations and individuals. Its members share the conviction that witnessing for peace and non-violence as recorded in the Gospels are among the most significant characteristics of the Church and the Christian community. The network provides mutual support in non-violent conflict resolution and other activities for peace and reconciliation.

Church and Peace continually endeavours to re-examine and reformulate the theological basis for Christian peace work and thus to help conceive of ways in which these theological convictions can be implemented in non-violent service for peace and reconciliation.

Church and Peace encompasses around eighty-five member organisations and individual members in nine European countries. They belong to a wide range of confessions: Mennonites, Quakers, Church of the Brethren, Anglicans, Baptists, Methodists, Moravians, Lutherans, Reformed and members of the Roman Catholic Church. That is why the ecumenical dialogue, particularly the development of a common peace ethic, is of the highest priority for Church and Peace. For this reason, the network is an associated member of the Conference of European Churches and works together with the Ecumenical Church Council in Geneva. It is currently focused on networking Christian peace activists and groups in the Balkans, participating in the "Ten Days of Peace" and in the promotion and further development of peace services.

Church and Peace has an international office in Schöffengrund/Germany which is also responsible for the German-speaking countries. It has further regional contacts in Lyon (French-speaking countries), London (Great Britain and Ireland), and Székesfehévár in Hungary (Eastern Europe).

Church & Peace e.V.

D Internationale Geschäftsstelle | Ringstr.14 | 35641 Schöffengrund
☎+49-(0)6445-5588 -5070 IntlOffice@church-and-peace.org
www.church-and-peace.org

Communauté de Grandchamp

CH 2015 Areuse
☎+41-(0)32842-2492 -2474

→Basisgemeinde Wulfshagenerhütten (D)

→Brot & Rosen. Diakonische Basisgemeinschaft. (D)

Hofgemeinschaft Bittelbronn

D c/o Martin und Heidi Haußecker | Mosbacher Str. 9 | 74219 Möckmühl-Brittelbronn
☎+49-(0)6298-1769 -929483 Hofgemeinschaft.bittelbronn@t-online.de

Hofgemeinschaft Guggenhausen e.V.

D Hauptstr.14 | 88379 Guggenhausen
☎+49-(0)7503-1889/-2642 -9167073
www.hofgemeinschaft.com

→Laurentiushof Wethen (D)

Communauté de Caulmont

F Froberville | 76400 Fécamp
☎+33-(0)3527-3172 -3667

→Communauté de l'Arche La Borie (F)

Communauté de Pomeyrol

F 13103 Saint-Etienne-du-Grès
☎ +33-(0)49049-1888 📠-1076

→Monastère de Cantauque (F)

→Community for Reconciliation (UK)

→Darvell Bruderhof (UK)

London Mennonite Centre

UK 14 Shepherds Hill | N6 5AQ Highgate, London
☎ +44-(0)181-3408775 📠-3416807 💻www.btinternet.com/~lmc

The Ammerdown Centre

UK Radstock | Bath | BA3 53W Somerset
☎ +44-(0)1761-433709 📠-433094

BOCS Foundation

H P.O. Box 7 | 8003 Székesfehérvár
☎ +36-(0)22-501844 📠-501843 ✉bocs@c3.hu 💻http://bocs.hu

Kommuniteit Spe Gaudentes

NL Pastorie Oudezijds 100 | O.Z. Achterburgwal 100 | 1012 DS Amsterdam
☎ +31-(0)20-266634

Come Together Netzwerk

This network of German speaking communities used to be a loose coalition of people from around fifty ecological, self-determined communities. Since 2003 it has been going through a reorientation process.

The communities' needs and contacts have developed in such a way that interest in our central mass meetings (one-week summer meetings), which we have been regularly staging every year in a variety of community projects, has lagged. Thus in 2003 – for the first time – we held no summer meeting at all.

Our other activities, such as healers' conferences, attending the Church Congress, arranging lectures etc. are no longer being centrally organised by the Come Together Network but are being attended to by smaller networks.

Our "Come Together News" newsletter appeared until 2003. The website has to be redesigned for 2004.

We have continued on as a network and we have maintained a contact address, as well as an Internet mailing list containing around 120 addresses of community projects and dedicated individuals. In addition, we maintain our membership and contacts as well as a good exchange of information with the Global Ecovillage Network (GEN) and HOLON. Important information goes onto our mailing list.

We respond to enquiries and requests for contact from both Germany and abroad.

Come Together Netzwerk

D c/o Dieter Federlein | Sieben Linden 1 | 38486 Bandau
☎ +49-(0)39000-907939
✉ dieter.federlein@web.de; cometogether.de@web.de

→Agnus Dei (D)

→Club99 (D)

→Delphin-Gemeinschaft - Wege zu Gott (D)

→Gemeinschaft in Güstritz (Wendland) (D)

→Holderbusch (D)

Kuhmuhne

D Dorfstr. 12 | 37318 Schönhagen
☎ +49-(0)36083-40796, -41081 ✉ info@kuhmuhne.de
www.kuhmuhne.de

→Lahn-Taunus Gemeinschaft (D)

→Lebens- und Agrarkulturelle Initiative e.V. (D)

→Lebensgarten Steyerberg (D)

→Lebensgut Pommritz (D)

→Ökodorf Sieben Linden (D)

→ÖkoLeA (D)

→Stamm der Likatier (D)

→Argayall (E)

→Francischu (F)

→Comunauté Vitulettu (F)

Common Life Network

is a network designed to help found and encourage Christian life communities in Switzerland. The "Common Life Network" was launched in 2001 with the goal of promoting relations between Christian communities in Switzerland and helping to pave the way for new communities.

We believe that a shared and committed life is an important part of what Jesus taught. This life can not only be realised in a shared lifestyle. In fact, living together makes many things more lively and tangible. Throughout the history of the Church, communities have continually provided important impulses and we think that their significance is growing within our individualistic society.

As a network we offer the following:

- Internet access (http://www.commonlife.ch) as an up-to-date information platform with resources, links etc.
- Meetings for people who are interested in the communal life

But the most important part of our work are the personal contacts and friendships that develop. Ultimately, this is the only way to pass on the things which make up a communal life in the first place: vision, practical assistance, relationships, prayer, learning from one another and encouragement.

Common Life Network

CH info@commonlife.ch www.commonlife.ch

Communities of the Twelve Tribes

We are people of many races and nationalities. We are a spiritual people, consisting of twelve tribes which are located in different places all over the earth. In Europe we have communities in Germany, France, Spain and England. The life in the communities of the Twelve Tribes is the result of the salvation that we have experienced. It enables us to live together in peace and to love one another. This salvation is one person: Yahshua*, the Messiah, the Son of God who became man. His sacrificial death and his resurrection have the power to cleanse our conscience of all our unrighteous deeds and to give us a new life. This new life is a life in community where people care for each other. In our communites we no longer live for ourselves. Now we have the power to love one another from the heart, to be open with each other and to tear down all the walls that exist in the human heart and which want to alienate us from one another. There are neither poor nor needy people among us because we share our possessions. We make our living by working in our own cottage industries. Our children grow up in stable and healthy families and are educated at home. We hope that what started 30 years ago with one community and has grown ever since, will develop into a spiritual 12-tribed Israel with many more communites. This is a foretaste of the new age when all human beings will live in peace with one another. If you are interested in this life (in a community which really works) and want to become acquainted with Jahschua*, the creator of this new social order, then each of our communities gives you its most heartfelt invitation. You can find all current world-wide addresses and much additional information about us on our website: http://www.Zwoelf-Staemme.de

*Jahschua is the Hebrew name for Jesus

→Gemeinschaft in Klosterzimmern (D)

Communidad de San Sebastian

E Paseo de Ulia 375 | 20014 San Sebastian

☎ +34-(0)943-580029

→Comunidad de Irún (E)

→Communauté de Sus (F)

→Stentwood Farm (UK)

Emmaus

The Emmaus Movement began in Paris in 1949. Following the Second World War, thousands of families suffered from poverty and hopelessness. Abbé Pierre, a French priest and member of parliament, opened his house to some poor people and asked them to help him to help others. Together they began building houses for the needy – sometimes illegally. In order to finance these activities, they began collecting, sorting, repairing and selling things which had either been thrown away or which had been donated to them. This work provided the useless objects with new value. And what was even more important: the members of this first Emmaus Community regained their dignity and self-esteem. By living and working together, by sharing the fruits of their labour with others and thereby feeling useful, they discovered a new meaning in their lives. Inspired by these positive experiences in Paris, further Emmaus Communities cropped up in France. Groups which had been active for similar goals in Asia and South America joined the movement. More Emmaus Communities arose in Europe and around the world. Emmaus's work easily fit into the various cultural and social conditions it encountered.

Today, the Emmaus Movement reflects a broad range of solidarity-based activities in which the emergence of marginal social groups and homelessness is combated at all levels by supporting people in their endeavours to take an active part in their own development, by reintegrating people into society through communal life, through informal training, courses and social undertakings. Recycling remains the main source of income for most Emmaus groups world-wide. It is a concrete measure against consumption and waste and for a sustainable lifestyle.

Today, the Emmaus Movement encompasses 450 groups and dependants in thirty-eight countries and on five continents. Because of the great number of Emmaus Communities, we have decided not to publish them all in this directory. Instead, we would like to refer you to our websites <www.emmaus.nl> and <www.emmaus-international.org>, and to the International Emmaus Secretariat.

Secretariat General d'Emmaus International

F 183 bis, rue vaillant coutorier | 94140 Alfortvillle
☎ +33-(0)148-932950 🖷 -531926 ✉ contact@emmaus-international.org 💻 www.emmaus-international.org

→Emmaus Gemeinschaft in Köln (D)

→Haus der Gastfreundschaft (D)

→Emmaus-Peupins (F)

→Emmaus-Jokioinen (SF)

→Emmaus Langeweg (NL)

→Stichting Emmaus Eindhoven (NL)

GEN - Global Ecovillage Network

We envision a planet with a variety of life cultures, united by the intention to develop communities living in harmony with each other and with the earth for the good of this and coming generations. In a time of rising unemployment and loss of meaning, of the loss of biodiver-sity and of climate change, our common goal is to create living and valuable examples of a healthy, fulfilling and sustainable way of life.

The community and ecovil-lage movement is rising to this challenge. Ecovillages are rural and urban communities which combine co-operative social relations with an ecological lifestyle. Ecovillages are concerned with renewing life-sustaining systems, promoting the development of each individual person, and research on a way of life in which harmony between people and between humans and nature can be promoted.

One of GEN's main activities is to link together a number of initiatives and individuals in order to promote the exchange of information and co-operation. For example:

- Networking communities and arranging contacts between them.
- Linking institutions and organisations concerned with sustainable ways of life or sustainable technologies with GEN and/or striving for co-operation.
- Channelling and/or networking interested persons world-wide.
- Lobbying political decision-makers.

GEN uses various tools to spread information on realised ecovillage concepts and practical examples. It places particular value on holistic project approaches integrating social and technological sustainability, ecology, spirituality, (political) education and alternative social practices. GEN publishes and supports training programmes, courses and consultation offered by individual communities: e.g. on the topics of community development, peace work, conflict resolution, permaculture, ecovillage and town planning, natural health care, personal development as well as the development of micro-businesses.

This work is conducted by three large regional offices: Global Ecovillage Network of the Americas (ENA), GEN-Europe e.V. (including also Africa and the Near East) and GEN Oceania/Asia (GENOA with its head office in Australia and another office specially for Asia in Sri Lanka). GEN maintains very active websites for networking and information purposes. They can be found at: www.ecovillage.org. It also publishes newsletters for various regions and publishes books, videos and CD-ROMs.

Future developments

Alongside publicity work, the focus of GEN's future work will centre on further education and mutual learning in so-called "Living and Learning Centres" (see below). The already existing programmes will be complemented by additional exchange programmes. GEN is seeking co-operation partners with an active interest in sustainable communities, alternative economic structures, renewable energies, ecological building as well as training and qualification in all of these areas. GEN will develop a "consultation and specialist data bank" on these issues. In 2004 it plans to begin conferring an (annual) "Ecovillage Excellence Award". It will honour outstanding contributions in the development and propagation of the community idea as a living model for the future.

Living and Learning Centres

- an initiative by GEN, Global Ecovillage Network

Created to spread information on sustainable lifestyles and make them tangible, the Living & Learning Centres are at the core of GEN. Teaching and learning in existing communities provides people with an opportunity to learn something about sustainable living through direct and practical experience and then take this knowledge elsewhere. Many Living and Learning Centres offer both training on the subject of community development and a large range of themes which are significant for the development of ecovillages on a material, organisational and social level. Visit these places, get involved, take your experiences home with you, share them with others and turn them into something new! Ecovillages are models of global significance for changes we all need to make.

"Yellow-barrel-houses" in Findhorn

You can find Living and Learning Centres on all continents. In Europe:

→Findhorn in Scotland provides holistic educational programmes. These include a one-month ecovillage training course, permaculture workshops, courses on personal development, spirituality, arts and crafts.

→ZEGG in Germany provides courses on social communication, conflict resolution, social networks and peace work. The annual ZEGG Summer Camp offers courses on virtually all ecovillage topics, from child-rearing to changing our consumption habits, all the way to the resolution of planetary crises.

In →Damanhur (Italy) courses are provided on community formation, communication methods and personal spiritual development alongside wide-ranging offerings on healing methods and arts and crafts.

These and additional current offerings (workshops, seminars, semester programmes) can be found on the GEN websites under http://www.gen-europe.org and http://gen.ecovillage.org and in the "Living and Learning" brochure, which is available either at the website or from GEN directly.

The "continental" offices:

GEN Europe e.V.

D Twinoffice: ZEGG (D) / Findhorn (UK) | Rosa-Luxemburg-Str. 89 | 14806 Belzig
☎+49-(0)33841-44766 📠-44768 ✉info@gen-europe.org
💻www.gen-europe.org

GEN-Europe organises 92 communities and 16 national networks.

Ecovillage Network of the Americas (ENA)

USA 556 Farm Road, P.O. Box 90 | Summertown TN 38483-0090
☎+1 (0)931-964 4324 📠-964 2200 ✉ecovillage@thefarm.org
💻http://ena.ecovillage.org

The ENA-website shows 113 communities.

GEN Oceania and Asia (GENOA)

AUS 59 Crystal Waters, 65 Kilcoy Lane | Conondale Qld 4552
☎+61-(0)75494-4741 📠-4578 ✉genoa@genoa.org.au 💻http://genoa.ecovillage.org

GENOA comprises 35 communities.

GEN South-East Asia

Thailand Jonggon Duangsri | 31 Chiangmai - Lamphun Rd., Tamboon Watkeat | 50000 A. Muang, Chiangmai
☎+66-(0)53-247374, +66-(0)53-241504 📠-241504
✉info@chiangmaigreen.com 💻www.chiangmaigreen.com; http://genoa.ecovillage.org/genoceania

The national offices:

Austrian National Contact

A Martin Kirchner | Albrechtsbergerstr. 32 | 3390 Melk
☎ +43-(0)676 352 33 69

GEN Oceania and Asia (GENOA)

AUS 59 Crystal Waters, 65 Kilcoy Lane | 4552 Conondale Qld
☎ +61-(0)75494-4741 📠 -4578 ✉ genoa@genoa.org.au 🖳 http://genoa.ecovillage.org

Czech Republic Ecovillage Network

CZ c/o Max Jensen | Svojanov 3 | 78325 Bouzov
☎ +420-(0)585-152010 🖳 www.permalot.org

Come Together Netzwerk

D c/o Dieter Federlein | Sieben Linden 1 | 38486 Bandau
☎ +49-(0)39000-907939
✉ dieter.federlein@web.de; cometogether.de@web.de

GEN Europe e.V.

D Zwillingsbüro: ZEGG (D) / Findhorn (UK) | Rosa Luxemburg-Str. 89 | 14806 Belzig
☎ +49-(0)33841-44766 📠 -44768 ✉ info@gen-europe.org
🖳 www.gen-europe.org

LØS (Landsforeningen for Økosamfund)

DK Allan Elm | Landsbyvænget 11, Herskind | 8464 Galten
☎ +45-(0)8754-6020 📠 -6021 ✉ los@pip.dknet.dk
🖳 http.//europe.ecovillage.org/denmark/network

Selba Vida sostenible - Red Ibérica de Ecoaldeas

E Artosilla | 22600 Sabiñánigo (Huesca)
✉ info@selba.org 🖳 www.selba.org

Réseau Français des Eco-Villages (RFEV)

F Jean Michel Pochat |
✉ jeanmi3@hotmail.com

GEN-Finland

SF c/o Liisa Jääskeläinen | Haapaniemenkatu 16 C 385 | 00530 Helsinki
☎ -358-(0)50-3070340 ✉ hhattila@saunalahti.fi

Eco-Village Network UK - EVNUK

UK PO BOX 1410 | CREATE Centre / B Bond Warehouse / Smeaton Rd | BS99 3J Bristol P
☎ +44-(0)117-373 0346, -953 1256 📠 -929 7283
✉ evnuk@gaia.org 🖳 http://evnuk.ecovillage.org

Hungarian National Contact

H Robert Gerzsany | Csendes u. 23, Oroshaza | 5900 Bekes

Rete Italiana dei Villagi Ecologici - RIVE

I c/o AAm Terra Nuova | Via Ponte di Mezzo 1 | 50127 Firenze
☎ +39-055 321 57-29 🖷 -29 ✉ redazione@aamterranuova.it

Israel National Contact

IL Michael Livni, c/o Kibbutz Lotan | D.N. Chevel Eilot 88855
☎ +972-(0)8 6356888 ✉ ml-lotan@zahav.net.il

Rede Portuguesa de Eco-aldeias

P Filipe Espina | Largo Ana de Castro Osório, 13-5° Esq, Alfornelos | 2700-054 Amadora
☎ +35-(0)121474-4535 🖷 -4535

WAS Polish Ecovillage Network

PL Nicole Grospierre | Dabrówka 30 | 21132 Kamionka
☎ +48-(0)81 756 7012 ✉ wasnicole@wp.pl

Russian Ecovillage Network

RUS Vasudeva Kirbiatiev | Basseinaya ul, 59-106 | 196235 St. Petersburg
☎ +7-(0)812-2944 189 🖷 -1135 896 ✉ Vasudeva@mail.spb.org

Romania National Contact

RO Teodora Borghoff | Str. Alex Martha 6/16 | Timisoara 1900
☎ +40-(0)256-437226 ✉ visator@home.ro, teo@ngo.ro

NJORD - The Swedish umbrella for eco-villages

S c/o Gunlaug Östbye | Gebers väg 26 | 12865 Stockholm-Sköndal
☎ +46-(0)8-605-4092 🖷 -4092 ✉ njord@telia.com

GEN South-East Asia

THAI Jonggon Duangsri | 31 Chiangmai - Lamphun Rd., Tamboon Watkeat | 50000 A. Muang, Chiangmai
☎ +66-(0)53-247374, +66-(0)53-241504 🖷 -241504
✉ info@chiangmaigreen.com 💻 www.chiangmaigreen.com; http://genoa.ecovillage.org/genoceania

Ekilat (Turkish network)

TR Dr. Demet Irkli Eryildiz |
✉ idemet@metu.edu.tr

Ecovillage Network of the Americas (ENA)

US Ecovillage Training Center at The Farm | 556 Farm Road, P.O. Box 90 | 38483-0090 Summertown TN
☎ +1 (0)931-964 4324 🖷 -964 2200 ✉ ecovillage@thefarm.org
💻 http://ena.ecovillage.org

Member-communities of GEN presented in this directory:

- →Keimblatt Ökodorf Info-Büro Wien (A)
- →Tchamla Kingdom (BG)
- →PermaLot (CZ)
- →Delphin-Gemeinschaft - Wege zu Gott (D)
- →Lebensgarten Steyerberg (D)
- →Ökodorf Sieben Linden (D)
- →Stamm der Likatier (D)
- →ZEGG - Zentrum für experimentelle Gesellschaftsgestaltung (D)
- →Fjordvang (DK)
- →Hertha Levefællesskab (DK)
- →Argayall (E)
- →Keuruu Ecovillage (SF)
- →Suomineito-yhteisö (SF)
- →Steward Community Woodland (UK)
- →The Findhorn Foundation (UK)
- →Gyürüfü Alapítvány (H)
- →Ökodorf Máriahalom (H)
- →Associazione Culturale Torri Superiore (I)

Healing biotop Tamera in Portugal

→Federazione di Damanhur (I)

→La Comune di Bagnaia (I)

→Upacchi Ecovillaggio (I)

→Kibbutz Lotan (IL)

→Tamera (P)

ISKCON

The International Society for Krishna Consciousness was founded in New York City by Bhaktivedenta Srila Prabhupada, a holy man from northern India, in 1996, and has since spread across the entire world. It represents one of the oldest religions of humankind. The teachings of the Vedas go far beyond such terms as Hinduism. God is neither a Hindu, nor a Moslem, nor a Christian. According to the Vedas, we are all eternal spiritual souls, tiny particles or children of the same God. In many cities and countries the "Hare Krishnas" are well known, above all in their public performances of chanting (singing the holy names of God), distributing Prasadam (vegetarian foods consecrated to God), and their regular efforts to make Vedic literature available to as broad a public as possible. In Germany there is a farm project in the Bavarian Woods (Abentheuer, see below), a village-like settlement near Trier, and various contact addresses and/or large and small centres. Membership in Germany numbers some one thousand people, whereby the majority of them work in their professions and practice Bhakti Yoga at home. But common public events, festivals and celebrations take place constantly (especially on Sundays) to which all are sincerely invited to learn more about the movement's philosophy and lifestyle. Everyone who is interested in this path of devotion to God can simply go to the nearest address and "look around" some more. Initiated members live according to four regulating principles: No meat, fish or eggs; no intoxicating substances; no exploitative sexuality; no games of chance. They practice daily mantra meditation of the holy name. There are various instances and committees which come to decisions through majority votes and organise the movement on a local and trans-regional basis, whereby the various interests of the circle of friends are taken into consideration. The movement maintains itself through income and donations by its members and friends, especially through publications and the sale of vegetarian foods. Further information and addresses are available from:

Goloka Dhama

D Hujetsmühle | Böckingstr. 8 | 55767 Abentheuer
☎ +49-(0)6782 98043-6 ℻-7 gaura-bhavini.sns@bbt.se
www.goloka-dhama.de

→ISKCON Heidelberg (D)

ISKCON Köln e.V.

D Taunusstr.40 | 51105 Köln

☎ +49-(0)221-8303778 💻 www.iskcon.de

→ simhacalam academy (D)

La Nouvelle Mayapour

F Domaine d'Oubaisse | 36360 Lucay le Male

☎ +33-(0)54402-418 📠 -823

Bhaktivedanta Manor

UK International Society for Krishna Consciousness | Aldenham, Near Watford | WD2 8EZ Herts

☎ +44-(0)1923-857244 📠 -852896

→ ISKCON: Govindadwipa Dhama (UK)

→ Somogyvámos (H)

→ Hare Krishna Temple (I)

→ ISKCON: The Bhaktivedanta Book Trust (S)

Lebenshäuser

Our social system is increasingly being overwhelmed by the challenge of providing people in crisis situations with the human security they need. This was the motivation behind the founding of the "Lebenshaus – Oekumenische Gemeinschaft für soziale Integration e.V." ("Houses of Life – Ecumenical Community for Social Integration Association") in Trossingen, Tuttlingen District, in 1985. The founding members were almost all involved in peace groups and in various churches and/or were members in the "Internationaler Versöhnungsbund" ("International Fellowship of Reconciliation"). The association's goal is to provide people seeking a protective community for social or psychological reasons with an appropriate framework. During the limited stay of our "guests", we support them in their efforts to deal with their "life crises" and join them in searching for further life opportunities. In 1987 we moved into a former factory building, which has been rebuilt and is under a preservation order. Since then, additional Lebenshäuser have arisen in South Germany. They largely pursue the same goals as the Lebenshaus in Trossingen and form part of a shared network, although they do not belong to a common "association". We meet once a year to share ideas and experiences.

Lebenshaus Trossingen

D Oekumenische Gemeinschaft für Soziale Integration e.V. | Kirchstr. 23 | 78647 Trossingen

☎ +49-(0)7425-1446 ✉ lebenshaus@t-online.de

Lebenshaus Heitersheim e.V.

D Staufenerstr.1a | 79423 Heitersheim

☎ +49-(0)7634-551719 📠-552089 ✉lebenshaus.hh@t-online.de 💻www.lebenshaus-heitersheim.de

Lebenshaus im Chiemgau

D ökumenisches Netzwerk für soziale Integration e.V. | Am Breitenfeld 30 | 83024 Rosenheim

☎ +49-(0)8031-86744 📠-892330 ✉e-mail@lebenshaus-im-chiemgau.de 💻www.lebenshaus-im-chiemgau.de

Lebenshaus Schwäbische Alb

D Gemeinschaft für soz. Gerechtigkeit, Frieden & Ökologie | Bubenhofenstr. 3, Postfach 1145 | 72501 Gammertingen

☎ +49-(0)7574-2862 ✉info@lebenshaus-alb.de 💻www.lebenshaus-alb.de

Lebenshaus Trossingen

D Oekumenische Gemeinschaft für Soziale Integration e.V. | Kirchstr. 23 | 78647 Trossingen

☎ +49-(0)7425-1446 ✉lebenshaus@t-online.de

LVCW: Landelijke Vereniging Centraal Wonen

LVCW is the Dutch association for co-housing, in which forty-eight communities – most of them co-housing projects – are members.

Centraal wonen (co-housing) is a form of intentional community in which each household basically owns its own house and also shares various facilities with others. Co-housing projects normally consist of thirty to fifty households. The smallest known community is made up of three, the largest of 150 households. Half of the projects can be broken down into groups of four to 7 households. Most projects rent their houses from building societies, but some own their property. In all of them, the community decides on accepting new members.

LVCW's main functions are: to provide a platform for community members; to advise new initiatives; to maintain contacts with administrative institutions. In addition to co-housing, the LVCW also offers itself to other forms of intentional communities. LVCW publishes its own newspaper (Gewoon Anders), has a network of experienced people at its disposal for neighbourhood assistance, maintains an office and conducts three membership assemblies every year.

LVCW is a member of the Netherlands Association for Communal Living (Nederlandse Federatie Gemeenschappelijk Wonen). This is an umbrella organisation uniting three Dutch community networks: LVCW, LVGO (communities for people over fifty-five) and WSB (communities of older people living on a farm).

Some 200 to 300 associations are members in one of these networks respectively and are thus members of the umbrella organisation.

LVCW: Landelijke Vereniging Centraal Wonen

NL Korte Elisabethstraat 13 | 3511 JG Utrecht
☎ +31-(0)30-2612585 ✉ info@lvcw.nl 🖳 www.lvcw.nl

→ Centraal Wonen Lismortel (NL)

LØS - Landforeningen Økologisk Samfund

The many ecological threats and social hardships currently visible in Denmark are being countered by a steadily expanding ecovillage movement. LØS is continually expanding its activities both within the network and also through its public relations work: LØS supports new projects and directs political attention to the hurdles which hamper the development of ecovillages. It attempts to focus the public eye on finding ways in which the existing laws and financial structures can be meaningfully transformed. In 1999, LØS co-operated with five ministries in developing a competition for the "Best Sustainable Settlement for the 21st Century", in which fifty-three groups participated. The outstanding and inspiring contributions have been collected in the book Welcome to the Future. This competition has led to many well-attended events on the topic of "free zones and settlements". These activities have moved LØS to prepare a draft law on experimental ecological free zones in which it is investing high hopes. Furthermore, a co-operative relationship between Danish educational institutions and the ecovillages is under discussion. The research and educational communities have indicated great interest in every approach with a high social and ethical content, an area where the ecovillage movement with its many innovative developments in both the technological and social fields has a great deal to offer.

Thirty-eight ecovillages and 350 other persons and institutions are currently members of LØS.

LØS (Landsforeningen for Økosamfund)

DK Allan Elm | Landsbyvænget 11, Herskind | 8464 Galten
☎ +45-(0)8754-6020 📠 -6021 ✉ los@pip.dknet.dk 🖳 http.// europe.ecovillage.org/denmark/network

A-70 Toustrup Mark

DK Lykkegårdsvej 354 | 8472 Sporup
☎ +45-(0)8696-8361 📠 -8133

Andelsforeningen Baungården

DK Hover Kirkevej 49B, 1 | 7100 Vejle
☎ +45-(0)-76418949 📠 -75853806 ✉ finn.agger@private.dk

→Andelsforeningen Møllegården (DK)

Andelssamfundet Hjortshøj

DK Gl. Kirkevej 70 | 8530 Hjortshøj
+45-(0)86228061 -(0)86741289 le@homebase.dk
www.andelssamfundet.dk

Båring Højskole

DK Højskolevej 2 | 5466 Asperup
+45-(0)64 48 11 08 www.baaringhoejskole.dk

Boform 2000

DK Alkenvej 63 | 8660 Skanderborg
+45-(0)86 93 84 28 connisophia@mail.dk

Boligforeningen Vedaparken

DK Astilbehaven 152, 1 | 2830 Virum
+45 -(0)48 14 21 73 benteostergaard@yahoo.dk

→Den Selvforsynende Landsby (DK)

→Fjordvang (DK)

Foreningen Den Selvejende Institution Pionergruppen

DK Kragebjerg 4 | 4296 Nyrup
+45-(0)27 28 13 91

Fri & Fro

DK c/o N.P. Nielsen | Vestergade 29 F, 1. th. | 5600 Faaborg
+45-(0)62 61 78 88 npn@organiskform.dk www.friogfro.dk

Hallingebjerg

DK Valsømaglevej 73 | 4100 Ringsted
+45-(0)57 53 82 24 post@landsby2000.dk
www.hallingebjerg.dk

Hare Krishna Samfundet

DK Sørningevej 39, Skamstrup | 4440 Mørkøv
+45-(0)59 27 19 30

→Hertha Levefællesskab (DK)

Hesbjerg Beboerforeningen

DK Hesbjerg Slot | Hesbjergvej 50 | 5491 Blommenslyst
+45-(0) 65 96 84 02 -(0)65967490

Kirstinelund

DK Bjedstrupvej 21 | 8660 Skanderborg
+45-(0)86 57 74 27

Købmandsgården

DK Socialpædagogisk landsbyinitiativ | Poststræde 16 | 9460 Brovst

☎ +45-(0)9823-3520 KMG@post10.tele.dk

Munksøgård

DK Økologisk Bofællesskab | Munkesøgård 20 | 4000 Roskilde

☎ +45-(0)77410120

thomas.lejre@munkesoegaard.dk, mikkel.strange@munksoegaard.dk

www.munkesoegaard.dk

Ottrupgård

DK Ottrupgård 11 | 9520 Skørping

☎ +45-(0)98 39 29 07 / Mobil: -27 20 16 74

Råd og Dåd Butikken

DK Hovedgaden 23 | 9460 Brovst

☎ +45-(0)98 23 06 60 -98 23 06 60

Sættedammen

DK Sættedammen 15, 1. | 3400 Hillerød

☎ +45-(0)48 25 40 15

Snabegaard

DK Snabegaardvej 11 | 8654 Bryrup

☎ +45-(0)7575-7222 det.gronne.hus@get2net.dk

→Svanholm (DK)

Thylejren – Det Ny Samfund

DK Gl. Aalborgvej 16 | 7741 Frøstrup

☎ +45-(0)97 99 13 14, -19 almar@paradis.dk

Tigerens Rede

DK Fællesskab - kursuscenter, meditation og spiritualitet | c/o Vestervej 4, Vestervej 1 | 8751 Gedved

☎ +45-(0)76 68 90 32 -75 66 5684

annesophie@tigerensrede.dk www.tigerensrede.dk

Tornsbjerggård

DK Tornsbjergvej 98 | 8350 Hundslund

☎ +45-(0)86 55 04 05

Tranehøj

DK Skippingevej 25 | 4460 Snertinge

☎ +45-(0)59 26 29 36, -20 93 00 36 gitte.jakobsen@private.dk

www.tranehoej.dk

→Udgården - Lading Andelsboligforening (DK)

Vaarst Vestervang

DK Staerhoj 14 | 9620 Gistrup

+45-(0)-96 77 50 40

Økosamfundet Dyssekilde

DK Tidl. „Økologisk Landsbysamfund“ | Hågendrupvej 6, Torup | 3390 Hundested

+45-(0) 47 98 86 57 -7046

oekosamfundet.dyssekilde@worldonline.dk www.torup-by.dk

RIVE - Rete Italiana dei Villaggi Ecologici

The vision:

We envision a world of complete transparency, trust and harmony. A world of communities which care for the world and its people and who know how to share with one another. For in the embrace of various cultures, the creative act harmonises with the earth and gives breath to our voices – as if they were cells in this great organism which naturally respects every form of life.

The task:

The Network of Italian Ecovillages – RIVE – believes that the existing experiments of a communal life are genuine and adequate experimental laboratories for social issues and the development of a better world. RIVE

- recognises social justice as the foundation of its own actions. This justice is founded on spiritual, economic and ecological harmony

- promotes the propagation of experiences made by existing communities and ecovillages and supports projects in the founding stage

- supports and co-operates with everything and everyone who stands up for a culture of peace, mutual recognition, respect for variety and solidarity

Rete Italiana dei Villagi Ecologici - RIVE

I c/o AAm Terra Nuova | Via Ponte di Mezzo 1 | 50127 Firenze

+39-055 321 57-29 -29 redazione@aamterranuova.it

→Associazione Archeus (I)

Associazione Basilico

I c/o Marilia Zappalà | Via dell'Agnolo 64 | 50122 Firenze

+39-0552-41522 marizap@supereva.it

→Associazione Culturale Torri Superiore (I)

→Az. Agr. Acquasanta (I)

→Comunella Casagatti (I)

→Comunità Coop. Villaggio Verde (I)

Ecovillaggio Crespina
I Val di Sonzi | 56042 Crespina (PI)
☎+39-05086852 ✉LisabettaMatteucci@virgilio.it

→Il Popolo Elfico della Valle dei Burroni (I)

→Inspira (I)

→La Comune di Bagnaia (I)

Mogliazze
I Loc. Mogliazze | 29022 Bobbio (PC)
☎+39-0523-936633 ✉mogliazze@libero.it 💻www.mogliazze.it

→Upacchi Ecovillaggio (I)

→Utopiaggia (I)

V.E.S.. – Villaggio Ecologico e Solidale
I Via S. Bartolomeo di Caifa 34 | 61034 Fossombrone (PU)
☎+39-0721726008 ✉ecosolidale@tiscali.it 💻www.sostenibile.org

→Villaggio Ecologico Solidale (I)

Soshona Freundeskreis

We Soshonas are an open circle of friends, currently around fifty people in the greater Frankfurt/Main area. Our concern is to provide a trusting framework for (among other things) encounter, exchange and experiences regarding the following themes: love, friendship, community, spirituality, healing, children and personal development.

Our group meetings, which we have been conducting regularly since 1997, attract around fifteen to twenty-five people. A team of around six persons, which assembles twice a year, prepares the framework for our fourteen-day meetings. Aside from the group meetings, work groups come together regularly, e.g. organising women's, men's or partnership groups centring on relationship issues.

By the end of 2003, our circle gave rise to two community projects. Two further ones are currently being developed. In the summertime we organise our own summer camp or take part in other camps which we set up together with other communities in the Southwest. We celebrate the seasonal holidays with campfires and rituals, and at New Year's we meet with friends from the network for community days in our region. Come visit us! Interested persons are heartily welcome!

Soshona

D **c/o Heiko Kußman | Hauptstraße 7 | 63165 Mühlheim a.M.**
☎+49-(0)6108-795703 ✉heiko.kussmann@bahn.de
💻www.soshona.de

→Casa Soluna (D)

→Projektzentrum Maibacher Schweiz (D)

The Family

is an international network of independent Christian missionary communities. We have over 1,350 Family Communities in 88 countries on 6 continents with 91 different nationalities. We believe that the Bible is the given Word of God, that Jesus Christ is his only son, born of the Virgin Mary, and that through His death Christ brought humankind salvation. A further foundation of our faith is that we belong to the generation which will experience the visible return of Christ to earth, and that before His return a powerful world government will arise which will be led by a maniacal dictator, known as the Antichrist.

The most important goals of The Family are to share with others the life giving message of love, hope, and salvation which is to be found in the Bible, and to be a living example of the love which we preach. The Family takes active part in humanistic relief work in many countries of the world, as well as in support work in regions struck by natural catastrophes. We not only provide relief through material assistance, but also through the loving care and encouragement of the victims. We also try to ensure that each of our children enjoys an education pleasing to God, in the best possible environment we can provide.

The Family International

UK **European Family Information Department | Office 11, Whitehill House, 6 Union Street | LU13AN Luton, Beds**
☎+44-(0)15820-450493 📠+44-(0)1582-400166
✉info@thefamilyeurope.org
💻www.thefamilyeurope.org | www.thefamily.org

Vereniging Ecodorp

It is often said that in the Netherlands everything is "so well-organised". That is simply a question of securing enough air to breath, or else keeping from drowning in a country where most people live below sea level. However, until recently this did not look like an environment conducive to the development of ecovillages. To build an ecovillage in the Netherlands you not only need the consent of the people who want to live in it. You also need the consent of society and – even harder – that of the institutions responsible for that sort of thing. But times are changing, and we are increasingly receiving support and understanding for the goals which we hope to achieve.

By "we" we mean the "Vereniging Ecodorp", an association with more than 400 members who are endeavouring to establish ecovillages in the Netherlands. Vereniging Ecodorp was created in 1999 by a small group of people who are deeply rooted in alternative ways of living and working (Hobbitstee, Waterman, Memo, Osho Friends). In 2003 the first large project was realised: Het Carré, near the historic town of Delft. Ecodorp can be viewed as a Dutch movement aimed at developing various projects where spirituality, ecology and a sense of community are placed (back?) into the centre of our lives. Other projects are on the way.

We envision a Dutch path of development, founding ecovillages between our "polders". This is occurring in close co-operation with the established institutions, which are increasingly understanding the indispensable nature of what we are creating. Today it is becoming more and more obvious that ecovillages are not just an alternative but the only path toward a sustainable future.

Vereniging Ecodorp

NL Postbus 932 | 3160 AC Rhoon
☎+31-(0)10-4723242 🖷+31-(0)10-4723242 🖂info@ecodorp.nl
💻www.ecodorp.nl

Roderholdtshof

D Schaarweg 28 | 47533 Kleve-Warbeijen
☎+49-(0)2821-980248

Ecodorp Het Carré

NL PO box 932 | 3160 AC Rhoon
☎+31-(0)10-4723242 🖷+31(0)10-4723242 🖂info@ecodorp.nl
💻http://carre.ecodorp.nl/

→Vlierhof (NL)

Useful addresses

In this appendix you will find addresses of institutions, organisations, individual persons and networks which we consider pertinent to the topic of "living in community" and which could be of use for the development of communal and alternative lifestyles. The descriptions either come from the persons and groups themselves or else we have developed them with the help of the information available to us.

The addresses have been listed alphabetically according to country and name. Explanations of the symbols and abbreviations used here can be found at the end of the book. Except for the country signature, the addresses are listed the way they would appear on an envelope, whereby a vertical beam (|) indicates the start of a new line. Please don't forget to include the country's name at the bottom of the address.

If you cannot find the term you are looking for, please refer to the **index**.

Austria

BioVegaN

A Biologisch-Veganes Netzwerk für Garten- und Landbau | Altenmarkt 95 | 8333 Riegersburg

☎ +43 (0)676-9221433 📠 +43 (0)676-9221434

✉ dialog@biovegan.org 💻 www.biovegan.org

Permakultur Austria

A Sapphogasse 20/1 | 1100 Wien

☎ +43-(0)1-9138313 📠 -9138313 ✉ buero@permakultur.net

Denmark

Den Almenyttige Andelskasse Merkur

DK Vejgårdmøllevej 3, Postboks 2036 | 8000 Ålborg

☎ +45-981018-35 📠 -53 ✉ merkurbank@merkurbank.dk

A bank which among other things supports alternative projects

WWOOF-Dänemark: Willing Workers On Organic Farms

DK VHH-Denmark | Asenvej 35 | 9881 Bindslev

☎ +45-98-938607 ✉ info@wwoof.dk 💻 http://www.wwoof.dk/

We publish a list of (mostly Danish) organic farms offering working guests free room and board.

France

Alliance Vert

F Andrea Dickewied | 32420 Simorre

I can offer myself as an information clearing house and help arrange internships on organic farms. Sometimes people are needed for construction projects or housekeeping. I am planning to set up an Internet forum where people can exchange information and also see for themselves who's looking for whom for what.

Éditions du Fraysse

F Les Immosines | 82230 Monclar de Quercy

☎ +33-(0)05 6330-3355 📠 -3439 ✉ lecuyer.philippe@wanadoo.fr

Éditions du Fraysse is a publishing house for books on ecology and health which are printed on recycled paper.

Passerelles Eco

F 42, rue du Faubourg-Figuerolles | 34070 Montpellier

☎ +33-(0)467065279 💻 www.passerelleco.info

Association, journal and network with the goal of gathering ecological practises and new lifestyles, and developing a new and respectful relationship towards our planet and its inhabitants.

Germany

Allmende e.V.

D Verein für Zusammenkunft und Gemeinschaft | Am See 1 | 17440 Klein Jasedow

☎ +49-(0)38374-75255 📠 -75223 ✉ info@allmende-ev.de
💻 www.allmende-ev.de

The association supports communities in their founding phase by (among other things) providing them with land which it has bought out. The association's members pay a monthly fee of 5 to 15 Euros, which the Allmende people think everyone can afford, to help improve the world. This money and other donations finance the buyout. The association is also active in the field of permaculture.

Anstiftung GmbH

D Daiserstr. 15 Rgb. | 81371 München

☎ +49-(0)89-747460-0 📠-30 ✉info@anstiftung.de

💻www.anstiftung.de

„We develop, test and spread ideas and projects in the areas of independent work, self-sufficiency and health."

Auroville International Deutschland e.V.

D Solmsstrasse 6 | 10961 Berlin

☎ +49-(0)30-42 80 31 50 📠-92 09 13 76 ✉info@auroville.de

💻www.auroville.de

World-wide network of the large, international, eco-spiritual Auroville settlement in India. Further contact info for Europe under www.auroville-international.org

Bruderschaft Salem GmbH

D Christliches gemeinnütziges Hilfswerk | Salem-Lindenhof | 95346 Stadtsteinach

☎ +49-(0)9225-809-0 📠-8161 ✉info@lindenhofsalem.de

💻www.saleminternational.org

The Salem-Friedenswerk supports children's and youth villages, organic guest houses and spa clinics the world over.

Bundesverband der freien Alternativschulen

D Wermelhauserstraße 270 | 44779 Bochum

☎ +49-(0)2356-2955170

Federation of Free Schools in Germany

BVN

D Bio-Veganes Netzwerk | Sieben Linden 1 | 38486 Poppau

☎ +49-(0)39000-90621 📠-51232 ✉biovegan@web.de

BVN, the German contact of the international Vegan Organic Networks (VON), is committed to the development and spread of ethical and ecological alternatives to animal exploitation in farming.

co:büro - Büro für Kooperation

D c/o Thomas Kalka | Nansenstr. 7 | 14471 Postdam

☎ +49-(0)331 - 5505795 📠-78714547 ✉post@co-buero.de

💻www.co-buero.de

The (o:büro supports projects and individuals through project consultation, support, and training in the fields of: new and efficient technologies; information systems (IT infrastructure, telephone); database publishing; Internet publishing. Software development in the fields of: co-operation support software; knowledge management. Technological and structural development in the field of co-operative economics.

Das Verden-Projekt

D Ökozentrum | Artilleriestr. 6 | 27283 Verden/Aller
☎ +49-(0)4231 957-590 Fax -400 ✉ buero@oekozentrum.org
www.oekozentrum.org; www.verbunt-netzwerk.de

In and around the small town of Verden/Aller near Bremen a network of self-administered, ecological businesses, residential projects and initiatives is emerging. This network includes a biological building materials store and workshops, gastronomy, a conference centre, ballet studio, environmental institute, vegetable subscription service, children's group, residential co-op, ecological architectural office, consultancy for small businesses, the Allmende permaculture project and offices for political campaigns. Its global activities include the movement foundation, Attac, the "Articulation" cultural project as well as ÖkologieGlobal. Most of these institutions have their headquarters in the Ökozentrum. Over the past two years we have renovated the Ökozentrum in an exemplary fashion following the most state-of-the art ecological principles. We share the idea of a self-administered, democratic economy, emphasising both ecology and social goals. We want to start living a future-oriented lifestyle today. For many of us, political involvement and lived alternatives are one and the same. We have a variety of plans for expansion: more people with concrete plans are sincerely welcome.

Forum Zukunft

D Helen Bathrellos | Papenschlade 13 | 57413 Finnentrop
☎ +49-(0)2395/212917 ✉ HelenB@gmx.de

Günther Wieland, a qualified psychologist, and Helen Bathrellos, a non-traditional practitioner (psychotherapy), conduct depth-psychology oriented group work and supervision for ecological and socio-innovative communities.

Gemeinschaftsberatung Tonio Keller

D ☎ +49-(0)4531-896475 ✉ tonio58@gmx.de

Offers community consultation and the seminar „Four Principles of Community Formation"; published the book „Gemeinschaft - ein Traum auf dem Prüfstand" („Community - a Dream Put to the Test") together with Holger Seyer. (Also see article on community formation in the front section of the book)

GLS Gemeinschaftsbank eG

D Oskar-Hoffmann-Str. 25 | 44789 Bochum
☎ +49-(0)234-5797-0 Fax -133 ✉ info@gemeinschaftsbank.de
www.gls-bank.de

Community bank for loans and gifts. The first ethical-ecological bank in Germany. The focus of its activity is on the financing of social, cultural and ecological projects.

Hand in Hand

D eurotopia-Gemeinschaftsberatungen | c/o Ökodorf Sieben Linden | 38486 Poppau

☎ +49-(0)39000-90866 or -905918 Fax -51232

✉ handinhand@siebenlinden.de

💻 www.gemeinschaftsberatung.de

First-hand community experience, tools for community development , supporting one's own path by residents of the Ecovillage Sieben Linden. Events and lectures, consultation and supervision, seminars and workshops, travels to communities (see advertisement on p. 413).

ijgd - Internationaler Jugendgemeinschaftsdienst e. V. -

D Bundesverein | Kasernenstr. 48 | 53111 Bonn

☎ +49-(0)228-2280011,-12, -13 Fax -2280010

✉ intern.workcamp.exchange@ijgd.de 💻 www.ijgd.de

Organises international c. 3-week work camps at home and abroad for youth groups made up of 15 volunteers (16-30 years) with the goal of international understanding through encounters in everyday situations.

Komm-Rat

D Beratungsgruppe in der Kommune Niederkaufungen | Kirchweg 1 | 34260 Kaufungen

☎ +49-(0)5605-80070 Fax -800740

✉ info@kommune-niederkaufungen.de (subject: Komm-Rat)

We offer competent project consultation for beginning or already existing groups. We can draw on our long-term community experience. The focal points of our consultation are: legal forms, finances, building, work, organising everyday life, pension schemes, group dynamics, non-violent communication. Depending on needs and issues, we provide support through supervision, moderation and future workshops.

KURVE Wustrow

D Kirchstr. 14 | 29462 Wustrow

☎ +49-(0)5843-9871-0 Fax -11 ✉ info@kurvewustrow.org

💻 www.kurvewustrow.org

The focal points of our peace work are: educational work, including the preparation of trainers in non-violent conflict resolution; anti-racism seminars; sending peace experts into the world's crisis regions, as well as the organisation and supervision of a voluntary year in many countries.

Lebensform Gemeinschaft

D Marita Bergmann & Heidi Gehring | Pappelweg 3 | 19217 Carlow
☎ +49-(0)38873-20969 /-20770 ℻ -20948
✉ b-g-seminare@t-online.de

Provides identification, consultancy, guidance and training for persons seeking communities, for groups in the founding process and for existing communities in the form of seminars and supervision (see article „How to begin – and what then?" on p. 50).

Netzwerk Selbsthilfe e.V.

D Netzwerkbüro | Leonrodstr.19 / Werkhaus III.Stock | 80634 München
☎ +49-(0)89-168116

An association for the promotion of self-administered projects and political, cultural and social initiatives. They distribute subsidies and loans.

Offene Häuser

D Kastanienallee 77 | 10435 Berlin
☎ +49-(0)44045411 / -0172 7746913 ℻ -85 11 17
✉ info@openhouses.de 🖳 www.openhouses.de

Offene Häuser provides hostels for pilgrims and backpackers in seven places, along with art projects, craftsman weeks and work camps. Active participation is welcome, but please call first.

Ökodorf-Institut für Wohnprojekte

D Im Wiesengrund 2 | 79691 Neuenweg
☎ +49-(0)7673-887886 ℻ please ask
✉ oekodorf@gemeinschaften.de 🖳 www.gemeinschaften.de

Providing support for community search/foundation since 1980: address exchange (over 25,000 contacts), interspiritual Ecovillage Festivals (encounters with communities, founding initiatives & interested persons), e-mail newsletters to some 3,000 persons interested in the community movement, media (mail-order books, videos, CDs, games...), real estate information. Consultations and seminars are also offered with co-operation partners in other parts of Germany and neighbouring countries. Request complete info with stamped self-addressed envelope (2 Euros) or order via e-mail.

Osterberg Institut

D Karl Kübel Stiftung für Familie und Kind | Am Hang | 24306 Niederkleveez
☎ +49-(0)4523-99290

Seminars on community building and social competence.

Permakultur Akademie

D Birkenallee 35 | 26197 Huntlosen
☎ +49-(0)4487-99969-0 ℻ -1 ✉ info@pk-akademie.de
🖳 www.permakultur-akademie.de

Courses and training for permaculture (designing self-sufficiency systems, communities etc.).

Politischer Salon - Netzwerkbüro ZEGG

D Ina Meyer-Stoll, Sarah Vollmer | Rosa Luxemburg Str. 89 | 14806 Belzig

☎+49-(0)33841-595-30 /-22 📠-12

Consultation, supervision and communication training (especially forum courses) for emerging and existing communities. Organisation of the International Community Meeting, networking young people in communities.

Schlafbuch der Erdenbürger

D Übernachtungsverzeichnis auf Gegenseitigkeit | Postfach 1110 | 14801 Belzig

☎+49-(0)33841-380371 📠-380377 ✉schlafbuch@web.de

💻www.schlafbuch.de

A Schlafbuch („sleep book") is a collection of addresses of hospitable people who are happy to provide other people with free or inexpensive (modest) accommodation for a few days.

SCI (Service Civil International)

D Blücherstr. 14 | 53115 Bonn

☎+49-(0)228-212086 📠-264234

Organises international work camps, some of them in communities.

Solvitur ambulando

D c/o Eva Scharnweber | Elsternweg 19 | 21423 Winsen an der Luhe

☎+49 (0)4171-690870

Eco-community on a pilgrimmage. Each year we put together a new group of participants.

Stiftung Mitarbeit

D Bornheimer Str.37 | 53111 Bonn

☎+49-(0)228-604240 📠-6042422 ✉info@mitarbeit.de

💻www.mitarbeit.de

Promotes democratic development from below, self-help activities

Stiftung TRIAS

D Gemeinnützige Stiftung für Boden - Ökologie - Wohnen | Postach 10 21 74 | 44721 Bochum

☎+49-(0)2324-9022213 📠-596705 ✉info@stiftung-trias.de

💻www.stiftung-trias.de

The Trias Foundation promotes initiatives concerning challenges to our treatment of the land and property, ecological behaviour and new lifestyles. It realises its goals in conjunction with co-operation partners within the framework of non-profit goals.

TAK AÖ - Theoriearbeitskreis für Alternative Ökonomie

D c/o Burghard Flieger | Erwinstr.29 | 79102 Freiburg

☎+49-(0)761-709023 📠-709084

Informal structure of persons interested in alternative economic forms, who meet quarterly and publish a circular.

Wuppertal Institut

D Postfach 100480 | 42004 Wuppertal

☎+49-(0)202-24920 📠-2492108 ✉info@wupperinst.org

💻www.wupperinst.org/Gutes_Leben

"Images of a good life": practised model projects for a life which is compatible with nature and society and also good.

WWOOF-Deutschland: freiwillige Helfer auf ökologischen Höfen e.V.

D Postfach 210259 | 01263 Dresden

✉info@wwoof.de 💻www.wwoof.de

WWOOF Germany provides its members with a list of organic farms offering free room and board in exchange for work. Application via e-mail / WWW

Great Britain/Northern Ireland

Anglican Religious Communities Year Book

UK c/o The Editor | ARCYB, Hilfield | Dorchester, Dorset DT2 7BE

☎+44-(0)1300-341345

Diggers & Dreamers

UK c/o Edge of Time Ltd. | BCM Edge | London WC1N 3XX

☎+44-(0)7000-780536 📠+44-(0)870-163 4661

✉info@diggersanddreamers.org.uk 💻www.diggersanddreamers.org.uk

Directory of English communities

FWBO - Friends of the Western Buddhist Order

UK London buddhist centre | 51 Roman Road | London E2 0HU

☎+44-(0)845 458 4716 📠-(0)20 8980 1960 ✉info@lbc.org.uk

💻www.lbc.org.uk

The Friends of the Western Buddhist Order are a world-wide Buddhist movement dedicated to the goal of expressing the essential truths of the Buddhist tradition in forms which correspond to the modern world. The FWBO teaches meditation and Buddhism in 20 countries.

ISEC - International Society for Ecology and Culture

UK incorporating The Ladakh Project | Apple Barn, Week, Dartington | Devon TQ9 6JP

☎+44-(0)1803-868-650 🖷-651 🖂isecuk@gn.apc.org

💻www.isec.org.uk

ISEC pursues two principle goals: Challenging economic globalisation and current notions of progress, as well as promoting the local initiatives within which communities are supported and the natural environment is restored.

PeopleFinder

UK Ecovillage Network UK | P.O. Box 1410 | Bristol BS99 3JP

☎+44-(0)117 373 0346 🖂office@evnuk.org.uk

💻http://evnuk.ecovillage.org/index.htm, www.evnuk.org.uk

Group of volunteers serving some of the basic networking needs of UK ecovillages. We are regularly asked to help individuals find suitable ecovillage projects, both existing and embryonic.

Permaculture Association

UK BCM Permaculture Association | London WC1N 3XX

☎+44-(0)113 2307461, -(0)845 4581805 🖷+44-(0)113 2307461, -(0)845 4581805 🖂office@permaculture.org.uk

💻www.permaculture.org.uk

The Permaculture Association supports people and projects through training, networking and research according to the ethics and principles of permaculture. They are publishing a directory of European PC projects in the internet (summer 2000).

Permanent Publications

UK Hyden House Ltd. | The Sustainability Centre | GU32 1HR East Meon, Hampshire

☎+44-(0)1730-82331, (0)845-4584150 🖷-823322

🖂enquiries@permaculture.co.uk 💻www.permaculture.co.uk

Permanent Publications, Publishers of Permaculture magazine - Solutions for Sustainable Living, published quarterly: incorporating Global Ecovillage Network News and Bulletin Board; and The Earth Repair Catalogue containing over 450 specially selected books, journals, videos, music CDs and products covering many aspects of sustainable living.

Radical Routes (General Enquiries)

UK Cornerstone Housing Coop | 16 Sholebroke Avenue | Chapeltown, Leeds LS7 2HB

☎+44-(0)113-2629365 ✉info@radicalroutes.org.uk
🖳www.radicalroutes.org.uk

A network of housing co-ops in Great Britain; publishes a directory.

The neighbourhood Initiatives Foundation

UK The Poplars | Lightmoore | Telford TF4 QN
☎+44-(0)1952-590777

Helping grassroots groups all over the world to develop their neighbourhoods together – the "planning for real" simple planning method.

VOT — Vegan Organic Trust

UK Vegan Organic Trust | 161 Hamilton Road, Longsight | Manchester M13 0PQ
☎+44-(0)161-248 9224 ✉veganorganic@riseup.net
🖳www.veganorganic.net

VOT exists to promote a system of farming that is organic, does not use animal inputs (such as blood, bones and manure), and so is free of violence and killing. We publish a journal and seek to educate people in vegan organic methods

WWOOF-International

UK PO Box 2675 | Lewes BN7 1RB
🖳www.wwoof.org

Finds jobs on organic farms the world over for room and board (charges a fee). Infos at website.

Greece

New Humanity Centre

GR Eleonon Road | 24100 Akroyali Avias / Kalamata
☎+30-(0)21-58172 📠-58035

A humanistic and cultural non-profit organisation which provides services for the well-being of international guests. There is a guest house with a cultural centre, a holistic-philosophical library, a spiritual retreat centre and much more.

Israel

International Communes Desk

IL Kibbutz Tzora | 99803 D. N. Shimshon
✉solrene@tzora.co.il 🖳www.communa.org.il

Contact office between communes, kibbutzim, co-housing, ecovillages and other intentional communities. We produce a biannual journal, CALL (Communities At Large Letter), and have an English/Hebrew website: www.communa.org.il

Italy

AAM Terra Nuova

I CP 199 | 50032 Borgo S. Lorenzo

☎ +39-55-3215729 ✉ redazione@aamterranuova.it

Network journal of the Italian community project network (RIVE).

Libera Universitá di Medicina Naturale - LUMEN

I Via Polignano 5 | 29010 San Pietro in Cerro

☎ +39-0523-83 81 72 Fax -83 81 89

Netherlands

EYFA: European Youth For(est) Action

NL Postbus 94115 | 1056 RK Amsterdam

☎ +31-(0)20-6657743 Fax -6657743

Organises "Ecotopia", the annual meeting of "alternative" European young people; co-ordination centre of the leftist-alternative European youth scene; publish "The Verge" magazine.

Solidair Association

NL Lauwerecht 55 | 3515 GN Utrecht

☎ +31-(0)30 276 09 30 Fax +31 (0)30 272 15 32

✉ info@solidair.nl 💻 www.solidair.nl

Movement for co-operation and solidarity.

The Dutch organization is a movement for everyone who is looking for an answer to the madness of the market economy and the destructive effects of economic growth.

VAKgroep

NL Federatie Verenigde Arbeids Kollektieven | Lauwerecht 55 | 3515 GN Utrecht

☎ +31-(0)30-2721660 ✉ amf@xs4all.nl

An association of small firms, volunteer projects and house collectives.

Vereniging voor Ecologics Wonen

NL Nyensteinheerd 69 | 9736 TE Groningen

☎ +31-(0)50-412643

Poland

Wydawnictwo „Zielone Brygady"

PL Slawkowska 12/24 | 31-014 Krakow

☎ +48-(0)12-4222147 ✉ zb@zb.most.org.pl 💻 www.most.org.pl/zb

The magazine "Green Brigades" has appeared 127 times since 1998. It is a networking and information pamphlet which is published by a volunteer staff. It deals with topics such as environmentalism, animal rights, vegetarianism, wild animal conservation, healthy living etc. and promotes an intellectual exchange transcending political, religious and philosophical boundaries. It also publishes special issues on these topics.

Spain

Selba Vida sostenible - Red Ibérica de Ecoaldeas

E Artosilla | 22600 Sabiñánigo (Huesca)

✉ info@selba.org 💻 www.selba.org

Seeks to spread the ecovillage concept and to promote the organisation of discussions, courses and meetings in connection with this idea. Clearing house for documentation, research and useful addresses (see website!). Upon request we will send you our monthly e-magazine on ecovillages, conflict guidance and resolution, solidarity-based economies, child-raising, ecological building...

Switzerland

Bioversität (Ursus Schwarz)

CH c/o Namaste-Stiftung für inneren und äusseren Frieden | Postfach 302 | 8260 Stein am Rhein

☎ +41-(0)-52 741 44 39 oder -741 17 47 📠 -52 741 56 12

✉ uur@gmx.ch; info@namaste.ch 💻 www.spiritofnature.ch

It is an initiative for comprehensive bio-teaching, a training programme for theory and praxis in holistic culture, community and a future-compatible lifestyle: bio-house, gardening and farming, permaculture, renewable energy, adapted technology, natural therapy, environmental and socially compatible economics/ finances, social consciousness, art, development, handicrafts, teamwork and communty, self-administration and survival strategies and back-to-nature potential. We are looking for people and places to help in the practical implementation in Europe or to take part in our pilot project in New Zealand. See website.

Holon

CH c/o Dynamik 5 | Postfach 7965 | 3001 Bern

☎ +41 (0)31 398 80 52 📠 +41 (0)31 398 80 51

✉ info@holon.ch, holon_ffm@yahoo.de 💻 http://www.holon.ch

A political-spiritual network of various initiatives, organisations and communities for the development of a European movement. Developed out of Beaulieu.

IARD International Association for Rural Development

CH Postfach 226 | 3414 Oberburg

Address network for dropouts and emigrants.

Reiche Dörfer

CH FairWork GmbH | Postfach 9510 | 8036 Zürich

☎ +41-(0)793766336 ✉ info@fairwork.ch 💻 www.reiche-doerfer.ch

Consultation, networking and locating experts for community projects: general problems in the founding and development phase, business and legal forms, team development, entry/exit, decision-making structures, hierarchies and conflicts, economics etc.

Talent

CH Postfach | 5001 Aarau

☎ +41-(0)62-8228486 ✉ info@talent.ch 💻 www.talent.ch

Alternative barter systems. Seize the opportunity to satisfy your (basic) needs through your own talents!

Zentrum Waldegg

CH Schitzwald | 3832 Wengen

☎ +41-(0)33855-4422 📠 -5068

International course and community centre.

United States

FEC: Federation of Egalitarian Communities

US HCR BOX 3370 | MO 65760 Tecumseh

☎ +1-(0)417-679-4682

North American commune network

Fellowship for Intentional Community (FIC)

US RR 1 Box 155-W | 63563-9720 Ruthledge MO

☎ +1-(0)660-883-5545 📠 -5545 ✉ fic@ic.org, newsletter@ic.org
💻 www.fic.org

Network of American communities and communes – the FIC publishes the voluminous Communities Directory with a North American and international section, and is an important institution for international community information.

Recommended reading list

This bibliography contains books which in our opinion have a direct bearing on the topic of living in community. Many of them have been written by community-members. We have added some annotations to the listing of the titles to give you some more information about their contents. We would like to thank the Fellowship for Intentional Communities for supporting us with their list of recommended books in English.

This list isn't complete, so if you know of other titles, please let us know. The most actual and manifold resource for further information is the Internet.

Some of the recommended books are no longer available in book shops, unless – with a bit of luck – you can find them in a used book store or in libraries (Internet).

Addresses for ordering some of the books:

* this book can be ordered through GEN International Secretariat: gen@gaia.org

** this book can be ordered through LØS, The Danish Association for Sustainable Communities, Landsbyvænget 10, 8464 Galten, Dänemark (see also Index)

This bibliography is organised according to the following categories:

- **Indexes of Communities & Ecovillages**
- **Other Alternative Indexes**
- **Communities & Ecovillages in the Past and Present**
- **Individual Communities and Their Publications**
- **Sustainability & Ecology**
- **Alternative Lifestyles & Movements in General**
- **Studying and Building Community**
- **Women in Community**
- **Decision Making**
- **Alternative Economics**

Indexes of Communities & Ecovillages

Anglican Religious Communities Year Book. c/o The Editor, ARCYB, Hilfield, DT2 7EB Dorchester, Dorset, Great Britain, Tel: +44-(0)1300-341345

Diggers & Dreamers 2004/5. The Guide to co-operative Living.

Edge of Time | BCM Edge | WC1 N3XX London | Great Britain
e-mail: edgeoftime@compuserve.com *Thorough overview of community scene in Great Britain; a real pocket-book for even the smallest pockets!*

eurotopia - Directory of Intentional Communities and Ecovillages in Europe (edition 2000/2001). Ökodorf Sieben Linden 2000; ISBN 3-00-007080-X; Euro 16,80 (only some copies left) *Former edition to the present 2005 edition with descriptions of about 150 communities that are not listed this time (mainly because they didn't respond to the research in the years 2004/2005).*

Fellowship for Intentional Community: **Communities Directory - A guide to Cooperative Living.** Fellowship for Intentional Community, Rutlegde, Missouri 2000; ISBN 0 9602714 4 9. The book costs US$ 34.00 ($42 overseas) with discounts available at our website, the video/DVD costs $33.00 ($38 overseas) available in NTSC/PAL format. *Thorough review of the community scene in the USA; descriptions and addresses of over 500 projects; including up to date (2000) information about: over 500 North American intentional communities, more than 50 communities on other continents and over 250 alternative resources and services; also 31 articles about community living. The book is supplemented by the video "Visions of Utopia", an over two hour long documentary including reports on 9 different communities.*

Greenaway, McMurray & Colyer: **Utopianz** - A guide to Intentional Communities and communal Living in Aotearoa New Zealand. 77 pages; Christchurch 2004; 20 NZ-Dollars, order at: The Straw Umbrella Trust | Po Box 33208 Barrington | Otautahi / Christchurch | Aotearoa / New Zealand. *Illustrated directory with descriptions about 30 communities in NZ with maps, some articles about the subject and some additional information.*

Kennedy & Grindheim: **Directory of Eco-Villages in Europe**. Publisher: GEN Europe; ISBN 3 9802184 3 0; Steyerberg 1998. (Thorough description of 57 ecovillage projects) *For eco-villagers to get to know each other and to exchange with existing and new projects within the Global Ecovillage Network (GEN) - Europe. The first directory that was published by GEN; not reprinted and up-dated since then.*

LØS: "**Økosamfund i Danmark**" (Ecovillages in Denmark), Danish, costs dkr. 20.- ($4.00)+ postage**

LØS: **Velkommen til fremtiden: Baeredygtige Bosaetninger i Danmark.** Published by Forlaget Modtryk; in Danish; 1998; ISBN 87 7394 539-0; Dkr. 148.- + postage** *Sustainable settlements in Denmark*

NACCAN: **Index of British Christian Communities.** Community House | Eton Road | NP19 0BL Newport | Great Britain; Tel: +44-(0)1633-265468

Nolte, Wolfram & Co.: **eurotopia 97/98**. Leben in Gemeinschaft. 365 Adressen und Beschreibungen von europäischen Gemeinschaften. ISBN 3-00-001311-3; in German; still available for Euro 3.50 plus postage as long as supplies last at Ökodorf Buchversand *The first edition of the eurotopia-directory, only available in German.*

Olivares, Manuel: **Comuni, Comunità ed ecovillaggi in Italia.** In Italian/Italiano ! 132 pages; Edizioni Malatempora, Rome 2003. *Descriptions of several communities and ecovillages made by the author and partially the communities themselves; detailed articles on the history of the anarchistic and communitiarian movement; no table of contents, no index.*

Other Alternative Indexes

Permaculture Association Britain: **Permaculture directory.** BCM Permaculture Association Britain | UK-WC1N 3XX London | Great Britain; e-mail: directory@permaculture.org.uk, Website: www.permaculture.org.uk

Schindler: **Klosterführer.** 2004; Euro 15,70 *German descriptions of 270 spiritual centres of various religions in D, A, CH.*

Vida alternativa en España. Spanish descriptions of 52 alternative projects in Spain. Send EUR 5,- as banknote to
Monika Frank | Venta Remedios | E-29461 Faraján/Málaga | Spain

Communities & Ecovillages in the Past and Present

Boice, Judith L.: **At one with all live: A personal journey in Gaian communities**. Findhorn Press 1990 *In this work the author shares travels to the Bear tribe, to Findhorn in Scotland, to Auroville in India and to the Australian desert in search of Earth-centered leaderless groups.*

Dare, Phillip N.: **American Communes to 1860: A Bibliography** (Bibliographies on Sects and Cults in America Series, Vol. 12). Garland Publishing 1990 *Nearly 50 collective settlements are represented in this bibliography by the nearly 2,000 references to articles, dissertations, monographs, bibliographs, and to primary archival material if accessible.*

Jackson, Hildur & Svensson, Karen: **Ecovillage Living - Restoring the Earth and Her People**. Green Books; Devon, UK 2002 *The editors collected a rainbow of articles written by people living in ecovillages all over the world. These articles comprise authentic information about many different aspects of living in ecovillages, illustrated with hundreds of colourful pictures showing people that live it!*

Kozeny, Geoph: **Utopia 101: Intentional Communities ... the Cooperative Quest to Build a Better World**. Video, Community Catalyst Project 2000. *Geoph Kozeny hast spent nearly three yeras creating this documentary about intentional communities. Now you can see how 18 communities look „up close", while you listen to community members, in their own words, tell stories about their communities, including their candid thoughts on what has worked and what hasn't.*

Metcalf, Bill: **Shared Visions, Shared Lives: Communal Living around the Globe.** Findhorn Press 1996; ISBN 1 899171 01 0* *16 stories of long-term residents of communities around the world, who on average have lived 30 years in communities. Bill Metcalf is an Australian historian and sociologist.*

Metcalf, Bill: **From Utopian Dreaming to communal Reality: Co-operative lifestyles in Australia.** University of new South Wales Press, Sydney 1995

Miller, Timothy: **American Communes, 1860-1960: A Bibliography** (Sects and Cults in America Bibliographical Guides, Vol. 13). Garland Publishing 1990 *Books, articles, theses, dissertations and some manuscripts are covered in this book on communes after 1860, including later communes that are the direct offspring of their predecessors.*

Morgan, Griscom (editor): **Guidebook for Intentional Communities**. 44 p, Editor 1988. *Revised from "An Intentional Community Handbook" this is a wonderfully eclectic collection of essays and personal observations on community life.*

Pepper, David: **Communes and the Green Vision.** 1991 *Counterculture, Lifestyle and the New Age. A comprehensive description of 12 communes in Great Britain.*

Sam O'Brien (producer/director), Video: **Findhorn Foundation: Straight From the Heart.** Sam and Assoc. Production 1995; *Through the voices and images of its people, captured on film, the story of building community is told: working with people, education, ecological building, environmental work, global networking, and infusing everyday life with spiritual values.*

Claude Whitmyer, editor: **In the Company of Others: Making Community in the Modern World.** Jeremy P. Tarcher, Inc. 1993; *A collection of some of the best articles and stories on community from the past 50 years, these essays offer practical advice about communication, authority, and decision making, and profile successful communities of all kinds.*

Benjamin Zablocki: **Joyful Community, The.** Penguin Books Inc. 1971; *Zablocki's story of the "Bruderhof", an experiment in Christian communal living, highlights their everyday life and relation to humankind's undying quest for brotherhood.*

Paul Hawken: **Magic of Findhorn. The.** Bantam Books 1975 *This is Hawken's account of the legendary community where he lived for a year: how it began, who lived there at the time, and what it means to the troubled world outside.*

William Edgerton, translator: **Memoirs of Peasant Tolstoyans in Soviet Russia.** Indiana University Press 1993; *Around 1900, rural communities influenced by Leo Tolstoy's ideas on personal and social renewal flourished in Russia and eastern Europe. Eventually Soviet policy forced the communities to move to western Siberia, and as members refused to take part in policies that they disagreed with, most of the adult members were interred in forced labor camps. Much of this material was written in secret and hidden from the authorities.*

Fritz Leonard, Video: **Story of ZEGG, The.** Center for Experimental Cultural Design 1992; *This film is an exploration of the German communtity of ZEGG, a succesful community of 100 people living, working, loving, laughing, and learning together, struggling toward a single goal -- the creation of a world without fear or violence.*

Ron Morrison: **We Build the Road as We Travel.** Essential Book Publishers 1991; *Morrison's book shares the story of the successful Mondragon cooperatives in Spain.*

Individual Communities and Their Publications

Auroville:

The Auroville Adventure. Published by: Auroville Today, Sri Aurobindo Press; Pondicherry, India 1998. *Selections from ten years of "Auroville Today", a monthly journal which provides information about Auroville. Auroville is an emerging international township of over 1500 people from India and 30 other nations, situated in South India. It is based upon the vision of the Mother.*

Damanhur:

Jeff Merrifield: **Damanhur, The real Dream.** Thorsons, an Imprint of harper Collins Publishers; London, 1998; ISBN 0 7225 3496 5 *The story of the extraordinary Italian artistic and spiritual community.*

Hjortshøj:

Eco-village Hjortshøj, danish, costs dkr. 20,- ($4) + postage**

Findhorn:

Alex Walker: **The Kingdom Within - A Guide to the Spiritual Work of the Findhorn Community.** Findhorn Press, 1994; ISBN 0 905249 99 2* *A selection of key ideas about the philosophical background and spiritual beliefs of the Findhorn Community (Scotland), together with important factual information, particularly about the history of the Foundation.*

Riddel, Carol: **The Findhorn Community: Creating a Human Identity for the 21st Century**. 290 pages; Findhorn Press 1991 *Carol has written a chronicle of the past, present and future of one of the world's most renowned "new age" communities.*

The Farm:

Rupert Fike: **Voices from The Farm: Adventures in Community Living**. From 1970 to the present, the Farm (Tennessee, USA). The Book Publishing Co. ISBN 1 57067 051 X

Sustainability & Ecology

Eco Villages & Sustainable Communities: Models for 21st Century Living. Findhorn Press, 1996. ISBN 1-899171 21 5 *Based on the main talks and workshops presented during the Conference "Eco villages and Sustainable Communities" in 1995 at Findhorn*

Kennedy and Kennedy: **Designing Ecological Settlements.** Dietrich Reimer Verlag, Berlin 1998;

ISBN 3 496 02630 8 *Ecological Planning and Building: Experiences in new housing and in the renewal of existing housing quarters in European countries.*

Korten, David: **The Post Corporate World.** Berett Koehler Publishers Inc. 1999, www.kpbooks.com or www.bkpub.com (If you would like to join an e-mail discussion group send information to: Positive Futures Network, P.O. Box 10818, Bainbridge Island. WA 98110, or e-mail: postcorporate@futurenet.org) *This book takes us to the roots of our cultural crises and shows us the way forward: withhold resources from the institutions of capitalism and build community based alternatives for meeting our needs.*

Mayur & Hernandez: **Learning for the New Millennium: Challenges of education for the 21st century.** Essays by a.o. Bertrand Russell, Paolo Freire, E.F. Schumacher, Ivan Illich, Theodore Roszak. International Institute for Sustainable Future and Bgaratiya Vidya Bhavan, Mumbai, India 1997*; *Provides new approaches to learning.*

McLaughlin and Davidson: **Builders of the Dawn: Community Lifestyles in a Changing World** Book Publishing Company Surnmertown, Tennessee 1990; ISBN 0 913990 68 X. *Presents an overview of community lifestyles based on interviews with many community founders. It offers workable guidelines for those interested in building communities.*

Norberg-Hodge, Helena: **Ancient Futures: Learning from Ladakh** Sierra Club Books, San Francisco 1991; ISBN 0 87156 559 5*. *This book raises important questions about the whole notion of progress and explores the root causes of the malaise of industrial society. At the same time, the story of Ladakh serves as a source of inspiration for our own future.*

Pedagogy of the Earth: Education for a sustainable future. Publishers: Bharatiya Vidya Bhavan and International Institute for Sustainable Future; 1999; ISBN 81 87404 00 01* *Ideas and information by some of the finest ecologists, developmentalists, thinkers, scientists, poets and even philosophers from around the world.*

Register and Peeks: **Village Wisdom, Future Cities.** Publishers: Ecocity Builders, Oakland, California. ISBN 0 9655732-0 6 *Represents material from The Third International Ecocity and Ecovillage Conference held in Senegal, 1996. Save the Village, Restore the Earth.*

Trainer, Ted: **Saving the Environment** University of New South Wales 1998; ISBN 0 868406 48 1

Alternative Lifestyles & Movements in General

Ariyaratne: **Collected Works. Volume I VI** Edited by Sarvodaya Shramadana Movement. *Volume IV gives an overview of the philosophical and historical bases and of the programs for the Sarvodaya movement on Sri Lanka, a peace and sustainability movement linking 13,000 villages and now also housing a GEN office.*

McCamant & Durett: **Cohousing, A temporary Approach to Housing Ourselves.** Ten Speed Press 1988, sold through Airlift Books; ISBN: 0-89815-539-8 *The "Bible" of the co-housing movement in Denmark, the USA and world-wide.*

Studying and Building Community

Breton, M.: "We're in Charge" **CoHousing Communities of Older People in the Netherlands: Lessons for Britain?** 88p, Policy Press, Bristol 1998. *A valuable resource for local authorities, coummunity care agencies, community groups, policy makers and academics, this book provides important information for older people thinking about future options.*

Butcher, Allan: **Community Tools: Resources on Communitarian Values and History and for Community Design, Management and Education**. Fourth World Services 1995 *This is a thorough listing of books, articles, conferences, classes and workshops. The author also analyzes and categorizes communities.*

Cohen, L. & Arkin, L.: **Cooperative Housing Compendium: Resources for Collaborative Living.** Co-op Resources and Services Project 1993 *This book covers all the building blocks of putting together a community, be it a small shared living space or an entire ecovillage. Topics include: legal issues, community structure, land development, resources and financing.*

Gilman, B. & D.: **Eco-Villages and Sustainable Communities**. Context Institute 1991. *Offering excellent suggestions for starting new communities, this book is primarily about ecovillages — what they are, why we need them and how to create them.*

Jackson, Hildur: **Creating Harmony: Conflict Resolution in Communities.** Permanent Publications 1999, hello@permaculture.co.uk or: gen@gaia.org ISBN 1 85623 014 7* *An anthology with 25 interesting case studies from ecovillages and GEN members around the world, from a number of leading people on this subject.*

Popenoe, C. & O: **Seeds of Tomorrow: New Age Communities That Work**. 289 p, Harper and Row 1984. *This book surveys and analyzes a range of communities, examining their origins, the principals and beliefs that motivate them, their administrative structures, business and financial resources, as well as obstacles faces and methos for overcoming them.*

Shaffer, C. R. & Anundsen, K.: **Creating Community Anywhere: Finding Support and Connection in a Fragmented World**. Tarcher/Putnam/PerigreeBooks 1993. *The authors explain in this book how to create community spirit without having to move to community, through living, working, playing and sharing together. They discuss how to develop support groups, social clubs, ritual groups, neighbourhood associations, workplace teams and spiritual communities.*

Arche following Jean Vanier, translated by Ann Shearer: **Community and Growth.** *Written by the founder of the L'arche International Federation of communitities, this inspirational Christian work concerns love, healing, service, family and community. It addresses the problem of increasing alienation, isolation, and loneliness in our modern technological world.*

M. Scott Peck: **Different Drum: Community-Making and Peace, The.** Simon and Schuster 1988; *In "The Road Less Traveled", M. Scott Peck took readers on a personal journey of psychological and spiritual development. In "The Different Drum", he takes the next step -- to the larger experience of living and working in community.*

Women in Community

Melford E. Spiro: **Kibbutz, Venture in Utopia.** Harward University Press 1955; *This is an anthropological study of an Israeli kibbutz that raises broad questions about the nature and limits of cooperative societies.*

WomenFutures: **Counting Ourselves In: A Women's Community Economic Development Handbook.** Women Futures 1993; *This is a basic, practical, and encouraging guide for women getting involved in the broad area of community economic development. It includes suggestions for workshops to help women get community economic development projects started, with mostly Canadian resources and examples.*

Lionel Tiger and Joseph Shepher: **Women in the Kibbutz.** Harcourt, Brace and Jovanovich 1975; *Based on the lives of 34,000 kibbutz dwellers, this sociological study covers sexual ideologies, child rearing, money and more, through the examination of the lives of three generations of kibbutz women.*

Decison Making

Corrine McLaughlin and Gordon Davidson: **Builders of the Dawn: Community Lifestyles in a Changing World.** Stillpoint Publishing 1985 *Mc Laughlin and Davidson's book offers workable guidelines for those interested in building tomorrow's communities and covers such topics as: self-reliance and healing, relationships, patterns of governance, leadership, and diversity of economic systems.*

Michael A. Mantell, Stephen F. Harper; and Luther Propst: **Creating Successful Communities, A Guidebook to Growth Management Strategies.** Island Press 1989 *Developed for civic activists, policy makers, and planners, this book gives practical guidelines for developing workable action plans for restoring distinctiveness and livability to communities, and provides strategies for effective paticipation in growth-management decision making.*

John Gastil: **Democracy in Small Groups: Participation, Decision Making and Communication.** New Society Publishers 1993 *Gastil's book explores the dynamics of the following: practicing democracy; the relationship between speaking rights and listening responsibilities; full access to information; agenda setting; surveys on consensus; majority rule; proportional outcomes; and ways to practice democracy in personal, family, and neighborhood life.*

Sam Kaner: **Facilitator's Guide to Participatory Decision-Making.** New Society Publishers 1996; *In this work, Kaner provides helpful hints for group leaders, the dynamics and processes of decision making, group process skills, agenda design, discussion techniques, and more.*

Roger Fisher and William Ury: **Getting to Yes: Negotiating Agreement Without Giving In.** Penguin 1981; *Getting to Yes is a step-by-step guide to mutually acceptable problem solving in difficult situations. It's about getting your principles straight, using them, and what to do in difficult real-world situations.*

Dee Kelsey and Pam Plumb: **Great Meetings! How to Facilitate Like a Pro.** Hanson Park Press 1997; *This is a user-friendly resource book designed to help meeting leaders, facilitators, and paticipants understand the important steps for planning and facilitating a great meeting.*

Michael Doyle and David Straus: **How to Make Meetings Work.** Berkeley Publishing Group 1993; *Tested on more than 10,000 participants, the Interaction Method of conducting meetings demonstrates how time and people can be better used in meetings and is proven to increase productivity by up to 15 percent.*

Tova Green, Peter Woodrow, with Fran Peavy: **Insight and Action: How to Discover and Support a Life of Integrity and Commitment to Change.** New Society Publishers 1994; *Three valuable processes for overcoming periods of doubt, indecision, and discouragement are presented here. Section I: Support Groups, Section II: Clearness for Individual Decision Making, Section III: Strategic Questioning.*

Bruce Kokopeli and George Lakey: **Leadership for Change: Toward a Feminist Model.** New Society Publishers; *A concise overview of the strategies used to break free of patriarchal patterns and behaviors, this short book empowers groups seeking both personal and political change,*

Leland P. Bradford: **Making Meetings Work: A Guide for Leaders and Group Members.** Pfeiffer and Co. 1976; *This is a classic, still-valuable book for group-centered leadership. especially chapter three: "Clues to Group Dysfunction."*

Brian Auvine, et al: **Manual for Group Facilitators, A.** Fellowship for Intentional Community 1978; *Originally published by the Center for Conflicts Resolution, and now published by FIC, this manual is a Straightforward and comprehensive guide to a very important community skill. Topics include the following: sample agendas, how to get a meeting started and on the right track, group process, communication, dynamics, conflict in groups, crisis intervention, and creative problem solving.*

Marshall B. Rosenberg: **Model for Nonviolent Communication, A.** 1983; *This is an examination of the clear and concise use of language as a means of peaceful and cooperative problem solving.*

Marshall Rosenberg: **Nonviolent Communication, A Language of Compassion.** Center for Nonviolent Communication; *This is a complete, step-by-step guide to the nonviolent communication method, with plenty of examples and exercises.*

CT Butler and Amy Rothstein: **On Conflict and Consensus: A Handbook on Formal Consensus.** Food Not Bombs Publishing 1987; *CT Butler, a political activist and consensus trainer, developed the Formal Consensus process as a more structured method for refining a proposal and handling objections to it than the more common Quaker-derived consensus method.*

William Polowniak: **On Creating a Community: A Guide for Organizations, Personal Productivity and International Peace.** Quantum Publishers 1994; *This is a helpful guidebook for understanding the process of building community. Introducing the "Trust Level Theory", the author gives practical advice on dealing with defense mechanisms, on the obstacles to expect and how to overcome them, and on problems with leadership.*

Center for Alternatives: **Planning a Meeting.** Center for Alternatives, Berkeley CA; *This book demonstrates how to plan and effective meeting and create an agenda, and dramatizes a "before" picture of a haphazard, conflictladen meeting, and an "after" picture of a productive facilitated meeting.*

Roger Schwarz: **Skilled Facilitator: Practical Wisdom for Developing Effective Groups, The.** Jossey-Bass Inc. 1994; *In his book, Schwarz shows what makes a group effective and how a facilitator can improve group effectiveness by identifying patterns of behavior that are getting in the way, helping the group stick to a few critical ground rules, and encouraging them to deal more openly with conflict.*

Alternative Economics

Douthwaite, Richard: **Short Circuit Strengthening Local Economies for Security in an Unstable World**. Lilliput Press 1996

Hawken, Lovins & Lovins: **Natural Capitalism: The Next Industrial Revolution.** Earthscan Publications, London. 1999; ISBN 185383 461 0; *Three leading business visionaries explain how the world is on the verge of a new industrial revolution that promises to transform our fundamental notions about the way to do business.*

Korten, David: **When Corporations Rule the World.** Earthscan Publications, London 1995; *A well argued, sober case for strengthening local communities and weakening the multinationals, by this former consultant to the US Agency for International Development, and well known critic of World Bank policies.*

Lietaer, Bernard: **The Future of Money and The Mystery of Money.** Random House, London.

Exchanging clothes:
Normally anyone can find something that fits...
Normally ...

10 GIFTS TO MY COMMUNITY

When I speak of others in their absence, I am aware that I may be giving form to a reality which does not exist. I speak about myself and others in such a way that it serves me and the others in their development.

Before I speak with someone about organisational matters outside of his/her field of work, I pause a moment and ask myself if this is the right time and place.

I constantly view myself as part of the whole, and I consider what I can do for the growth and well-being of the entire community.

I develop dreams of a new home and create that which I would like to receive from the others.

I do not burden the others with my bad mood. I either transform it into something constructive or discuss it openly.

I care for the place where I live. I spread beauty, and in this way I link myself to this place.

Every day I am open to others. I do not tie them down to past images and experiences. I see them in their most beautiful form.

When I do not like something, I examine it to see if I cannot use it to make a suggestion for the good of everyone else. For "the superior man, if he sees good, he imitates it; if he has faults, he rids himself of them.". (I Ging)

I use energy, water, warmth and food conscientiously. I only take what I really need.

I do not take myself too seriously – but that which needs to be done.

Index

In this index you will find a list of the names of all the communities and institutions,
- which are described in the chapter "**Communities - self-descreptions**", (the page numbers are printed in **bold** letters)
- which can be found in the chapter **"Addresses from the 2000/2001 edition"**
- which are listed in the chapter **"Networks of communities & ecovillages"**
- which are listed and perhaps described in the chapter **"Useful addresses"**.

If we know that a community has **changed its name**, then you will also find a reference to the new name under the old one.
If a community has a name which can be **alphabetised in different ways**, you can find it under different categories. In this case the **squiggle** (~) stands for the keyword. For example: "Le Levain" is also listed as "Levain, Le ~ ".

The symbols used in this section:
(A-Z) country abbreviations, which are explained on **page 415.**
→ see entry in the index
X this community no longer exists or is no community any more (to our knowledge)

A

C

D

E

F

G

J

K

L

M

N

O

P

R

S

Response Coupon

Please complete and send to:

eurotopia | Ökodorf Sieben Linden | 38486 Poppau | Germany
Fax: +49-(0)39000-51232

☐ I know of existing or planned communities which are not listed in the ***eurotopia*** directory; I have included information on them (e.g. their address).

☐ We are a ☐ community or a commune / an ☐ ecovillage / an ☐ organisation and would like to be contacted for the next edition of ***eurotopia***. Our contact address:

Name:

....

Address:

....

....

Tel./Fax:

....

Email:

....

*(**eurotopia** does not publish any community addresses without permission. All communities are written to and then decide for themselves whether they want to appear in **eurotopia**.)*

☐ The information in the ***eurotopia*** directory is incorrect or has changed. Please consider/check the following information (please include the page number and name of the community):

....

....

....

....

Additional information for the response coupon:

Hand in Hand – Eurotopia – Community Consultation

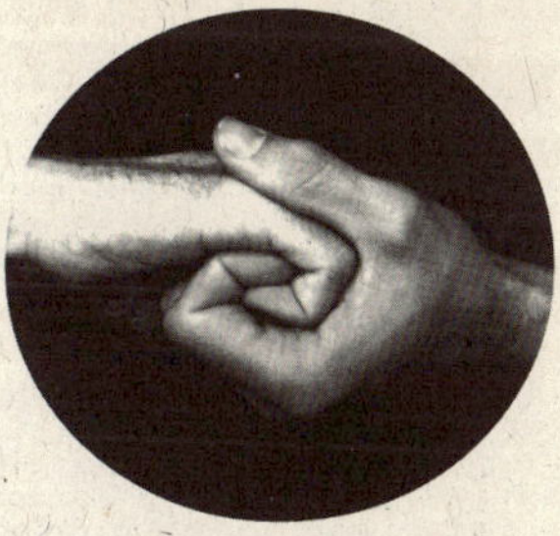

First hand community experience – Tools to build community – Support for the realisation of dreams and visions

Our team lives in the ecovillage of Sieben Linden.
We wish to seed positive and succesful communication experiences in groups and projects. We choose methods that integrate body, mind and spirit, so that humans can be and grow together in meaningful and healthy depth. Our vision of community implies the unfolding and development of individuality within a lively and diverse whole.

Our team brings together a combination of important qualifications and abilities needed to strengthen ecovillages and communities in all stages of development: A deep knowledge of different spiritual pathways and tools for inner work, breadth of visionary scope, methods of planning, financing and realising projects, practice of succesful communication methods, support for the individual development of participants.

We offer:

- Events, lectures, talks on the subjects of communal life and the development of a future-compatible lifestyle and a forward-looking society – complemented with music, songs and other group-experiences.
- Consultation, supervision, coaching – support for the realisation of projects – for individuals and groups.
- Seminars and Workshops – basic requirements for the building of community– a 3-week long community course and weekend seminars on different subjects.
- Accompanied and organised tours to visit communities.

Possible subjects:

Consensus and decision making processes, visionary work, spiritual work (group ceremonies, sweatlodges and vision quests, meditation, yoga), deep ecology and deep democracy, communication methods for peace and mutual understanding, sharing of community life experience, cooperative planning methods and project management, ecological building and settlement, legal forms and financing concepts...

In cooperation with the Global Ecovillage Network (GEN) and Eurotopia. **Contact**: see p. 377.

The Hand in Hand - Team

Legend

community in planning
ecovillage
ecosettlement
AZ indicates the location of the community on the map
| start a new line when writing the mailing address
telephone number
fax number
Email
homepage
founding year
located in the city
located in a town/suburb
located in the countryside
behind it: size of the property (1 ha =10,000 m², 1ac =4,050 m²)
( ) *behind it in brackets:* the nearest large town
♀ number of women
♂ number of men
number of children
total number of members
languages spoken in the community (besides the national language): g=German, e=English, f=French, i=Italian, s/sp=Spanish
How many work inside the community?
Who makes important decisions?
( ) *in brackets:* How are these decisions made?
type of financing
owner (of building/land)
ideological/spiritual principles
main areas of activity
catchwords
☺ new members are basically welcome
behind it: admission requirements for new members
welcome work ing guests in exchange for board and lodging
( ) *in brackets:* do not explicitly offer board and lodging
is part of the networks listed here
X this community no longer exists or is no community any more
A-Z country abbreviations, which are explained on **page 415.**
→ see entry in the index

Country abbreviations

These are the country abbreviations as we use them in this directory - mostly according to the usual abbreviations used by postal systems. When sending letters please write out the country's name in full as the last line of the address.

A	Austria
AL	Albania
ARG	Argentina
AUS	Australia
B	Belgium
BG	Bulgaria
BRA	Brazil
CH	Switzerland
CZ	Czech Republic
D	Germany
DK	Denmark
E	Spain
EE	Estonia
F	France
FIN	Finland
GR	Greece
H	Hungary
HR	Croatia
I	Italy
IL	Israel
IND	India
IRL	Ireland
IS	Iceland
J	Japan
L	Luxembourg
LT	Lithuania
LV	Latvia
N	Norway
NL	Netherlands
P	Portugal
PL	Poland
RO	Rumania
RUS	Russia
S	Sweden
SF	Finland
SK	Slovakia
SLO	Slovenia
SRL	Sri Lanka
TR	Turkey
UE	Ukraine
UK	Great Britain/Northern Ireland